PSYCHE

MERIDIAN

Crossing Aesthetics

Werner Hamacher

Editor

Edited by Peggy Kamuf and Elizabeth Rottenberg

*Stanford
University
Press*

*Stanford
California
2008*

PSYCHE

Inventions of the Other, Volume II

Jacques Derrida

Stanford University Press
Stanford, California

Psyche originally appeared in French as *Psyché: Inventions de
l'autre, tomes I et II*, by Jacques Derrida.
Copyright © Éditions Galilée 1987/2003.

Printed in the United States of America
on acid-free, archival-quality paper

Library of Congress Cataloging-in-Publication Data

Derrida, Jacques.
[Psyché. English]
Psyche : inventions of the other / Jacques Derrida.
p.   cm.—(Meridian: crossing aesthetics)
Includes bibliographical references.
ISBN 978-0-8047-4798-1 (cloth : v. 1 : alk. paper)
ISBN 978-0-8047-4799-8 (pbk. : v. 1 : alk. paper)
ISBN 978-0-8047-5766-9 (cloth : v. 2 : alk. paper)
ISBN 978-0-8047-5767-6 (pbk. : v. 2 : alk. paper)
1. Soul.   2. Narcissism.   3. Other minds.
(Theory of knowledge)   I. Title.
B2430.D483P7813 2007
194—dc22
2006037117

Contents

§ 1   Letter to a Japanese Friend

Dear Professor Izutsu,

At our last meeting I promised you some schematic and preliminary reflections on the word "deconstruction." What we discussed were prolegomena to a possible translation of this word into Japanese, one that would at least try to avoid, if *possible*, a negative determination of its meanings or connotations. The question would be therefore what deconstruction is not, or rather *ought* not to be. I underline these words ("possible" and "ought"). For if the difficulties of translation can be anticipated (and the question of deconstruction is also through and through *the* question of translation, and of the language of concepts, of the conceptual corpus of so-called Western metaphysics), one should not begin by naïvely believing that the word "deconstruction" corresponds in French to some clear and univocal meaning. There is already in "my" language a serious [*sombre*] problem of translation between what here or there can be envisaged for the word and the usage itself, the reserves of the word. And it is already clear that even in French, things change from one context to another. More so in the German, English, and especially American contexts, where the *same* word is already attached to very different connotations, inflections, and emotional or affective values. Their analysis would be interesting and warrants a study of its own.

When I chose this word, or when it imposed itself upon me—I think

---

This letter, first published in Japanese, as was my intention, before being published in other languages, appeared in French in *Le Promeneur* 42 (1985): 2–4. Toshihiko Izutsu is a well-known Japanese Islamologist.

it was in *Of Grammatology*—I little thought it would be credited with such a central role in the discourse that interested me at the time. Among other things I wished to translate and adapt to my own ends the Heideggerian words *Destruktion* or *Abbau*. Both words signified in this context an operation bearing on the *structure* or traditional *architecture* of the fundamental concepts of ontology or of Western metaphysics. But in French the term "destruction" too obviously implied an annihilation or a negative reduction much closer perhaps to Nietzschean "demolition" than to the Heideggerian interpretation or to the type of reading I was proposing. So I ruled that out. I remember having looked to see if the word *déconstruction* (which came to me it seemed quite spontaneously) was good French. I found it in *Littré*. The grammatical, linguistic, or rhetorical senses [*portées*] were, I found, bound up with a "mechanical" sense [*portée "machinique"*]. This association appeared very fortunate and fortunately adapted to what I wanted at least to suggest. Perhaps I could cite some of the entries from *Littré*. "*Deconstruction:* Action of deconstructing. / Grammatical term. Disarranging of the construction of words in a sentence. 'Of deconstruction, common way of saying construction,' Lemare, 'De la manière d'apprendre les langues [On the Way of Learning Languages],' chapter 17 of *Cours de langue latine. To deconstruct:* 1. To disassemble the parts of a whole. To deconstruct a machine to transport it elsewhere. 2. Grammatical term . . . To deconstruct verse, rendering it, by the suppression of meter, similar to prose. / Absolutely. 'In the system of prenotional sentences, one also starts with translation and one of its advantages is never needing to deconstruct,' Lemare, ibid. 3. *To self-deconstruct* [*se déconstruire*]: . . . to lose its construction. 'Modern scholarship has shown us that in a region of the timeless East, a language reaching its own state of perfection is deconstructed [*s'est déconstruite*] and altered from within itself according to the single law of change, natural to the human mind,' Villemain, Preface to the *Dictionnaire de l'Académie*."[1]

Naturally it will be necessary to translate all of this into Japanese, but that only postpones the problem. It goes without saying that if all the meanings enumerated by *Littré* interested me because of their affinity with what I "meant" ["*voulais-dire*"], they are concerned, metaphorically, so to say, only with models or regions of meaning and not with the totality of what deconstruction aspires to in its most radical ambition. This is not limited to a linguistico-grammatical model, nor even a semantic model, let alone a mechanical model. These models themselves have to be submitted to a deconstructive questioning. It is true then that these "models" have been behind a number of misunderstandings about the concept and term "deconstruction" because of the temptation to reduce it to these models.

It must also be said that the word was rarely used and was largely unknown in France. It had to be reconstructed in some way, and its use value was determined by the discourse that was then being attempted around and on the basis of *Of Grammatology*. It is to this use value that I am now going to try to give some precision and not some primitive meaning or etymology sheltered from or outside of any contextual strategy.

A few more words on the subject of "the context." At that time, structuralism was dominant. "Deconstruction" seemed to be going in the same direction, since the word signified a certain attention to *structures* (which themselves were neither simply ideas, nor forms, nor syntheses, nor systems). To deconstruct was also a structuralist gesture, or in any case a gesture that assumed a certain need for the structuralist problematic. But it was also an antistructuralist gesture, and its fortune rests in part on this ambiguity. Structures were to be undone, decomposed, desedimented (all types of structures, linguistic, "logocentric," "phonocentric"—structuralism being especially at that time dominated by linguistic models and by a so-called structural linguistics that was also called Saussurian—socio-institutional, political, cultural, and above all and from the start philosophical). This is why, especially in the United States, the motif of deconstruction has been associated with "poststructuralism" (a word unknown in France until its "return" from the United States). But the undoing, decomposing, and desedimenting of structures, in a certain sense more historical than the "structuralist" movement it called into question, was not a negative operation. Rather than destroying, it was also necessary to understand how a "whole" was constituted and to reconstruct it to this end. However, the negative appearance was and remains much more difficult to erase than is suggested by the grammar of the word (*de-*), even though it can designate a genealogical derivation rather than a demolition. That is why this word, at least on its own, has never appeared satisfactory to me (but what word is?) and must always be girded by an entire discourse. It is difficult to erase it afterward because, in the work of deconstruction, I have had to, as I have to here, multiply the cautionary indicators and put aside all the traditional philosophical concepts, while reaffirming the necessity of returning to them, at least under erasure. Hence, this has been called, precipitously, a type of negative theology (this was neither true nor false, but I shall not enter into the debate here).[2]

All the same, and in spite of appearances, deconstruction is neither an *analysis* nor a *critique*, and its translation would have to take that into consideration. It is not an analysis in particular because the dismantling of a structure is not a regression toward a *simple element*, toward an *undecomposable origin*. These values, like that of analysis, are themselves philosophemes subject to deconstruction. No more is it a critique, in a general sense or in a Kantian sense. The instance of *krinein* or *krisis* (decision, choice, judgment, discernment) is itself, as is all the apparatus of transcendental critique, one of the essential "themes" or "objects" of deconstruction.

I would say the same about *method*. Deconstruction is not a method and cannot be transformed into one. Especially if the technical and procedural significations of the word are stressed. It is true that in certain circles (university or cultural, especially in the United States) the technical and methodological "metaphor" that seems necessarily attached to the very word "deconstruction" has been able to seduce or lead astray. Hence the debate that has developed in these circles: Can deconstruction become a methodology for reading and for interpretation? Can it thus let itself be reappropriated and domesticated by academic institutions?

It is not enough to say that deconstruction could not be reduced to some methodological instrumentality or to a set of rules and transposable procedures. Nor will it do to claim that each deconstructive "event" remains singular or, in any case, as close as possible to something like an idiom and a signature. It must also be made clear that deconstruction is not even an *act* or an *operation*. Not only because there is something "patient" or "passive" about it (as Blanchot says, more passive than passivity, than the passivity that is opposed to activity). Not only because it does not return to an (individual or collective) *subject* who would take the initiative and apply it to an object, a text, a theme, and so on. Deconstruction takes place, it is an event that does not await the deliberation, consciousness, or organization of a subject, or even of modernity. *It deconstructs itself. It can be deconstructed* [Ça se déconstruit]. The "it" [ça] is not here an impersonal thing that is opposed to some egological subjectivity. *It is in deconstruction* [en déconstruction] (*Littré* says: "to deconstruct itself [se déconstruire] . . . to lose its construction"). And the *se* of *se déconstruire*, which is not the reflexivity of an ego or of a consciousness, bears the whole enigma. I recognize, my dear friend, that in trying to make a word clearer so as to assist its translation, I am only thereby increasing the difficulties: "the impossible task of the translator" (Benjamin). This too is what is meant by "deconstruction."

If deconstruction takes place everywhere it [*ça*] takes place, where there is something (and is not therefore limited to meaning or to the text in the current and bookish sense of the word), we still have to think through what is happening in our world, in modernity, at the time when deconstruction is becoming a motif, with its word, its privileged themes, its mobile strategy, and so on. I have no simple and formalizable answer. All my essays are attempts to have it out with this formidable question. They are modest symptoms of it, quite as much as attempts at interpretation. I would not even dare to say, following a Heideggerian schema, that we are in an "epoch" of being-in-deconstruction, of a being-in-deconstruction that manifests or dissimulates itself at one and the same time in other "epochs." This thinking of "epoch" and especially that of a gathering of the destiny of being and of the unity of its destination or its dispersion (*Schicken, Geschick*) can never give rise to any certainty.

To be very schematic, I would say that the difficulty of *defining* and therefore also of *translating* the word "deconstruction" stems from the fact that all the predicates, all the defining concepts, all the lexical significations, and even the syntactic articulations, which seem at one moment to lend themselves to this definition or to that translation, are also deconstructed or deconstructible, directly or otherwise, and so on. And that goes for the *word*, the very unity of the *word* deconstruction, as for every *word*. *Of Grammatology* questioned the unity "word" and all the privileges with which it was credited, especially in its *nominal* form. It is therefore only a discourse or rather a writing that can make up for the incapacity of the word to be equal to a "thought." All sentences of the type "deconstruction is X" or "deconstruction is not X" a priori miss the point, which is to say that they are at least false. As you know, one of the principal things at stake in what is called in the texts "deconstruction" is precisely the delimiting of onto-logic and above all of the third person present indicative: S *is* P.

The word "deconstruction," like any other, acquires its value only from its inscription in a chain of possible substitutions, in what is so blithely called a "context." For me, for what I have tried and still try to write, the word has interest only within a certain context, where it replaces and lets itself be determined by so many other words such as "writing [*écriture*]," "trace," "differance," "supplement," "hymen," "*pharmakon*," "margin," "cut [*entame*]," "*parergon*," and so on. By definition, the list can never be closed, and I have cited only nouns, which is inadequate and done only for reasons of economy. In fact, I should have cited the sentences and the interlinking of sentences that in their turn determine these nouns in some of my texts.

What deconstruction is not? everything of course!

What is deconstruction? nothing of course!

I do not think, for all these reasons, that it is a *good word* [un bon mot]. It is certainly not elegant [*beau*]. It has definitely been of service in a highly determined situation. In order to know what it was that imposed it in a chain of possible substitutions, despite its essential imperfection, this "highly determined situation" would need to be analyzed and deconstructed. This is difficult, and I am not going to attempt it here.

One final word to hasten the conclusion of this letter, which is already too long. I do not think that translation is a secondary and derived event in relation to an original language or text. And, as I have just said, "deconstruction" is a word that is essentially replaceable in a chain of substitutions. This can also be done from one language to another. The chance for (a) "deconstruction" would be that another word (the same word and an other) be *found* or *invented* in Japanese to say the same thing (the same and an other), to speak of deconstruction, and to lead it elsewhere, to its being written and transcribed. In a word that will also be more beautiful.

When I speak of this writing of the other that will be more beautiful, I clearly understand translation as involving the same risk and chance as the poem. How to translate "poem"? a "poem"? . . .

Please be assured, dear Professor Izutsu, of my gratitude and of my most cordial feelings.

—Translated by David Wood and Andrew Benjamin

§ 2 *Geschlecht* I: Sexual Difference, Ontological Difference

To Ruben Berezdivin

Of sex, one can readily remark, yes, Heidegger speaks as little as possible, perhaps he has never spoken of it. Perhaps he has never said anything, by that name or the names under which we recognize it, about the "sexual-relation," "sexual-difference," or indeed about "man-and-woman." This silence, therefore, is easily remarked. Which means that the remark is somewhat facile. A few indications, concluding with "everything happens as if . . . ," would suffice. The dossier could then be closed, avoiding trouble, if not risk: it is as if, according to Heidegger, there were no sexual

---

This essay (first published in the issue of the *Cahier de l'Herne* devoted to Heidegger and edited by Michel Haar in 1983), like the following one ("Heideggger's Hand [*Geschlecht* II]"), will have to content itself with sketching in a preliminary fashion an interpretation to come in which I would like to situate *Geschlecht* in Heidegger's path of thought. In the path of his writing as well—and the impression, or inscription, marked by the word *Geschlecht* will not have been there for nothing. I will leave this word in its own language for reasons that should impose themselves on us in the course of the reading. And it certainly is a matter of "*Geschlecht*" (the *word* for sex, race, family, generation, lineage, species, genre), and not of *Geschlecht* as such: one will not so easily clear away the mark of the word ("*Geschlecht*") that blocks our access to the thing itself (the *Geschlecht*); in that word, Heidegger will much later remark the imprint of a blow or a stroke (*Schlag*). He will do so in a text we will not speak of here but toward which this reading is heading, and by which, in truth, I know it is already being drawn as toward a magnet: "Die Sprache im Gedicht: Eine Erörterung von Georg Trakls Gedicht" (1953), in *Unterwegs zur Sprache* (Pfullingen: Neske, 1959); "Language in the Poem: A Discussion on Georg Trakl's Poetic Work," in *On the Way to Language*, trans. Peter D. Hertz (New York: Harper & Row, 1971).

difference, and nothing of this aspect in man, which is to say in woman, to interrogate or suspect, nothing worthy of questioning (*fragwürdig*). It is as if, one might continue, sexual difference did not rise to the height [*hauteur*] of ontological difference: it would be on the whole as negligible, with regard to the question of the meaning of Being, as any other difference, a determinate distinction or an ontic predicate. Negligible for *thought*, of course, even if it is not at all negligible for science or philosophy. But insofar as it is open to the question of Being, insofar as it has a relation to Being, in that very reference, *Dasein* would not be sexiferous [*sexifère*]. Discourse on sexuality would thus be abandoned to the sciences or philosophies of life, to anthropology, sociology, biology, or perhaps even to religion or morality.

Sexual difference, we were saying or heard ourselves saying, would not rise to the height of ontological difference. But knowing that it will not be a question of heights, since the thinking of difference is not up to it, has the effect of heightening this silence. One might even find this silence to be, precisely, haughty, arrogant, or provocative in a century in which sexuality, the commonplace of all chatter, has also become the currency of philosophical and scientific "knowledge," the inevitable *Kampfplatz* of ethics and politics. And yet not a word from Heidegger! One might find that this scene of stubborn mutism at the very center of the conversation has a certain grand air to it, in the uninterrupted and distracted buzzing of the colloquium. In itself, it has the value of being alert and sobering (but what exactly is everyone talking about around this silence?): Who, indeed, around or even long before him, has not chatted about sexuality as such, if one could say that, and by that name? All the philosophers in the tradition have done so, from Plato to Nietzsche, who for their part were irrepressible on the subject. Kant, Hegel, Husserl all reserved a place for it; they at least touched on it in their anthropology or in their philosophy of nature, and in fact everywhere.

Is it imprudent to trust Heidegger's apparent silence? Will this apparent fact later be disturbed in its nice philological assurance by some known or unpublished passage when some reading machine, while combing through the whole of Heidegger, manages to hunt out the thing and snare it? Still, one must think of programming the machine, think, think of it and know how to do it. What will the index be? What words will it rely on? Will it be only on nouns? And on what syntax, visible or invisible? Briefly, by what signs will you recognize his speaking or remaining silent about what you nonchalantly call "sexual difference"? What is it you are thinking behind those words or through them?

What would be a sufficient basis, in most cases, for noting such an impressive silence today? What measure would suffice to allow the silence to appear as such, marked and marking? Undoubtedly this: Heidegger apparently said nothing about sexuality by name in those places where the best educated and endowed "modernity" would have fully expected it, given its panoply of "everything-is-sexual-and-everything-is-political-and-reciprocally" (note in passing that the word "political" is rarely used, perhaps never, in Heidegger, another not insignificant matter). Without any statistics, the case would already have been settled. But there are good reasons for believing that the statistics here would only confirm the verdict: Heidegger remained silent about what we glibly call sexuality. A transitive and significant silence (he has silenced sex), one that belongs, as he says about a certain *Schweigen* ("hier in der transitiven Bedeutung gesagt"), to the path of a speech he seems to interrupt. But what are the places of this interruption? Where does the silence work on that discourse? And what are the forms and determinable contours of that non-said [*non-dit*]?

We can wager that nothing is at a standstill in these places where the arrows of the aforesaid panoply would pin things down with a name: omission, repression, denial, foreclosure, even the unthought.

But then, if the wager were lost, wouldn't the trace of that silence warrant the detour? The silence does not silence just anything and the trace does not come from just anywhere. But why the wager? Because, as we will see, before predicting anything whatever about "sexuality," one must invoke chance, the aleatory, destiny.

Let us imagine, then, a so-called modern reading, an investigation armed with psychoanalysis, an inquiry enabled by a vast anthropological culture. What is it looking for? Where does it look? Where does it think it has the right to expect at least a sign, an allusion, however elliptical, a reference, to sexuality, the sexual relation, sexual difference? To begin with, in *Sein und Zeit*. Was the existential analytic of *Dasein* not close enough to a fundamental anthropology to have given rise to so many misunderstandings or mistakes regarding its supposed "human reality [*réalité-humaine*]" as it was translated in France? Yet even in the analyses of being-in-the-world as being-with-others, of care as in itself and as *Fürsorge*, one searches in vain, it seems, for the beginnings of a discourse on desire and sexuality. One might conclude from this that sexual difference is not an essential trait, that it does not belong to the existential structure of *Dasein*. Being-there, being *there*, the *there* of Being as such, bears no sexual mark. The same goes for the reading of the meaning of Being, since, as *Sein und Zeit* clearly states (§ 2), *Dasein* remains the exemplary being in such a reading.[1] Were it even admitted that all reference to sexuality was not erased or remains implied, this would only be to the degree that such a reference, among so many others, presupposes very general structures (*In-der-Welt Sein als Mit- und Selbstsein, Räumlichkeit, Befindlichkeit, Rede, Sprache, Geworfenheit, Sorge, Zeitlichkeit, Sein zum Tode*). Yet sexuality would never be the guiding thread for a privileged access to these structures.

There the case rests, it might be said. And yet! *Und dennoch!* (Heidegger uses this rhetorical turn more often than one would think: and yet! exclamation point, next paragraph).

And yet the matter was so little or so ill understood that Heidegger had to explain himself right away. He was to do so in the margins of *Sein und Zeit*, if we may call marginal a lecture course given at the University of Marburg/Lahn in 1928.[2] There he recalls certain "guiding principles" on "*The problem of transcendence and the problem of* Being and Time" (§ 10). The existential analytic of *Dasein* can occur only within the perspective of a fundamental ontology. That is why it is not a matter of an "anthropology" or an "ethics." Such an analytic is only "preparatory," while the "metaphysics of *Dasein*" is not yet "the central focus" of the endeavor, clearly suggesting that it is nevertheless on the program.

It is by the *name* of *Dasein* that I will here introduce the question of sexual difference.

Why call the being that constitutes the theme of this analytic *Dasein*? Why is *Dasein* the "term" given to this thematic? In *Sein und Zeit*, Heidegger had justified the choice of the exemplary entity for the *reading* of the meaning of Being: "In *which* entities is the meaning of Being to be discerned?" (*SZ* 7; 26). In the last instance, the response leads to the "modes of Being for those particular entities which we, the inquirers, are ourselves" (*SZ* 7; 26–27). If the choice of that exemplary entity, in its "priority," becomes the object of a justification (whatever one may think of it and whatever may be its axiomatics), Heidegger on the contrary seems to proceed by decree, at least in this passage, when it becomes a matter of *naming* that exemplary entity, of giving it once and for all its terminological title: "This entity which each of us is himself and which includes inquiring as one of the possibilities of its Being [*die Seinsmöglichkeit des Fragens*], we shall denote [we grasp it, arrest it, apprehend it 'terminologically,'] by the term '*Dasein*' [*fassen wir terminologisch als Dasein*]" (*SZ* 7; 27). This "terminological" choice undoubtedly finds its profound justification in the whole enterprise and in the whole book by making explicit a *there* and a *being-there* that (almost) no other predetermination could command. But that does not remove the decisive, brutal, and elliptical appearance from this preliminary statement, this declaration of name. On the contrary, it happens that in the Marburg lecture course, the term *Dasein*—its sense as well as its name—is more patiently qualified, explained, evaluated. Now, the first trait that Heidegger underlines is its *neutrality*. First directive principle: "The term 'man [*Mensch*]' was not used for that being which is the theme of the analysis. Instead the neutral term *Dasein* was chosen" (*MA* 171; 136).

The concept of neutrality seems very general at first. It is a matter of reducing or subtracting, by means of that neutralization, every anthropological, ethical, or metaphysical predetermination so as to keep nothing but a relation to itself, a bare relation, to the Being of its being. This is the minimal relation to itself as relation to Being, the relation that the being which we are, as questioning, maintains with itself and with its own proper essence. This relation to self is not a relation to an "ego" or to an individual, of course. Thus *Dasein* designates the being that, "in a definite sense," is not "indifferent" to its own essence, or to whom its own being is not indifferent. Neutrality, therefore, is first of all the neutralization of everything but the naked trait of this relation to self, of this interest for its own being in the widest sense of the word "interest." The latter implies an interest or a precomprehensive opening in the meaning of Being and in the questions organized around it. And yet!

And yet this neutrality will be rendered explicit by a leap, without transition and in the very next item (second guiding principle) in the direction of *sexual* neutrality, and even of a certain *sexlessness* (*Geschlechtslosigkeit*) of being-there. The leap is surprising. If Heidegger wanted to offer examples of determinations to be left out of the analytic of *Dasein*, especially of anthropological traits to be neutralized, he had many to choose from. Yet he begins with, and in fact never gets beyond, sexuality, or more precisely sexual difference. Sexual difference thus holds a privilege and seems to belong in the first place—if one follows the statements according to their logical connections—to that "factual concretion" that the analytic of *Da*-

sein should *begin* by neutralizing. If the neutrality of the term *Dasein* is essential, it is precisely because the interpretation of this being—which *we* are—must be carried out *prior to* and *outside* of a concretion of this kind. The *first* example of "concretion" would then be the belonging to one or the other of the sexes. Heidegger does not doubt that they are two: "This neutrality *also* indicates [my emphasis—JD] that *Dasein* is neither of the two sexes [*keines von beiden Geschlechtern ist*]" (*MA* 172; 136).

Much later, at any rate thirty years later, the word *Geschlecht* will be charged with all its polysemic richness: sex, genre, family, stock, race, lineage, generation. Heidegger will pursue in language, along irreplaceable pathways [*frayages*] (that is, inaccessible to common translation), along labyrinthine, seductive, and disquieting ways, the imprint of paths that are often closed. Here they are still closed by the two. Two: that cannot count anything but the sexes, it seems, what are called the sexes.

I have stressed the word *also* ("this neutrality *also* indicates . . . "). By its place in the logical and rhetorical chain, this "also" recalls that, among the numerous meanings of that neutrality, Heidegger judges it necessary not so much to begin with sexual neutrality—which is why he also says "also"—but, nevertheless, *immediately after the only* general meaning that has marked neutrality up until this point in the passage, namely, its *human* character, the term *Mensch* for the theme of the analytic. This is the only meaning that up until this point he has excluded or neutralized. Hence there is here a kind of precipitation or acceleration that cannot itself be neutral or indifferent: among all the traits of man's humanity that are thus neutralized, along with anthropology, ethics, or metaphysics, the first that the very word "neutrality" makes one think of, the first that Heidegger thinks of in any case, is sexuality. The incitement cannot come merely from grammar, it goes without saying. To pass from *Mensch*, indeed from *Mann*, to *Dasein*, is certainly to pass from the masculine to the neuter, while to think or to say *Dasein* and the *Da* of *Sein* on the basis of the transcendent that is *das Sein* ("Sein ist das transcendens schlechthin" [*SZ* 38]), is to pass into a certain neutrality. Furthermore, such neutrality derives from the nongeneric and nonspecific character of Being: "Being, as the basic theme of philosophy, is no class or genus [*keine Gattung*] of entities . . . " (*SZ* 38; 62). But once again, even if sexual difference cannot be without relation to saying, speech, and language, it still cannot be reduced to a grammar. Heidegger designates, rather than describes, this neutrality as an existential structure of *Dasein*. But why does he all of a sudden insist on it with such alacrity? Whereas he says nothing in *Sein und Zeit* of sexlessness (*Geschlechtslosigkeit*), it figures here at the forefront of the traits to be mentioned when recalling *Dasein*'s neutrality, or rather the neutrality of the term *Dasein*. Why?

A first reason comes to mind. The very word *Neutralität* (*ne-uter*) induces a reference to binarity. If *Dasein* is neutral, and if it is not man (*Mensch*), the first consequence to draw from this is that it does not submit to the binary partition one most spontaneously thinks of in such a case, namely, "sexual difference." If "being-there" does not mean "man" (*Mensch*), a fortiori it designates neither "man" nor "woman." But if the consequence is so near common sense, why recall it? Above all, why would one have such difficulty, later in the lecture course, in getting rid of anything so clear and secure? Should one conclude that sexual difference does not depend so simply on all that the analytic of *Dasein* can and must neutralize: metaphysics, ethics, and especially anthropology, or indeed any other domain of ontic knowledge, for example, biology or zoology? Ought one to suspect that sexual difference cannot be reduced to an ethical or anthropological theme?

Heidegger's precautionary insistence leads one to think, in any case, that these things are not a matter of course. Once anthropology (fundamental or not) has been neutralized and once it has been shown that anthropology cannot engage the question of Being or be engaged with it as such, once it has been observed that *Dasein* is reducible neither to human being, nor to the ego, nor to consciousness, nor to the unconscious, nor to the subject, nor to the individual, nor even to an *animal rationale*, one might have thought that the question of sexual difference did not have a chance of measuring up to the question of the meaning of Being or of the ontological difference, that even its dismissal did not deserve privileged treatment. Yet unquestionably it is the contrary that happens. Heidegger has barely finished recalling *Dasein*'s neutrality when right away he has to clarify: neutrality *also* as to sexual difference. Perhaps he was responding to more or less explicit, naïve or enlightened, questions on the part of his readers, students, or colleagues, who were still, whether they liked it or not, wholly within anthropological space: What about the sexual life of your *Dasein*? they might still have asked. And after having answered the question on that front by disqualifying it, in sum, after having recalled the asexuality of a being-there that is not the *anthropos*, Heidegger wanted to preempt another question, even perhaps a new objection. That is where the difficulties begin to increase.

Whether one speaks of neutrality or sexlessness (*Neutralität, Geschlechtslosigkeit*), the words strongly emphasize a negativity that manifestly runs counter to what Heidegger is trying thus to mark. It is not a matter here of linguistic or grammatical signs at the surface of a meaning that, for its part, remains untouched. By means of such manifestly negative predicates, one must be able to read what Heidegger does not hesitate to call a "positivity [*Positivität*]," a richness, and even, in a heavily charged code, a "potency [*Mächtigkeit*]." This clarification suggests that the sexless neutrality does not desexualize; on the contrary, its *ontological* negativity is not deployed with respect to *sexuality itself* (which it would instead liberate), but with respect to the marks of difference, or more precisely to *sexual duality*. There would be no *Geschlechtslosigkeit* except with respect to the "two"; sexlessness would be determined as such only to the degree that sexuality is immediately understood as binarity or sexual division. "But here sexlessness is not the indifference of an empty void [*die Indifferenz des leeren Nichtigen*], the weak negativity of an indifferent ontic nothing. In its neutrality *Dasein* is not the indifferent nobody and everybody, but the primordial positivity [*ursprüngliche Positivität*] and potency of the essence [*Mächtigkeit des Wesens*]" (*MA* 172; 136–37).

If *Dasein* as such belongs to neither of the two sexes, that does not mean that it is deprived of sex. On the contrary: here one must think of a pre-differential, or rather a pre-dual, sexuality—which, as we shall see later, does not necessarily mean unitary, homogeneous, and undifferentiated. And beginning with that sexuality, more originary than the dyad, one may try to think at its source a "positivity" and a "potency" that Heidegger is careful not to call "sexual," fearing no doubt to reintroduce the binary logic that anthropology and metaphysics always assign to the concept of sexuality. But it would indeed be a matter here of the positive and powerful source of every possible "sexuality." *Geschlechtslosigkeit* would not be more negative than *alētheia*. One might recall what Heidegger says regarding the "Würdigung des 'Positiven' im 'privativen' Wesen der *Alētheia*."[3]

From this point on, the lecture course sketches out a quite singular movement. It is very difficult to isolate the theme of sexual difference in it. I am tempted to interpret this as follows: by some strange yet very necessary displacement, sexual division itself leads us to negativity; and neutralization is *at once* the effect of such negativity and the erasure to which a thinking must submit this negativity so that an originary positivity can appear. Far from constituting a positivity that the asexual neutrality of *Dasein* would annul, sexual binarity itself would be responsible, or rather would belong to a determination that is itself responsible for this negativation. To radicalize or formalize all too quickly the meaning of this movement before retracing it more patiently, we might propose the following schema: it is sexual difference itself *as binarity*, it is the discriminative belonging to one or the other sex, that destines (to) or determines a negativity that must then be accounted for. Going further still, one might even associate sexual difference thus determined (one out of two), negativity, and a certain "impotence [*impuissance*]." When returning to the originarity of *Dasein*, of this *Dasein* said to be sexually neutral, "original positivity" and "potency [*puissance*]" can be recovered. In other words, despite appearances, the asexuality and neutrality that must first of all be subtracted from the binary sexual mark, in the analytic of *Dasein*, are in fact on the same side, on the side of *that* sexual difference—the binary one—to which one might have thought them simply opposed. Would this interpretation be too violent?

The next three subparagraphs or items (3, 4, and 5) develop the motifs of neutrality, positivity, and primordial potency, the originary itself, without explicit reference to sexual difference. The "potency" becomes that of an origin (*Ursprung, Urquell*), and moreover Heidegger will never directly associate the predicate "sexual" with the word "potency," the first remaining all too easily associated with the whole system of sexual difference that may, without much risk of error, be said to be inseparable from every anthropology and every metaphysics. More than that, the adjective "sexual" (*sexual, sexuell, geschlechtlich*) is never used, at least to my knowledge, only the nouns *Geschlecht* or *Geschlechtlichkeit*: this is not without importance, since these nouns can more easily radiate toward other semantic zones. Later we will follow some of these other paths of thought.

But without speaking of it directly, these three subparagraphs prepare the return of the theme of *Geschlechtlichkeit*. First of all they erase all the negative signs attached to the word "neutrality." Neutrality is not the void of an abstraction; rather, it leads back to the "potency of origin" that bears in itself the intrinsic possibility of humanity in its concrete facticity. *Dasein*, in its neutrality, must not be confused with the existent. *Dasein* only exists in its factual concretion, to be sure, but this very existence has its primal source (*Urquell*) and intrinsic possibility in *Dasein* as neutral. The analytic of this origin does not treat the existent itself. Precisely because it precedes them, such an analytic cannot be confused with a philosophy of existence, with wisdom (which could be established only within the "structure of metaphysics"), with prophecy or preaching that teaches this or that "worldview." It is therefore not at all a "philosophy of life." Which is to say that a discourse of this order on sexuality (wisdom, knowledge, metaphysics, philosophy of life or existence) falls short of every require-ment of an analytic of *Dasein* in its very neutrality. Has there ever been a discourse on sexuality that belonged to none of these registers?

It must be recalled that sexuality is named neither in this last paragraph nor in the one that will treat (we will return to this) a certain "isolation" of *Dasein*. It is named in the same year (1928) in a paragraph in "Vom Wesen des Grundes" that develops the same argument. The word occurs in quotation marks, in a parenthetical clause. The logic of the a fortiori raises the tone somewhat there. For, in the end, if it is true that sexual-ity must be neutralized "à plus forte raison [with all the more reason]" as Henry Corbin's translation reads, or a fortiori, *erst recht*, why insist? Where would be the risk of misunderstanding? Unless the matter is not at all obvious, and there is still a risk of confusing once more the question of sexual difference with the question of Being and ontological difference? In this context, it is a matter of determining the ipseity of *Dasein*, its *Selbstheit*, its selfhood. *Dasein* exists only for the sake of itself, if one can put it that way (*umwillen seiner*), but this means neither the for-itself of consciousness, nor egoism, nor solipsism. It is starting from *Selbstheit* that an alternative between "egoism" and "altruism" has any chance of arising and appearing, as well as a difference between an "I-self" and a "you-self" (*Ichsein/Dusein*). Always presupposed, ipseity is therefore also "neutral" with respect to being an "I" and being a "you," "and above all with respect to such things as 'sexuality' [*und erst recht etwa gegen die 'Geschlechtlichkeit' neutral*]."[4] The movement of this a fortiori is logically irreproachable on only one condition: on condition that the said "sexuality" (in quotation marks) be the certain predicate of whatever is made possible by or from ipseity, here, for example, the structures of "me" and "you," yet that it not belong, as "sexuality," to the structure of ipseity, of an ipseity not as yet determined as human being, me or you, conscious or unconscious subject, man or woman. Yet if Heidegger insists and underlines ("and above all"), it is because a suspicion continues to weigh on him: What if "sexuality" already marked the most originary *Selbstheit*? What if it were an ontological structure of ipseity? What if the *Da* of *Dasein* were already "sexual"? And what if sexual difference were already marked in the opening to the question of the meaning of Being and to ontological difference? And what if neutralization, which does not happen all by itself, were a violent operation? "And above all" may hide a weaker reason. In any case, the quotation marks always signal some kind of quotation. The current meaning of the word "sexuality" is "mentioned" rather than "used," one might say in the language of speech act theory; it is cited to appear, warned if not accused. Above all, one must protect the analytic of *Dasein* from the risks of anthropology, of psychoanalysis, even of biology. Yet there still may be a way open for other words, or another usage and another reading of the word *Geschlecht*, if not the word "sexuality." Perhaps another "sex" or rather another "*Geschlecht*" will come to inscribe itself in ipseity, or will come to disturb the order of all derivations, for example, that of a more originary *Selbstheit*, one that would make possible the emergence of the ego and of the you. Let us leave this question suspended.

Although this neutralization is implied in every ontological analysis of *Dasein*, this does not mean that the "*Dasein* in man," as Heidegger often says, need be an "egocentric" singularity or an "ontic isolated individual" (*MA* 172; 137). The point of departure in neutrality does not lead back to the isolation or insularity (*Isolierung*) of man, to his factical and existential solitude. And yet the point of departure in neutrality does indeed mean, Heidegger clearly says it, a certain original isolation of man: not, precisely, in the sense of factical existence, "as if the one philosophizing were the center of the world," but as the "*metaphysical isolation* of the human being" (*MA* 172; 137). It is the analysis of this isolation that again brings out the theme of sexual difference and of the dual partition within *Geschlechtlichkeit*. At the center of this new analysis, the very subtle differentiation of a certain lexicon already signals translation problems that will only get worse for us. It will always be impossible to consider them as either accidental or secondary. At a certain moment we will even come to see that the thinking of *Geschlecht* and the thinking of translation are essentially the same. The lexical swarm [*essaim*] brings together (or scatters [*essaime*]) the series "dissociation," "distraction," "dissemination," "division," "dispersion." The *dis-* is then supposed to translate, though only by means of transfer and displacement, the *zer-* of *Zerstreuung, Zerstreutheit*,

Zerstörung, Zersplitterung, Zerspaltung. But an inner and supplementary frontier splits the lexicon again: *dis-* and *zer-* often have a negative sense, yet sometimes also a neutral or nonnegative sense (I would hesitate here to say positive or affirmative).

Let us attempt to read, translate, and interpret as literally as possible. *Dasein* in general hides, harbors in itself the intrinsic possibility of a factical dispersion or dissemination (*faktische Zerstreuung*) into bodiliness (*Leiblichkeit*) and "thus into sexuality [*und damit in die Geschlechtlichkeit*]" (*MA* 173; 137). Every body is sexed, and there is no *Dasein* without bodiliness. But the sequence proposed by Heidegger seems very clear: the dispersing multiplicity is not primarily due to the sexuality of the body; it is bodiliness itself, the flesh, the *Leiblichkeit*, that originally draws *Dasein* into dispersion and *thus* into sexual difference. This "thus" or "concomitantly [*damit*]" is insistent a few lines later, as if *Dasein* were supposed to have or be a priori (as its "intrinsic possibility") a bodiliness that *happens* to be sexed and affected by sexual division.

Here again, Heidegger insists that, like neutrality, dispersion (and all the meanings in *dis-* or *zer-*) not be understood in a negative mode. The "metaphysical" neutrality of isolated man as *Dasein* is not an empty abstraction drawn from or in the sense of the ontic; it is not a "neither . . . nor," but rather what is the authentic concreteness of the origin, the "not-yet" of factical dissemination, of dissociation, of dissociated-being or of factical dissociality: *faktische Zerstreutheit* here and not *Zerstreuung*. This dissociated being, un-bound, or desocialized (for it goes together with the "isolation" of man as *Dasein*) is not a fall or an accident, a degeneration that has supervened. It is an originary structure of *Dasein* that affects it—along with a body, and *thus* with sexual difference—with multiplicity and unbinding, these two meanings remaining distinct though joined in the analyses of dissemination (*Zerstreuung* or *Zerstreutheit*). Assigned to a body, *Dasein* is separated in its facticity, subjected to dispersion and division (*zersplittert*), and concomitantly (*in-eins damit*) always disunited, disaccorded, split, divided (*zwiespältig*) by sexuality into a particular sex (*in eine bestimmte Geschlechtlichkeit*). These words undoubtedly sound negative at first: dispersion, splitting, division, dissociation, *Zersplitterung, Zerspaltung*, just like *Zerstörung* (demolition, destruction), says Heidegger; this resonance is associated with negative concepts from an ontic point of view, which immediately entails a meaning of lesser value. "But here we are dealing with something else" (*MA*

173; 137). What? Something that marks the fold of a "multiplication." We can read the characteristic sign (*Kennzeichnung*) by which one recognizes such a multiplication in the isolation and factical singularity of *Dasein*. Heidegger distinguishes this multiplication (*Mannigfaltigung*) from a simple multiplicity (*Mannigfaltigkeit*), from a diversity. One must also avoid the representation of a large primal being whose simplicity was suddenly dispersed (*zerspaltet*) into many singularities. It is rather a matter of clarifying the intrinsic possibility of multiplication for which *Dasein*'s own embodiment represents an "organizing factor." The multiplicity in this case is not a simple formal plurality of determinations or of determinities (*Bestimmtheiten*); it belongs to Being itself. An "originary *dissemination* [*urspüngliche* Streuung]" already belongs to the being of *Dasein* in general, "in its metaphysically neutral concept" (*MA* 173; 138, translation modified). This primordial dissemination (bestrewal, *Streuung*) becomes, from an altogether determined point of view, *dispersion* (*Zerstreuung*): here a difficulty of translation forces me to distinguish somewhat arbitrarily between dissemination and dispersion, in order to mark out by a convention the subtle trait that distinguishes *Streuung* from *Zerstreuung*. The latter is the intensive determination of the former. It determines a structure of intrinsic possibility, dissemination (bestrewal, *Streuung*), according to all the meanings of *Zerstreuung* (dissemination, dispersion, scattering, diffusion, dissipation, distraction). The word *Streuung* occurs but once, it seems, and it designates this intrinsic possibility, this disseminality, so to speak. Subsequently, the word is always *Zerstreuung*, which would add—but it is not so simple—a mark of determination and negation, had Heidegger not just warned us against negative evaluations. Yet, even if not rigorously legitimate, it is difficult to avoid a certain contamination by negativity, that is, by ethico-religious associations that would come to align this dispersion with a fall or some sort of corruption of the pure, originary possibility (*Streuung*), which would seem to be affected by some sort of supplementary turn. It will also be necessary to elucidate the possibility or fatality of this contamination. We will return to this later.

Some indications of this dispersion (*Zerstreuung*). First of all, *Dasein* never relates to *one* object, to a single object. If it does, it is always in the mode of abstraction or abstention with regard to other beings that always co-appear at the same time. This multiplication does not supervene because there is a plurality of objects; actually, it is the reverse that takes place. It is the originary, disseminal structure, the dispersion of *Dasein*, that makes possible this multiplicity. And the same holds for *Dasein*'s re-lation to itself: it is dispersed, which is consistent with the "structure of historicity in the broadest sense" (*MA* 173; 138) to the extent that *Da-sein* occurs as *Erstreckung,* a word whose translation remains very risky. The word "extension" could all too easily be associated with "*extensio,*" which *Sein und Zeit* interprets as "basically definitive ontologically for the world" according to Descartes (§18). Here something very different is at stake. *Erstreckung* names a spacing that, "prior to" the determination of space as *extensio,* comes to extend or stretch out being-there, the *there* of being, *between* birth and death. As an essential dimension of *Dasein,* the *Erstreckung* opens the *between* that binds it at once to its birth and to its death, the movement of suspense by which it itself *tends* and extends itself *between* birth and death, these two receiving their meaning only from that intervallic movement. *Dasein* affects itself with this movement, and this auto-affection belongs to the ontological structure of its histori-cality; "Die spezifische Bewegtheit des *erstreckten Sicherstreckens* nennen wir das *Geschehen* des Daseins" (§ 72). The fifth chapter of *Sein und Zeit* brings together precisely this intervallic tension and dispersion (*Zerstreu-ung*) (see, in particular, § 75). *Between* birth and death, the spacing of the *between* marks at once the gap and the relation, but the relation according to a kind of distension. This "between-two" as *relation* (*Bezug*) having a *connection* [trait] with both birth and death belongs to the very being of *Dasein,* "prior to" any biological determination, for example ("Im Sein *des Daseins liegt schon das 'Zwischen' mit Bezug auf Geburt und Tod*" [*SZ* 374; 426]). The relation thus enter-tained, inter-drawn [*entre-tenu, entre-tendu*] between, over, or through the dis-tance between birth and death, speaks *with* and supports itself *through* [*s'entretient lui-même* avec] dispersion, dissociation, unbinding (*Zerstreuung, Unzusammenhang,* etc.; see *Sein und Zeit* [390; 441], for example). This relation, the between, *could not take place* without them. Yet to interpret them as negative forces would be to precipitate the interpretation, for example, to dialectize it.

The *Erstreckung* is thus one of the determinate possibilities of essen-tial dispersion (*Zerstreuung*). The "between" would not be possible with-out dispersion, yet it constitutes only one of its structural dependencies, namely, temporality and historicality. Another dependency, another pos-sibility—connected and essential—of originary dispersion is the originary spatiality of *Dasein,* its *Räumlichkeit.* The spatial or spacing dispersion is manifested, for example, in language. Every language is first determined by spatial meanings (*Raumbedeutungen*).[5] The phenomenon of these so-called spatializing metaphors is not at all accidental nor does it fall within the scope of the rhetorical concept of "metaphor." It is not some external fatality. Its essential irreducibility cannot be elucidated outside of this existential analytic of *Dasein*, of its dispersion, its historicality, and its spatiality. The consequences of this must therefore be drawn, in particular for the very language of the existential analytic: all the words that Heidegger uses also necessarily refer back to these *Raumbedeutungen*, beginning with the word *Zerstreuung* (dissemination, dispersion, distraction), which nevertheless names the origin of spacing at the moment when, as language, it submits to its law.

The "transcendental dispersion," as Heidegger calls it, thus belongs to the essence of *Dasein* in its neutrality. "Metaphysical" essence, as we are told in the lecture course, which at the time presents itself as, above all, a metaphysical ontology of *Dasein*, whose very analytic would merely constitute a phase, no doubt a preliminary one. This must be taken into account to situate what is said here about sexual difference in particular. Transcendental dispersion is the possibility of all dissociation and all splitting (*Zersplitterung, Zerspaltung*) in factical existence. It is itself "based" on that primordial feature of *Dasein* that Heidegger then calls *Geworfenheit*. One would have to spend time with this word, subtracting it from so many usages, current interpretations or translations (for example, dereliction, being-thrown). This should be done in anticipation of what the interpretation of sexual difference—which will soon follow—retains in itself of that *Geworfenheit* and, "based" on it, of transcendental dispersion. There is no dissemination that does not presuppose this "thrownness," this *Da* of *Dasein* as thrown. Thrown "prior to" all the modes of thrownness that will later come to determine it: the project, the subject, the object, the abject, the reject, the trajectory, dejection; thrownness that *Dasein* cannot make its own in a project, in the sense of *throwing itself* like a subject master of the throw. *Dasein* is *geworfen*: this means that it is thrown before any project on its part, but this being-thrown is not yet *submitted* to the alternative of activity or passivity, this alternative being still too much in solidarity with the couple subject-object and hence with their opposition, one could even say with their objection. To interpret thrownness as passivity could reinscribe it within the later problematic of subjecti(vi)ty (active or passive). What does "to throw" mean before any of these syntaxes? And being-thrown even before the image of the fall, be it Platonic or Christian? There is a thrownness of *Dasein* even "before" there *appears*—or befalls it, there—any thought of throwing that would amount to an operation, activity, or initiative. And the thrownness of *Dasein* is not a thrownness *in* space, in the already-there of a spatial element. The primordial spatiality of *Dasein* depends on thrownness.

It is at this point that the theme of sexual difference reappears. The disseminal thrownness of being-there (understood still in its neutrality) is particularly manifest insofar as "*Dasein* is *Mitsein* with *Dasein*" (*MA* 174; 139, translation modified). As always in this context, Heidegger's first gesture is to recall an order of implication: sexual difference, or belonging to a genre, must be elucidated starting from being-with, in other words, from a disseminal thrownness, and not the reverse. Being-with does not arise from some factical connection; "it is not explained solely on the basis of the supposedly more primordial species-being" (*MA* 174–75; 139) a being whose own body would be split by sexual difference (*geschlechtlich gespaltenen leiblichen Wesen*). On the contrary, a certain species-like unification (*gattungshafte Zusammenstreben*), the union of genres (their unification, rapprochement, *Einigung*), "metaphysically presupposes" the dissemination of *Dasein* as such, *and thus Mitsein*.

The *mit* of *Mitsein* is to be understood existentially, not categorially, and the same holds for the adverbs of place (see *Sein und Zeit*, § 26). What Heidegger calls here the fundamental metaphysical character of *Dasein* cannot be derived from any generic organization or from a community of living beings as such.

How is this question of *order* important to a "situation" of sexual difference? Thanks to a prudent derivation that in turn becomes problematic for us, Heidegger can at least reinscribe the theme of sexuality, in rigorous fashion, within an ontological questioning and an existential analytic.

Sexual difference remains to be thought, from the moment one no longer pins one's hopes on a common *doxa* or a bio-anthropological science, both of which are sustained by a metaphysical pre-interpretation. But the price of that prudence? Is it not to distance sexuality from all originary structures? To deduce it? Or in any case to derive it, and thus to confirm the most traditional philosophemes by repeating them with the force of new rigor? And did this derivation not begin with a neutralization, the negativity of which was laboriously denied? And once the neutralization was effected, did one not accede once again to an ontological or "transcendental" dispersion, to that *Zerstreuung* the negative value of which was so difficult to erase?

In this form, these questions remain no doubt summary. But they cannot be elaborated in a simple exchange with the passage in the Marburg lectures that names sexuality. Whether it be a matter of neutralization, negativity, dispersion, or distraction (*Zerstreuung*), all of which are, if we follow Heidegger, indispensable motifs here for posing the question of sexuality, it is necessary to *return* to *Sein und Zeit*. Although sexuality is not named there, these motifs are treated in a way that is more complex, more differentiated, which does not mean—on the contrary—easier.

We must content ourselves here with a few preliminary indications. Resembling a methodical procedure in the lectures, neutralization is not unrelated to what in *Sein und Zeit* is called the "privative Interpretation" (§ 10). One could even speak of a method, since Heidegger appeals to an ontology that is accomplished "by way of" or "on the way to" a privative interpretation. This way allows one to bring out the a priori's, and, as a note on the same page (crediting Husserl) tells us, we know that "'*a-priorism*' is the method of every scientific philosophy which understands itself" (*SZ* 50; 75). In this context, it is a question, precisely, of psychology and biology. As sciences, they presuppose an ontology of being-there. This mode-of-being that is life is accessible, essentially, only through being-there. It is the ontology of life that requires a "privative interpretation": "life" being neither a pure "*Vorhandensein*" nor a "*Dasein*" (Heidegger says this without considering that the matter might require more than an affirmation: it seems to go without saying for him), it is accessible only by a negative operation, by subtraction. One may very well wonder what the being of a life is that is *but* life, which is neither this nor that, neither *Vorhandensein* nor *Dasein*. Heidegger never elaborates this ontology of life, but one can imagine all the difficulties it would have run into, since the "neither . . . nor" that conditions it excludes or overflows the most structuring concepts (categorial or existential) of the entire existential analytic. It is the entire problematic organization that is here in question, the one that subjects positive cognitions to regional ontologies, and these regional ontologies to a fundamental ontology, which was itself (at that time) first opened by the existential analytic of *Dasein*. It is no accident (once more, one might say and show) that the mode-of-being of the *living*, the animate (hence also of the psychical) is what raises and situates this enormous problem, or in any case gives it its most recognizable name.

We cannot go into this matter here, but by underlining its all too often unnoticed necessity, let us at least observe that the theme of sexual difference cannot be dissociated from it.

Let us for the moment keep to the "way of privation," an expression that Heidegger returns to in § 12, once again to designate the a priori access to the ontological structure of the living. Once the remark is made, Heidegger enlarges upon the question of these negative statements. Why do negative determinations impose themselves so often in this ontological characteristic? It is not at all "accidental." It is because one must remove the originality of the phenomena from what has dissembled, disfigured, displaced, or covered them over, from the *Verstellungen* and *Verdeckungen*, from all the pre-interpretations whose negative effects must in their turn be annulled by the negative statements, the genuine "sense" of which is in fact "positive." This is a schema we encountered earlier. The negativity of the "characterization" is thus not any more fortuitous than the necessity of the alterations or dissimulations that it attempts in some sense *methodically* to correct. *Verstellungen* and *Verdeckungen* are necessary movements in the very history of Being and its interpretation. They cannot be avoided, like contingent mistakes, any more than one can reduce inauthenticity (*Uneigentlichkeit*) to a mistake or a sin into which one should not have fallen.

And yet. If Heidegger easily uses the word *negativ* when it is a matter of qualifying statements or a characterization, he never uses it, it seems to me (or, let me be more prudent here, he uses it much less often and much less easily), to qualify the very thing that, in the pre-interpretations of Being, nevertheless makes necessary those methodical corrections that take a negative or neutralizing form. *Uneigentlichkeit, Verstellungen,* and *Verdeckungen* are not of the order of negativity (the false or the evil, error or sin). And one can well understand why Heidegger carefully avoids speaking in this case of negativity. By claiming to go back "further" or higher, he thus avoids religious, ethical, indeed even dialectical schemas.

It should then be said that no negative signification is ontologically attached to the "neutral" in general, particularly not to this transcendental dispersion (*Zerstreuung*) of *Dasein*. Thus, without being able to speak of negative value or of value in general (Heidegger's distrust of the value of value is well known), we must take into account the differential and hierarchizing emphasis that regularly comes in *Sein und Zeit* to mark the neutral and dispersion. In certain contexts, dispersion marks the most general structure of *Dasein*. We saw this in the lectures, but it was already the case in *Sein und Zeit*, for example in § 12: "Dasein's facticity is such that its Being-in-the-world [*In-der-Welt-Sein*] has always dispersed [*zerstreut*] itself or even split [*zersplittert*] itself up into definite ways of Being-in [*In-Sein*]" (*SZ* 56; 83). Heidegger proposes a list of these ways and of their irreducible multiplicity. Yet elsewhere dispersion and distraction (*Zerstreuung* in both senses) characterize the inauthentic ipseity of *Dasein*, that of *Man-selbst*, of the *One* that has been "distinguished" from authentic, proper (*eigentlich*) ipseity (*Selbst*). As "*one*," *Dasein* is dispersed or distracted (*zerstreut*). The whole of that analysis is well known; we are only detaching from it that which concerns dispersion (cf. § 27), a concept one finds again at the center of the analysis of curiosity (*Neugier*, § 36). The latter, let us recall, is one of the three modes of falling (*Verfallen*) of *Dasein* in its everyday-being. Later we will have to return to the precautions Heidegger takes: falling, alienation (*Entfremdung*), and even downfall (*Absturz*) would not be the theme of a "moralizing critique," a "philosophy of culture," a dogmatic, religious account of the fall (*Fall*) from a "primal status" (of which we have no ontic experience and no ontological interpretation) and the "corruption of human nature." Much later, we will have to recall these precautions and their problematic character, when, in the "discussion" of Trakl, Heidegger interprets the decomposition and the de-essentialization (*Verwesung*), that is to say, also a certain corruption, of the figure of man. It will again be a matter, even more explicitly this time, of a thinking of "*Geschlecht*" or of *Geschlecht*. (I put it in quotation marks because it is as much about the name as what it names, and it is here just as imprudent to separate them as to translate them). As we shall see, what is at stake is the inscription of *Geschlecht* and of the *Geschlecht* as inscription, stroke, and imprint.

Dispersion is thus marked *twice*: as general structure of *Dasein* and as mode of inauthenticity. One might say the same of the neutral: no hint of the negative or pejorative when it is a question of *Dasein's* neutrality in the lectures; whereas in *Sein und Zeit*, the "neutral" may also be used to characterize the "one," that is, what becomes of the "who" in everyday ipseity: the "who," then, becomes the neuter (*Neutrum*), "*the one* [le on]" (§ 27).

This brief recourse to *Sein und Zeit* has perhaps allowed us to better understand the meaning and necessity of the *order of implications* that Heidegger wants to preserve. Among other things, that order may also account for the predicates used by all discourse on sexuality. There is no properly sexual predicate; at least there is none that does not refer back, in its meaning, to the *general* structures of *Dasein*. So that to know what one is talking about, and how, when one names sexuality, one must indeed rely on the very thing described by the analytic of *Dasein*. Inversely, so to speak, that disimplication allows the general sexuality or sexualization of discourse to be understood: sexual connotations can mark discourse, to the point of complete takeover, only to the extent that they are homogeneous with what every discourse implies, for example the topology of those irreducible "spatial meanings" (*Raumbedeutungen*), but also so many other traits we have situated in passing. What would a "sexual" discourse or a discourse "on-sexuality" be that did not evoke remoteness [*éloignement*], the inside and the outside, dispersion and proximity, the here and the there, birth and death, the between-birth-and-death, being-with and discourse?

This order of implications opens thinking to a sexual difference that would not yet be sexual duality, difference as dual. As we have already observed, what the lectures neutralized was less sexuality itself than the "generic" mark of sexual difference, belonging to one of the two sexes. Hence, in leading back to dispersion and multiplication (*Zerstreuung, Mannigfaltigung*), might one not begin to think of a sexual difference (without negativity, let us be clear) that would not be sealed by the two? Not yet sealed or no longer sealed? But the "not yet" or the "already no longer" would yet signify, would already signify a submission to the control and inspection of reason [*quelque arraisonnement*].

The retreat of the dyad leads to the other sexual difference. It may also prepare us for other questions. For instance, this one: How did difference get deposited in the two? Or again, if one insisted on consigning difference within dual opposition, how does multiplication get arrested in difference? And in sexual difference?

In the lectures, for the reasons given above, *Geschlecht* always names sexuality such as it is rendered by *opposition* or by the dual. Later (and earlier) matters will be different, and this opposition is called decomposition.[6]

—Translated by Ruben Bevezdivin and Elizabeth Rottenberg

§ 3   Heidegger's Hand (*Geschlecht* II)

[T]hinking is genuine activity [*handeln*], genuine taking a hand, if to take a hand [*Hand*] means to lend a hand to the essence, the coming to presence, of Being. This means: to prepare (build) for the coming to presence of Being that abode in the midst of whatever is into which Being brings itself and its essence to utterance in language. *Language* first gives to every purposeful deliberation its ways and its byways.

—Heidegger, *The Question Concerning Technology* (my emphasis— JD)

What is very beautiful, and so precious in this painting, is the *hand*. A hand without deformation, a particular structure, one that seems to speak, like a *language of fire*. Green, like the dark part of a flame that carries in it all the agitations of life. A hand for caressing and for making graceful gestures. One that lives like a clear thing in the red shadow of the painting.

—Antonin Artaud, *Messages révolutionnaires. La peinture de Maria Izquierdo* (my emphasis—JD)

I must begin with some precautions. They all come down to asking for your leniency and your indulgence for what in particular touches on the form and status of this "lecture," on all the presuppositions I must ask you to accept. I am assuming, in fact, that you have read a brief and modest essay published under the title "*Geschlecht* I: Sexual Difference, Ontological Difference." This essay, published and translated more than a year ago, was the beginning of a project that I have taken up again only this year in the course of a seminar I am giving in Paris under the title "Philosophical Nationality and Nationalism." For lack of time I can reconstitute neither the introductory article entitled "*Geschlecht* I" (it discusses the motif of sexual difference in a course almost contemporary with *Sein und Zeit* [Chapter 2 above, "*Geschlecht* I: Sexual Difference, Ontological Dif-

This essay was first given as a lecture in March 1985 at Loyola University Chicago on the occasion of a colloquium organized by John Sallis, whose proceedings have since been published in *Deconstruction and Philosophy*, ed. John Sallis (Chicago: University of Chicago Press, 1987).

ference"]), nor all the developments that form, in my seminar on "Philo-sophical Nationality and Nationalism," the contextual landscape of the reflections I will present to you today. Nevertheless I will try to make the presentation of these few reflections, which are still preliminary, as intel-ligible and independent of all these invisible contexts as possible. Another precaution, another call for your indulgence: for lack of time, I will pres-ent only a part, or rather several fragments, at times a little discontinuous, of the work I am pursuing this year at the slow pace of a seminar engaged in a difficult reading—one I would like to be as meticulous and prudent as possible—of certain texts of Heidegger's, notably *Was heisst Denken?* and above all the lecture on Trakl in *Unterwegs zur Sprache.*

I

We are going to speak then of Heidegger.

We are also going to speak of monstrosity.

We are going to speak of the word *Geschlecht.* I am not going to trans-late it for the moment. Probably I will not translate it at any point. But according to the contexts that come to determine this word, it can be translated by "sex," "race," "species," "genus," "gender," "stock," "family," "generation" or "genealogy," or "community." In the seminar on "Philo-sophical Nationality and Nationalism," before studying certain texts by Marx, Quinet, Michelet, Tocqueville, Wittgenstein, Adorno, and Hannah Arendt, we encountered the word *Geschlecht* in a very preliminary reading of Fichte: "was an Geistigkeit und Freiheit dieser Geistigkeit glaubt, und die ewige Fortbildung dieser Geistigkeit durch Freiheit will, das, wo es auch geboren sey und in welcher Sprache es rede, ist unsers Geschlechts, es gehört uns an und es wird sich zu uns thun" (seventh of the *Addresses to the German Nation* [*Reden an die Deutsche Nation*]).[1] The French transla-tion neglects to translate the word *Geschlecht,* no doubt because the trans-lation was done during or just after the war, I think, by S. Jankélévitch, and under conditions that made the word "race" particularly dangerous and moreover not pertinent for translating Fichte. But what does Fichte mean when he develops in this way what he calls his fundamental prin-ciple (*Grundsatz*), namely, that of a circle (*Kreis*) or of an alliance (*Bund*), of an engagement (we spoke at length about this engagement in the early sessions of the seminar) that precisely constitutes membership in "our *Geschlecht*"? "Whoever believes in spirituality and in the freedom of this spirituality, and who wills the eternal development of this spirituality by freedom [*die ewige Fortbildung*: and if Fichte is "nationalistic" in too enigmatic a sense for us to be able to speak of it very quickly here, it is as a *progressive*, a republican, and a cosmopolitan; one of the themes of the seminar I am currently working on concerns precisely the paradoxical but regular association of nationalism with cosmopolitanism and with humanism], wherever he may have been born and whatever language he speaks . . . he is of our *Geschlecht* and will come over to our side" (*RD* 121; 108, translation modified). So this *Geschlecht* is not determined by birth, native soil, or race; it has nothing to do with the natural or even the linguistic, at least not in the usual sense of this term, for we were able to recognize in Fichte a kind of claim of the idiom, of the idiom of the German idiom. Certain citizens, German by birth, remain strangers to this idiom of the idiom; certain non-Germans can have access to it since, engaged in this circle or this alliance of spiritual freedom and its infinite progress, they belong to "our *Geschlecht.*" The sole analytic and unimpeachable determination of *Geschlecht* in this context is the "we," the belonging to the "we" to whom we are speaking at this moment, at the moment that Fichte addresses himself to this supposed but still to be constituted community, a community that, strictly speaking, is neither political, nor racial, nor linguistic, but that can receive his allocution, his address, or his apostrophe (*Rede an . . .*), and can think with him, can say "we" in some language and from a particular birthplace. *Geschlecht* is a whole, a gathering (one could say *Versammlung*), an organic community in a nonnatural but spiritual sense, one that believes in the infinite progress of the spirit through freedom. So it is an infinite "we," a "we" that announces itself to itself from the infinity of a *telos* of freedom and spirituality, and that promises, engages, or allies itself according to the circle (*Kreis, Bund*) of this infinite will. How is *Geschlecht* to be translated under these conditions? Fichte uses a word that *already* has a vast wealth of semantic determinations in his language, and he speaks *German*. Despite what he says: anyone, in whatever language he speaks, "*ist unsers Geschlechts,*" he says it in German, and this *Geschlecht* is an essential *Deutschheit*. Even if the word *Geschlecht* acquires a rigorous content only from out of the "we" instituted by that very address, it also includes connotations indispensable to the minimal intelligibility of discourse, and these connotations belong irreducibly to German, to a German more essential than all the phenomena of empirical Germanness, but to a certain German [*à de l'allemand*]. All these connoted senses are co-present in the use of the word *Geschlecht*, they appear virtually in that use, but no sense is fully satisfying. How is one to translate? One may recoil before the risk and omit the word, as the French translator did. One might also judge the word to be so open and undetermined by the concept it designates, namely, a "we" as spiritual freedom engaged in the infinity of its progress, that the omission of this word does not lose much. The "we" finally comes down to the humanity of man, to the teleological essence of a humanity that is announced par excellence in *Deutschheit*. *Menschengeschlecht* is often used for "humankind," "human species," "human race." In the Heidegger text we will be looking at in a few minutes, the French translators at times use "humankind [*genre humain*]" for *Geschlecht* and at times simply "species [*espèce*]."

For here the question is nothing less, I venture to say, than the problem of man, of man's humanity, and of humanism. But situated in a place where language no longer lets itself be erased. Already, for Fichte, it is not the same thing to say the "humanity" of man and *Menschlichkeit*. When he says "ist unsers Geschlechts," he is thinking of *Menschlichkeit* and not of *Humanität* with its Latin derivation. The fourth *Discourse* is consonant with those Heidegger texts to come on Latinness. Fichte distinguishes between the dead language "cut off from the living root" (*RD* 65; 55) and the living language animated by an inspiriting breath. When a language, from its first phonemes, arises from the common and uninterrupted life of a people whose intuitions that language continues to espouse, the invasion of a foreign people changes nothing; the intruders cannot rise to the level of this primordial language, unless one day they can assimilate the intuitions of the *Stammvolkes*, of the people-stock for whom these intuitions are inseparable from the language: "und so bilden nicht sie die Sprache, sondern die Sprache bildet sie [they do not form the language, the language forms them]" (*RD* 63; 53). Conversely, when a people adopts another language developed for the designation of suprasensible things, without however totally handing itself over to the influence of this foreign language, the sensible language is not altered by this event. In all peoples, Fichte notes, children learn that part of the language turned toward sensible things as if the signs for those things were arbitrary (*willkürlich*). They must reconstitute the past development of the national language. But in this sensible sphere ("in diesem sinnlichen Umkreise"), each sign (*Zeichen*) can become altogether clear, thanks to vision or the immediate contact with the designated or signified thing (*bezeichnete*). Here I stress the sign (*Zeichen*), for in a moment we shall come to the sign as monstrosity. In this passage, Fichte uses the word *Geschlecht* in the narrow sense of generation: "At most, the result of this would be that the first generation [*das erste Geschlecht*] of a people which thus changed its language would be compelled when adult [*l'âge d'homme*, adulthood: *Männer*] to go back to the years of childhood" (*RD* 64; 54).

Here Fichte is bent on distinguishing between *Humanität* and *Menschlichkeit*. For a German, these words of Latin origin (*Humanität, Popularität, Liberalität*) resound as if they were void of sense, even if they appear sublime and make one curious about their etymology. Moreover, it is the same with the Latin or neo-Latin peoples who know nothing of the etymology and believe these words belong to their mother tongue (*Muttersprache*). But say *Menschlichkeit* to a German, he will understand you without any other historical explanation ("ohne weitere historische Erklärung"). Besides, it is useless to state that a man is a man and to speak of the *Menschlichkeit* of a man about whom one knows very well that he is not an ape or a savage beast. A Roman would not have responded in that way, Fichte believes, because, for the German, *Menschheit* or *Menschlichkeit* always remains a sensible concept (*ein sinnlicher Begriff*), whereas for the Roman *humanitas* had become the symbol (*Sinnbild*) of a suprasensible (*übersinnliche*) idea. From their origins, the Germans have also joined together concrete intuitions in an intellectual concept of humanity, always opposed to animality; and one would surely be wrong to see in the intuitive relation they preserve with *Menschheit* a sign of inferiority with respect to the Romans. Nevertheless, the artificial introduction of words of foreign origin, singularly Roman, into the German tongue risks debasing the moral level of their own way of thinking ("ihre sittliche Denkart . . . herunterstimmen"). But there is concerning language, image, and symbol (*Sinnbild*) an "ineradicable nature" of the "national imagination [*Nationaleinbildungskraft*]" (*RD* 65–66; 55–56).

This schematic reminder seemed necessary to me for two reasons. On the one hand, in order to underline the difficulty of translating this sensible, critical, and sensitive [*névralgique*] word *Geschlecht*; on the other hand, in order to indicate its irreducible bond to the question of humanity (versus animality), and of a humanity whose name, as the bond of the name to the "thing," if one can say that, remains as problematic as that of the language in which the name is inscribed. What does one say when one says *Menschheit, humanitas, Humanität, mankind*, and so on, or when one says *Geschlecht* or *Menschengeschlecht*? Is one saying the same thing? In passing, I would also recall the criticism Marx addressed in *The German Ideology* to the socialist Karl Grün, whose nationalism, Marx observed ironically, claimed to represent a "human nationality" better than the nationalisms of other (French, American, Belgian) socialists.

In the letter addressed to the Academic Rectorate of Albert-Ludwigs-Universität in November 1945, Heidegger explains his own attitude during the Nazi period. He had thought, he said, that he would be able to distinguish between the national and nationalism, that is, between a national and a biological-racial ideology:

> I believed that Hitler, after he assumed responsibility for the whole nation in 1933, would rise above the party and its doctrine and everything would come together, through a renewal and a rallying, in an assumption of responsibility for the West. This belief proved erroneous, as I recognized from the events of June 30, 1934. It had brought me in 1933/34 to the intermediate position where I affirmed the national and the social (not the nationalistic) and rejected its spiritual and metaphysical grounding on the basis of the biologism of the Party doctrine, because the social and the national, as I saw them, were not essentially tied to a biological-racial ideology.[2]

The condemnation of biologism and racism, and of the whole ideological discourse of Rosenberg, inspires numerous Heidegger texts, whether it be the Rectoral Address or the lectures on Hölderlin and Nietzsche, or the question of technology that is always put in perspective against the utilization of knowledge for technical and utilitarian ends, against the Nazis' professionalization and marketing of university knowledge. I will not reopen today the dossier of Heidegger's "politics." I have done so in other seminars, and we have today a rather large number of texts available for deciphering the classic and henceforth academic dimensions of this problem. But everything I will try to do now will maintain an indirect relation to another, perhaps less visible, dimension of the *same* drama. Today, I will begin then by speaking of that monstrosity I announced a few moments ago. This will be another detour through the question of man (*Mensch* or *homo*) and of the "we" that gives its enigmatic content to a *Geschlecht*.

Why "monster"? Not in order to make the thing pathetic, nor because we are always close to some monstrous *Unheimlichkeit* when we are prowling around the nationalist thing and the thing named *Geschlecht*. What is *un monstre*, a monster? You know the polysemic gamut of this word, the uses that can be made of it, for example, concerning norms and forms, species and genus: thus concerning *Geschlecht*. I will begin by privileging here another course. It goes in the direction of a lesser-known meaning, since in French "la *monstre*" (a change of gender, sex, or *Geschlecht*) has the poetico-musical sense of a diagram that *shows* [montre] in a piece of music the number of verses and the number of syllables assigned to the poet. *Monstrer* is *montrer* [to show or demonstrate], and *une monstre* is *une montre* [a watch]. I am already settling into the untranslatable idiom of my language, for I certainly intend to speak to you about translation. *La monstre*, then, prescribes the divisions of a line of verse for a melody. *Le monstre* or *la monstre* is what shows [*montre*] in order to warn or put on guard. In the past *la montre*, in French, was written *la monstre*.

Why this melo-poetic example? Because the monster I am going to speak to you about comes from a well-known poem of Hölderlin's, "Mnemosyne," which Heidegger often contemplates, interrogates, and interprets. In the second of its three versions, the one that Heidegger cites in *Was heisst Denken?*, one reads the famous stanza:

Ein Zeichen sind wir, deutungslos,
Schmerzlos sind wir und haben fast
Die Sprache in der Fremde verloren[3]

Among the three French translations of this poem, there is one by Aloys Becker and Gérard Granel, the translators of *Was heisst Denken?* Translating Hölderlin in Heidegger, this translation uses the word *monstre* (for *Zeichen*), in a style that at first seemed to me a little mannered and gallicizing, but that, on reflection, seems thought-provoking in any case.

Nous sommes un monstre privé de sens
Nous sommes hors douleur
Et nous avons perdu
Presque la langue à l'étranger[4]

[We are a monster void of sense
We are outside sorrow
And have nearly lost
Our tongue in foreign lands]

Leaving aside the allusion to the tongue lost in foreign lands, which

would lead me back to the seminar on nationality too quickly, I would
first like to stress the "we . . . monster." We are a monster, in the singular,
a sign that shows and warns, but all the more singular since, showing,
signifying, designating, this sign is void of sense (*deutungslos*). *It calls itself*
void of sense, simply and doubly monster, this "we": we are a sign—showing, informing, warning, pointing as sign toward, but in truth toward
nothing, a remote sign [*à l'écart*], at a distance from the sign [*en écart
par rapport au signe*], a display [*montre*] that deviates from the display or
monstration, a monster that shows [*montre*] nothing. Isn't such a gap in
the sign's relation to itself and to its so-called normal function already a
monstrosity of monstrasity [*monstrosité*], a monstrosity of monstration?
And this is we, we inasmuch as we have nearly lost our tongue in foreign
lands, perhaps in a translation. But this "we," the monster, is it man?

The translation of *Zeichen* by *monstre* has a triple virtue. It recalls a motif at work ever since *Sein und Zeit*: the bond between *Zeichen* and *zeigen*
or *Aufzeigung*, between the sign and monstration. Paragraph 17 ("Ver-
weisung und Zeichen") analyzes the *Zeigen eines Zeichens*, the showing of
the sign, and touches in passing on the question of the fetish. In *Unterwegs
zur Sprache, Zeichen* and *Zeigen* are linked to *Sagen*, more precisely to the
High German idiom *Sagan:* "'Sagan' heisst: zeigen, erscheinen-, sehen-
and hören-lassen."[5] Further on: "In keeping with the most ancient use of
the word we understand saying [*die Sage*] in terms of showing, pointing
out, signaling [*die Zeige: la monstre*]" (*US* 253; 123, a word underlined by
Heidegger who has moreover just cited Trakl, to whom we will return
in a moment). The second virtue of the French translation by "*monstre*"
has value only in the Latin idiom, since the translation stresses this gap
in relation to the normality of the sign, a sign that for once is not what
it should be, shows or signifies nothing, shows the *pas de sens*, no-sense,
and announces the loss of the tongue. The third virtue of this translation
poses the question of man. Omitting a long digression here, which I had
thought necessary, on how humanism, nationalism, and Europocentric
universalism are in some sense profoundly linked, let me quickly move
on to the interpretation of "Mnemosyne" by Heidegger. The "we" of "Ein
Zeichen sind wir," is it indeed a "we men"? Numerous indications would
lead one to think that the response of the poem remains rather ambiguous. If "we" were "we men," this humanity would indeed be determined
in a way that was rather monstrous, apart from the norm, and notably
from the humanist norm. But Heidegger's interpretation that prepares

and gives access to this Hölderlin quotation says something about man, and then too about *Geschlecht*, about the *Geschlecht* and the word *"Geschlecht"* that still awaits us in the text on Trakl in *Unterwegs zur Sprache*.

In a word, to save time, let me just say that it is about the hand, about the hand of man, about the relation of the hand to speech and to thought. And even if the context is not at all classical, at issue is an opposition that is posed very classically, very dogmatically and metaphysically (even if the context is far from dogmatic and metaphysical), between a man's hand and an ape's hand. Also at issue is a discourse that says everything about the hand or the gift as a site of sexual desire, as one says, of the *Geschlecht* in sexual difference.

The hand: the proper characteristic of man as sign, *monstre* (*Zeichen*). "The hand reaches and extends, receives and welcomes—and not just things: the hand extends itself, and receives its own welcome in the hands of the other. The hand holds. The hand carries. The hand designs and signs, presumably because man is a sign [*Die Hand zeichnet, vermutlich weil der Mensch ein Zeichen ist*]" (*WD* 51; 16). Does the *Phenomenology of Spirit* say anything different?

This seminar of 1951–52 is later than the "Letter on Humanism," which withdraws the question of Being from the metaphysical or ontotheological horizon of classic humanism: *Dasein* is not the *homo* of this humanism. So we are not going to suspect Heidegger of simply falling back into that humanism. On the other hand, the date and the thematic of this passage bring it into agreement with the thinking of the gift, of giving, and of the *es gibt* that goes beyond the earlier formulation of the question of the meaning of Being, without overturning it.

In order to situate more precisely here what one might call the thinking of the hand, but also the hand of thinking, a thinking of the human *Geschlecht*, a thinking that claims to be nonmetaphysical, let us remark that this thinking is developed at a point in the seminar ("Summary and Transition" from the first to the second hour [*WD* 48ff.; 12ff.]) that repeats the question of the teaching of thinking, in particular in the university, as the place of sciences and technology. It is in this passage that I cut out, so to speak, the form and the passage of the hand: Heidegger's hand. The issue of *L'Herne* in which I first published "*Geschlecht* I" bore on its cover a photograph of Heidegger holding his pen with both hands above a manuscript—a studied and significant choice. Even if he never used it, Nietzsche was the first thinker of the West to have a typewriter, of which we have a photograph. Heidegger himself could write only with the pen, with the hand of a craftsman and not a mechanic, as the text that we are going to look at prescribes. Since then I have studied all the published photographs of Heidegger, especially in an album bought in Freiburg when I gave a lecture on Heidegger there in 1979. The play and the theater of hands in the album would deserve an entire seminar. Were I not to renounce this project, I would stress the deliberately craftsmanlike staging of the hand play, of the monstration and demonstration that is exhibited there, whether it be a matter of the handling [*maintenance*] of the pen, of the wielding of the cane, which points rather than supports, or of the water bucket near the fountain. The demonstration of hands is as gripping in the accompanying discourse. On the cover of the catalogue, the only thing that overflows the frame, the frame of the window but also of the photograph, is Heidegger's hand.

The hand is monstrasity [*monstrosité*], the proper characteristic of man as the being of monstration. This distinguishes him from every other *Geschlecht*, and above all from the ape.

One cannot talk about the hand without talking about technology.

Heidegger has just recalled that the problem of university teaching results from the fact that the sciences belong to the essence of technology: not to technology, but to the essence of technology. Technology remains plunged in a fog, for which no one is responsible, neither science, nor the scientists, nor man in general. Simply what is most thought-provoking (*das Bedenklichste*) is that *we* still do not think. Who, we? All of us, Heidegger specifies, including him who speaks here and even him first of all ("der Sprecher mit einbegriffen, er sogar zuerst"). To be the first among those who are still not thinking—is that to think more or less the "still not" of what is most thought-provoking, namely, that we are still not thinking? The first, here, the one who speaks and *shows himself* in speaking thus, designating himself in the third person, *der Sprecher*, is he the first because he is already thinking (what) we are still not thinking and already says so? Or indeed is he the first who is still not thinking, thus the last to be already thinking (what) we are still not thinking, which would not prevent him, however, from speaking in order to be the first to say this? These questions would deserve long developments on the auto-situation, the self-monstration of a speech [*parole*] that claims to teach while speaking of teaching and claims to think what learning is and first of all learning to think. "This is why," Heidegger continues, "we are here attempting to learn thinking [*Darum versuchen wir hier, das Denken zu lernen*]" (*WD* 49; 14). But what is learning [*apprendre*]? The answer, untranslatable in its literalness, passes through a very subtle craft work, a work of the hand and of the pen among the words *entsprechen, Entsprechung, zusprechen, Zuspruch.* Let me, instead of translating, roughly paraphrase: to learn, *apprendre*, is to relate what we are doing to a correspondence (*Entsprechung*) in us with what is essential (*wesenhaft*). To illustrate this attunement [*accord*] with essence, we are given the traditional example of philosophical didactics, that of the joiner, of the apprentice joiner. Heidegger chooses the word *Schreiner* rather than *Tischler*, for he intends to speak of an apprentice joiner (*Schreinerlehrling*) who works on a cabinet (*Schrein*). And later he will say: "Perhaps thinking, too, is just something like building a cabinet [*wie das Bauen an einem Schrein*]" (*WD* 50; 16). The apprentice cabinetmaker learns not only to use tools, not only to familiarize himself with the use, the utility, the toolness [*outilité*] of things for making. If he is a "true cabinetmaker [*ein echter Schreiner*]," he inclines [*se porte*] or relates himself to the different ways of the wood itself, is attuned to the forms that sleep in the wood as it enters man's dwelling ("in das Wohnen des Menschen"). The true joiner is attuned to the hidden plenitude of the wood's essence, and not to the tool or to use value. But to the hidden plenitude insofar as it enters the inhabited site (I stress here this value of *site* [lieu] for reasons that will appear later), and inhabited by *man*. There is no craft, *métier*, of joiner without this correspondence between the essence of the wood and the essence of man as the being who inhabits. In German, *métier* is *Handwerk*, work of the hand, handiwork, handling, if not maneuver. When French must translate *Handwerk* by *métier*, perhaps it is legitimate and unavoidable, but it is a risky maneuver, in the craft of translation, because in it the hand is lost. And reintroduced in this translation is what Heidegger wants to avoid, the service rendered, utility, the office, the *ministerium*, from which, perhaps, the word *métier* comes. *Handwerk*, the noble craft, is a manual craft that cannot, like other professions, be put to public use or to the pursuit of profit. This noble craft, as *Handwerk*, is also that of the thinker or the teacher [*l'enseigneur*] who teaches thinking (the teacher [*l'enseigneur*] is not necessarily the teacher [*l'enseignant*], the professor of philosophy). Without this attunement to the essence of wood, itself attuned to man's dwelling, the activity would be empty. It would remain just activity (*Beschäftigung*) oriented by trade (*Geschäft*), commerce, and the taste for profit. Though merely implicit, the hierarchy and the evaluation are very clear: on the one hand, but also higher, on the side of what is best, handiwork (*Handwerk*) guided by the essence of the human dwelling, by the wood of the hut [*la hûte*] rather than by the metal or glass of the city; on the other hand, but also lower, the activity that cuts the hand off from the essential, useful activity, utilitarianism guided by capital. Indeed, as Heidegger himself recognizes, the inauthentic can always contaminate the authentic; the authentic cabinetmaker can become a furniture dealer for "large stores" (supermarkets), the artisan of the dwelling or habitat can become the international corporation called, I believe, "Habitat." The hand is in danger. Always: "All handiwork [*Handwerk*], all human dealings [*Handeln*] are constantly in that danger. The writing of poetry [*das Dichten*] is no more exempt from it than is thinking [*das Denken*]" (*WD* 50; 14–15, translation modified). The analogy is double: between *Dichten* and *Denken* on the one hand, but also, on the other, between the two, poetry and thought, and authentic handiwork (*Handwerk*). To think is a handiwork, Heidegger says explicitly. He says it without any detour and without even that "perhaps [*vielleicht*]" that had moderated the analogy of thought with the manufacture of the cabinet, which is "perhaps" like thought. Here, without analogy and without "perhaps," Heidegger declares: "At any rate, it [thinking, *das Denken*] is a craft, a 'handicraft' [*Es ist jedenfalls ein Hand-Werk*], a work of the hand, in two words" (*WD* 50–51; 16).

This does not mean that one is thinking *with* one's hands, as we say in English and French, that one speaks *with* one's hands when one's discourse is accompanied by voluble gestures, or that one thinks *with* one's feet, *avec ses pieds*, when one is, as we say in French, "bête comme ses pieds," literally, as stupid as one's feet, that is, too stupid for words. What does Heidegger mean then, and why does he choose the hand, whereas elsewhere he more readily links thought to light or to *Lichtung*, one might say to the eye, or else to hearing and the voice?

Three remarks in preparation for a response:

1. I have chosen this text in order to introduce a reading of *Geschlecht*. In this text, Heidegger links thinking [*le penser*], and not only philosophy, to a thought [*une pensée*] or to a situation of the body (*Leib*), of the body of man and of the human being (*Menschheit*). This will allow us to glimpse a dimension of *Geschlecht* as sex or sexual difference in relation to what is said or not said about the hand. Thinking is not cerebral or disincarnate; the relation to the essence of Being is a certain *manner* of *Dasein*

as *Leib*. (I take the liberty of referring to what I have said on this subject in my first article on *Geschlecht*.

2. Heidegger privileges the hand when, speaking of the relationship between thinking and the craft of teaching, he distinguishes between the everyday profession (an activity, *Beschäftigung*, oriented by useful service and the pursuit of profit, *Geschäft*), and, on the other hand, the authentic *Hand-Werk*. And yet to define *Hand-Werk*, which is not a profession, one must think *Werk*, *œuvre*, work, but also *Hand* and *handeln*, which cannot be translated simply by "acting [*agir*]." The hand must be thought. But it cannot be thought as a thing, a being, even less as an object. The hand thinks before being thought; *it is thought*, a thought, thinking.

3. My third remark will be more narrowly tied to a classic treatment of Heidegger's "politics" in the National Socialist context. In all his self-justifications after the war, Heidegger presents his discourse on the essence of technology as a protest, an act of *resistance* barely disguised *against* (1) the professionalization of university studies on which the Nazis and their official ideologues embarked. Heidegger recalls this in connection with his Rectoral Address, which, in fact, condemned the professionalization that is also a technologization of study; and (2) the submission of National Socialist philosophy to the empire and imperatives of technological productivity. The meditation on authentic *Hand-Werk* also has the sense of an artisanal protest against the hand's effacement or debasement in the industrial automation of modern mechanization. This strategy has, one might suspect, equivocal effects: it leads to an archaistic turn to the rustic artisan class and denounces business or capital, notions whose associations were then well known. In addition, with the division of labor, what is called "intellectual work" is what implicitly finds itself thus discredited.

Having said this, I still want to underscore the idiomaticity of what Heidegger says to us about the hand: "Mit der Hand hat es eine eigene Bewandtnis" (*WD* 51; 16). With the hand one is dealing with a thing entirely particular, proper, singular. *Une chose à part* (a thing apart), as the French translation says, running the risk of having one think of a separate thing, of a separate substance, and Descartes says of the hand that it is a part of the body but a part endowed with such independence that it could also be considered a substance unto itself and almost separable. It is not in this sense that Heidegger says that the hand is a thing apart. What is proper or particular (*eigene*) to the hand is not that it is a part of the organic body, as the common representation (*gewöhnliche Vorstellung*) claims and against which Heidegger invites us to think.

The being of the hand (*das Wesen der Hand*) does not let itself be determined as a bodily organ of prehension (*als ein leibliches Greiforgan*). It is not an organic part of the body intended to grasp, take hold, or indeed grip [*griffer*], and let us add grasp [*prendre*], comprehend, conceive, if one moves from *Greif* to *begreifen* and to *Begriff*. Heidegger could not help but let the thing be said, and here one could follow, as I have tried to elsewhere, the entire problematic of the philosophical "metaphor," in particular in Hegel, who presents the *Begriff* as the intellectual or intelligible structure "relieving" (*aufhebend*) the sensible act of grasping (*begreifen*), of comprehending by taking hold, by laying one's hands on, by mastering and manipulating. If there is a thinking of the hand or a hand of thinking, as Heidegger gives us to think, it is not of the order of a conceptual grasping. Rather the thinking of the hand belongs to the essence of the *gift*, of a giving that would give, if this is possible, without taking anything. If the hand is also, and no one can deny this, an organ of prehension (*Greiforgan*), that is not its essence, that is not the hand's essence for the human being. This critique of organicism and biologism also has the political destination I spoke of a moment ago. But is this enough to justify the critique?

Here in fact there occurs a sentence that seems to me both symptomatic and dogmatic. Dogmatic, that is to say, also metaphysical, related to one of those "common representations" that risks compromising the force and necessity of the discourse in this place. This sentence comes down to distinguishing the human *Geschlecht*, our *Geschlecht*, and the animal *Geschlecht*, the *Geschlecht* that is called "animal." I believe, and I have often believed I must underscore this, that the manner, lateral or central, in which a thinker or scientist speaks of so-called animality constitutes a decisive symptom regarding the essential axiomatic of the given discourse. No more than anyone else, classic or modern, does Heidegger seem to me here to escape this rule when he writes: "Apes, *for example* [my emphasis—JD], have organs that can grasp, but they do not have hands [*Greiforgane besitzt z.B. der Affe, aber er hat keine Hand*]" (*WD* 51; 16).

Dogmatic in its form, this traditional statement presupposes an empirical or positive knowledge whose titles, proofs, and signs are never shown. Like most of those who speak of animality as philosophers or persons of good sense, Heidegger takes no account of a certain "zoological knowledge" that grows, becomes differentiated and more refined regarding what is brought together under this so general and confused word "animality." He does not criticize it and does not even examine it here in terms of the sorts of presuppositions—metaphysical or other—that it may also harbor. This nonknowledge raised to the status of settled knowledge, then exhibited as an essential proposition about the essence of the ape's prehensile organs, an ape that supposedly has no hand, this is not only, in its form, a kind of empirico-dogmatic hapax, misled or misleading in the middle of a discourse that holds itself to the highest level of the most demanding thought, beyond philosophy and science. In its very content, this statement marks the text's essential scene. It marks it with a humanism that is certainly supposed to be nonmetaphysical (Heidegger underscores this in the following paragraph), but this humanism nonetheless inscribes—between a human *Geschlecht* that one wants to withdraw from biologistic determinations (for the reasons I mentioned earlier) and an animality that one encloses in its organico-biological programs—not *some* differences but an absolute, oppositional limit. Elsewhere I have tried to show that, like every opposition, this absolute oppositional limit erases differences and leads back to the homogeneous, according to the most resistant metaphysico-dialectical tradition. What Heidegger says of the ape deprived of hand—and thus, as we are going to see, deprived of thought, of language, of gift—is not only dogmatic in its form because Heidegger knows nothing about it and does not want to know anything about it here.[6] It is serious because it traces a system of limits within which everything he says about man's hand takes on meaning and value. From the moment such a delimitation is problematic, the name of man, his *Geschlecht,* itself becomes problematic. For it names that which has the hand, and thus thought, speech or language, and the opening to the gift.

Thus man's hand would be a thing apart, not as separable organ, but because it is different, dissimilar (*verschieden*) from all prehensile organs (paws, claws, talons); it is infinitely (*unendlich*) removed from these through the abyss of its being, "durch einen Abgrund des Wesens."

This abyss is speech and thought. "Only a being who can speak, that is, think, can have hands and can handily [*in der Handhabung*] achieve works of handicraft [*Nur ein Wesen, das spricht, d.h. denkt, kann die Hand haben and in der Handhabung Werke der Hand vollbringen*]" (*WD* 51; 16). The hand of man is thought on the basis of thinking [*depuis la pensée*], but thinking is thought on the basis of speech or language. That is the order Heidegger opposes to metaphysics: "[O]nly when man speaks, does he think—not the other way around, as metaphysics still believes [*Doch nur insofern der Mensch spricht, denkt er; nicht umgekehrt, wie die Metaphysik es noch meint*]" (*WD* 51; 16).

The essential moment of this meditation opens onto what I will call the hand's double *vocation*. I use the word vocation to recall that, in its destination (*Bestimmung*), the hand holds (on to) speaking. This vocation is double but gathered or crossed in the same hand: the vocation to show [*montrer*] or to sign (*zeigen, Zeichen*) and to give or give itself, in a word, the monstrasity [*monstrosité*] *of the gift or of what gives itself.*

> But the craft of the hand [*das Werk der Hand*] is richer than we commonly imagine [*meinen*: we believe, are of the opinion]. The hand does not only grasp and catch [*greift und fängt nicht nur*], or push and pull. The hand reaches and extends, receives and welcomes [*reicht und empfängt*—the German consonances must be heard: *greift, fängt/reicht, empfängt*]—and not just things: the hand extends itself, and receives its own welcome in the hands of the other. The hand holds [*hält*]. The hand carries [*trägt*]. (*WD* 51; 16)

This passage from the transitive gift, if one can say this, to the gift of what gives *itself*, which gives itself as being-able-to-give, which gives the gift, this passage from the hand that gives something to the hand that gives *itself* is clearly decisive. We find a passage of the same type or of the same structure in the following sentence: not only does man's hand sign and show, but man is himself a sign or a monster [*monstre*], and this is what begins the quotation and the interpretation of "Mnemosyne," on the following page:

> The hand designs and signs [*zeichnet*], presumably because man is a sign [*ein Zeichen*]. Two hands fold into one [*falten sich*: also, join together], a gesture meant to carry man into the great oneness [*Einfalt*; I am not sure I understand this sentence, which plays on *sich falten* and *Einfalt*; whether it be a question of prayer—the hands of Dürer—or of more common gestures; what matters above all is that the hands touch each other as such, auto-affect each other, even at the touch of the other's hand in the gift of the hand, and that the hands also be able to *show themselves*]. The hand is all this, and this is the true handicraft [*das eigentliche Hand-Werk*]. Everything is rooted here that is commonly known as handicraft [*Handwerk*], and commonly we go no further. But the hand's gestures [*Gebärden*: a word that Heidegger has studied in other texts as well] run everywhere through language [or through the tongue], in

their most perfect purity precisely when man speaks by being silent. And only when man speaks, does he think—not the other way around, as metaphysics still believes. Every motion of the hand in every one of its works carries itself [*trägt sich*] through the element of thinking, every bearing of the hand bears itself [*gebärdet sich*] in that element. All the work of the hand is rooted in thinking. Therefore, thinking [*das Denken*] itself is man's simplest, and for that reason hardest, handiwork [*Hand-Werk*], if it would be accomplished at its proper time [*eigens*: properly]. (*WD* 51; 16–17)

The nerve of the argument seems to me reducible, *in the first place and at first sight*, to the assured opposition between *giving* and *taking*: man's hand *gives and gives itself*, like thinking or like what gives itself to be thought and that we are still not thinking, whereas the organ of the ape or of man as a simple animal, indeed as an *animal rationale*, can only *take, grasp, lay hold of the thing*. Because of time constraints, I must refer to an older seminar ("Donner le temps" [1977]) in which this opposition was already problematized. Nothing is less assured than the distinction between *giving* and *taking*, both in the Indo-European languages that we speak (here I am referring to a famous text by Benveniste, "Gift and Exchange in the Indo-European Vocabulary")[7] and in the experience of an *economy*—symbolic or imaginary, conscious or unconscious, all these values remaining precisely to be reelaborated from the precariousness of that opposition of the gift and of the grip, of the gift that presents or makes a gift [*fait présent*] and the gift that takes, keeps, or holds back, of the gift that does good and of the gift that does bad, of the present [*cadeau*] and of the poison (*gift/Gift* or *pharmakon*, etc.).

But in the end this opposition would refer, in Heidegger, to the opposition between giving/taking-the-thing *as such* and giving/taking without this *as such*, and finally without the thing itself. One might say that the animal can only take or manipulate the thing insofar as it is not dealing with the thing *as such*. It does not let the thing be what it is in its essence. The animal does not have access to the essence of Being *as such* (see Heidegger, *Gesamtausgabe*, vols. 29–30: 290). More or less directly, the hand or the word *Hand* plays an immense role in the whole Heideggerian conceptuality since *Sein und Zeit*, notably in the determination of presence according to the mode of *Vorhandenheit* or *Zuhandenheit*. The first has been translated more or less well in French by *étant subsistant* and better in English by "presence-at-hand"; the second by *être disponible* [being available], like a tool or implement, and better, since the English can keep the hand, by "ready-to-hand," "readiness-to-hand." *Dasein* is neither *vorhanden* nor *zuhanden*. Its mode of presence is other, but it must indeed have a hand in order to relate itself to other modes of presence.

The question posed by *Sein und Zeit* (§ 15) gathers the greatest force of its economy in the German idiom and, in that idiom, in the Heideggerian idiom: is or is not *Vorhandenheit* founded (*fundiert*) on *Zuhandenheit*? Literally: what is, in the two relations to the hand, the one that founds the other? How is one to describe this foundation *according to the hand* in what returns *Dasein* to the Being of beings that it is not (*Vorhandensein* and *Zuhandensein*)? Which hand founds the other? The hand that is related to the thing as maneuverable tool or the hand as relation to the thing as subsisting and independent object? This question is decisive for the whole strategy of *Sein und Zeit*. The stakes: nothing less than Heidegger's original procedure for deconstructing the classical order of foundation (the end of § 15). This entire passage is also an analysis of *Handeln*, of action or practice as gesture of the hand in its relation to sight, and thus a new putting into perspective of what is called the *praxis/theoria* opposition. Let us recall that for Heidegger "'practical' behavior is not "'atheoretical.'"[8] And I am only going to quote a few lines in order to draw out two guiding threads:

> The Greeks had an appropriate term for "Things" [*Dinge*]: *pragmata*—that is to say, that which one has to do with [*zu tun*] in one's concernful dealings [*im besorgenden Umgang*] (*praxis*). But ontologically, the specifically "pragmatic" character of the *pragmata* is just what the Greeks left in obscurity [*im Dunkeln*: in short the Greeks were beginning to leave the *Zuhandenheit* of the tool in obscurity to the advantage of the *Vorhandenheit* of the subsisting object: one could say that they were inaugurating all of classical ontology by leaving a hand in the dark, by leaving a hand to bring umbrage to the other, by substituting, in a violent hierarchy, one experience of the hand for another]; they thought of these "proximally" as "mere Things [*blosse Dinge*]." We shall call those entities which we encounter in concern [*im Besorgen*] "*equipment* [Zeug]." In our everyday dealings [in everyday life, *im Umgang*, in our daily and social surroundings] we come across equipment for writing, sewing, working, transportation, measurement [these are inadequate translations of *Schreibzeug, Nähzeug, Werk-, Fahr-, Messzeug*]. The kind of Being which equipment [*Zeug*] possesses must be exhibited. The clue for doing this lies in our first defining [*Umgrenzung*: delimitation] what makes an item of equipment—namely, its equipmentality [*Zeughaftigkeit*]. (*SZ* 68; 96–97)

This mode of being is precisely *Zuhandenheit* (readiness-to-hand). And Heidegger will begin, in order to speak about it in the following paragraph, by taking examples that he has, in some sense, near at hand: the writing desk (*Schreibzeug*), pen (*Feder*), ink (*Tinte*), paper (*Papier*), what is happily called *le sous-main* in French, the blotting pad (*Unterlage*), the table, lamp, furniture, and, his eyes rising above his hands writing, the windows, doors, the room.

Here now are the two threads I would like to draw, by hand, from this text, in order to make them guiding threads or in order to sew and also write a little in my own way.

A. The first concerns *praxis* and *pragmata*. I had already written all this when John Sallis, whom I would like to thank here, drew my attention to a much later passage in Heidegger. It punctuates in a gripping way this long maneuver that makes the *path of thinking* and the question of the meaning of Being a long and continuous meditation *on* the hand. Heidegger always says of thinking that it is a path, on the way (*Unterwegs*); but on the way, on the march, the thinker is unceasingly occupied with thinking the hand. Long after *Sein und Zeit*, which does not speak *thematically* of the hand when analyzing *Vorhanden-* and *Zuhandenheit*, but ten years before *Was heisst Denken?*, which thematizes the hand, there is the seminar on Parmenides (*Parmenides*, in *Gesamtausgabe*, vol. 54) that, in 1942–43, once again takes up the meditation on *pragma* and *praxis*. Although the German word *Handlung* is not the literal translation of *pragma*, it is on target, if correctly understood, it encounters "the originally essential essence of *pragma* [*das ursprünglich wesentliche Wesen von* pragma]," since these *pragmata* present themselves, as *Vorhandenes* and *Zuhandenes*, within the reach of the hand (*im Bereich der "Hand"*).[9] All the motifs of *Was heisst Denken?* are already in place. Only a being that, like man, "has" speech (*Wort, mythos, logos*) can and must have hands thanks to which prayer can come about, but also murder, greeting and thanks, oath and signal (*Wink*), *Handwerk* in general. I underscore for reasons that will appear later the allusion to *Handschlag* (the handshake or what is called "shaking on it") that "grounds," Heidegger says, the alliance, the accord, the engagement (*Bund*). The hand comes into its essence (*west*) only in the movement of truth, in the double movement of concealment and disclosure (*Verbergung/Entbergung*). Moreover, the whole seminar is devoted to the history of truth (*alētheia, lethē, lathon, lathēs*). When he says, in this same passage, that the animal has no hand, that a hand can never originate from a paw or claws, but only from speech, Heidegger specifies that "man does not 'have' hands," but that *the* hand occupies man's essence in order to dispose of it ("Der Mensch 'hat' nicht Hände, sondern die Hand hat das Wesen des Menschen inne") (*P* 118–19; 80).

B. The second thread leads back to writing. If man's hand is what it is only from out of speech or the word (*das Wort*), the most immediate, the most originary manifestation of this origin will be the hand's gesture for making the word manifest, namely, handwriting, manuscripture (*Handschrift*), which shows [*montre*]—and inscribes the word for the gaze. "The word as what is inscribed [*eingezeichnete*] and what thus appears to the gaze [*und so dem Blick sich zeigende*] is the written word, i.e., script [*d.h. die Schrift*]. And the word as script is handwriting [*Das Wort als die Schrift aber ist die Handschrift*]" (*P* 119; 80). Instead of handwriting, let us say rather manuscripture, for, let us not forget, the writing of the typewriter against which Heidegger is going to lodge an implacable indictment is also a handwriting. In the brief "'history' of the art of writing [*'Geschichte' der Art des Schreibens*]" he sketches out in a paragraph, Heidegger sees the fundamental motif of a "destruction of the word" or of speech (*Zerstörung des Wortes*). Typographic mechanization destroys this unity of the word, the integral identity, the proper integrity of the spoken word that manuscripture—both because it appears closer to the voice or to the body proper and because it joins the letters together—conserves and gathers together. I insist on this gathering motif for reasons that will also become clear in a moment. The typewriter tends to destroy the word: the typewriter "tears [*entreisst*] writing from the essential realm of the hand, i.e., the realm of the word [of speech]" (*P* 119; 81). The "typed" word is only a copy (*Abschrift*), and Heidegger recalls those beginnings of the typewriter when a typed letter offended good manners. Today, it is the manuscripted letter that seems culpable: it slows down reading and seems outmoded. The manuscripted letter obstructs what Heidegger considers a veritable degradation of the word by the machine. The machine "degrades [*degradiert*]" the word or the speech it reduces to a simple means of transport (*Verkehrsmittel*), to an instrument of commerce and communication. Furthermore, the machine offers the advantage, for those who desire this degradation, of dissimulating manuscripted writing and "character." "The typewriter makes everyone look the same," Heidegger concludes (*P* 119; 81).

One would have to follow closely the paths along which Heidegger's denunciation of the typewriter becomes more serious and more pro-nounced (*P* 124ff.; 84ff.). In the end, the typewriter would dissimulate the very essence of writing and of script ("Die Schreib-maschine verhüllt das Wesen des Schreibens and der Schrift" [*P* 126; 85]). This dissimula-tion is also a movement of withdrawal or subtraction (the words *entz-iehen, Entzug* often recur in this passage). And if in this withdrawal the typewriter becomes *zeichenlos*, signless, unsignifying, a-signifying, that is because it loses the hand. It threatens in any case what, in the hand, holds speech or holds for speech the relation of Being to man and of man to beings. "The hand acts": *die Hand handelt.* The essential co-belonging (*Wesenszusammengehörigkeit*) of hand and speech, man's essential distinc-tion, manifests itself in this, that the hand discloses what is concealed (*die Hand Verborgenes entbirgt*). And the hand does this precisely in its relation to speaking by pointing and by writing, by making signs, signs that show, or rather by giving *forms* called writing to these signs or to these *monstres* ("sie zeigt und zeigend zeichnet und zeichnend die zeigenden Zeichen zu Gebilden bildet. Diese Gebilde heissen nach dem 'Verbum' *graphein* die *grammata*"). This implies, as Heidegger expressly says, that writing is manuscripture in its originating essence ("Die Schrift ist in ihrer We-sensherkunft die Hand-schrift"). And I will add—what Heidegger does not say but which seems to me more decisive still—a manuscripture that is *immediately* bound to speech, or, what is more likely, to a *system of phonetic writing*, unless what gathers together *Wort, zeigen,* and *Zeichen* does not necessarily pass through the voice and unless the speech Hei-degger speaks of here is essentially distinct from all *phonē*. The distinction would be strange enough to warrant emphasis. And yet Heidegger does not breathe a word of this. He insists, on the contrary, on the essential and originary co-belonging of *Sein, Wort, legein, logos, Lesen, Schrift* as *Hand-schrift*. Moreover, this co-belonging that gathers them together stems from the very movement of gathering that Heidegger always reads, here as elsewhere, in *legein* and in *Lesen* ("das 'Lesen', d.h. Sammeln" [*P* 125; 85]). This gathering motif (*Versammlung*) governs the meditation of *Geschlecht* in the text on Trakl that I will evoke briefly in a moment. Here, the protest against the typewriter also belongs, it goes without saying, to an interpretation of technology and to an interpretation of politics on the basis of technology. Just as *Was heisst Denken?* will name Marx a few pages after discussing the hand, so this seminar of 1942–43 situates Lenin and "Leninism" (the name Stalin gave to this "metaphysics"). Heidegger recalls Lenin's remark: "Bolshevism is Soviet power + electrification" (127;

86). He writes this just as Germany is entering the war against Russia and the United States, a country that is also not spared in this seminar—but there was no electric typewriter yet.

This apparently positive evaluation of manuscripture does not exclude, on the contrary, a devalorization of writing in general. This devalorization makes sense given the general interpretation of the art of writing as the growing destruction of the word or of speech. The typewriter is only a modern aggravation of the evil. This evil comes not only through writing but also through literature. Just before the quotation of "Mnemosyne," *Was heisst Denken?* advances two trenchant affirmations: (1) Socrates is "the purest thinker of the West. This is why he wrote nothing [*der reinste Denker des Abendlandes. Deshalb hat er nichts geschrieben*]" (*WD* 52; 17). He knew how to place himself in the draft and in the withdrawing movement of what gives itself to be thought (*in den Zugwind dieses Zuges*). In another passage, which also discusses this withdrawal (*Zug des Entziehens*), Heidegger again distinguishes man from animal, this time from migratory birds. In the very first pages of *Was heisst Denken?* before quoting "Mnemosyne" for the first time, he writes: "Once we are drawn into the withdrawal [*Zug des Entziehens*], we are . . . like migratory birds, but in an entirely different way, caught in the pull of what draws, attracts us by its withdrawal" (*WD* 5; 9). The choice of the example here stems from the German idiom: "migratory bird" is *Zugvogel* in German. We, men, are in the pull (*Zug*) of this withdrawal, *nur ganz anders als die Zugvögel.* (2) Second trenchant affirmation: thought declines the moment one begins to write, *on leaving* [au sortir *de*] thought, *by escaping* [en sortant *de*] thought in order to seek refuge from it, as from the draft. This is the moment when thought entered literature (*Das Denken ging in die Literatur ein*) (*WD* 52; 18). Sheltered from thought, this entry into writing and literature (in the broad sense of the word) would have decided the fate of Western science as much by the way of the *doctrina* of the Middle Ages (teaching, discipline, *Lehre*) as by the science of modern times. At issue naturally is what constructs the dominant concept of discipline, teaching, and the university. Thus one sees all the traits—whose incessant recurrence I have elsewhere recalled under the names logocentrism and phonocentrism—being organized around the hand and speech, with great coherence. Logocentrism and phonocentrism dominate a certain very continuous discourse of Heidegger's—whatever the lateral or marginal motifs that shape it simultaneously—and they dominate from the moment of the repetition of the question of the meaning of Being, the destruction of classic ontology, the existential analytic that redistributes the (existential and categorial) relations among *Dasein, Vorhandensein,* and *Zuhandensein.*

The economy imposed on me by this lecture prevents my going beyond this first point of reference in the Heideggerian interpretation of the hand. In order to link, in a more differentiated coherence, what I am saying here to what I have said elsewhere about Heidegger, in particular in "*Ousia* and *Grammē*," one would have to reread a certain page of "The Anaximander Fragment," that is, a text that also cites "Mnemosyne" and with which "*Ousia* and *Grammē*" is engaged. This page recalls that in *chreon*, which is generally translated as "necessity," the hand speaks *ē cheir*: "*chraō* means: I get involved with something, I reach for it, extend my hand to it [*ich be-handle etwas*]."[10] The rest of the paragraph, too difficult to translate because it works so closely within the German idiom (*in die Hand geben, einhändigen, aushändigen*: to hand back, and then hand over, give up, *überlassen*), removes the participle *chreōn* from the values of constraint and obligation (*Zwang, Müssen*). And it does the same for the word *Brauch* with which Heidegger proposes to translate *to chreōn* and which means, in everyday German, "usage." Thus it is not necessary to think the hand on the basis of "usage." *Der Brauch* is translated into French as *le maintien*, which, besides many shortcomings or false meanings, exploits the chance of a double allusion: to the hand and to the now, the *maintenant*—specific concerns that preoccupy this text. If indeed *brauchen* translates, as Heidegger says it does, the *chreōn* that allows one to think the present in its presence (*das Anwesende in seinem Anwesen*), if it names a trace (*Spur*) that disappears in the history of Being as that history unfolds itself as Western metaphysics, if *der Brauch* is indeed "the gathering (*Versammlung*): *o logos*" (*H* 340; 54–55), then, before all technology of the hand, all surgery, the hand is not there for nothing [*la main n'y est pas pour rien*].

II

The hand of *man* [La *main de l' homme*]: you will certainly have noticed that Heidegger does not only think the hand as a very singular thing that rightfully belongs only to man. He always thinks the hand *in the singular,* as if man did not have two hands but, this monster, a single hand. Not a single organ in the middle of his body, like the Cyclops who had a single eye in the middle of his forehead, although this representation, which leaves something to be desired, also gives one to think. No, *the* hand of man, this signifies that we are no longer dealing with prehensile organs or instrumentalizable limbs that *hands* are. Apes have prehensile organs that resemble hands; the man of the typewriter and of technology in general uses two hands. But the man who speaks and the man who writes by hand, as one says, is he not the monster with a single hand? Thus, when Heidegger writes: "Der Mensch 'hat' nicht Hände, sondern die Hand hat das Wesen des Menschen inne" ("Man does not 'have' hands, but the hand holds the essence of man"), this supplementary precision does not just concern, as we saw in the first instance, the structure of "having," a word Heidegger places in quotation marks and whose relation he proposes to invert (man does not *have* hands, it is the hand that *has* man). The precision concerns the difference between the plural and the singular: *nicht Hände, sondern die Hand.* What comes to man through *logos* or speech (*das Wort*) can be only a single hand. Hands—this is already or still organic or technological dispersion. Thus one should not be surprised by the absence of all allusion, for example of the Kantian kind, to the play of difference between right and left, to the mirror, or to the pair of gloves. This difference can only be *sensible.* For my part, having already discussed the pair of shoes, the left foot and the right foot in Heidegger,[11] I will not go any further today on this path. I will content myself with two remarks. *On the one hand,* as you say in English, the only sentence in which Heidegger, to my knowledge, names man's hands in the plural seems to concern precisely the moment of prayer, or in any case the gesture in which the two hands join together (*sich falten*) to make themselves one in simplicity (*Einfalt*). It is always the gathering (*Versammlung*) that Heidegger privileges. *On the other hand,* nothing is ever said of the caress or of desire. Does one make love, does man make love, with a hand or with hands? And what about sexual difference in this regard? We can imagine Heidegger's protest: this question is derivative; what you call desire or love presupposes the coming [*avènement*] of *the* hand from speech, and as soon as I allude to the hand that gives, gives itself, promises, lets go, gives up, hands over, and engages in the alliance or oath, you have at your disposal everything you need to think what you commonly call making love, caressing, or even desiring. —Perhaps, but why not say it then?[12]

[This last remark will have to serve as a transition to the word, the mark *Geschlecht* that we ought now to have taken up in another text. I will not give this part of my lecture, which should have been titled "*Geschlecht* III" and whose (typed) manuscript has been photo*copied* and distributed to some of you so that a discussion of it might be possible. I will confine myself then to a very cursory sketch of it.]

I just said "the word '*Geschlecht*'": that is because I am not sure it has a determinable and unifiable referent. I am not sure that one can speak of *Geschlecht* beyond the word "Geschlecht"—which is then necessarily cited, between quotation marks, mentioned rather than used. And I leave the word in German. As I have already said, no word, no word for word will suffice to translate this word that gathers, in its idiomatic meaning, stock, race, family, species, genus, generation, sex. And then, after saying the word "*Geschlecht*," I amended or corrected myself: the "mark '*Geschlecht*,'" I clarified. For the theme of my analysis would come down to a sort of composition or decomposition that affects, precisely, the unity of this word. Perhaps it is no longer a word. Perhaps one must begin by gaining access to it from its disarticulation or its decomposition, in other words, its formation, its information, its deformations or transformations, its translations, the genealogy of its body unified on the basis of or according to the split [*partage*] of pieces of words. We are going then to concern ourselves with the *Geschlecht* of *Geschlecht*, with its genealogy or its generation. But this genealogical composition of "*Geschlecht*" will be inseparable, in the text of Heidegger we should be looking at now, from the decomposition of the human *Geschlecht*, from the decomposition of man.

In 1953, one year after *Was heisst Denken?*, Heidegger published "Die Sprache im Gedicht" in the journal *Merkur* under the title "Georg Trakl," with a subtitle that will not change, so to speak, when the text is taken up again in 1959 in *Unterwegs zur Sprache*: "Eine Erörterung seines Gedichtes." All these titles are already practically untranslatable. I will nevertheless have recourse, rather frequently, to the invaluable translation published by Jean Beaufret and Wolfgang Brokmeier in the *Nouvelle Revue Française* (January–February 1958), reprinted in *Acheminement vers la parole*.[13] At each step, the risk of thinking remains intimately engaged with the language, the idiom, and translation. I salute the daring venture that such a translation constituted in its very discretion. Our debt here goes in the direction of a gift that gives much more than what is called a

French version. Each time I will have to diverge from it, it will be without the least intention of evaluating it, even less of amending it. Rather, we will have to multiply the drafts, harass the German word, and analyze it according to several waves of touches, caresses, or blows. A translation, in the usual sense of what is published under this name, cannot indulge itself in this. But we, on the contrary, have the duty to do this every time the calculation of word for word, one word for another, that is, the conventional ideal of translation, is defied. Moreover, it would be legitimate—in appearance mundane, but in truth essential—to take this text on Trakl as a discussion [*Erörterung*] of what we call "translating." At the heart of this situation, of this site [*Ort*], *Geschlecht*, the word or the mark. For it is the composition and the decomposition of this mark, the work of Heidegger in his language, his hand and artisanal writing, his *Hand-Werk*, that these extant translations (the French and, I suppose, the English) tend inevitably to erase.

Before any further preliminaries, I will jump immediately to the middle of the text, in order to throw light as from a first flash on the place that interests me. On two occasions, in the first and the third parts, Heidegger declares that the word *Geschlecht* has in German, "in our language" (it is always a question of "we"), a multitude of meanings. But this singular multitude must gather itself in some way. In *Was heisst Denken?*, just after the passage on the hand, Heidegger protests more than once against one-track thinking or the one-track path. While recalling here that *Geschlecht* is open to a kind of polysemy, he heads, before and after all, toward a certain unity that gathers this multiplicity. This unity is not an identity, but it preserves the simplicity of the same, even in the form of the fold. Heidegger wants to think this originary simplicity beyond all etymological derivation, at least according to the strictly philosophical sense of etymology.

1. The first passage (*US* 49–50; 170; *AP* 53) quotes the next to last stanza of the poem "Autumnal Soul [*Herbstseele*]." I will read it in the French translation that will pose some problems for us later on:

Bientôt fuient poisson et gibier
Âme bleue, obscur voyage
Départ de l'autre, de l'aimé
Le soir change sens et image [*Sinn und Bild*]

[Fish and game soon glide away.
Soon blue soul and long dark journey
Parted us from loved ones, others
Evening changes image, sense]

Heidegger comments: "The wanderers who follow the stranger soon find themselves parted 'from loved ones [*von Lieben*]' who to them are 'others' [*die für sie 'Andere' sind*]. The 'others'—that is the cast of the decomposed form of man [in the French translation: *Les 'Autres,' entendons la souche défaite de l'homme*]."

The last sentence translated in this way is "der Schlag der verwesten Gestalt des Menschen." *Schlag* means several things in German. In the literal sense, as the dictionary would say, it is a *blow* [coup] with all the associated meanings; but in the figurative sense, says the dictionary, it is also race or species, stock [*la souche*] (the word chosen by the French translators). Heidegger's meditation will let itself be guided by the relation between *Schlag* (at once blow and stock) and *Geschlecht*. "Der Schlag der verwesten Gestalt des Menschen" implies a *Verwesen* in the sense of what is "decomposed," if it is understood literally, along the lines of the usual code of bodily putrefaction, but also in another sense of the corruption of Being or essence [*Wesen*] that Heidegger is not going to stop retracing and recalling. Here he opens a paragraph that begins with "Unsere Sprache": "Our language calls [*nennt:* names] the humanity [*Menschenwesen*] that has received the imprint of a striking [*das aus einem Schlag geprägte*] and is cast in this striking [*und in diesen Schlag verschlagene:* and in fact *verschlagen* means commonly to specify, separate, cast adrift, partition, board-up, distinguish, differentiate] . . . '*Geschlecht*'" (translation modified). The word is in quotation marks. I will go to the end of this paragraph whose context will have to be reconstituted later: "The word [*Geschlecht*, then] refers to mankind as a whole [*Menschengeschlecht*] as well as to humanity [*Menschheit*] in the sense of race, tribe, family—all of these in turn cast [*dies alles wiederum geprägt:* cast or struck in the sense of what receives the imprint, the *typos*, the typical mark] in the [generic] duality of the sexes [*in das Zwiefache der Geschlechter*]." "Dualité générique des sexes" is the risky translation in French. Heidegger, it is true, is speaking this time of the *sexual* difference that comes again, in a second blow [*wiederum geprägt*], to hit, to strike (also in the sense that one says in French to strike coins) the *Geschlecht* in all the senses just enumerated. My questions will focus on this second blow. But Heidegger does not say "generic duality." And as for the word *das Zwiefache*, the double, the dual, the duplicitous, it carries the whole enigma of the text that plays itself out between, on the one hand, *das Zwiefache*, a certain duplicity, a certain fold of sexual difference or *Geschlecht*, and, on the other hand, *die Zwietracht der Geschlechter*, the duality of sexes as dissension, war, disagreement, opposition, the duel of violence and of declared hostilities.

(2) The second passage is taken from the third part (*US* 78; 195; *AP* 80) in the course of a trajectory that will indeed have displaced many things:

The "*one*" [in quotation marks and italics in the German text: "*das 'Ein'*"] in "*one* generation" [*im Wort* "Ein *Geschlecht*": quotation of a verse of Trakl; this time the French translators chose, without apparent or satisfactory justification, to translate *Geschlecht* as *race*] does not mean "one" as opposed to "two" [*meint nicht "eins" statt "zwei"*]. Nor does it mean the monotony of dull equality [*das Einerlei einer faden Gleichheit*: on this point I take the liberty of referring to the first part of my essay entitled "*Geschlecht* I"]. "*One* generation" [*das Wort* "Ein *Geschlecht*"] here does not refer to a biological fact at all [*nennt hier . . . keinen biologischen Tatbestand*], neither to a "unisexuality" [*weder die* "Eingeschlechtlichkeit"] nor to an "indifferentiation of the sexes" [*noch die* "Gleichgeschlechtlichkeit"]. In the emphatic "*one* generation" [emphasized by Trakl] [*In dem betonten* "Ein *Geschlecht*"] there is hidden the unifying force that unifies [*einigt*] by virtue of the ghostly night's gathering blue [*l'azur appareillant*; this is incomprehensible if one does not take into consideration, as I try to do in the part of the presentation I will not give, the symphonic or synchromatic reading of the blues or of the blue of the azured sky in Trakl's poems, and if one does not take into consideration that what the French translators are translating by *appareillant* is the word *versammelnd*: gathering, collecting in the same or the "similar {*pareil*}" what is not identical]. The word [namely, the word *Ein* in "Ein *Geschlecht*"] speaks from the song [*Das Wort spricht aus dem Lied*] that sings of evening [or of the West: *worin das Land des Abends gesungen wird*]. Accordingly, the word "generation [*Geschlecht*]" retains here the full manifold meaning [*mehrfältige Bedeutung*] mentioned earlier. For one thing, it names the historical generation of man, mankind [*das geschichtliche Geschlecht des Menschen, die Menschheit*] as distinct from all other living beings (plants and animals) [*im Unterschied zum übrigen Lebendigen* (*Pflanze und Tier*)]. Next the word "generation [*Geschlecht*]" names the races [*Geschlechter*, in the plural: the word *Geschlecht* names the *Geschlechter*], tribes, clans, and families of mankind [*Stämme, Sippen, Familien dieses Menschengeschlechtes*]. At the same time, the word [*Geschlecht*] always refers [*überall:* throughout; Heidegger does not specify "all these distinctions" that the French translation introduces by analogy with the first definition, but no matter] to the twofoldness of the sexes [*die Zwiefalt der Geschlechter:* the French translation here does not name sexuality, which is nonetheless evident, whereas above it translated *Zwiefache der Geschlechter* by *dualité générique des sexes* {generic duality of the sexes}].

Thus Heidegger has just recalled that, *at the same time (zugleich), Geschlecht* names, surnames sexual difference, in addition to all the other meanings. And he begins the following paragraph with the word *Schlag,* which the French translation renders as *frappe* (blow), and which presents a double drawback. On the one hand, the translation misses the reference to the Trakl verse whose word *Flügelschlag* is precisely translated as "wing-beat [*coup d'aile*]." On the other hand, in using two different words, *coup* and *frappe,* to translate the same word *Schlag,* the translation erases what authorizes Heidegger to recall the affinity between *Schlag* and *Geschlecht* in the two verses he is in the process of reading. That affinity supports the whole demonstration. These verses are excerpted from a poem titled "Occidental Song [*Abendländisches Lied*]." Another is titled "Evening Land" or "Occident [*Abendland*]," and the decline of the West, *as* Occident, is at the center of this meditation.

> O der Seele nächtlicher Flügelschlag:
> Ô de l'âme nocturne coup d'aile:
> O the nocturnal wingbeat of the soul: (*US* 77; 194; *AP* 79)

Following these two verses, a colon (two points) and two very simple words: "*Ein* Geschlecht." "*Ein*": the only word that, in his whole corpus, Heidegger notes, Trakl ever stressed. To stress is *betonen.* The word thus underlined (*Ein*) gives the fundamental tone, the fundamental note (*Grundton*). But it is the *Grundton* of *Gedicht* and not of *Dichtung,* for Heidegger regularly distinguishes *Gedicht,* which always remains unspoken (*ungesprochen*), silent, from poems (*Dichtungen*) that say and speak in proceeding from *Gedicht. Gedicht* is the silent source of written and spoken poems (*Dichtungen*) from which one must indeed begin if one is to situate (*erörtern*) the place (*Ort*), the source, namely, *Gedicht.* That is why Heidegger says of "*Ein* Geschlecht" that it shelters the *Grundton* from which the *Gedicht* of this poet keeps the secret (*Geheimnis*) silent (*schweigt*). Thus the paragraph that begins with *Der Schlag* can point not only to a philological decomposition but to what happens in the verse, in Trakl's *Dichtung*: "The force [*Der Schlag*] which marks the tribes of mankind as the simple oneness of 'one generation' [*der sie in die Einfalt des* 'Einen *Geschlechts*' *prägt*], and thus restores them and mankind itself [*die Sippen des Menschengeschlechtes*] to the stiller childhood, strikes [*einge-schlagen lässt*] by prompting the soul to set out toward the 'blue spring' [this is a quotation of Trakl indicated by the quotation marks omitted in the French translation]" (*US* 78–79; 195; *AP* 80).

These, then, are the two passages, still out of context, in which Heidegger thematizes both the polysemy and the focal simplicity of *Geschlecht* in "our language." This language, which is ours, German, is also the language of "our *Geschlecht*," as Fichte would say, if *Geschlecht* also means family, generation, stock. And yet what is written and played out in the writing of this word, *Geschlecht*, in our *Geschlecht* and in our language (*unsere Sprache*) is idiomatic enough in its possibilities to remain almost untranslatable. The affinity between *Schlag* and *Geschlecht* takes place and is thinkable only from this "*Sprache*." Not only from the German idiom, which I hesitate to call a "national" idiom here, but from the overdetermined idiom of a singular *Gedicht* and *Dichten*, here Trakl's, then on top of that overdetermined by the idiom of a *Denken* that passes through Heidegger. I am indeed saying *Dichten* and *Denken*, poetry and thinking. You recall that for Heidegger *Dichten* and *Denken* are a work of the hand exposed to the same dangers as the handicraft (*Hand-Werk*) of the cabinetmaker. We also know that Heidegger never puts philosophy and science on the same level as thinking and poetry. Thinking and poetry, although radically different, are relatives and parallels, parallels that cut across and breach one another, that cut each other in a place that is also a kind of signature (*Zeichnung*), the incision of a cut (*Riss*) (*US* 196; 90).[14] Philosophy, science, and technology are, so to speak, excluded from this parallelism.

What is one to think of this text? How is one to read it?

But is it still a matter of a "lecture," in the French or English sense of the word? No, and for at least two reasons. *On the one hand*, it is too late, and rather than continue to read the hundred or so pages I have devoted to this text on Trakl—and whose first French version, incomplete and provisional, has been communicated to some of you—I will simply take a few minutes and outline their principal concern, inasmuch as it can be translated into a series of suspended or suspensive questions. I have grouped them, more or less artificially, around *five* foci. But, *on the other hand*, one of these foci concerns the concept of *reading*, which does not seem adequate to me, without being completely reelaborated, either for naming what Heidegger is doing in his *Gespräch* with Trakl or in what he calls the authentic *Gespräch* or the *Zwiesprache* (two-speaking) of one poet with another poet or of a thinker with a poet, or for naming what I am trying to do or what interests me in this *explication with (Auseinandersetzung mit)* this particular text of Heidegger's.

My most constant concern is obviously the "mark" *Geschlecht* and what in it *remarks* the mark, the stroke, the impression, a certain writing as *Schlag, Prägung,* and so on. This *re-mark* seems to me to entertain an essential relation with what, a little arbitrarily, I put in the first place among the five foci of questioning:

1. *Concerning man and animality.* The text on Trakl also proposes a thinking of the difference between animality and humanity. At issue here would be the difference between two sexual differences, difference, the relation between the 1 and the 2, and divisibility in general. At the focus of this focus, the mark *Geschlecht* in its polysemy (species or sex) and in its dissemination.

2. Another focus of questioning concerns exactly what Heidegger says of polysemy and that I want to distinguish from dissemination. On several occasions, Heidegger shows himself receptive to what could be called a "good" polysemy, that of poetic language and of the "great poet." This polysemy must let itself be *gathered* in a "higher" univocity and in the oneness of a harmony (*Einklang*). Heidegger thus valorizes *for once* a "*Sicherheit*" of poetic rigor, thus stretched by the force of the gathering. And he opposes this "security [*Sicherheit*]" both to the errancy of mediocre poets who give in to bad polysemy (the polysemy that does not let itself be gathered in a *Gedicht* or in a unique site [*Ort*]) and to the univocity of exactitude (*Exaktheit*) in technoscience. This motif seems to me at once traditional (properly Aristotelian), dogmatic in its form, and symptomatically contradictory of other Heideggerian motifs. For I never "criticize" Heidegger without recalling that this can be done from other places in his own text. His text is not homogeneous, and it is written with two hands, at least.

3. This question, which I entitle *polysemy and dissemination*, communicates with another focus where several *questions of method* intersect. What

is Heidegger doing? How does he "operate" and along what paths, *odoi*, which are not yet or already no longer *methods?* What is Heidegger's step [*pas*] on this path? What is his rhythm in this text that explicitly pronounces itself on the essence of *rhuthmos*, and also what is his *manner*, his *Hand-Werk* of writing? These questions beyond-method [*d'outre-méthode*] are also questions about the relation that this Heidegger text (and the text I am writing in turn) entertains with what is called hermeneutics, interpretation or exegesis, literary criticism, rhetoric or poetics, but also with all the bodies of knowledge of the human or social sciences (history, psychoanalysis, sociology, politology, etc.). Two oppositions or distinctions, two couples of concepts support the Heideggerian argument—and I will question them. There is, *on the one hand*, the distinction between *Gedicht* and *Dichtung*. *Gedicht* (an untranslatable word, once more) is, in its place, what gathers together all the *Dichtungen* (the poems) of a poet. This gathering is not that of a complete corpus, of the complete works, but a unique source that is not present in any part of any poem. It is the place of origin from which and toward which the poems tend according to a "rhythm." It is not elsewhere, not some other thing, and yet it cannot be confused with the poems insofar as they say (*sagen*) something. The *Gedicht* is "unspoken [*ungesprochen*]." What Heidegger wants to indicate, to announce rather than show, is the unique Site (*Ort*) of this *Gedicht*. That is why Heidegger presents his text as an *Erörterung*, that is to say, according to the awakened literalness of this word, a *situating* that localizes the unique site or the proper place of the *Gedicht* from which the poems of Trakl sing. Whence, *on the other hand*, a second distinction, between the *Erörterung* of the *Gedicht* and an *Erläuterung* (clarification, elucidation, explication) of the poems (*Dichtungen*) themselves, with which one must indeed begin. I am following thus all the difficulties that result from this double starting point and from what Heidegger calls *Wechselbezug*, the relation of reciprocity or exchange between discussion (*Erörterung*) and clarification (*Erläuterung*) (*US* 37–38; 160–61). Does this *Wechselbezug* coincide with what is called the hermeneutic circle? And how does Heidegger practice or play, *in his manner*, this *Wechselbezug*?

4. This last formulation, which is always directed at Heidegger's *manner* or, as one also says in French, with another connotation, *ses manières*, his manners, no longer lets itself be separated—no more than the hand according to Heidegger—from the implementation of the language, its

mise en œuvre. In this case, then, from a certain maneuver of writing. This maneuver is such that it always resorts at decisive moments to a resource that is idiomatic, in other words, untranslatable, if one trusts in the common concept of translation. This resource, overdetermined by the idiom of Trakl and by that of Heidegger, is not only the resource of German, but most often of an idiom of the High or Old German idiom. In my manner, that is, following the injunctions and the economy of other idioms, I retrace and remark all these recourses by Heidegger to Old German, every time he begins by saying: "In our language [*in unserer Sprache*] such and such a word originally means [*bedeutet ursprünglich*]. . . . " Here, in this quick overview, I can only give the list of words, of the pieces of words, or of the sentences beside which I will mark a slightly longer stop.

(a) First, naturally, there is the word *"Geschlecht"* and all of its *Geschlecht*, all of its family, its roots, its offshoots, legitimate or not. Heidegger convokes them all and gives to each its role. There is *Schlag, einschlagen, verschlagen* (to separate, partition), *zerschlagen* (to break, smash, dismantle), *auseinanderschlagen* (to separate while striking one another), and so on. Instead of redeploying the whole Heideggerian maneuver here, the one he forces on us, I will quote, as a sign of thanks, a paragraph that David Krell devotes in English to this word in chapter 11 of his book. The chapter is entitled "Strokes of Love and Death," and from it I take the following:[15]

"Strokes of love and death": *Schlag der Liebe, Schlag des Todes.* What do the words *Schlag, schlagen* mean? Hermann Paul's *Deutsches Wörterbuch* lists six principal areas of meaning for *der Schlag*; for the verb *schlagen* it cites six "proper" senses and ten "distant" meanings. Deriving from the Old High German and Gothic *slahan* (from which the English word "slay" also derives) and related to the modern German word *schlachten*, "to slaughter," *schlagen* means to strike a blow, to hit or beat. A *Schlag* may be the stroke of a hand, of midnight, or of the brain; the beating of wings or of a heart. *Schlagen* may be done with a hammer or a fist. God does it through his angels and his plagues; a nightingale does it with his song. One of the most prevalent senses of *schlagen* is to mint or stamp a coin. *Der Schlag* may therefore mean a particular coinage, imprint, or type: a horse dealer might refer to *einem guten Schlag Pferde*. It is by virtue of this sense that *Schlag* forms the root of a word that is very important for Trakl, *das Geschlecht*. Paul lists three principal meanings for *Geschlecht* (Old High German *gislahti*). First, it translates the Latin word *genus*, being equivalent to *Gattung*: *das Geschlecht* is a group of people who share a common ancestry, especially if they constitute a part of the hereditary nobility. Of course, if the ancestry is traced back far enough we may speak of *das menschliche Geschlecht*, "humankind." Second, *das Geschlecht* may mean one generation of men and women who die to make way for a succeeding generation. Third, there are male and female *Geschlechter*, and *Geschlecht* becomes the root of many words for the things males and females have and do for the sake of the first two meanings: *Geschlechts-glied* or *-teil*, the genitals; *-trieb*, the sex drive; *-verkehr*, sexual intercourse; and so on.

(b) Next there is the noun *Ort*. When Heidegger recalls, from the first page, that this word "Originally . . . suggests [*Ursprünglich bedeutet*]" the point of the spear (*die Spitze des Speers*), it is first and foremost (and there is much to say on this "first and foremost") to insist on its power of gathering. Everything *concurs* and converges toward the point (*in ihr läuft alles zusammen*). The site is always the site of a gathering, the gathering, *das Versammelnde*. This definition of site, besides implying the recourse to an "original meaning" in a determined language, governs the whole course of the *Erörterung*, the privilege granted to unicity and to indivisibility in situating the *Gedicht* and what Heidegger calls a "great poet"—great insofar as he is related to that unicity of gathering and resists the forces of dissemination or dislocation (*US* 37; 160). Naturally, I would multiply the questions around this value of gathering.

(c) Next there is the idiomatic and untranslatable opposition between *geistig* and *geistlich*, which plays a determinant role.[16] This opposition authorizes withdrawing the *Gedicht* or the "site" of Trakl both from what is gathered together by Heidegger under the title of "Western metaphysics" (*la* "métaphysique occidentale") and its Platonic tradition, which distinguishes between the "sensible" material and the "intelligible" spiritual (*aisthēton/noeton*), and from the Christian opposition between the spiritual and the temporal. Heidegger again refers to the "original meaning [*ursprüngliche Bedeutung*]" of the word *Geist* (*gheis*): to be lifted, transported outside of oneself, like a flame (*aufgebracht, entsetzt, ausser sich sein*) (*US* 60; 178–79). At issue is the ambivalence of the fire of the spirit, whose flame can be both Good and Evil.

(d) There is still the word *fremd*, which does not mean the foreign, in the Latin sense of what is outside of, extra, *extraneus*, but properly (*eigentlich*), according to the High German *fram*: toward elsewhere, forward, under way toward . . . the encounter with what is reserved for it in advance ("anderswohin vorwärts, unterwegs nach . . . dem Voraufbehaltenen entgegen"). This allows one to say that the Stranger does not wander [*erre*] but has a destination ("es irrt nicht, bar jeder Bestimmung, ratlos umher") (*US* 41; 163); the Stranger is not without destination.

(e) In addition, there is the word *Wahnsinn*, which does not mean, as is often thought, a mind filled with delusions. If one takes *Wahn* back to the High German, *wana* means *ohne, sans, without*, the "Wahnsinnige," the madman is the one who remains *without* the sense of others. He is of another sense, and *Sinnan* "bedeutet ursprünglich" originally means "reisen, streben nach . . . eine Richtung einschlagen," to travel, to strive toward, to fray a direction with a blow. Heidegger invokes the Indo-European root *sent, set*, which would mean *Weg*, path (*US* 53; 173). Here things get complicated, since it is the very sense of the word *sense* that seems untranslatable, tied to an idiom. And it is then this value of sense that, governing nonetheless the traditional concept of translation, suddenly finds itself rooted in a single language, family, or *Geschlecht* of languages, outside of which it loses its original meaning.

If the "situation [*Erörterung*]" of *Gedicht* is thus found to depend at crucial moments on the recourse to the idiom of *Geschlecht* and to the *Geschlecht* of the idiom, how is one to think the relation between the unspoken of *Gedicht* and its belonging—the appropriation of its very silence—to a language and to a *Geschlecht*? This question concerns not only the German *Geschlecht* and the German language, but also those that are recognized in the West, in Western man, since this whole "discussion" is preoccupied with the concern for the place, path, and destination of the West. This brings me to the fifth focus. I multiply the foci in order to "give a change of scenery [*dépayser*]" to an atmosphere that is perhaps a bit too "landed [*paysante*]"; I do not say "peasant [*paysanne*]," even for Trakl . . .

5. What happens to *Geschlecht* as its decomposition (*Verwesung*), its corruption, is a *second blow* that comes to strike the sexual difference and to transform it into dissension, war, savage opposition. The originary sexual difference is tender, gentle, peaceful. When that difference is struck by a "curse" (*Fluch*, a word of Trakl's taken up and interpreted by Heidegger), the duality or the duplicity of the two becomes unleashed, indeed bestial, opposition (*US* 50; 170). Heidegger claims that this schema, which I reduce here to its most summary expression, is, despite all the appearances and signs of which he is well aware, neither Platonic nor Christian. It is neither a question of metaphysical theology nor of ecclesial theology. But the originarity (pre-Platonic, pre-metaphysical, or pre-Christian) to which

Heidegger recalls us and in which he situates the proper place of Trakl has *no other content and even no other language* than that of Platonism and Christianity. It is simply that from which something like metaphysics and Christianity become possible and thinkable. But what constitutes their archi-matinal [*archi-matinale*] origin and their ultra-Western horizon is nothing other than this hollow of a repetition, in the strongest and strangest sense of the term. And the form or "logic" of this repetition is readable not only in this text on Trakl, but in everything that, after *Sein und Zeit*, analyzes the structures of *Dasein*, the fall (*Verfall*), the call (*Ruf*), and care (*Sorge*), and regulates this relation of the "most originary" with what is presumed to be less originary, notably Christianity. In this text, the argument (especially the one used to demonstrate that Trakl is not a Christian poet) takes some particularly laborious and at times very simplistic forms, which I cannot reconstitute in this schema. Just as Heidegger requires a unique gathering place for Trakl's *Gedicht*, so must he presuppose that there is a single place, unique and univocal, for Metaphysics [*LA métaphysique*] and Christianity [*LE christianisme*]. But does this gathering take place? Has it a place, a unity of place? That is the question I will leave suspended thus, just before the *chute*. In French one sometimes calls the end of a text a *chute*. One also says, in place of *chute*, the *envoi*.

—*Translated by John P. Leavey Jr. and Elizabeth Rottenberg*

§ 4   The Laws of Reflection:
Nelson Mandela, in Admiration

I

Admirable Mandela.

Period, no exclamation. I am not using this punctuation to moderate my enthusiasm or to quell my fervor. Instead of speaking only in honor of Nelson Mandela, I will say something about his honor without succumbing, if this is possible, to loftiness, without proclaiming or acclaiming.

The homage will perhaps be more just, as will its tone, if it seems to surrender its impatience—without which there would be no question of admiring—to the coldness of an analysis. Admiration reasons, despite what people say; it works things out with reason; it astonishes and interrogates: how can one be Mandela? Why does he seem exemplary—and admirable in what he thinks and says, in what he does or in what he suffers? Admirable in himself, as well as for what he conveys in his *testimony*, another word for martyrdom, namely, the experience of his people?

"My people and I," he always says, without speaking like a king.

Why does he also *force* one to admire him? This word presupposes some resistance, for his enemies admire him without admitting it. Unlike those who love him among his people and along with his inseparable Winnie, from whom they have always kept him separated in vain, these enemies

This essay was first published in *Pour Nelson Mandela* ("Quinze écrivains saluent Nelson Mandela et le combat dont sa vie porte témoignage [Fifteen writers salute Nelson Mandela and the fight to which his life bears witness]" (Paris: Gallimard, 1986). I thank Antoine Gallimard for permission to reprint it here.

fear him. If his most hateful persecutors secretly admire him, this proves that, as one says, he compels admiration.

So, this is the question: where does this force come from? Where does it lead? For what is it used, or to what is it applied? Or rather: what does it cause to *fold*? What form is to be recognized in this fold? What line?

First of all we will see there, and let us say it without further premise, the *line of a reflection*. It is first of all a force of reflection. What is obvious right away is that Mandela's political experience or passion can never be separated from a theoretical reflection: on history, culture, and above all, law. An unremitting analysis enlightens the rationality of his acts, his demonstrations, his speeches, his strategy. Even before being constrained to withdraw [*au repli*] by prison—and during a quarter century of incarceration, he has not ceased to act and direct the struggle—Mandela has always been a man of reflection. Like all great politicians.

But in "force of reflection" there is something else that can be heard, something that signals toward the literality of the mirror and the scene of speculation. Not so much toward the physical laws of reflection as toward specular paradoxes in the experience of the law. There is no law without mirror. And in this properly reversible structure, we will never avoid the moment of admiration.

Admiration, as its name indicates, one will say, and so on. No, no matter what its name or the fact that it always enables us to *see*, admiration does not only belong to sight. It translates emotion, astonishment, surprise, interrogation in the face of what oversteps the measure: in the face of the "extraordinary," says Descartes, and he considers it a passion, the first of the six primitive passions, before love, hate, desire, joy, and sadness. It enables understanding. Outside of it, there is only ignorance, he adds, and in it resides "a great deal of force" of "surprise" or of "sudden arrival [*arrivement subit*]." The admiring look is astonished; it questions its intuition; it opens itself to the light of a question, but of a question received no less than asked. This experience lets itself be traversed by the ray of a question, which in no way prevents its reflection. The ray comes from the very thing that forces admiration; it thus splits admiration into a specular movement that seems strangely fascinating.

Mandela becomes admirable for having known how to admire. And what he has learned, he has learned in admiration. He fascinates too, as we shall see, for having been fascinated.

In a certain way that we will have to understand, *he says this*. He says what he does and what has happened to him. Such a light, its reflected passage, experience as the departure-return of a question, would thus also be the eruption [*éclat*] of a voice.

Nelson Mandela's voice—what does it evoke, ask, enjoin? What would it have to do with sight, reflection, admiration, I mean the energy of this voice but also of what sings in its name? (hear the clamor of his people when this people demonstrates in his name: Man-de-la!).

Admiration of Nelson Mandela, as we might say the passion of Nelson Mandela. Admiration of Mandela, a double genitive: the one he inspires and the one he feels. The two have the same focus, they are reflected in it. I have already stated my hypothesis: he becomes admirable for having admired, with all his strength, and for having made a force of his admiration—an inflexible and irreducible fighting power. The law itself, the law above other laws.

For in fact what has he admired? In one word: the Law.

And what inscribes it in discourse, in history, in the institution, namely, Right.

A first quotation—a lawyer is speaking, during a trial, his trial, the one where he is also prosecuting, the one in which he prosecutes those who accuse him, in the name of the law:

> The basic task at the present moment is the removal of race discrimination and the attainment of democratic rights on the basis of the Freedom Charter. . . . From my reading of Marxist literature and from conversations with Marxists, I have gained the impression that communists regard the parliamentary system of the West as undemocratic and reactionary. But, on the contrary, *I am an admirer* of such a system.
>
> The *Magna Carta*, the Petition of Rights, and the Bill of Rights are documents which are held in veneration by democrats throughout the world.
>
> *I have great respect* for British political institutions, and for the country's system of justice. I regard the British Parliament as the most democratic institution in the world, and the independence and impartiality of its judiciary never fail to *arouse my admiration*.[1]

He admires the law, he says it clearly, but is this law, which commands constitutions and declarations, essentially a thing of the West? Does its formal universality retain some irreducible link with European or even Anglo-American history? If it were so, we would of course still have to consider this strange possibility: that its formal character would be as essential to the universality of the law as the event of its presentation in a determined moment and place in history. How could we conceive of such a history? The struggle against *apartheid*, wherever it takes place and such as Mandela carries it on and reflects it, would this remain a sort of specular opposition, an internal war that the West would maintain in itself, in its own name? An internal contradiction that would suffer neither radical alterity nor true dissymmetry?

In this form, such a hypothesis still implies too many indistinct presuppositions. We will try to identify them later on. For the moment, let us retain an obvious, more limited but also more certain fact: what Mandela admires and says he admires is the tradition inaugurated by the Magna Carta, the Universal Declaration of the Rights of Man in its different forms (he frequently appeals to "the dignity of man," to man "worthy of the name"); it is also parliamentary democracy and, still more precisely, the doctrine of the separation of powers, the independence of justice.

But if he admires this tradition, does it mean that he is its heir, its simple heir? Yes and no, depending on what is meant here by inheritance. One can recognize an authentic heir in the one who conserves and reproduces, but also in the one who respects the *logic* of the legacy even to the point of turning it on occasion against those who claim to be its guardians, to the point of revealing, against the usurpers, what has never been seen in the inheritance: to the point of giving birth, by the unheard-of *act* of a reflection, to what had never seen the light of day.

2

This inflexible logic of reflection was also Mandela's practice. Here are at least two signs of it.

1. *First sign.* The African National Congress, of which he was one of the leaders after having joined it in 1944, succeeded the South African National Congress. Now, the structure of the latter already reflected that of the American Congress and the House of Lords. It included in particular a High Chamber. The paradigm was thus already the parliamentary democracy that Mandela admired. The Freedom Charter, which he promulgated in 1955, also enunciates those democratic principles inspired by the Universal Declaration of the Rights of Man. And yet, with an exemplary rigor, Mandela nonetheless refuses a pure and simple alliance with the liberal whites who want to maintain the struggle within the constitutional framework, such at least as it was established then. Indeed, Mandela re-

calls a truth: the establishment of this constitutional law had not only, in fact and as always, taken the form of a singular *coup de force*, the violent act that *both* produces *and* presupposes the unity of a nation. In this case, the *coup de force remained* a *coup de force*, thus, a bad blow [*coup*]—the failure of a law that is unable to establish itself. Its authors and beneficiaries were only the particular wills of a part of the population, a limited number of private interests, those of the white minority. The latter becomes the privileged subject, indeed the only subject of this anticonstitutional constitution. In fact, one might say that such a *coup de force* always marks the advent of a nation, state, or nation-state. The properly *performative* act of such an institution must in effect produce (proclaim) that which it claims, declares, assures it is describing according to a *constative* act. The simulacrum or fiction then consists in bringing to the light of day, *in giving birth to*, that which one claims to reflect so as to take note of it [*en prendre acte*], as though it were a matter of recording what will *have been there*, the unity of a nation, the founding of a state, whereas one is in the act of producing that event. But legitimacy, indeed legality, becomes permanently installed; it recovers its originary violence, and is forgotten only on certain conditions. Not all performatives, a theoretician of speech acts would say, are "felicitous." That depends on a great number of conditions and conventions that form the context of such events. In the case of South Africa, certain "conventions" were not respected, the violence was too great, *visibly too great*, at a moment when this visibility extended to a new international scene, and so on. The white community was *too* much in the minority, the disproportion of wealth *too* flagrant. From then on this violence remains both excessive and powerless, insufficient in its result, lost in its own contradiction. It cannot be forgotten, as in the case of states founded on genocide or quasi-extermination. Here, the violence of origin must repeat itself indefinitely and imitate right in a legislative apparatus whose monstrosity fails to allay suspicion: a pathological proliferation of juridical prostheses (laws, acts, amendments) destined to legalize down to the smallest detail the most everyday effects of fundamental racism, of a state racism, the only and last state racism in the world.

The constitution of such a state cannot, then, refer to the popular will with enough verisimilitude. As the Freedom Charter recalls: "South Africa belongs to all its inhabitants, black and white. No government can prevail over an authority that is not founded on the will of the entire nation." Referring to the general will, which cannot be reduced to the sum of the wills of the "entire nation," Mandela often reminds us of Rousseau, even if he never quotes him. And he thus contests the authority, the legality, the constitutionality of the constitution. He refuses the proposal of—and the alliance with—the white liberals who would struggle against *apartheid* and yet claim to respect the legal framework: "The credo of the liberals consists in 'the use of democratic and constitutional means, rejecting the different forms of totalitarianism: fascism and communism.' Only a people already enjoying democratic and constitutional rights has any grounds for speaking of democratic and constitutional means. This makes no sense for those who do not benefit from them."[2]

What does Mandela oppose to the *coup de force* of the white minority that has instituted a supposedly democratic law to the advantage of a single ethnonational entity? The "entire nation," that is to say, another ethnonational entity, another popular collectivity formed of all the groups, including the white minority, that inhabits the territory named South Africa. This other entity could not have instituted nor in the future will it be able to institute itself as the subject of the state or of the constitution of "South Africa" except by a performative act. And the latter will not appear to refer to any prior, fundamental law, but only to the "convention" of a geographic and demographic division [*découpage*] effected, in large measure, by white colonization. This fact cannot be erased. The will of the "entire nation," or at least the general will, should of course exclude all empirical determination. Such is at least its regulative ideal. And it seems no more attainable here than elsewhere. The definition of the "entire nation" registers—and thus seems to reflect—the event of the *coup de force* that was white occupation, followed by the founding of the South African Republic. Without this event, how could we see even the slightest relationship between a general will and what the Freedom Charter calls the "will of the entire nation"? The latter finds itself paradoxically united by the violence done to it, which tends to disintegrate or to destructure it forever, down to its most virtual identity. This phenomenon marks the establishment of almost all states after decolonization. Mandela knows that: no matter how democratic it is, and even if it seems to conform to the principle of the equality of all before the law, the absolute establishment of a state cannot presuppose the previously *legitimized* existence of a national entity. The same is true for a first constitution. The total unity of a people can only be identified for the first time by contract—whether formal or not, written or not—that institutes some fundamental law. Now this contract is never signed, in fact, except by the supposed representatives of the supposedly "entire" people. This fundamental law cannot, either by right or in fact, simply precede that which at once institutes it and yet presupposes it: projects it and reflects it! It can in no way precede this extraordinary performative by which a signature authorizes itself to sign, in a word, legalizes itself on its own initiative [*de son propre chef*] without the guarantee of a preexisting law. This autographic violence and fiction are to be found at work just as surely in what we call individual autobiography as in the "historical" origin of states. In the case of South Africa, the fiction lies in this—and it is fiction against fiction: the unity of the "entire nation" could not correspond to the division effected by the white minority. It should now constitute a whole (the white minority + all the inhabitants of "South Africa") whose configuration was only established, or in any case identified, on the basis of minority violence. That such a unity might then oppose this violence changes nothing about this implacable contradiction. The "entire nation," a unity of "all the national groups," will grant itself existence and legal force only by the very same act to which the Freedom Charter appeals. This Charter speaks in the present, a present that one supposes to be founded on the *description* of a past given that should be recognized in the future; and it also speaks in the future, a future that has the value of a *prescription*:

> South Africa belongs to all its inhabitants, black and white. No government can prevail over an authority that is not founded on the will of the entire nation.
> —The people will govern.
> —All the national groups will enjoy equal rights. . . .
> —All will be equal before the law.[3]

The Charter does not annul the founding act of the law, an act that is necessarily a-legal in itself, which finally institutes South Africa and can only become legal afterward, in particular if it is ratified by the law of the international community. No, the Charter refounds it, or in any case intends to refound it, by *reflecting*, against the white minority, the principles by which it claimed to be inspired, whereas *in fact* it never ceased to betray them. Democracy, yes, South Africa yes, but this time, says the Charter, the "entire nation" must include all the national groups, such is the very logic of the law to which the white minority claimed to appeal. On the territory thus delimited, all human beings, all human beings "worthy of the name," will then effectively become the subjects of law.

2. *Second sign.* The declared "admiration" for the model of parliamentary democracy of the Anglo-American kind and for the separation of powers, the faithfulness of the Charter to all the principles of such a democracy, the logic of a radicalization that opposes these very principles to the Western defenders of *apartheid*, all of this might seem to resemble the *coup de force* of a simple specular inversion: the struggle of the "black" community (of non-"white" communities) would be undertaken in the name of an imported law and model—a law and model that were betrayed, in the first place, by their first importers. A terrifying dissymmetry. But it seems to reduce itself, or rather to reflect itself to the point of withdrawing from every objective representation: neither symmetry nor dissymmetry. This is because there would be no importation, no simply assignable origin for the history of law, only a reflecting apparatus, with projections of images, inversions of trajectories, *mises en abîme*, effects of history for a law whose structure and whose "history" consist in carrying off [*emporter*] the origin. Such an apparatus—and by this word I only mean that this X is not natural (which does not necessarily define it as an artifact brought forth by human hands)—cannot be represented in objective space. For at least *two reasons* that I will relate to the case that concerns us here.

A. The first reason concerns the structure of the law, of the principle, or the model being considered. Whatever the historical place of its formation or formulation, of its revelation or presentation, a structure of this kind tends toward universality. Here we have, as it were, its intentional content: its meaning requires that it immediately exceed the historical, national, geographical, linguistic, and cultural limits of its phenomenal origin. Everything should begin with uprooting. The limits would then appear to be empirical contingencies. They might even dissimulate what, it seems, they let appear. Thus one might think that the "white minority" of South Africa occults the essence of the principles to which it claims to appeal; it privatizes them, particularizes them, appropriates them, and in this way subjects them to the inspection of reason [*les arraisonne*] against their very reason for being, against reason itself. Whereas, in the struggle against *apartheid*, the "reflection" of which we are speaking here makes visible what was no longer even visible in the political phenomenality dominated by whites. It obliges us to see what was no longer seen or was not yet to be seen. It tries to open the eyes of whites; it does not reproduce the visible, it produces it. This reflection makes visible a law that in truth it does more than reflect, because this law, in its phenomenon, was invisible: had become invisible or was still invisible. By bringing the invisible into the visible, this reflection does not proceed from the visible; rather it passes through understanding. More precisely, it gives us to understand what exceeds understanding and accords only with reason. This was a first reason, reason itself.

B. The second reason seems more problematic. It concerns precisely this phenomenal apparition, the historical constitution of the law, of democratic principles, and of the democratic model. Here again, the experience of declared admiration, this time of an admiration that is also said to be *fascinated,* follows the fold of a reflection. Always a reflection on the law: Mandela perceives, he *sees,* others might say that he *projects and reflects without seeing,* the very presence of this law inside African society. Even before "the arrival of the white man."

In what he himself says about this subject, I will underline three motifs:

(a) that of *fascination:* fixed attention of the gaze transfixed, as if petrified by something that, without being simply a visible object, looks at you, already concerns you, understands you, and orders you to continue to observe, to respond, to make yourself responsible for the gaze that gazes at you and calls you beyond the visible: neither perception nor hallucination;

(b) that of the *seed:* it furnishes an indispensable schema for interpretation. It is on account of its virtuality that the democratic model would have been present in the society of ancestors, even if it was not to be revealed, *developed* as such for reflection, until afterward, after the violent irruption of the "white man," the bearer of the same model;

(c) that of the South African *homeland* [patrie], the birthplace of all the national groups called upon to live under the law of the new South African Republic. This homeland is not to be confused either with the state or with the nation:

> Many years ago, when I was a boy brought up in my village in the Transkei, I listened to the elders of the tribe telling stories about the good old days, *before the arrival of the white man.* Then our people lived peacefully, under the *democratic* rule of their kings and their *amapakati,* and moved freely and confidently up and down the country without let or hindrance. Then the country was ours. . . . I hoped and vowed then that, among the treasures that

life might offer me, would be the opportunity to serve my people and make my own humble contribution to their freedom struggles.

The structure and organization of early African societies in this country *fascinated* me very much and greatly influenced the evolution of my political outlook. The land, then the main means of production, belonged to the whole tribe, and there was no individual ownership whatsoever. There were no classes, no rich or poor, and no exploitation of man by man. All men were free and equal and this was the foundation of government. Recognition of this general principle found expression in the constitution of the council. . . .

There was much in such a society that was primitive and insecure and it certainly could never measure up to the demands of the present epoch. But in such a society are contained *the seeds of a revolutionary democracy* in which none will be held in slavery or servitude, and in which poverty, want, and insecurity shall be no more. (149–50)

It is common knowledge that the conference decided that, in place of the unilateral proclamation of a republic by the white minority of South Africans only, it would demand in the name of the African people the calling of a truly national convention representative of all South Africans, irrespective of their color, black and white, to sit amicably round a table, to debate a new constitution for South Africa, which was in essence what the government was doing by the proclamation of a republic, and furthermore, to press on behalf of the African people, that such a new constitution should differ from the constitution of the proposed South African Republic by guaranteeing democratic rights on a basis of full equality to all South Africans of adult age. (148)

What fascination seems to bring into view here, what mobilizes and immobilizes Mandela's attention, is not only parliamentary democracy, whose principle presents itself *for example but not exemplarily* in the West. It is the *already virtually* accomplished passage, if one can say this, from parliamentary democracy to revolutionary democracy: a society without class and without private property. We have just encountered, then, a supplementary paradox: the *effective* accomplishment, the fulfillment of the democratic form, the *real* determination of the formality, *will only have taken place* in the past of this non-Western society, in the form [*sous l'espèce*] of virtuality, in other words, of "seeds." Mandela lets himself be *fascinated* by what he sees being reflected in advance, by what is not yet to be seen, what he fore-sees: the properly revolutionary democracy of which the Anglo-American West, in sum, would have delivered only an incomplete, formal, *and thus also potential* image. Potentiality against potentiality, power against power. For if he "admires" the parliamentary systems of the most Western West, he also declares his "admiration," and this is still his word, always the same word, for the "structure and organization of early African societies in this country." It is a question of "seed" and of preformation, according to the same logic or the same rhetoric, a sort of genoptics. The figures of African society prefigure; they give one to see in advance what still remains invisible in its historical phenomenon, that is to say, the "classless" society and the end of the "exploitation of man by man": "Today I am attracted by the idea of a classless society, an attraction that springs in part from Marxist reading and, in part, from *my admiration* of the structure and organization of early African societies in this country. The land, then the main means of production, belonged to the tribe. There were no rich or poor, and there was no exploitation of man by man" (150).

3

In all the senses of this term, Mandela remains, then, a *man of law*. He has always appealed to right even if, in appearance, he had to oppose himself to this or that determinate legality, and even if certain judges made of him, at certain moments, an outlaw.

A man of law, he was this first *by vocation*. On the one hand, he always appeals to the law. On the other hand, he was always attracted, called by the law before which he was asked to appear. He accepted moreover to appear before the law, even if he was also forced to do so. He seized the occasion, not to say the chance. Why chance? Let us reread his "defense," which is in truth an indictment. We will find in it a political autobiography, his own and that of his people, indissociably. The "I" of this autobiography founds itself and justifies itself, reasons and signs in the name of "we." He always says "my people," as we have already noted, especially when he raises the question of the subject responsible *before the law*:

I am charged with inciting people to commit an offence by way of protest against the law, a law that neither I nor any of my people had any say in preparing. The law against which the protest was directed is the law which established a republic in the Union of South Africa. . . . But in weighing up the decision as to the sentence which is to be imposed for such an offence, the court must take into account the question of responsibility, whether it is I who am responsible or whether, in fact, a large measure of the responsibility does not lie on the shoulders of the government which promulgated that law, knowing that my people, who constitute the majority of the population of this country, were opposed to that law, and knowing further that every legal means of demonstrating that opposition had been closed to them by prior legislation, and by government administrative action. (148)

Thus he himself presents himself. He presents himself, himself in his people, *before the law*. Before a law he impugns, certainly, but that he impugns in the name of a higher law, the one he declares to admire and before which he agrees *to appear*. In such a presentation of self, he justifies himself by gathering his history—that he reflects in a single focal point, a single and double focal point, his history and that of his people. Appearance: they appear together, he gathers himself by appearing before the law that he summons as much as he is summoned by it. But he does not present himself *in view of* a justification that would follow. The self-presentation is not *in the service* of law; it is not a means. The unfolding of this history is a *justification*; it is possible and has meaning only before the law. He only is what he is, Nelson Mandela, he and his people, he has presence only in this movement of justice.

Memories and confessions of an attorney-advocate. The advocate "avows" a fault from the point of view of legality, even as he justifies it, even to the point of assuming it proudly. Taking as his witness humanity as a whole, he addresses himself to the universal justice over the heads of those who are but his judges for a day. Whence this paradox: one can perceive a sort of joyous trembling in the narrative of this martyrdom. And at times one can make out the inflexion of Rousseau in these confessions, a voice that never ceases to appeal to *the voice of conscience*, to the immediate and unfailing feeling of justice, to this law of laws that speaks in us before us because it is inscribed in our heart. In the same tradition, it is also the place of a categorical imperative, of a morality incommensurate with the hypotheses and conditional strategies of interest, as it is with the figures of this or that civil law:

> I do not believe, Your Worship, that this court, in inflicting penalties on me for the crimes for which I am convicted, should be moved by the belief that penalties deter men from the course that they believe is right. History shows that penalties do not deter men when their *conscience* is aroused. (158)
>
> Whatever sentence Your Worship sees fit to impose upon me for the crime for which I have been convicted before this Court, may it rest assured that when my sentence has been completed, I will still be moved, as men are al-

ways moved, by their *consciences*; I will still be moved by my dislike of the race discrimination against my people when I come out from serving my sentence, to take up again, as best I can, the struggle for the removal of those injustices until they are finally abolished once and for all. (159)

It was an act of defiance of the law. We were aware that it was, but, nevertheless, that act had been forced on us against our wishes, and we could do no other than to choose between compliance with the law and compliance with our *consciences*. (151)

[We] were faced with this *conflict between the law and our conscience*. In the face of the complete failure of the government to heed, to consider, or even to respond to our seriously proposed objections and our solutions to the forthcoming republic, what were we to do? Were we to allow the law, which states that you shall not commit an offence by way of protest, to take its course and thus betray our conscience? . . . [I]n such a dilemma, men of honesty, men of purpose, and men of public morality and of conscience can only have one answer. They must *follow the dictate of their conscience* irrespective of the consequences which might overtake them for it. We of the Action Council, and I particularly, as Secretary, *followed our conscience*. (153–54)

Conscience and consciousness of the law, these two make only one. Presentation of oneself and presentation of one's people, these two make only a single history in a single reflection. In both cases, as we have said, a single and double focus. And it is that of admiration, since this conscience presents itself, gathers itself, collects itself by reflecting itself before the law. That is to say, let us not forget, before what is admirable.

The experience of admiration is also *doubly internal*. It reflects reflection and draws from it all the strength that it turns against its Western judges. For it proceeds, dramatically, from a double internalization. Mandela first internalizes, he takes into himself an ideal thought of the law that may appear to come from the West. Mandela also interiorizes, at the same time, *the principle of interiority* in the figure that the Christian West has given to it. All its traits are to be found in the philosophy, the politics, the right and morality that dominate in Europe: the law of laws resides in the most intimate conscience; we must in the final instance judge the intention, goodwill, and so on. Before any juridical or political discourse, before the texts of positive law, the law speaks in the voice of conscience or is inscribed in the furthest reaches of the heart.

A man of law *by vocation*, then, Mandela was also a man of law by profession. We know that he first studied law on the advice of Walter Sisulu, the then secretary of the African National Congress. In particular, it was a matter of mastering Western law, this weapon to turn against the oppressors. The latter misrecognize, in the end, in spite of all their legal ruses, the true force of a law that they manipulate, violate, and betray.

To inscribe himself in the system, and above all in the faculty of law, Mandela takes courses *by correspondence*. He wants to obtain first a degree in letters. Let us stress this episode. Since he cannot have immediate access to direct, "live" exchanges, he has to begin by *correspondence*. Mandela will complain about this later on. The context will certainly be different, but it will always be about a politics of voice and writing, of the difference between what is said "aloud" and what is written, between the "live voice" and "correspondence."

> We have been conditioned by the history of White governments in this country to accept the fact that Africans, when they make their demands strongly and powerfully enough to have some chance of success, will be met by force and terror on the part of the government. This is not something we have taught the African people, this is something the African people have learned from their own bitter experience. . . . Already [1921–23] there are indications in this country that people, my people, Africans, are turning to deliberate acts of violence and of force against the government, in order to persuade the government, in the only language which this government shows, by its behavior, that it understands.
>
> Elsewhere in the world, a court would say to me, "You should have made representations to the government." This Court, I am confident, will not say so. Representations have been made, by people who have gone before me, time and time again. Representations were made in this case by me; I do not want again to repeat the experience of those representations. The court cannot expect a respect for the process of representation and negotiation to grow amongst the African people, when the government shows every day, by its conduct, that it despises such processes and frowns upon them and will not indulge in them. Nor will the court, I believe, say that, under the circumstances, my people are condemned forever to say nothing and to do nothing. (155–56)

In order not to hear, not to understand, the white government requires that one write to it. But it intends thereby not to answer and first of all not to read. Mandela reminds us of the letter that Albert Luthuli, then the president of the ANC, addressed to Prime Minister J. G. Strijdom. It was a lengthy analysis of the situation, accompanied by a request for a consultation. Not the slightest response. "The standard of behavior of the South African government towards my people, and its aspirations, has not always been what it should have been, and is not always the standard which is to be expected in serious high-level dealings between *civilized* peoples. Chief Luthuli's letter was not even favored with the courtesy of an acknowledgment from the Prime Minister's office" (153).

White power does not think it has to respond, does not hold itself responsible to the black people. The latter cannot even assure itself, by return mail, by an exchange of words, looks or signs, that any image of it has been formed on the other side, an image that might then return to it in some way. For white power does not content itself with not answering. It does worse: it does not even acknowledge receipt. After Luthuli, Mandela experiences it himself. He has just written to Verwoerd to inform him of a resolution voted on by the National Action Council, of which he is then the secretary. He also requests that a national convention be convoked before the deadline determined by the resolution. No answer, no acknowledgment of receipt:

> In a *civilized* country one would be outraged by the failure of the head of government even *to acknowledge receipt of a letter*, or to consider such a reasonable request put to him by a broadly representative collection of important personalities and leaders of the most important community of the country. Once again, government standards in dealing with my people fell below what the *civilized world* would expect. No reply, no response whatsoever, was received to our letter, no indication was even given that it had received any consideration whatsoever. Here we, the African people, and especially we of the National Action Council, who had been entrusted with the tremendous *responsibility* of safeguarding the interests of the African people, were faced with *this conflict between the law and our conscience.* (153)

Not to acknowledge receipt is to betray the laws of civility but first of all those of civilization: a primitive behavior, a return to the state of nature, a presocial phase, *before the law*. Why does the government return to this noncivilized practice? Because it considers the majority of the people, the "most important community," to be noncivilized, before or outside the law. By acting in this way, by interrupting the correspondence in a unilateral fashion, the white man is no longer respecting his own law. He is blind to the evidence: a letter received signifies that the other is appealing to the law of the community. By scorning his own law, the white man makes law contemptible:

> Perhaps the court will say that despite our human rights to protest, to object, to make ourselves heard, we should stay within the letter of the law. I would say, Sir, that it is the government, its administration of the law, which *brings the law into such contempt and disrepute* that one is no longer concerned in this country to stay within the letter of the law. I will illustrate this from my own experience. The Government has used the process of law to handicap me, in my personal life, in my career, and in my political work, in a way which is calculated, in my opinion, to bring about *contempt of the law*. (156)

This contempt for the law (the symmetrical inverse of the *respect* for the moral law, as Kant would say: *Achtung/Verachtung*) is not his, is not Mandela's. By accusing, by responding, by acknowledging receipt, he reflects, in a sense, the contempt of the whites for their own law. It is always a reflection. Those who, one day, made him an outlaw simply did not have the right: they had already placed themselves outside the law. By describing his own outlaw condition, Mandela analyzes and reflects the being-outside-the-law of the law in the name of which he will have been not judged but persecuted, prejudged, taken for a criminal beforehand, as if, in this endless trial, the trial had *already* taken place, before the investigation, whereas it is being endlessly adjourned:

> I was made, by the law, a criminal, not because of what I had done, but because of what I stood for, because of what I thought, because of my conscience. Can it be any wonder to anybody that such conditions make a man an outlaw of society? Can it be wondered that such a man, having been outlawed by the government, should be prepared to lead the life of an outlaw, as I have led for some months, according to the evidence before this court? . . . But there comes a time, as it came in my life, when a man is denied the right to live a normal life, when he can only live the life of an outlaw because the government has so decreed to use the law to impose a state of outlawry upon him. (157)

Mandela thus accuses white governments of never *answering*, while at the same time demanding that blacks be quiet and make written representations: resign yourself to correspondence and to corresponding all alone.

The sinister irony of counterpoint: after his conviction, Mandela is kept in solitary confinement twenty-three hours a day in Pretoria Central Prison. He is employed in sewing mailbags.

4

A man of law by vocation, Mandela submits the laws of his profession, the professional code of ethics, its essence and its contradictions, to the same reflection. This lawyer, enjoined by that code of ethics "to observe the laws of this country and to respect its traditions," how could he have conducted a campaign and incited others to strike against the politics of this same country? He himself raises this question before his judges. The answer requires nothing less than the story of his life. The decision to conform or not to conform to a code of ethics does not depend on ethics *as such*. The question of what to do about the professional code of ethics, "should one respect it or not?" is not of a professional order. The response is a decision that engages one's whole existence in its moral, political, and historical dimensions. In a way, one has to recount one's life to explain or rather to justify the transgression of a professional rule: "In order that the court shall understand the frame of mind which leads me to action such as this, it is necessary for me to explain the background to my own political development and to try to make this court aware of the factors which influenced me in deciding to act as I did. Many years ago, when I was a boy brought up in my village in the Transkei . . . " (149).

Is Mandela treating his professional obligations lightly? No, he is trying to think his profession, which is not just one profession among others. He reflects the deontology of deontology, the deep meaning and the spirit of deontological laws. And once again, out of admiring respect, he decides to come down on the side of a deontology of deontology that is also a deontology beyond [*au-delà*] deontology, a law beyond [*par-delà*] legality. But the paradox of this reflection (the deontology *of* deontology), which carries *beyond* what it reflects, is that responsibility takes its meaning again from *inside* the professional apparatus. It is reinscribed within it, for Mandela decides, to all appearances against the code, to exercise his profession exactly when they want to stop him from doing so. As an "attorney worth his salt," he sets himself *against the code in the code*, by reflecting the code, and thereby making visible what the code in force makes unreadable. Once again his reflection exhibits what phenomenality still dissimulates. It does not re-produce, it produces the visible. This production of light is justice—moral or political. For phenomenal dissimulation must not be confused with a natural process; there is nothing neutral about it, nothing innocent or fatal. It translates here the political violence of the whites; it holds to their interpretation of the laws, to that proliferation of juridical purviews whose letter is destined to contradict the spirit of the law. For example, because of the color of his skin and his membership in the ANC, Mandela cannot occupy any professional premises in the city. He must therefore, unlike any white lawyer, have a special authorization from the government, in accordance with the Urban Areas Act. Authorization refused. And then a waiver that is not renewed. Mandela must from then on practice in a "native location," accessible only with difficulty to those who need his counsel in the city:

> This was tantamount to asking us to abandon our legal practice, to give up the legal service of our people, for which we had spent many years training. No attorney *worth his salt* will agree easily to do so. For some years, therefore, we continued to occupy premises in the city, illegally. The threat of prosecution and ejection hung menacingly over us throughout that period. It was an act of *defiance of the law.* We were aware that it was, but, nevertheless, that act had been forced on us against our wishes, and we could do no other than to choose between compliance with the law and compliance with our consciences. . . . I regarded it as a duty which I owed, not just to my people, but also to my profession, to the practice of law, and *to justice for all mankind,* to cry out against this discrimination which is essentially unjust and opposed to the whole basis of the attitude towards justice which is part of the tradition of legal training in this country. (151)

A man of the law by vocation: it would be greatly simplifying things to say that he places respect for the law and a certain categorical imperative above professional ethics. The "profession of attorney" is not just any job. It professes, one might say, that to which we are all bound, even outside the profession. An attorney is an expert in respect or admiration; he judges himself or submits to judgment with added rigor. Or in any case he should. Mandela must then find, *inside* professional deontology, the best reason for failing a legislative code that was already betraying the principles of every *good* professional deontology. As if, through reflection, he also had to repair, supplement, reconstruct, add something to a deontology where the whites in fact showed themselves to be deficient.

Twice, then, he confesses to a certain "contempt for the law" (this is always his expression) in order to hold out to his adversaries the mirror in which they will have to recognize and see their own scorn for the law reflected. But with this *supplementary inversion*: on Mandela's side, the apparent contempt signifies an added respect [*un surcroît de respect*] for the law.

And yet he does not accuse his judges, not immediately, at least not at the moment he appears before them. Certainly, he will have begun by challenging them: on the one hand, there was not a single black on the court and thus the court could not guarantee the necessary impartiality ("The South African Government affirms that the Universal Declaration of the Rights of Man is applied in this country but, in truth, equality before the law in no way exists in relation to the concerns of our people"); on the other hand, the presiding judge remained, between sessions, in contact with the political police. But once in front of his judges, these objections not having been sustained, of course, Mandela no longer accuses the tribunal. First, he continues to observe his deeply respectful admiration for those who exercise a function that is exemplary in his eyes and for the dignity of a tribunal. Moreover, the respect for the rules allows him to confirm the ideal legitimacy of an instance before which he also must *appear*. He wants to seize the occasion, and I dare not say once again the chance, of this trial in order to *speak*, to give to his word a space of *public* and virtually universal resonance. His judges must indeed represent a universal instance. He will thus be able to speak to them, while speaking over their heads. This double opportunity permits him to gather together the meaning of his history, his and that of his people, in order to articulate it in a coherent narrative. The image of what ties his story to that of his people must be formed in this double focal point, which at the same time welcomes [*accueille*] it, takes it in [*recueille*] by gathering it, and preserves [*garde*] it, yes, preserves it above all: the judges here present who are listening to Mandela, and behind them, rising high and far above them, the universal court. And in a moment we will rediscover the man and the philosopher of this tribunal. For once, then, there will have been the spoken discourse *and* the correspondence, the written text of his plea, which is also an indictment: it has come down to us, here it is, we are reading it at this very moment.

5

This text is both unique and exemplary. Is it a *testament?* What has become of it in the past twenty years? What has history done, what will history do with it? What will become of the example? And Nelson Mandela himself? His jailers dare speak of exchanging him, of negotiating for his freedom! Of bargaining for his freedom and that of Sakharov!

There are at least two ways of receiving a testament—and two meanings of the word, two ways, in short, of acknowledging receipt. One can inflect it toward what *bears witness* only to a past and knows itself condemned to reflecting that which will not return: a kind of West in general, the end of a race that is also the trajectory from a luminous source, the close of an epoch, for example that of the Christian West (Mandela speaks its language, he is also an English Christian). But, another inflection, if the testament is always made in front of witnesses, a witness in front of witnesses, it is also so as to open and to enjoin, it is to confide in others the responsibility of a future. To testify, to test, to attest, to contest, to present oneself before witnesses—for Mandela, it was not only to show himself, to give himself to be known, himself and his people, it was also to re-institute the law for the future, as if, at bottom, the law had never taken place. As if, having never been respected, it had remained, this arch-ancient thing that had never been present, the future itself—still invisible. To be reinvented.

These two inflections of the testament are not opposed: they meet in the exemplarity of the example when it concerns respect for the law. Respect for a person, Kant tells us, is first addressed to the law of which this person only gives us the example. Strictly speaking, respect is only due the law, which is its sole cause. And yet, it is the law, we must respect the other for himself, in his irreplaceable singularity. It is true that, as a person or a reasonable being, the other always testifies, in his very singularity, to the respect for the law. He is exemplary in this sense. And still reflecting—according to the same optic, that of admiration and respect—these figures of the gaze. Some might be tempted to see in Mandela the witness or the martyr of the past. He let himself be captured (literally, imprisoned) in the perspective [*optique*] of the West, as in the machination of its reflecting apparatus; he not only internalized the law, as we were saying, he internalized the principle of interiority in its testamentary tradition (Christian, Rousseauist, Kantian, etc.).

But one could say the opposite: his reflection lets us see—in the most singular geopolitical situation, in this extreme concentration of all human history that are today the places or the stakes called "South Africa," or "Israel," for example—the promise of what has never yet been seen or heard, in a law that only presented itself in the West, at the Western border, in order to disappear immediately. What will be decided in these so-called "places"—which are also formidable metonymies—would decide everything, if there were still that; they would decide the whole.

Thus the exemplary witnesses are often those who distinguish between the law and laws, between the respect for the law that speaks immediately to conscience and submission to positive law (historical, national, instituted). Conscience is not only memory but promise. The exemplary witnesses who make us think about the law they reflect are those who, in certain situations, *do not respect* the laws. They are sometimes torn between their conscience and the laws; at times they let themselves be condemned by the tribunals of their country. And there are witnesses of this kind *in every country*, which proves that the place of appearance or formulation is for the law also the place of the first uprooting. *In every country*, thus, for example, yet again, in Europe, for example in England, for example, among philosophers. The example chosen by Mandela, the most exemplary of the witnesses he seems to call to the bar is an English philosopher, a peer of the realm (still this admiration for the most elevated forms of parliamentary democracy), the "most respected philosopher in the Western world" who knew how, in certain situations, not to respect the law, how to put "conscience," "duty," "belief in the morality of the essential rightness of the cause" before the "respect for the law." It is out of respect that he did not show respect: (no) more respect. Respect for the sake of respect. Can we regulate some optical model on what such a possibility promises? Admiration of Mandela—for Bertrand Russell:

> Your Worship, I would say that the whole life of any thinking African in this country drives him continuously to a conflict between his conscience on the one hand and the law on the other. This is not a conflict peculiar to this country. The conflict arises for men of conscience, for men who think and who feel deeply in every country. Recently in Britain, a peer of the realm, Earl Russell, probably *the most respected* philosopher of the Western world, was sentenced, convicted for precisely the type of activities for which I stand before you today, for following his conscience in defiance of the law, as a protest against a nuclear-weapons policy being followed by his own government. For

him, his duty to the public, his belief in the morality of the essential rightness of the cause for which he stood, rose superior to his *high respect for the law.* He could not do other than to oppose the law and to suffer the consequences for it. Nor can I. Nor can many Africans in this country. The law as it is applied, the law as it has been developed over a long period of history, and especially the law as it is written and designed by the Nationalist government, is a law which, in our view, is immoral, unjust, and intolerable. Our consciences dictate that we must protest against it, that we must oppose it, and that we must attempt to alter it. (152)

To oppose the law, to then try and transform it: once the decision is made, the recourse to violence should not take place without measure and without rule. Mandela explains in minute detail the strategy, the limits, the progress reflected upon and observed. First, there was a phase during the course of which, all legal opposition being forbidden, the infraction had nevertheless to remain nonviolent: "All lawful modes of expressing opposition to this principle had been closed by legislation, and we were placed in a position in which we had either to accept a permanent state of inferiority or to defy the government. We chose to defy the law. We first broke the law in a way which avoided any recourse to violence" (162).

The infraction still manifests the absolute respect for the supposed spirit of the law. But it was impossible to stop there. For the government invented new legal devices to repress these nonviolent challenges. To this violent response, which was also a nonresponse, the transition to violence was in its turn the only possible response. Response to the nonresponse: "When this form was legislated against, and then the government resorted to a show of force to crush opposition to its policies, only then did we decide to answer violence with violence" (162).

But there again, the violence remains subject to a rigorous law, "a strictly controlled violence." Mandela insists, he underlines these words at the point where he explains the genesis of Umkonto we Sizwe (Spear of the Nation) in November 1961. In founding that combat organization, he intends to submit it to the political directives of the ANC, whose statutes prescribe nonviolence. In front of his judges, Mandela describes in detail the rules of action, the strategy, the tactics, and above all the limits imposed on the militants charged with sabotage: to wound or kill no one, either in the preparation or the execution of the operations. The militants must not bear arms. If he recognizes "having prepared a plan of sabotage," it was neither through "adventurism" nor through any "love of violence in itself." On the contrary, he wanted to interrupt what is so oddly called the cycle of violence, one entailing the other because first of all it answers, reflects, sends it back its image. Mandela meant to limit the risks of explosion by controlling the actions of the militants and by constantly devoting himself to what he calls a "reflective" analysis of the situation.

He was arrested four months after the creation of Umkonto, in August 1962. In May 1964, at the conclusion of the Rivonia Trial, he was sentenced to life imprisonment.

P.S. The postscript is for the future—in what is most undecided about it today. I wanted to speak, of course, of Nelson Mandela's future, of what does not allow itself to be anticipated, caught, captured by any mirror. Who is Nelson Mandela?

We will never stop admiring him, him and his admiration. But we do not yet know whom to admire in him, the one who, in the past, will have been the captive of his admiration or the one who, in a future anterior, will always have been free (the freest man in the world, let us not say that lightly) for having had the patience of his admiration and having known, passionately, what he had to admire. Going so far as to refuse, again yesterday, a conditional freedom.

Would they thus have imprisoned him, for almost a quarter century now, in his very admiration? Was that not the very *objective*—I mean that in the sense of photography and of the optical machine—the right to oversee [*le droit de regard*]? Did he *let* himself be imprisoned? Did he *get* himself imprisoned? Was it an accident? Perhaps we must place ourselves at a point where these alternatives lose their meaning and become the justification and the starting point for new questions. Then we must leave these questions open, like doors. And what remains to come in these questions, which are not only theoretical or philosophical, is also the figure of Mandela. Who is it? Who is coming there?

We have looked at him through words that are sometimes the devices for observation, or can in any case become that if we are not careful. What we have described, while trying precisely to escape speculation, is a kind of great historical mirador or watchtower. But there is nothing that permits us to rest assured of the unity, still less of the legitimacy of this optic of reflection, of its singular laws, of the Law, of its place of institution, of presentation or of revelation, for example, of what we gather too quickly under the name of the West. But does this presumption of unity not produce something like an effect (I am not attached to this word) that so many forces, always, try to appropriate for themselves? An effect visible and invisible, like a mirror, hard also, like the walls of a prison.

Everything that still hides Nelson Mandela from our sight.

—Translated by Mary Ann Caws and Isabelle Lorenz

§ 5 No (Point of) Madness—
Maintaining Architecture

1. *Maintenant*, this French word will not be translated. Why? For reasons, a whole series of reasons, that will perhaps appear along the way, or even at the end of the road. For I am setting out on a road, or rather course, among other possible and concurrent ones: a series of cursive notations through the *Folies* of Bernard Tschumi, from point to point, notations that are hazardous, discontinuous, aleatory.

Why now, why maintaining, why *maintenant*? I put away or place in reserve, I set *aside* the reason for maintaining the seal or stamp of this idiom: it recalls the Parc de la Villette in France—and that a pretext there gave rise to these *Folies*. Only a pretext, no doubt, along the way, a station, a phase, or a pause in a trajectory, but the pretext was offered in France. In French, we say that *une chance est offerte*, a chance is offered, but also, let us not forget, *offrir une résistance*, "to offer resistance."

2. *Maintenant*, the word will not flutter like the banner of actuality; it will not lead to burning questions: What about architecture today? What are we to think about the current state of architecture? What is new in this field? For architecture no longer defines a field. *Maintenant*: neither a modernist signal nor even a salute to postmodernity. The "posts" and posters that proliferate today (poststructuralism, postmodernism, etc.)

This text is devoted to the work of the architect Bernard Tschumi, and more precisely to the *Folies* project, which was then under construction at the Parc de la Villette in Paris. It was first published in a bilingual edition in Bernard Tschumi's *La Case vide: La Villette*, a boxed set containing essays and plates (London: Architectural Association, 1986).

still surrender to the historicist compulsion. Everything marks an era, even the decentering of the subject: posthumanism. It is as if one wished yet again to order a linear succession, to periodize, to distinguish between the before and the after, to limit the risks of reversibility or repetition, transformation or permutation: a progessivist ideology.

3. *Maintenant*: if the word still designates what happens, has just happened, promises to happen *to* architecture as well as *through* architecture, this imminence of the *just* (*just* happens, *just* happened, is *just* about to happen) no longer lets itself be inscribed in the ordered sequence of a history: it is not a fashion, a period, or an era. The *juste maintenant* [just now] does not remain a stranger to history, of course, but the relation would be other. And if this *is happening to us*, we must be prepared to receive these words. On the one hand, it does not happen to a constituted *us*, to a human subjectivity whose essence would be arrested and would *then* find itself affected by the history of this thing called architecture. We appear to ourselves only through an experience of spacing that is already marked by architecture. What happens through architecture both constructs and instructs this *us*. The latter *finds itself* engaged by architecture before it becomes the subject of it: master and possessor. On the other hand, the imminence of what is happening to us now [*maintenant*] announces not only an architectural event: rather a writing of space, a mode of spacing that makes a place for the event. If Tschumi's work indeed describes an architecture of the event, it is not only by constructing places in which something should happen or only by making the construction itself be, as we say, an event. This is not what is essential. The dimension of the event is taken up in the very structure of the architectural apparatus: sequence, open seriality, narrativity, the cinematic, dramaturgy, choreography.

4. Is an architecture of the event possible? If what happens to us thus does not come from the outside, or rather if this outside engages us in the very thing we are, is there a now [*maintenant*] of architecture, and in what sense? Everything comes down, precisely, to the question of sense. We shall not reply by indicating a means of access, for example, through a given form of architecture: preamble, *pronaos*, threshold, methodical route, circle or circulation, labyrinth, flight of stairs, ascent, archaeological regression toward a foundation, and so on. Even less in the form of a

system, namely, of the *architectonic*: the art of systems, as Kant tells us. We will not reply by giving access to some final meaning, whose revelation would be finally promised to us. No, it is precisely a matter of what happens to sense: not in the sense of what would finally allow us to arrive at sense, but what happens to it, to sense, to the sense of sense. And this is the event, what happens to it through an event that, no longer deriving altogether or simply from sense, would have to do with something like madness [*la folie*].

5. Not Madness [*Non point la Folie*], the allegorical hypostasis of Unreason, Non-Sense, but *madnesses* [les folies]. We will have to take account of this plural. *Les folies*, then, the follies of Bernard Tschumi. Henceforth we will speak of them by metonymy—and in a metonymically metonymic way, since, as we will see, this figure carries itself off and gets carried away; it has no means of stopping within itself, any more than the number of Follies in the Parc de la Villette. Follies: this is first of all the name, a proper name in a way, and a signature. Tschumi names in this way the point grid [*trame ponctuelle*] that distributes a non-finite number of elements in a space that it in fact spaces but does not fill. Metonymy, then, since *folies*, at first, designates only a part, a series of parts, precisely the pinpoint of a whole that also includes lines and surfaces, a "soundtrack" and an "image track." We will return to the function assigned to this multiplicity of red points. Here, let us note only that it maintains a metonymic relation to the whole of the Parc. Beneath this proper name, in fact, the "follies" are a common denominator, the "largest common denominator" of this "programmatic deconstruction." But, in addition, the red point of each folly remains divisible in turn, a point without point, offered up in its articulated structure to substitutions or combinatory permutations that relate it to other follies as much as to its own parts. Open point and closed point, not opened and not closed [*point ouvert et point fermé*]. This double metonymy becomes abyssal when it determines or overdetermines what opens this proper name (the *Folies* of Bernard Tschumi) to the vast semantics of the concept of madness, the great name or common denominator of all that happens to sense when it leaves itself, alienates and dissociates itself without ever having been subject, exposes itself to the outside and spaces itself out in what is not itself: not the semantics but, first of all, the a-semantics of *Folies*.

6. The *folies*, then, these follies in every sense, *for once*, we will say that they are not on the road to ruin, the ruin of defeat or nostalgia. They do not amount to the "absence of the work"—that fate of *madness in the classical period* that Foucault speaks of. Instead, they make up a work [*font œuvre*], they put to work. How? How can we think that the work can possibly *maintain itself* in this madness? How can we think the now [*maintenant*] of the architectural work? Through a certain adventure of the point, we are coming to it, *maintaining/now* [maintenant] the work— maintaining/now is the point—in the very instant, at the point of its implosion. The follies put to work a general dislocation; they draw into it everything that, until now [*maintenant*], seems to have given architecture meaning. More precisely, everything that seems to have given architecture over to meaning. They deconstruct first of all, but not only, the semantics of architecture.

7. Let us not forget that there is an architecture of architecture. Down to its archaic foundation, the most fundamental concept of architecture has been *constructed*. This naturalized architecture is bequeathed to us: we inhabit it, it inhabits us, we think it is destined for habitation, and it is no longer an object for us at all. But we must recognize there an *artifact*, a *constructum*, a monument. It did not fall from the sky; it is not natural, even if it informs a specific scheme of relations to *physis*, the sky, the earth, the mortal, and the divine. This architecture of architecture has a history; it is historical through and through. Its heritage inaugurates the intimacy of our economy, the law of our hearth (*oikos*), our familial, religious, and political oikonomy, all the places of birth and death, temple, school, stadium, agora, square, sepulcher. It penetrates us [*nous transit*] to the point that we forget its very historicity: we take it for nature. It is good sense itself.

8. The concept of architecture is itself an inhabited *constructum*, a legacy that understands us even before we try to think it. Certain invariants remain through all the mutations of architecture. Impassable, imperturbable, an axiomatic traverses the whole history of architecture. An axiomatic, that is to say, an organized whole of fundamental and always presupposed evaluations. This hierarchy has fixed itself in stone; henceforth, it informs the entirety of social space. What are these invariants? I will distinguish four, the slightly artificial charter of four traits, let us say, rather,

of four points. They translate one and the same postulate: *architecture must have a meaning*, it must *present* this meaning, and hence *signify*. The signifying or symbolic value of this meaning must command the structure and syntax, the form and function of architecture. It must command it *from the outside*, according to a principle (*archē*), a grounding or foundation, a transcendence or finality (*telos*) whose locations are not themselves architectural. The anarchitectural topic of this semanticism from which, inevitably, *four points* of invariance derive:

—The experience of meaning must be the *dwelling* [habitation], the law of the *oikos*, the economy of men or gods. In its nonrepresentational presence, which, as distinct from the other arts, seems to refer only to itself, the architectural work seems to have been destined for the presence of men and gods. The arrangement, occupation, and investment of locations should be measured against this economy. Heidegger once again recalls this economy when he interprets homelessness (*Heimatlosigkeit*) as the symptom of ontotheology and, more precisely, of modern technology. He encourages us to think properly the real distress, poverty, and destitution of dwelling itself ("die eigentliche Not des Wohnens") behind the housing crisis. Mortals must first learn how to dwell ("sie das Wohnen erst lernen müssen"), how to listen to what *calls* them to dwell. This is not a deconstruction, but rather a call to repeat the very grounds of the architecture that we inhabit, that we should relearn how to inhabit, the origin of its meaning. Of course, if the "follies" think and dislocate this origin, they should not give in either to the jubilation of modern technology or to the maniacal mastery of its powers. That would be a new turn of the same metaphysics. Hence the difficulty of what precisely [*justement*]—now [*maintenant*]—arises.

—Centered and hierarchized, the architectural organization will have had to fall in line with the anamnesis of its origin and the basis of a foundation. Not only from the time of its founding on the ground of the earth, but also since its juridico-political founding, the institution that commemorates the myths of the city, the heroes or founding gods. Despite appearances, this religious or political memory, this historicism, has not deserted modern architecture. Modern architecture is still nostalgic for it: it is its destiny to be a guardian. An always hierarchizing nostalgia: architecture will have materialized this hierarchy in stone or wood (*hylē*); it is a hyletics of the sacred (*hieros*) and the principle (*archē*), an *archihieratics*.

—This economy remains, of necessity, a *teleology* of dwelling. It sub-scribes to all the regimes of finality. Ethico-political purposiveness, reli-gious duty, utilitarian or functional ends: it is always a matter of putting architecture *in service*, and *at the service of.* This end is the principle of the archi-hieratic order.

—Whatever its mode, period, or dominant style, this order ultimately depends on the *fine arts.* The value of beauty, harmony, and totality must still reign.

These four points of invariance cannot be juxtaposed. They delineate the map of a system from the angles of a frame. We will not say only that they come together and remain inseparable, which is true. They give rise to a specific experience of *gathering,* that of a coherent totality, a continu-ity, a system. Thus, they determine a network of evaluations; they induce and inform, even if indirectly, all the theory and criticism of architecture from the most specialized to the most trivial. Such evaluation inscribes the hierarchy in a hyletics, as well as in the space of a formal distribution of values. But this architectonic of invariable points also governs all of what is called Western culture, far beyond its architecture. Hence the con-tradiction, the *double bind,* or the antinomy that at once mobilizes and disturbs this history. On the one hand, this general architectonic *erases* or *exceeds* the sharp specificity of architecture; it is valid for other arts and regions of experience as well. On the other hand, architecture forms its most powerful metonymy; it gives it its most solid *consistency,* objective substance. By consistency, I do not mean only logical coherence, which implicates all dimensions of human experience in the same network: there is no work of architecture without interpretation, or even economic, reli-gious political, aesthetic, or philosophical decision. But by consistency I also mean duration, hardness, the monumental, mineral or ligneous sub-sistence, the hyletics of tradition. Hence the *resistance:* the resistance of materials like the resistance of consciousness and unconsciousness that establishes this architecture as the last fortress of metaphysics. Resistance and transference. A consistent deconstruction would be nothing if it did not take account of this resistance and this transference; it would do little if it did not take on architecture as much as the architectonic. To take it on: not in order to attack, destroy, or lead it astray, to criticize or disqual-ify it. Rather, in order to *think* it in fact, to take sufficient distance from it so as to apprehend it in a thought that carries beyond the theorem—and becomes an oeuvre in turn.

9. We will now take the measure of the follies, of what others would call the immeasurable hubris of Bernard Tschumi and what it gives us to think. These follies cause meaning to tremble, the meaning of meaning, the signifying whole of this powerful architectonic. They challenge, dislocate, destabilize, or deconstruct the edifice of this configuration. In this, they are "madness," one will say. For in a *polemos* without aggressivity, without the destructive drive that would still betray a reactive affect within the hierarchy, they take on the very meaning of architectural meaning, as it has been bequeathed to us and as we still inhabit it. Let us not elude the question: if this configuration presides over what in the West is called architecture, don't these follies wipe the slate clean? Don't they lead back to the desert of anarchitecture, to a degree zero of architectural writing where this writing would lose itself, henceforth without *telos*, without aesthetic aura, without grounding, without hierarchical principle, without symbolic signification, in short—a prose made up of abstract, neuter, inhuman, useless, uninhabitable, and meaningless volumes?

Precisely not. The "follies" affirm; they commit their affirmation beyond this ultimately annihilating, secretly nihilistic repetition of metaphysical architecture. They enter into the now [*maintenant*] of which I speak; they maintain, renew, and reinscribe architecture. They awaken, perhaps, an energy in it that was infinitely anaesthetized, walled-in, buried in a common sepulcher or sepulchral nostalgia. For we must begin by emphasizing this: the map or metaphysical frame whose configuration has just been sketched out was already, one might say, the end of architecture, its "reign of ends" in the figure of death.

It came to subject the oeuvre to reason [*arraisonner*]; it imposed on it norms or meanings that were extrinsic, if not accidental. It made its attributes into an essence: formal beauty, finality, utility, functionality, the value of habitation, its religious or political economy, all the *services*, so many nonarchitectural or meta-architectural predicates. By *now* [maintenant] suspending this command over architecture—what I keep naming thus, using a paleonym, so as to maintain a muted call—by ceasing to impose these alien norms on the work, the follies return architecture, faithfully, to what architecture, since the very eve of its origin, should have signed. The now [*maintenant*] that I speak of will be this signature—the most irreducible. It does not contravene the charter, but rather draws it into another text; it even subscribes and calls others to subscribe to, what we will later call a *contract*, another play of the trait, of attraction, and contraction.

A proposition that I do not make without precautions, admonitions, and warnings. Still, the signal of two red points:

—These follies do not destroy. Tschumi always talks about "deconstruction/reconstruction," particularly concerning the Madness and the generation of his cube (formal combinations and transformational relations). What is in question in Tschumi's *Manhattan Transcripts* is the invention of "new relations, in which the traditional components of architecture are broken down and reconstructed along other axes."[1] Without nostalgia, the most living act of memory. Nothing here of that nihilistic gesture that would fulfill, on the contrary, a certain theme of metaphysics; no reversal of values in view of an unaesthetic, uninhabitable, unusable, asymbolic, and unsignifying architecture, an architecture simply left vacant after the retreat of gods and men. And the follies—like madness in general—are anything but the chaos of anarchy. Yet, without proposing a "new order," they locate the architectural work elsewhere, a work that, at least in its principle, in its essential impetus, will no longer obey these external imperatives. Tschumi's "first" concern will no longer be to organize space as a function of or in view of economic, aesthetic, epiphanic, or techno-utilitarian norms. These norms will be taken into account, but they will find themselves subordinated and reinscribed in a place in the text and in a space that they will no longer dominate in the final instance. By pushing "architecture toward its limits," a place will be made for "pleasure"; each folly will be destined for a given "use," with its own cultural, playful, pedagogical, scientific, and philosophical purposiveness. I will say a little more about its powers of "attraction" later. All of this answers to a program of transfers, transformations, or permutations over which these external norms no longer have the final word. They will not have presided over the work [*œuvre*]; Tschumi has folded them into the general *mise en œuvre*.

—Yes, folded. What fold? By reinstituting architecture in what should have been singularly *proper* to it, the aim is not to reconstitute a *simple* of architecture, a simply architectural architecture, through a purist or integrationist obsession. It is no longer a matter of saving the proper in the virginal immanence of its economy and of returning it to its inalienable presence, a presence that, ultimately, is nonrepresentational, nonmimetic, and refers only to itself. This autonomy of architecture, which would thus claim to reconcile formalism and semanticism in their extremes, would only fulfill the metaphysics it was claiming to deconstruct. The invention here consists in crossing the architectural motif with what is most singular and most closely competing in other writings, which are themselves drawn into the said madness, in its plural, that of photographic, cinematographic, choreographic, and even mythographic writing. As *The Manhattan Transcripts* demonstrated (the same is true, though in a different way, of La Villette), a narrative montage of great complexity outwardly explodes the narrative that mythologies contracted or effaced in the hieratic presence of the monument "for memory." An architectural writing interprets (in the Nietzschean sense of active, productive, violent, transformative interpretation) events that are *marked* by photography or cinematography. Marked: provoked, determined *or* transcribed, captured, in any case always mobilized in a scenography of passage (transference, translation, transgression from one place to another, from a place of writing to another, graft, hybridization). Neither architecture nor anarchitecture: transarchitecture. It comes to terms with the event; it no longer offers its work to users, believers, or dwellers, to contemplators, aesthetes, or consumers. Instead, it calls on the other to *invent*, in turn, the event, to sign, consign, or *countersign*: advanced by an advance made to the other—and *maintaining* architecture, *now* architecture.

(I can hear a murmur: but doesn't this event you're talking about, an event that reinvents architecture in a series of "one time only's" that are always unique in their repetition, isn't this what takes place each time not *in* a church or a temple, or even *in* a political place, not *in* them, but rather *as* them, resuscitating them, for example, during each Mass when the body of Christ, and so on, when the body of the king or of the nation presents itself or announces itself? And why not, if this still could happen again, happen through architecture, or even to it? Without venturing further in this direction, although still acknowledging its necessity, I will say only that Tschumi's architectural "follies" *gives us to think* about what *takes place* when, *for example*, the Eucharistic event comes to penetrate [*transir*] a church, here, now, or when a date, a seal, the trace of the other finally comes into the body of stone [*vient au corps de la pierre*]—this time in the movement of its dis-appearance.)

10. Therefore, we can no longer speak of a *properly* architectural moment, the hieratic impassability of the monument, this hyle-morphic complex that is given once and for all, permitting no trace to appear any longer on its body because it affords no chance of transformations, permutations, or substitutions. In the follies we are talking about, on the contrary, the event undoubtedly undergoes this trial of the monumental moment; however, it inscribes it, as well, in a series of *experiences*. As its name indicates, an experience traverses: voyage, trajectory, translation, transference. Not in view of a final presentation, a presencing [*mise en présence*] of the thing itself, nor in order to complete an odyssey of conciousness, the phenomenology of mind as an architectural process. The course followed by the follies is undoubtedly prescribed, from point to point, to the extent that the point grid [*trame ponctuelle*] takes account of a *program* of possible experiences and new experiments (cinema, botanical garden, video workshop, library, skating rink, gymnasium). But the structure of the grid and of each cube—for these points are cubes—leaves room for chance, formal invention, combinatory transformation, wandering. Such chance is not given to the inhabitant or the believer, the user or the architectural theorist, but to whoever engages, in turn, in architectural writing: without reservation, which implies an inventive reading, the unease of a whole culture, and the signature of the body. This body would no longer be content simply to *walk*, circulate, stroll around *in* a place or *on* paths, but would transform its elementary motions by giving them place [*en leur donnant lieu*]; it would receive from this other spacing the invention of its gestures.

11. The madness does not stop: neither in the hieratic monument nor in the circular path. Neither the impassability nor the step [*pas*]. Seriality inscribes itself in stone, iron, or wood, but this seriality does not stop there. And it began earlier. The series of *épreuves* (trials or artist proofs, as we say), which are ingenuously called drawings, essays, photographs, models, films, or writings (for example, what is gathered together for a time in this volume) fully belongs to the *experience* of the follies: follies *at work*. We can no longer give them the value of documents, related illustrations, preparatory or pedagogical notes, the *hors-d'œuvre*, in short, or the equivalent of theatrical rehearsals. No—and this is what seems most threatening to the architectural desire that still inhabits us. The immovable mass of stone, the vertical glass or metal plane that we had taken to be the very object

of architecture (*die Sache selbst,* or "the real thing"), its undisplaceable effectivity is now apprehended in the voluminous text of multiple writings: superimpression of a *Wunderblock* (to signal to one of Freud's texts—and Tschumi exposes architecture to psychoanalysis, introducing the theme of transference, for example, and of splitting [*schize*]), palimpsest grid, supersedimented textuality, bottomless stratigraphy that is mobile, light and abyssal, foliated, foliform. Foliated folly, leafy [*feuille*] and mad [*folle*] because it does not seek reassurance in any solidity: not ground or tree, horizontality or verticality, nature or culture, form or foundation or finality. The architect who wrote with stones now places lithographs in a volume, and Tschumi speaks of them as *folios.* Something is being plotted in this "foliotage" whose stratagem, as well as randomness, reminds me of a suspicion harbored by Littré. Regarding the second meaning of the word *folie,* that of houses bearing the name of their signatory, the name of "the one who built them or the place in which they are located," Littré hazards the following, in the name of etymology: "Usually one sees in this the word *folie* [madness]. But this becomes doubtful when one finds in the texts from the Middle Ages: *foleia quae erat ante domum,* and *domum foleyae,* and *folia Johannis Morelli*; the suspicion arises that this involves an alteration of the word *feuillie* or *feuillée.*" The word *folie* has no commonsense meaning any more: it has lost even the reassuring unity of its meaning. Tschumi's follies no doubt play on this "alteration" and superimpose, over against the common meaning, this other meaning, the meaning of the other, of the other language, the madness of this asemantics.

12. When I discovered Bernard Tschumi's work, I had to dismiss an easy hypothesis: recourse to the language of deconstruction—to what in it could be coded, to its most insistent words and motifs, to some of its strategies—would only be an *analogical* transposition or even an architectural *application.* In any case, the impossible itself. For, according to the logic of this hypothesis (which did not last long), one might have asked oneself: What exactly would deconstructive architecture be? Isn't what deconstructive strategies begin or end by destabilizing precisely the structural principle of architecture (system, architectonic, structure, foundation, construction, etc.)? Instead, this last question led me toward another turn of interpretation: what *The Manhattan Transcripts* and the *Folies* of La Villette urge us toward is the *obligatory way* of deconstruction in one of its most intense, affirmative, and necessary *implementations*

[mises en œuvre]. Not deconstruction *itself,* there is never such a thing, but what carries the jolt beyond semantic analysis, beyond the critique of discourses and ideologies, concepts or texts, in the traditional sense of the latter term. Deconstructions would be weak if they were negative, if they did not construct, and above all if they did not first measure themselves against that which is most solid in institutions, *at the place of their greatest resistance:* political structures, levers of economic decision, the material and phantasmatic apparatuses that connect state, civil society, capital, bureaucracy, cultural powers and architectural teaching—a remarkably sensitive relay—but that also connect the arts, from the fine arts to the arts of war, science and technology, the old and the new. So many forces that are precipitated and begin to harden or cement in a large-scale architectural operation, particularly when it approaches the body of a metropolis and involves negotiations with the state. This is the case here.

13. War is not declared. Another strategy is woven, somewhere between hostilities and negotiation. Taken in its strictest, if not most literal, sense, the grid of the follies introduces a singular device into the space of the transaction. The proper meaning of the "grid" [*trame*] does not come together. It traverses. To "tramer" is to traverse, to go through a channel [*méat*]. It is the experience of a permeability. Moreover, the traversal does not move through an already existing material; it weaves, it invents the histological structure of a text, of what one would call in English a "fabric." *Fabrique,* let it be said in passing, is the French noun—with an entirely different meaning—that some decision makers had proposed substituting for the disquieting title of *folies.*

Architect-weaver. He weaves, twining the threads of the warp; his writing holds out a net. A weave always weaves in several directions, according to several meanings, and beyond meaning. A network stratagem, thus a singular device. Which?

A dissociated series of "points," red points, constitutes the grid [*trame*], spacing out there a multiplicity of matrices or engendering cells whose transformations will never let themselves be pacified, stabilized, installed, identified in a continuum. Divisible themselves, these cells also point to instants of rupture, discontinuity, disjunction. But simultaneously, or rather through a series of countertimes, rhythmed anachronies, or aphoristic gaps, the point of madness gathers together what it has just dispersed; it gathers it *as* dispersion. It gathers into a multiplicity of *red* points. Resemblance and gathering are not confined to color, but the *chromographic* reminder plays a necessary role in it.

What then, is a point, *this* point of madness? How does it stop the madness? For it suspends it, and, in this movement, brings it to a halt, but as madness. Arrest of madness: *point de folie*, no point of madness, no more madness, no madness. At the same time, it decides, but according to what decree, what warrant, and what aphoristic justice? What does the law do? Who makes the law? The law divides *and* arrests division; it *maintains* this point of madness, this chromosomal cell, as the engendering principle. How are we to think the architectural *chromosome*, its color, this work of division and individuation that no longer belongs to bio-genetics?

We are coming to that, but only after a detour. We must pass through one more point.

14. There are strong words in Tschumi's lexicon. They situate the points of greatest intensity. These are the words beginning with *trans-* (transcript, transference, etc.) and, above all, *de-* or *dis-*. These words say destabilization, deconstruction, dehiscence and, first of all, dissociation, disjunction, disruption, difference. An architecture of the heterogeneous, of interruption, of non-coincidence. But who will ever have built in this manner? Who will ever have counted solely on the energies in *dis-* or *de-*? No work can result from a simple displacement or dislocation alone. One must thus invent. One must clear a passage to another writing. Without renouncing the deconstructive affirmation whose necessity we have experienced, in order to relaunch it, on the contrary, this writing *maintains* the *dis-jointed* as such; it joins the *dis-* by maintaining the gap; it gathers together difference. This gathering will be singular. What maintains together does not necessarily take the form of a system; it does not always depend on an architectonic and does not have to obey the logic of synthesis or the order of syntax. The now (maintaining) of architecture would be this maneuver to inscribe the *dis-* and make it into a work as such. Standing and maintaining (now), this work does not pour difference into concrete; it does not erase the differential trait; it neither reduces nor sets this trait, the dis-tract or the abstract, in a homogeneous mass (*concrete*). The architectonic, or the art of the system, represents only one epoch, says Heidegger, in the history of being-together. It is only one determined possibility of gathering.

This, then, would be both the task and the wager, the concern of the impossible: to give dissociation its due, but to put it to work *as such* in the space of a gathering. A transaction in view of a spacing and a *socius* of dissociation that would, moreover, allow one to negotiate *that very thing*, difference, with the received norms, the politico-economic powers of the architectonic, the mastery of what one calls in French the *maîtres d'œuvre* [general contractors or chief architects]. This "difficulty" is Tschumi's experience. He does not hide it, "this is not without difficulty." "At La Villette, it is a matter of forming, of acting out dissociation. . . . This is not without difficulty. Putting dissociation into form necessitates that the underlying support (the Parc, the institution) be structured as a gathering system. The red point of the Folies is the focus of this dissociated space."[2]

15. A force joins and holds together the dis-jointed as such. It does not affect the *dis-* from the outside. The *dis-jointed* itself, maintaining architecture, the architecture that arrests madness in its dislocation. It is not only *a* point. An open multiplicity of red points no longer lets itself be totalized, even by metonymy. These points fragment perhaps, but I would not define them as fragments. A fragment still signals to a lost or promised totality.

Multiplicity does not open each point *from the outside*. To understand how multiplicity also comes from within, we must analyze the *double bind* whose knot the point of madness tightens, without forgetting what can tie a *double bind* to splitting [*schize*] and madness.

On the one hand, the point concentrates, folds back toward itself the greatest force of attraction, *contracting* the lines toward the center. Referring back only to itself, within a grid that is also autonomous, the point fascinates and magnetizes, seduces through what could be called its self-sufficiency and "narcissism." At the same time, by its force of magnetic attraction (Tschumi speaks here of a "magnet" that would "gather" the "fragments of an exploded system"), the point seems to bind, as Freud would say, the energy available, in a free state, within a given field. It exerts its attraction in its very punctuality, the *stigmē* of an instantaneous now toward which everything converges and where it seems to become indivisible; but also by the fact that, in stopping madness, it constitutes the point of transaction with an architecture that it in turn deconstructs or divides. A discontinuous series of instants and *attractions*: in each point of madness, the attractions of the Parc, the useful or playful activities, the purposes, meanings, economic or ecological investments, the services will again find their place on the program. Bound energy and semantic recharge. Hence, also, the distinction *and* transaction between what Tschumi terms the normality and deviance of the follies. Each point is a point of rupture: it interrupts, absolutely, the continuity of the text or of the grid. But the inter-ruptor maintains together *both* the rupture *and* the relation to the other, which is itself structured as both attraction *and* interruption, interference and difference: a relation without relation. What is contracted here signs a "mad" contract between the *socius* and dissociation. And this without dialectic, without the sublation or relief (*Aufhebung*) whose process Hegel explains to us and which can always reappropriate a now of this kind: the point denies space and, in this spatial negation of itself, generates the line in which it maintains itself by canceling itself (*als sich aufhebend*). Thus, the line would be the truth of the point, the surface would be the truth of the line, time, the truth of space, and, finally, the now, the truth of the point (*Encyclopedia*, § 256–7). Here I permit myself to refer to my text, "Ousia et grammē."[3] Under the same name, the now of which I am speaking would mark the interruption of this dialectic.

But, on the other hand, if dissociation does not come to the point from the outside, it is because the point is *both* divisible *and* indivisible. It appears atomic and thus has the function and individualizing form of the point only from a *point of view*, from the perspective of the serial whole that it punctuates, organizes, and upholds, without ever being its support. As it is seen, and seen from outside, it simultaneously scans and interrupts, maintains and divides, gives color and rhythm to the spacing of the grid. But this point of view does not see; it is blind to what happens *inside* the madness or the folly, for if we consider it *absolutely*, abstracted from the whole and in itself (it is also destined to abstract, distract, or subtract itself), the point is no longer a point; it no longer has the atomic indivisibility that is given to the geometrical point. Open on the inside to a void that gives play to the pieces, the point constructs/deconstructs itself like a cube exposed to formal combination. The articulated pieces disjoin themselves, compose, and recompose. By articulating the pieces that are more than pieces, pieces of a game, theater pieces, inhabitable pieces, at once places and spaces of *movement*, the *dis*-joint figures them as *promised* to events: in order for them to take place.

16. For it was necessary to speak of promise and pledge, of promise as affirmation, of the promise that provides the privileged example of a performative writing. More than an example, the very condition of such writing. Without accepting what theories of performative language and speech acts—relayed here by architectural praxis—continue to assume as presuppositions (for example, the value of presence, of the now as present), and without being able to discuss these things here, let us focus only on this trait: the provocation of the event of which I am speaking ("I promise," for example), that I describe or trace, the event that I *make* happen or *let* happen by marking it. One must insist on the mark or trait so as to remove this performativity from the hegemony of speech and of so-called human speech. The performative mark *spaces*: it is the event of spacing. The red points space; they maintain architecture in the dissociation of spacing. But this now does not only maintain a past or a tradition; it does not ensure a synthesis. It maintains the interruption, in other words, the relation to the other as such. To the other in the magnetic field of attraction, of the "common denominator" or "focus," to the other points of rupture as well, but first of all to the Other: the one through which the promised event will come or will not come. For the other is called, only called, to countersign the pledge [*gage*], the engagement, or the wager. This Other never presents itself and is not present, now. It can be represented by what we too quickly call Power, the politico-economic decision makers, users, representatives of fields, of cultural domination, and here, singularly, of a philosophy of architecture. This Other will be anyone, not yet [*point encore*] subject, ego or conscience, no man [*point d'homme*]; anyone who comes to answer the promise, who first answers *for* the promise: the to-come of an event that maintains spacing, the now in dissociation, the relation to the other as such. Not the maintained [*maintenue*] but the hand held out [*main tendue*] over the abyss.

17. Covered over by the entire history of architecture and open to the unanticipatable chance of a future, this other architecture, this architecture of the other, is nothing that is. It is not a present, the memory of a past present, the purchase on or pre-comprehension of a future present. It presents neither a (constative) theory nor a politics nor an ethics of architecture. Not even a narrative, although it opens this space to all narrative matrices, to sound tracks and image tracks. (As I write this, I am thinking of Blanchot's *Madness of the Day*, and of the demand for, and impossibil-

ity of narrative brought to light there. Everything I have written about it, most notably in *Parages*, is directly and sometimes literally concerned—I have become aware of this after the fact, thanks to Tschumi—with the madness of architecture: step, threshold, stair, labyrinth, hotel, hospital, wall, enclosures, edges, bedroom, the inhabitation of the uninhabitable. And since all of this, which concerns the madness of the line [*trait*], the spacing of "dis-traction," will be published in English, I also think of that idiomatic manner of referring to the fool, the absent-minded, the wanderer: *the one who is spacy, or spaced-out.*)

But if it presents neither theory, nor ethics, nor politics, nor narrative ("No, no narrative, never again," one reads in *The Madness of the Day*), it gives rise [*lieu*] to them all. It writes and signs in advance—maintaining a divided line on the edge of meaning, before any presentation, beyond it— that very thing, the other, that engages architecture, its discourse, political scenography, economy, and morality. Pledge but also wager, symbolic order and gamble: these red cubes are thrown like the dice of architecture. The throw not only programs a strategy *of* the event, as I suggested earlier, it goes out to meet the architecture to come. It runs that risk and gives us that chance.

—Translated by Kate Linker

§ 6 Why Peter Eisenman Writes Such Good Books

This title barely conceals a quotation, that of another title, a well-known one. It lifts out a fragment, or rather a person.

By transcribing the title "Warum ich so gute Bücher schreibe" ["Why I Write Such Good Books"] in the third person, by calling Nietzsche's *Ecce Homo* to the witness stand, I take it upon myself to clear Eisenman of all suspicion. It is not he who says it. It is I. I who write. I who, by means of displacements, samplings, fragmentations, play with people and their titles, with the integrity of their proper names.

Does one have the right to do this? But who will determine the right? And in whose name?

By abusing metonymy as much as pseudonymy, following Nietzsche's example, I propose to do several things. All at once, or one by one. But I will not reveal them all, and certainly not to begin with. Without giving away all the leads, I will at first indicate neither the path, nor the connections. Is this not the best condition for writing good texts? Those who assumed from a simple reading of my title that I was going to diagnose the paranoia of some Nietzsche of modern architecture have mistaken the address.

First, I propose to draw attention to the art with which Eisenman knows how to play with titles. We will take a few examples. First of all,

This text was originally written for the Japanese journal *Architecture and Urbanism*, a special issue devoted to the work of the architect Peter Eisenman (Tokyo, 1987); it was first published in English. [Bolded type indicates English in the original.—Eds.]

there are the titles of his books. They are made up of words. But what are words for an architect? Or books?

I also want to propose, with the allusion to *Ecce Homo*, that Eisenman is, in architecture, the most anti-Wagnerian creator of our time. What is Wagnerian architecture? Where are its remains today, or its disguises? These questions will remain unanswered here. But do such questions of art or politics not at least deserve to be prepared, if not posed?

I propose to speak of music, of musical instruments in one of Eisenman's works in progress. It is unnecessary to recall the fact that *Ecce Homo* is above all a book about music, and not only in its final chapter, "Der Fall Wagner, Ein Musikanten-Problem."

Finally, I propose to remind the reader that the value, that is, the very axiomatic of architecture that Eisenman begins by overturning, is the measure of man, that which proportions everything to a human, all too human, scale ("Menschliches, Allzumenschliches, Mit zwei Fortsetzungen," another chapter of *Ecce Homo*). Already at the entry to the labyrinth of *Moving Arrows, Eros, and Other Errors,*[1] one reads: "Architecture traditionally has been related to a human scale." For the "metaphysics of scale" that Eisenman's "scaling" means to destabilize is, first of all, a humanism or an anthropocentrism. A human, all too human, desire for "presence" and "origin." Even as far as its theological dimensions, and first of all under the law of representation and aesthetics, this architecture of originary presence returns to man: "In destabilizing presence and origin, the value that architecture gives to representation and the aesthetic object is also called into question" (*Moving Arrows*).

We should not, however, simply conclude that this architecture will be Nietzschean. Let us not borrow *themes* or *philosophemes* from *Ecce Homo*, but rather a few figures, stagings, apostrophes, and then a lexicon, like those computerized palettes from which one borrows colors by pressing a key before writing. So, I take the following, which in a moment you will read on my screen (I write on my computer and you know that Nietzsche was one of the first writers in the world to own a typewriter), it is at the beginning of *Ecce Homo*: a "labyrinth," the labyrinth of knowledge, his own, the most dangerous of all, to which some might wish to forbid entry: "man wird niemals in dies Labyrinth verwegener Erkenntnisse eintreten"; a little further on, there is a quotation from *Zarathustra*, and then an allusion to those who hold "Ariadne's thread with a cowardly hand." Between the two, one will also catch the allusion to those bold searchers who "embark on terrible seas [*auf furchtbare Meere*]" and to those whose souls are lured by flutes toward dangerous whirlpools ("deren Seele mit Flöten zu jedem Irrschlunde gelockt wird"). In short, let us say that what we retain from *Ecce Homo*, in the chapter "Why I Write Such Good Books," is only this: the seduction of music, the musical instrument, the sea or the abyss, and the labyrinth.

A strange introduction to architecture, you will say, and especially to that of Peter Eisenman. In which hand must the thread be held? And should it be held firmly or loosely?

It is true that this is doubtless not my subject. I will speak more readily of encounters, and of what *encounter* means, what takes *place* at the crossing of chance and program, of *the aleatory* and necessity.

When I met Peter Eisenman, still in my naïveté, I thought that discourse was on my side. And that architecture "properly speaking" was on his: places, space, drawing, silent calculation, stones, the resistance of materials. Of course, I was not so naïve; I knew that discourse and language did not count for nothing in the activity of architects and above all in his. I even had reason to think that discourse and language were more important to this activity than architects themselves realized. But I did not know the extent to which, and above all the way in which, this architecture began by taking on the very conditions of discourse, grammar, and semantics. Or why Eisenman is a writer, which, far from distancing him from architecture and making him one of those "theoreticians" who—as is said by those who do neither one nor the other, write more than they build—on the contrary, opens a space where two writings, the verbal and the architectural, are printed, the one in the other, outside the traditional hierarchies. What Eisenman writes "with words" is not limited to so-called theoretical reflection on the architectural object, what it has been or what it should be. Of course, it is also this, but there is still something else, something that does not simply develop like a metalanguage concerning a certain traditional authority of discourse in architecture. At issue is another treatment of the word, another "poetics," if you like, one that participates rightfully in the architectural invention without subjecting it to the order of discourse.

Our encounter was a chance for me. But the aleatory—which is what befalls [*advient*] in any encounter—must have been on the program, an abyssal program that I cannot risk trying to analyze here. Let us begin at the point when Bernard Tschumi proposed to both of us that we collaborate in the conception of what was called, by convention, a "garden" in the Parc de la Villette, a rather strange garden containing no vegetation, only liquids and solids, water and minerals. I will not elaborate here on my first contribution, a text on the *khōra* in Plato's *Timaeus*. The abyssal enigma of what Plato says of the architect demiurge, of locality, of the inscription that imposes on it the images of paradigms, and so on: all this seemed to me to merit being put to a kind of architectural test, a kind of challenge of rigor, with its poetic, rhetorical, and political stakes, with all the difficulties of reading that this text has posed to centuries of inter-pretation. But once again, I do not wish to speak here of what may have happened on my side, on the side of the proposal that I put forward, even as I put myself forward with the greatest misgiving. What counts here is what came from the other side, from the side of Peter Eisenman.

Things having begun with words and a book, I quickly had to give in to the obvious. Eisenman not only takes great pleasure, a jubilatory plea-sure, in playing with language, with languages, in the *encounter* of several idioms, welcoming chances, paying attention to the aleatory, to grafts, to the slippages and driftings of the letter. He takes this play seriously, if one can say this, and without giving it the principal, inductive role in a work that one hesitates to call properly or purely architectural, without setting up this play of the letter as a *determining origin* (there is no such a thing for Eisenman), he does not abandon it *outside the work*. For him, words are not epigraphs.

I will recall only two examples.

After he translated, or rather transferred, transformed, appropriated and made appropriate for himself, certain motifs of my text in a first architectural project, a bottomless palimpsest, with **scaling**, **quarry**, and "labyrinth," I insisted, and Eisenman fully agreed, on the need to give our work something like a title, and an inventive title. This title should not have as its sole function to gather meaning and produce those effects of legitimizing identification that one expects from titles in general. At the same time, precisely because what we were making was not a garden (the category under which the administration of La Villette ingenuously clas-sified the space that was entrusted to us), but something else, a place still without name, if not unnameable, it was necessary to give it a name, and with this naming make a new gesture, a supplementary piece of the work, something other than a simple reference to a thing that would exist in any case without its name, outside the name.

Three conditions seemed to be required.

1. That this title be as strong, as inclusive, as economical a designation of the work as possible. This was its "classic" and normally referential function as title and name.

2. That this title, while designating the work from its outside, also be part of the work, imprinting on it from the inside, if one can say this, an indispensable motion, in such a manner that the letters of the name would participate in the very body of architecture.

3. That the verbal structure maintain a relation to what was aleatory in the encounter such that no semantic order could stop the play, or totalize it from a center, an origin, or a principle.

Choral Work, this was the title invented by Eisenman.

Even though it surfaced at a moment when long discussions had already given rise to the first **drawings** and the principial schema of the work, this title seemed to impose itself all at once in a single stroke [*d'un seul coup*]; a stroke of luck [*coup de chance*] but also the result of a calculation. No contestation, no reservation was possible. The title was perfect.

1. It names in the most correct [*juste*] fashion, by means of the most efficient and *economic* reference, a work that in its own way interprets, in a dimension that is both discursive and architectural, a reading of the Platonic *khōra*. The word *khōra* is carried over into song (choral), or even into choreography. Ending in *l, chora l: khōra* becomes more liquid or more aerial, I dare not say more feminine.

2. It becomes indissociable from a construction, on which it imposes a new dimension from within: choreographic, both musical and vocal. Speech, and even song, are inscribed thus, take place within a rhythmic composition. To give rise to, or to take place is to make an architectural event out of music, or rather out of a chorus.

3. In addition to being a musical, or even a choreographic allusion to Plato's *khōra*, this title is more than a title. It also forms a signature, and the mark of a plural signature, written by both of us in chorus. Eisenman had just done what he said. The performance, the felicitous efficacy of the performative, consists in inventing all alone the form of a signature that not only signs for two but enunciates in itself the plurality of the choral signature, the co-signature or countersignature. He gives me his signature, as one says of someone who gives to a collaborator the "power" to sign in his place. The work becomes musical, an architecture

for many voices, at once different and attuned [*accordées*] in their very alterity. This forms a gift as precious as it is stony [*pierreux*], coral. As if water had naturally joined with mineral for this simulacrum of spontaneous creation in the unconscious depths of some divided ocean. *Ecce Homo*: the abyss of bottomless depths, music, a hyperbolic labyrinth. The law is both respected and outsmarted. For the task that we had been given also prescribed this: only water and stone should be used for this pseudo-garden and above all, no vegetation. So it was done, in a stroke [*d'un coup*], with a wave [*coup*] of a magic wand, in two words, so close to silence. The magic wand is also that of the orchestra conductor. I still hear it now, like the masterpiece of a maker of fireworks, the explosion of a firecracker. And how not think of the *Music for the Royal Fireworks*, of the chorale, of the influence of Corelli, of the "sense of architecture" that one always admires in Handel?

The elements are thus brought to light, exposed to the air: earth, water, and fire. As in the *Timaeus*, at the moment of the formation of the *cosmos*. But it is impossible to assign an order, a hierarchy, a principle of deduction or derivation, to all the meanings that intersect here as if through the effect of a chance encounter, in hardly more than ten letters, sealed, forged (**coined**) in the idiomatic forge (**forgery**) of a single language. The "title" gathers itself in the stamp, the seal or the paraph of this countersignature (for this was also a way of not signing while signing), but it does so by opening the whole to which it seems to belong. No capitalizing role for this title, which is open to other interpretations or, one might say, other performances, other musicians, other choreographers, or even other voices. Totalization is impossible.

We might draw on other threads, other chords in this labyrinthine skein. Eisenman often refers to the labyrinth to describe [*écrire*] the paths called for by certain of his works: "These superpositions appear in a labyrinth, which is located at the site of the castle of Juliet. Like the story of Romeo and Juliet, it is an analogic expression of the unresolved tension between fate and free will. Here the labyrinth, like the castle grounds, becomes a palimpsest." Like the work it names, the title *Choral Work* is at the same time palimpsest and labyrinth, a maze of superimposed structures (Plato's text, the reading of it that I proposed in my text, the slaughterhouses of La Villette, Eisenman's project for Venice, and Tschumi's *Folies*). In French, but this remains untranslatable, one says: the title *se donne carrière*. "Carrière" is **quarry**. But *se donner carrière* is also to give

free reign, to appropriate a space for oneself with a certain joyful inso-
lence. Literally, I mean it here in the sense of a quarry that at once gives
itself graciously, offers up its own depths, but belongs first and foremost
to the very space it enriches. How can one *give* in this way? How can one,
while drawing from it, enrich the whole to which one belongs? What is
this strange economy of the gift? In *Choral Work* and elsewhere, Eisenman
playfully sets up a part of the whole as a quarry—the word is his—as a
mine of materials to be displaced for the rest, on the inside of the whole.
The quarry is both inside and outside; the resource is included. And the
structure of the title obeys the same law; it has the same form of potentiality, the same power: the dynamic of an immanent invention. Everything
can be found inside, but it is more or less unpredictable.

For my second example, I must pull on another string. As if incorporat-
ing or quoting them in itself, this musical and choreographic architecture
was going to point to a poetic genre, namely, the lyric, and the stringed
instrument that corresponds to it, I mean the lyre.

The title had already been given and we had moved forward in the
preparation of *Choral Work*, when Eisenman suggested that I finally take
an initiative that was not only discursive, theoretical, or "philosophical"
(I place this word in quotation marks because my reading of the *khōra*
perhaps no longer belongs to philosophical thought, but we will leave
this aside). He wanted, rightly, our chorus to be more than the simple ag-
gregation of two soloists, a writer and an architect. The latter signed and
"de-signed," **designed** with words. I should for my part project or draw
visible forms. While returning from New York, in the airplane, I wrote
Eisenman a letter containing a drawing and its interpretation. Thinking
of one of the most enigmatic passages to my mind in Plato's *Timaeus*, I
wanted the figure of a *sieve* to be inscribed on the *Choral Work* itself, so
as to leave the memory of a synecdoche or an errant metonymy. Errant,
that is to say, without possibility of being taken up in some totality that it
would figure as a detached piece: neither fragment nor ruin. The *Timaeus*,
in effect, uses what one no doubt abusively calls a metaphor, that of the
sieve, in order to describe the way in which the place (the *khōra*) filters
the "kinds," the forces, or the seeds that are imprinted on it:

> [A]nd that wet nurse of becoming, being liquified and ignited and receiving
> the shapes of earth and air, and suffering all the other affections that follow
> along with these, appears in all sorts of ways to our sight. And because she's

filled with powers neither similar nor equally balanced, in no part of her is she equally balanced, but rather, as she sways irregularly in every direction, she herself is shaken by those kinds and, being moved, in turn shakes them back; and the kinds, in being moved, are always swept along this way and that and are dispersed—just like the particles shaken and winnowed out, by *sieves* and other instruments used for purifying grain: the dense and heavy are swept to one site and settle, the porous and light to another. So too, when the four kinds are shaken by the recipient, who, being herself moved, is like a *sieve*. (*Timaeus* 52d–53a; my emphases—JD)[2]

This is not the place to explain why I have always found this passage provocative but also fascinating because of its resistance to reading. That is not important for the moment. As if to give body to this fascination, I wrote this letter to Eisenman on the plane, a fragment of which I will quote here:

You remember what we envisioned together at Yale: that to conclude, I would "write," so to speak, *without* a single word, a heterogeneous piece, *without* origin or apparent destination, like a fragment that would come, *without* signaling toward any totality (lost or promised), to break the circle of reappropriation, the triad of the three sites (Eisenman-Derrida, Tschumi, La Villette), in short, the totalization, the still too historical configuration, in the form in which it would lend itself to a general decoding. And yet I thought that, without giving any assurance on this subject, some detached, enigmatic metonymy, rebelling against the history of these three sites and even against the palimpsest, should "recall" by chance, if one encountered it, something—the most incomprehensible of all—of *khōra*. For me, today, the most enigmatic, what resists and provokes the most, in the reading I attempt of the *Timaeus* is, I'll talk to you about this, the allusion to the figure of the *sieve* (*plokanon*, a braided work or rope, 52e), to the *khōra* as *sieve* (**sieve, sift**, I also love these English words). There is in the *Timaeus* a figural allusion that I do not know how to interpret and which nevertheless seems to me decisive. It refers to the movement, the shaking (*seiesthai, seien, seiomena*), the seism in the course of which a selection of forces or seeds *takes place*, a sorting, a filtering in the very place where, nevertheless, the place remains impassable, indeterminate, amorphous, and so on. This passage in the *Timaeus* is as erratic (it seems to me), as difficult to integrate, as deprived of origin and of manifest *telos* as the piece we imagined for our *Choral Work*.

Thus I propose the following "representation," "materialization," "formation" (more or less): in one or three examples (if there are three, then **with different scalings**), a gilded metal object (there is gold in the passage of the *Ti-*

maeus on the *khôra* and in your Venetian project) would be planted obliquely in the ground. Neither vertical, nor horizontal, a very solid frame that would resemble at once a web, a sieve, or a grill (**grid**) and a musical instrument with *strings* (piano, harp, lyre? **strings, stringed instrument, vocal chord,** etc.).

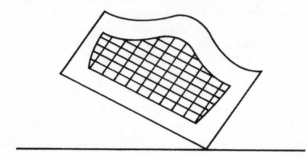

As grill, **grid**, and so on, it would have a certain relation with the filter (telescope or photographic developer, a machine fallen from the sky after having photographed, radiographed, filtered in an aerial view). An interpretive and *selective* filter that will have allowed one to read and to sift the three sites or the three layers (Eisenman-Derrida, Tschumi, La Villette). As a stringed instrument, it would gesture toward the concert and the multiple chorale, the *khôra* of *Choral Work.*

I do not think that anything should be inscribed on this sculpture (for it is a sculpture), unless, perhaps, the title and a signature were to figure on it somewhere (*Choral Work,* by . . . 1986), or one or two Greek words (*plokanon, seiomena,* etc.). To be discussed, among other things . . . (May 30, 1986).[3]

You will have noted in passing: the allusion to the filtering of a selective interpretation in my letter appealed to Nietzsche and to a certain scene played out between Nietzsche and the pre-Socratics, the very ones who seem to haunt this or that passage in the *Timaeus,* Democritus, for example.

So what does Eisenman do? He interprets, in turn, actively and selectively. He translates, transposes, transforms, and appropriates my letter, rewriting it in his language, in his *languages,* architectural and a few others. He gives another form to the architectural structure that is in process of being elaborated—but already very stabilized—another form, that of a lyre reclining on an oblique plane. Then, change of scale, he reinscribes it *inside* itself, a small lyre within a larger one. To destabilize the ruses of totalizing reason, he is not satisfied with a metonymy *en abyme,* at the bottom of the ocean where coral is deposited in sediments. Among all the stringed instruments evoked in my letter (piano, harp, lyre), he chooses one, whose play he reinvents in his own language, English. And in inventing another architectural device, he transcribes his linguistic reinvention, his own.

What happens exactly? First of all, he adds another justification and another dimension to the open title *Choral Work*, which is thereby enriched and overdetermined. Then, on all the semantic or even formal strings of the *word* "lyre"—a word that turns out to be homographic in French and English—we hear the resonance of different texts. These are added, superposed, superimposed *in* one another, *on* or *under* one another, according to an apparently impossible topology, nonrepresentable, through a partition [*paroi*]. An invisible partition, certainly, but one that is audible in the internal repercussion of several sound layers. These sound layers are also layers of meaning but, as you immediately notice, this is said in a quasi-homophonic way in the English word "layer" that both takes its place in the series of layers [*couches*] I have been discussing and also designates that series.

The strata of this palimpsest, its layers are thus bottomless, since, for the reasons I have just mentioned, they do not allow themselves to be totalized.

And yet this structure of the untotalizable palimpsest that draws on one of its elements as the resource for the others (their *carrière* or **quarry**), and that makes an irrepresentable and unobjectivizable labyrinth out of this play of internal differences (scale without end, **scaling** without hierarchy), is precisely the structure of *Choral Work*, its structure of stone and metal, the superposing of layers (La Villette, the Eisenman-Derrida project, Tschumi's *Folies*, etc.) sinking into the abyss of the "platonic" *khōra*. "Lyre," "Layer" is a good title, supertitle, or subtitle for *Choral Work*. And this title is inscribed *in* the work, as a piece of the very thing it names. It speaks the truth about the work in the body of the work; it speaks the truth in a word that is many, a kind of many-leaved book, but also the visible figure of a lyre, the visibility of an instrument that foments the invisible: music. And all that *lyrical*, in a word, gives us to hear.

But for these same reasons, the truth of *Choral Work*, the one that *lyre* or **layer** says, and does, and gives, is not a truth: it is not presentable, representable, totalizable; it never shows itself. It gives rise to no revelation of presence, still less to an adequation. It is an irreducible inadequation that we have just evoked. And a challenge to the subjectile: all these layers of meaning and form, of visibility and invisibility lie *in* one another, *on* or *under* one another, *before* or *behind* one another; but the truth of this relation is never established, never stabilized in any judgment. It always causes to be said, allegorically, something other than what is said. *In a word*, it makes one lie [*fait mentir*]. The truth of the work lies in this lying power,[4] this liar that accompanies all our representations (as Kant said of the "I think"), but that also accompanies them as a lyre can accompany a chorus.

Without equivalent and therefore without contrary. In this abyssal palimpsest, no truth can establish itself on any principial or final presence of meaning. In the labyrinth of this coral, truth is nontruth, the errance of one of those **errors** that belongs to the title of another labyrinth, another palimpsest, another **quarry**. I have been speaking of this other for some time now without naming it. I have been speaking of *Romeo and Juliet*—a story all about names and countertimes about which I have also written elsewhere[5]—of Eisenman's Romeo and Juliet, *Moving Arrows, Eros and Other Errors*. Have I not been lying? Have I not been speaking all this while, allegorically, about something other than what you thought? Yes and no. The lie has no contrary; it is absolute and null. It does not lead into error but into **moving errors** whose errance is both finite and infinite, aleatory and programmed. The **liar** remains thus unfindable in this lie without contrary. What remains "is" the unfindable, something altogether other than a conscious signatory assured of his mastery, something altogether other than a subject; what remains, rather, is an infinite series of subjectiles and countersignatories, you among them, ready to take, to pay for, or miss the pleasure given by the passage of Eros. **Liar** or lyre, this is the royal name, for the moment, one of the best names, namely, the homonym and the pseudonym, the multiple voice of this secret signatory, the cryptic title of *Choral Work*. But if I say that we owe this to language more than to Peter Eisenman, you will ask me: which language? There are so many. Do you mean the *encounter* of languages? An architecture that is at least tri- or quadrilingual, polygot stones or metal?

—But if I tell you that we owe this chance to Peter Eisenman, whose own name, as you know, carries within it stone and metal, would you believe me? And yet I am telling you the truth. It is the truth of this man of iron determined to break with the anthropomorphic scale, with "man the measure of all things": he writes such good books! I swear it to you!

—This is what all liars say; they would not be lying if they did not say that they were telling the truth.

—I see you do not believe me; let us consider things otherwise. What do I hope to have shown, on the subject of *Choral Work*, while, on the other hand, proposing an autobiographical description of my encounter with Peter Eisenman, in all of the languages at work in it? That all of this in truth referred to two other works, FIN D'OU T HOU S and *Moving Arrows, Eros and Other Errors*. What Jeffrey Kipnis rightly analyzes as "the endless play of readings"[6] applies to these three works. Each of the three is at the same time larger and smaller than the series, which no doubt also includes the Venice project and several other projects. I had to find an economic way of speaking of all three in one, and in the few pages that were allotted me. Similarly, at La Villette, we have little space, a single space with which we have to make do. We have already multiplied or divided it by three on the inside, and we hope to multiply it by three again in the future. For the moment we must find a structure that proliferates within a given economy, "faisant flèche de tout bois [making an arrow out of any wood]" as we say in French, using all available means. When meaning moves like an arrow, without ever letting itself be stopped or gathered, the errors to which it leads and which are no longer lies, can no longer be opposed to the true. Between **errors**, **eros**, and **arrows**, the transformation is endless, the contamination both inevitable and aleatory. None of the three presides at the encounter. They cross each other like arrows, making of **misreading**, or **misspelling**, a generative force that says pleasure, while procuring it. If I had the time and the space, I would analyze the strategies Peter Eisenman uses, what he has to do in his books, that is to say also in his constructions, to fly like an arrow while avoiding getting trapped in the oppositions with which he nevertheless must negotiate. The absence he speaks of in *Moving Arrows* is not opposed, especially not dialectically, to presence. Linked to the discontinuous structure of **scaling**, it is not the void. Determined by recursivity and by the internal-external difference of **self-similarity**, this absence "produces," it "is" (without being, being an origin or a productive cause) a *text*, better and something other than a "good book," more than a book, more than one book; a text like "an unending *transformation* of properties": "Rather than an aesthetic object, the object becomes a text . . . " What undoes [*déjoue*] the opposition presence/absence, and thus an entire ontology, must however advance in the language it transforms in this way, in which what this language literally contains *without* containing is found imprinted. Eisenman's architecture marks this *without*, which I prefer to write in English,

with/without, within and out, and so forth. We relate to this **without** of language by mastering it in order to play with it, and at the same time to submit to its law, which is the law *of* language, of languages, in truth of any mark. We are in this regard at the same time active and passive. And one could say something *analogous* about this active/passive opposition in Eisenman's texts; one could say something analogous about what he says about analogy. But one must know how to stop an arrow. He also knows how to do this.

One might be tempted to speak here of an architectural *Witz*, of a new textual economy (and *oikos* is the house; Eisenman also builds houses), an economy in which one no longer has to exclude the invisible from the visible, to oppose the temporal to the spatial, discourse and architecture. Not that we confuse them, but we distribute them according to another hierarchy, a hierarchy without archy, a memory without origin, a hierarchy without hierarchy.

What there is there (*il y a, es gibt*): a beyond the *Witz*, like a beyond the pleasure principle, at least if one hears behind these two words, *Witz* and *pleasure*, the intractable law of savings and economy.

The question of the book, once again, to conclude: it is sometimes implied, a little rashly, that architects who are "theoreticians," the most innovative among them, write books instead of building buildings. Those who hold to this dogma, let it just be said, generally do neither. Eisenman writes, in fact. But in order to break the norms and the authority of the existing economy, he needed, through what still resembles a book, *effectively* to clear a new space in which this aneconomy would be both possible and, up to a certain point, legitimized, negotiated. Negotiation takes place in time, and more time is always needed, with the powers and culture of the moment. For it is beyond economy, beyond the book, whose form still falls within this totalizing mania of discourse, that he writes something else.

This is a *topos*: the monument has often been compared to the book.[7] Eisenman's catalogues are, no doubt, no longer books. Nor are they so "good and beautiful." They exceed the measure of calligraphy or *callistics*, this ancient name for aesthetics. I will not say that they are sublime for all that. In its very measurelessness [*démesure*], the sublime is still a human measure.

Ecce Homo: end, the end of everything.

—*Translated by Sarah Whiting*

§ 7 Fifty-two Aphorisms for a Foreword

1. The aphorism decides, but as much by its substance as by its form, it determines by a play of words. Even if it speaks of architecture, it does not belong to it. That goes without saying, and the aphorism, which is part of discourse, often gives to the trivially obvious the authority of a sentence.

2. One expects the aphorism to utter the true. It prophesizes, at times vaticinates, proffers what is or what will be, arrests it in advance in a form that is monumental, to be sure, but also anarchitectural: dissociated and a-systemic.

3. If there is a truth of architecture, it appears doubly allergic to the aphorism: it is produced as such, for the most part, outside of discourse. It concerns an articulated organization, but a mute articulation.

4. To speak here of aphorisms and by means of aphorism is to place oneself in the analogy between rhetoric and architecture. One thereby assumes the problem has been resolved, one of the problems in the face of which all the texts assembled here risk themselves, each in its own way. The ana*logy* between *logos* (logic) and architecture is not just one anal-

This text originally appeared as a preface to *Mesure pour Mesure. Architecture et philosophie*, a special issue of the *Cahiers du CCI* (Georges Pompidou Center) in 1987 ("a first report of the work done between 1984 and 1986 at the initiative of the Collège International de Philosophie and the Centre de Création Industrielle").

ogy among others. Nor is it reducible to a single figure of rhetoric. The *problem* of analogy thus defines the space of this book, the opening given to its *project*.

5. A *problem*, the subject of a discussion or the theme of a research project, always outlines, it lays out the lines of a construction. It is often a protective architecture. *Problema*: that which one anticipates or *proposes* to oneself, the *object* one places before oneself, the armor, the shield, the obstacle, the garment, the rampart, the ledge, the promontory, the barrier. One always stands both *before* and *behind* the problem.

6. What is a *project* in general? And what is the "project" in architecture? How is one to interpret its genealogy, its authority, its politics—in short, its philosophy at work? If the texts collected in this volume often intersect around these questions, one might ask oneself what this particular "project" here may signify, what is exposed or gathered in a preface, the foreword or the fore-project [*l'avant-projet*] of a book on architecture and philosophy.

7. A text that presents itself as the simulacrum of a foreword, a discontinuous series, an archipelago of aphorisms: an intolerable composition in this place, a rhetorical and architectural monster. Demonstrate it. Then read this book. You will perhaps begin to have your doubts.

8. This is a word, a sentence, therefore this is not architecture. But prove it, present your axioms and your definitions and your postulates.

9. Here is architecture: a project that is unreadable and to come [*à venir*], a school still unknown, a style to be defined, an uninhabitable space, an invention of new paradigms.

10. *Paradeigma* means "architectural plan," for example. But *paradeigma* is also the example. It remains to be seen what happens when one speaks of an architectural paradigm for other spaces, other techniques, arts, writings. The paradigm as paradigm for any paradigm. Concerning the play on words in architecture—and whether the *Witz* is possible there.

11. Architecture does not tolerate the aphorism, it seems, ever since architecture has existed as such in the West. Perhaps the conclusion to be drawn from this is that, strictly speaking, an aphorism does not exist: it

does not appear, it does not give itself to be seen in space, neither traversed nor inhabited. It is not, even if there are aphorisms [*s'il y en a*]. How would it let itself be read? One never enters or leaves it; it has therefore neither beginning nor end, neither foundation nor end, neither up nor down, neither inside nor outside. These assertions only make sense on the condition of an analogy between discourse and all the so-called arts of space.

12. This is an aphorism, he says. And people will be content simply to quote it/him.

13. Concerning quotation: even if it is caught up there in a singular fashion, even if it does not imitate in the way a painting or a sculpture comes to represent a model, the architecture of "tradition" belongs to the space of *mimesis*. It is traditional; indeed it constitutes the tradition in this way. Despite appearances, the "presence" of an edifice does not refer only to itself; it repeats, signifies, evokes, convokes, reproduces, and also quotes. It *carries toward* the other and *refers* itself, it divides itself in its very *reference*. On quotation marks in architecture.

14. There has never been an architecture without "preface." The quotation marks signal here the risk of analogy. An architectural "preface" includes, among other preliminaries, the project or its analogues, the methodology that defines the paths and procedures, the principial or fundamental axiomatic preambles, the exposition of ends, and then the models for the execution of the work, and finally, in the work itself, all the modes of access, the threshold, the door, the space of the vestibule. But the preface (without quotation marks this time, the preface of a book) must announce the "architecture" of a work, and it is very difficult to say whether, yes or no, the preface belongs to it.

15. It is expected of a preface that it describe and justify the book's composition: why and how it was constructed in this way. No preface to a deconstruction, unless it is a preface in reverse [*à l'envers*].

16. Every preface is in reverse. It presents itself the right way round, as is required, but in its construction, it proceeds in reverse; it is developed (processed), as one says of photography and its negatives, from its end or supposed purpose: a certain conception of the architectural "project."

17. The analogy has always proceeded in both directions, this book demonstrates it: one speaks of the architecture of a book, but constructions in stone have often been compared to volumes to be deciphered.

18. The preface is not one institutional phenomenon among others. It presents itself as an institution through and through, the institution par excellence.

19. To ask for a preface is to put faith in a conjoined idea of the signature and of architecture: the law of the threshold, the law on the threshold or rather the law as the threshold itself, and the door (an immense tradition, the door "before the law," the door in the place of the law, the door making the law that it is), the right of entry, the presentations, the titles, the legitimation that, from the opening of the edifice, gives names, announces, anticipates, introduces, brings out a perspective on the whole, situates the foundations, recalls the order, calls one back to the order of the beginning and the end, from the commandment to the ends, from the *archē* in view of the *telos*.

20. A preface gathers, links, articulates, anticipates the passages, denies the aphoristic discontinuities. There is a genre forbidden to the preface— it is the aphorism.

21. This is not an aphorism.

22. The Collège International de Philosophie owed it to itself to make space for and give rise to [*donner lieu*] an *encounter*, a thinking *encounter*, between philosophy and architecture. Not so as to put them face to face, but rather in order to think what has always maintained them together in the most essential of cohabitations. They imply one another according to necessities that are derived not only from metaphor or rhetoric in general (architectonic, system, foundation, project, etc).

23. The Collège International de Philosophie is the true preface, the truth of the preface to this encounter and to this book. Its preface is in the right direction [*à l'endroit*] since in a certain way, this Collège does not yet exist; it has been searching for itself for at least the past four years; it is searching for the form of its community, its political model, which perhaps will no longer be political, and thus its architectural design, which

perhaps will no longer be an architecture. But to do this, to make space for and give rise to this encounter and to this book, it is supported by the forces of a solid, legitimate, open, friendly, institution: the Centre de Création Industrielle (CCI). This fact is a *problem*, that is, the most generous of "protections" (see aphorism 5): center, creation, industry.

24. An authentic aphorism must never refer to another. It is sufficient unto itself, a world or monad. But whether one wants it or not, whether one sees it or not, aphorisms interlink here *as* aphorisms, and in number, numbered. Their series obeys an *irreversible* order. Hence, it is without being architectural. Reader, visitor, get to work!

25. An aphorism never enjoins. It does not exclaim; it neither orders nor promises. On the contrary, it proposes, stops and says what is, period that's all [*un point c'est tout*]. A point that is not an exclamation mark.

26. The Collège International de Philosophie gave itself the task of thinking the institutionality of the institution, and first of all its own, in particular what connects architecture, the signature, and the preface (the question of names, titles, project, legitimation, right of access, hierarchies, etc.). But the strange thing is that if it has been able to *make space for and give rise to* such encounters and a book like this, it is perhaps to the extent to which it has as yet no space or architectural form of its own. That is due no doubt to the inherited limits of the old politico-institutional space, to its most tenacious and least avoidable constraints.

27. From its Fore-project [*Avant-projet*] the Collège International de Philosophie owed it to itself to think its own architecture, or at least its relation to architecture. It had to be prepared to invent, and not only for itself, a configuration of spaces that would not reproduce the philosophical topology [*topique*] that it is precisely a matter of interrogating or deconstructing. This topology reflects models or is reflected in them: socio-academic structures, politico-pedagogical hierarchies, forms of community that preside over the organization of spaces, or in any case never let themselves be separated from them.

28. To deconstruct the *artifact* called "architecture" is perhaps to begin to think it as *artifact*, to rethink artifacture on its basis, and thus technics [*la technique*] at the very point at which it remains uninhabitable.

29. To say that architecture must be subtracted from the ends that are assigned to it, and first of all from the value of habitation, is not to prescribe uninhabitable constructions, but to take an interest in the genealogy of an ageless contract between architecture and habitation. Is it possible to undertake a work without fitting it out to be habitable? Everything here passes by way of "questions to Heidegger" concerning what he thought he could say about this, which we translate in Latin by "inhabit."

30. The architecture of an institution—for example, of a philosophical institution—is neither its essence nor its attribute, neither its property nor its accident, neither its substance nor its phenomenon, neither its inside nor its outside. What follows from this, which is not nothing, is perhaps no longer a matter of the order of consequence in philosophy: architecture would not be.

31. In constructing—de-constructing—itself in this way, the Collège International de Philosophie owed it to itself, even before its fore-project, to open philosophy to other "disciplines" (or rather to other questions on the possibility of "discipline," on the space of teaching), to other theoretical and practical experiences. Not only in the name of a sacrosanct interdisciplinarity that presupposes attested competences and already legitimate objects, but in view of new "-jects [*jets*]" (projects, objects, subjects), of new and still unqualified gestures. What is "throwing [*jeter*]" for thought? And for architecture? What does "laying the foundations [*jeter les fondements*]" mean? What are "launching [*lancer*]," "sending [*envoyer*]," "soaring [*s'élancer*]," "erecting," "instituting"?

32. The deconstruction of the "project" in all its states and disarray [*dans tous ses états*]. Architecture *is without being* in the project—whether or not in the technical sense of this term.

33. A question analogous to that of the *subjectile* (for example, in painting, in the graphic or sculptural arts) must be posed to the architect. The question of the support or the substance, of the *subject*, of what is *thrown* [jeté] *under.* But also of what is thrown in front of or in advance of in the *project* (projection, program, prescription, promise, proposition), of everything that belongs, in the architectural process, to the movement of launching or of being-launched, of throwing or being-thrown (*jacere, ja-*

cio/jaceo). Horizontally or vertically: the foundation for the erection of an edifice that always soars toward the sky, where, in an apparent suspension of *mimesis*, there was nothing. A thesis poses something in the place of nothing or of the lack. It is the project as prosthesis. Another value of the *pro*: not in front of or in advance, neither the problem nor the protection, but what comes in the place of –. On architectural supplementarity.

34. The Collège International de Philosophie—and this was said even before the fore-project—owed it to itself to make room for and give rise to research called for convenience's sake *performative*. By this let us understand those moments where knowledge makes a work [*fait œuvre*], when the theoretical statement can no longer be dissociated from the event called "creation," "composition," "construction." It is not enough here to say that architecture is one of its best paradigms. The very word and concept of paradigm have an exemplarily architectural value.

35. The Collège International de Philosophie announced, in its fore-project, that it would not neglect anything that was at stake in what is called teaching, and this without limiting itself to the philosophical discipline. Every didactics includes a philosophy, a relation to philosophy, even if it is denied. What, in this country, is the philosophy practiced or ignored by the pedagogy of architecture, by the teaching of its history, by its techniques, its theory, its relations to the other "arts," other texts, other institutions, other politico-economic authorities? In this country and in others? France's situation is, in this regard, very singular, and this book, by attaching itself to certain philosophical premises, could contribute to a sort of general displacement of boundaries and to another experience of internationality. This is no doubt an urgent undertaking for architecture, and in any case an essential project for an international college.

36. Given what is taught of the architectural "project" in this book, one hesitates to speak of a "project" of the Collège International de Philosophie. To say that it does not have a project is not however to denounce its empiricism or its adventurism. In the same way, an architecture without project undertakes perhaps a more thoughtful work, more inventive, more propitious than ever for the coming of the event.

37. To say of architecture that it is not is perhaps to imply that it hap-

pens. It gives rise to itself with no return [*se donne lieu sans en revenir*]; this is the event.

38. There is no deconstructive project, no project for deconstruction.

39. The project: it is and is not the essence of architecture. It will perhaps have been the history of architecture, its order in any case.

40. Leave the aphorism at the threshold. There is no inhabitable place for the aphorism. The disjunctive force can only be put to architectural work at the instant when, by some secret or denied synergy, it lets itself be integrated into the order of a narrative, whatever its dimension, into an uninterrupted history, between the beginning and the end, the founding bedrock and the highest point, the cellar and the roof, the ground and the tip of the pyramid . . .

41. No housing [*habitat*] for the aphorism, but one does not inhabit an aphorism either, neither man nor god. The aphorism is neither a house, nor a temple, nor a school, nor a parliament, nor an *agora*, nor a tomb. Neither a pyramid nor above all a *stadium*. What else?

42. Whether we like it or not, the aphorism is irremediably edifying.

43. Nothing more architectural than a pure aphorism, says the other. Architecture in the most philosophical form of its concept: not a pure interruption, not a dissociated fragment, but a totality that claims self-sufficiency, the figure of the system (the architectonic is the art of systems, says Kant) in its most authoritative, peremptory, dogmatic eloquence, self-legitimating to the point of complacency, when it does everything to save itself [*faire économie*] a demonstration.

44. The aphorism summarizes, gathers everything in itself, like absolute knowledge. It no longer asks any questions. No question mark [*Point d'interrogation*]: impossible to punctuate thus a discourse that is or that produces its own method, includes within itself its preambles and vestibules. If architecture is dominated by the *logos*, then the character at once prescriptive and whole of the aphorism sees this logocentric philosophy of architecture triumph. The aphorism commands, it begins and ends: architectonic, archi-eschatology, and archi-teleology. It gathers in itself, organizes the fore-project, the project, the general contracting of the work

[*la maîtrise d'œuvre*], and the implementation of the work [*la mise en œu-vre*]. It denies the resistance of materials (here all the words ending in *r: la terre* [earth], *la matière* [matter], *la pierre* [stone], *le verre* [glass], *le fer* [iron], without which, so it is thought, there is no architecture that holds up, only *analogical* discourses on architecture). To verify this, we should not be content with what Hegel says about architecture itself, but also take into account that it is nothing, itself, once it is withdrawn from the teleology of absolute knowledge. In the same way, aphorisms can only multiply or be put in a series if they either confirm or contradict one another.

45. There is always more than one aphorism.

46. Despite their fragmentary appearance, they signal toward the memory of a totality, at the same time ruin and monument.

47. In their contradictory multiplicity, they can always become dialectical moments once again, absolute knowledge held in reserve in a thesis or antithesis. Preface to a short treatise on negativity in architecture. How an architectural interruption again takes on a meaning, a function, a finality (the work of the negative) in a new edification.

48. Contrary to appearances, "deconstruction" is not an architectural metaphor. The word would, it will have to name a thinking of architecture, a thinking at work. First of all, it is not a metaphor. There is no longer any reliance on the concept of metaphor here. Next, a deconstruction, as its name indicates, should first deconstruct the construction itself, the structural or constructivist motif, its schemas, its intuitions and concepts, its rhetoric. But also deconstruct the strictly architectural construction, the philosophical construction of the concept of architecture whose model governs the idea of the system in philosophy as well as the theory, practice, and teaching of architecture.

49. One is not deconstructing superstructures in order to reach the bottom, the original ground, the ultimate foundation of an architecture or a thinking of architecture. There is no return to a purity or to a proper propriety, to the essence of architecture *itself.* One challenges the schema of the fundamental and the oppositions it leads to: "depth/surface," "substance/quality," "essence/accident," "inside/outside," and especially "ba-

sic research / applied research," this last opposition being of great consequence here.

50. The commitment, the wager: taking account of the architectural or
anarchitectural necessity without destroying, without drawing only negative consequences from it. The without-ground of a "deconstructive" and
affirmative architecture can cause vertigo, but it is not the void, it is not
the gaping and chaotic remainder, the hiatus of destruction. Inversely, it
is no longer the Heideggerian *Destruktion*, even if that project must be
presupposed. Still less is it the improbable *désobstruction*, as it has been
recently dubbed in our language.

51. Neither Babel, nor Nimrod, nor the Flood. Between *khōra* and *archē*
perhaps, if there could be an architecture that was, in this *between*, neither
Greek nor Judaic. A still innumerable filiation, another series of aphorisms.

52. To maintain, despite the temptations, despite all the possible reappropriations, the chance of the aphorism, is to keep—in the interruption,
without interruption—the promise of making room for and giving rise
to, if it is necessary. But it is never given.

—*Translated by Andrew Benjamin*

§ 8   Aphorism Countertime

1. Aphorism is the name.

2. As its name indicates, aphorism separates, it marks dissociation (*apo*), it terminates, delimits, arrests (*orizō*). It brings to an end by separating, it separates in order to end [*finir*]—and to define [*définir*].

3. An aphorism is a name, but every name can take on the figure of aphorism.

4. An aphorism is exposure to contretemps.[1] It exposes discourse—hands it over to contretemps. Literally—because it is abandoning a word [*une parole*] to its letter.
(Already this could be read as a series of aphorisms, the alea of an initial anachrony. In the beginning there was contretemps. In the beginning there is speed. Word and deed are *overtaken*. Aphorism outstrips.)

5. To abandon speech [*la parole*], to entrust the secret to letters, this is the stratagem of the third party, the mediator, the Friar, the matchmaker who, without any other desire but the desire of others, organizes the contretemps. He counts on the letters without taking account of them:

In the meantime, against thou shalt awake,

First version published in *Roméo et Juliette* (Paris: Papiers, 1986) on the occasion of a production of *Romeo and Juliet* by Daniel Mesguich at the Théâtre Gérard-Philipe de Saint-Denis.

Shall Romeo by my letters know our drift,
And hither shall he come. (IV, i, 113–15)[2]

6. Despite appearances, an aphorism never arrives by itself, it doesn't come all alone. It is part of a serial logic. As in Shakespeare's play, in the trompe-l'oeil depth of its paradigms, all the *Romeo and Juliet*s that came before it, there will be several series of aphorisms here.

7. Romeo and Juliet, the heroes of contretemps in our mythology, the positive heroes. They missed each other, how they missed each other! Did they miss each other? But they also survived [*ont survécu*], *both of them*, survived *each other*, in their name, through a studied effect of contretemps: an unfortunate crossing, by chance, of temporal and aphoristic series.

8. Aphoristically, one must say that Romeo and Juliet will have lived, and lived on [*auront survécu*], through aphorism. *Romeo and Juliet* owes everything to aphorism. Aphorism can, of course, turn out to be a device of rhetoric, a sly calculation aiming at the greatest authority, an economy or strategy of mastery that knows very well how to potentialize meaning ("See how I formalize, in so few words I always say more than would appear.") But before letting itself be manipulated in this way, aphorism hands us over, defenseless, to the very experience of contretemps. Before every calculation but also across it, beyond the calculable itself.

9. The aphorism or discourse of dissociation: each sentence, each paragraph dedicates itself to separation, it shuts itself up, whether one likes it or not, in the solitude of its proper duration. Its encounter and its contact with the other are always given over to chance, to whatever may befall, good or ill. Nothing there is absolutely assured, neither the linking nor the order. One aphorism in the series can come before or after the other, before *and* after the other, each can survive the other—and in the other series. Romeo and Juliet *are* aphorisms, in the first place in their names, which they are not (Juliet: "'Tis but thy name that is my enemy." . . . Romeo: "My name, dear saint, is hateful to myself, / Because it is an enemy to thee. / Had I it written, I would tear the word" [II, ii, 38, 55–57]), for there is no aphorism without language, without nomination, without appellation, without a letter, even to be torn up.

10. Each aphorism, like Romeo and Juliet, each aphoristic series has its particular duration. Its temporal logic prevents it from sharing all its time with another place of discourse, with another discourse, with the discourse of the other. Impossible synchronization. I am speaking here of the discourse of time, of its marks, of its dates, of the course of time and of the essential digression that dislocates the time of desires and carries [*déporte*] the step of those who love one another off course. But that is not sufficient to characterize our aphorism, it is not sufficient that there be language or mark, nor that there be dissociation, dislocation, anachrony, in order for aphorism to take place. It still must have a determined form, a certain mode. Which? The bad aphorism, the *bad* of aphorism is sententious, but every aphorism cuts and delimits by virtue of its sententious character [*son caractère de sentence*]: it says the truth in the form of the last judgment, and this truth carries [*porte*] death. The death sentence [*l'arrêt de mort*], for Romeo and Juliet, is a contretemps that condemns them to death, both of them, but also a contretemps that arrests death, suspends its coming, secures for both of them the delay necessary in order to witness and survive the other's death.

11. Aphorism: that which hands over every rendezvous to chance. But desire does not lay itself open to aphorism by chance. There is no time for desire without aphorism. Desire has no place without aphorism. What Romeo and Juliet experience is the exemplary anachrony, the essential impossibility of any absolute synchronization. But *at the same time*, they live—as do we—this disorder of the series. Disjunction, dislocation, separation of places, deployment, or spacing of a story because of aphorism— would there be any theater without that? The survival of a theatrical work implies that, theatrically, it is saying something about theater itself, about its essential possibility. And that it does so, theatrically, then, through the play of uniqueness and repetition, by giving rise every time to the chance of an absolutely singular event as it does to the untranslatable idiom of a proper name, to its fatal necessity (the "enemy" that "I hate"), to the fatal necessity of a date and of a rendezvous. Dates, timetables, property registers, place names, all the codes that we cast like nets over time and space—in order to reduce or master differences, to arrest them, determine them—these are also contretemps traps. Intended to avoid contretemps, to be in harmony with our rhythms by bending them to objective measurement, they produce misunderstanding, they accumulate the op-

portunities for false steps or wrong moves, revealing and simultaneously increasing this anachrony of desires: *in the same time.* What is this time? There is no place for a question in aphorism.

12. Romeo *and* Juliet, the conjunction of two desires that are aphoristic but held together, maintained in the dislocated now of a love or a promise. A promise in their name, but across and beyond their given name, the promise of *another name,* its request rather: "O be some other name . . . " (II, ii, 42). The *and* of this conjunction, the theater of this "and," has often been presented, represented as the scene of fortuitous contretemps, of aleatory anachrony: the failed rendezvous, the unfortunate accident, the letter that does not arrive at its destination, the time of the detour prolonged for a purloined letter, the remedy that transforms itself into poison when the stratagem of a third party, a brother, Friar Laurence, proposes simultaneously the remedy and the letter ("And if thou dar'st, I'll give thee remedy. . . . In the meantime, against thou shalt awake, / Shall Romeo by my letters know our drift, / And hither shall he come . . . " [IV, i, 76, 113–15]). This representation is not false. But if this drama has thus been imprinted, superimprinted on the memory of Europe, text upon text, this is because the anachronous accident comes to illustrate an essential possibility. It confounds a philosophical logic that would like accidents to remain what they are, accidental. This logic, at the same time, rejects as unthinkable an anachrony of structure, the absolute interruption of history as deployment of *a* temporality, of a single and organized temporality. What happens to Romeo and Juliet, and remains in fact an accident whose aleatory and unforeseeable appearance cannot be effaced, at the crossing of several series and beyond common sense, can only be what it is, accidental, insofar as it has *already* happened, in essence, before it happens. The desire of Romeo and Juliet did not encounter the poison, the contretemps, or the detour of the letter by chance. In order for this encounter to take place, there must *already* have been instituted a system of marks (names, hours, maps of places, dates, and supposedly "objective" place names) to thwart, as it were, the dispersion of interior and heterogeneous durations, to frame, organize, put in order, render possible a rendezvous: in other words to deny, while taking note of it, noncoincidence, the separation of monads, infinite distance, the disconnection of experiences, the multiplicity of worlds, everything that renders possible a contretemps or the irremediable detour of a letter.

But the desire of Romeo and Juliet is born in the heart of this possibility. There would have been no love, the pledge would not have taken place, nor time, nor its theater, without discordance. The accidental contretemps comes to *remark* the essential contretemps. Which is as much as to say it is not accidental. It does not, for all that, have the signification of an essence or of a formal structure. It is not the abstract condition of possibility, a universal form of the relation to the other in general, a dialectic of desire or consciousnesses. Rather the singularity of an imminence whose "cutting point" spurs desire at its birth—the very birth of desire. I love because the other is the other, because his or her time will never be mine. The living duration, the very presence of the other's love remains infinitely distant from mine, distant from itself in what stretches it toward mine and even in what one might want to describe as amorous euphoria, ecstatic communion, mystical intuition. I can love the other only in the passion of this aphorism. Which does not happen, does not come about like misfortune, bad luck, or negativity. It has the form of the most loving affirmation—it is the chance of desire. And it not only cuts into the fabric of durations, it spaces. Contretemps says something about topology or the visible; it opens theater.

13. Conversely, no contretemps, no aphorism without the promise of a now in common, without the pledge, the vow of synchrony, the desired sharing of a living present. In order that the sharing may be desired, must it not first be given, glimpsed, apprehended? But this sharing is just another name for aphorism.

14. This aphoristic series crosses over another one. Because it traces, aphorism *lives on* [survit], it lives much longer than its present and it lives longer than life. Death sentence [*arrêt de mort*]. It gives and carries death, but in order to make a decision thus on a sentence [*arrêt*] of death, it suspends death, it stops it once more [*il l'arrête encore*].

15. There would not be any contretemps, nor any anachrony, if the separation between monads disjoined only interiorities. Contretemps is produced at the intersection between interior experience (the "phenomenology of internal time-consciousness," or space-consciousness) and its chronological or topographical marks, those which are said to be "objective," "in the world." There would not be any series otherwise, without the possibility of this marked spacing, with its social conventions and the

history of its codes, with its fictions and its simulacra, with its dates. With so-called proper names.

16. The simulacrum raises the curtain, it reveals, thanks to the dissociation of series, the theater of the impossible: two people each outlive the other [*se survivent*]. The absolute certainty that rules over the *duel* (*Romeo and Juliet is* the *mise-en-scène* of all duels) is that one must die before the other. One of them must see the other die. To no matter whom, I must be able to say: since we are two, we know in an absolutely ineluctable way that one of us will die before the other. One of us will see the other die, one of us will live on, even if only for an instant. One of us, only one of us, will carry the death of the other—and the mourning. It is impossible that we should each survive the other. That's the duel, the axiomatic of every duel, the scene that is the most common and the least spoken of—or the most prohibited—concerning our relation to the other. Yet *the impossible happens*, not in "objective reality," which has no say here, but in the experience of Romeo and Juliet. And under the law of the pledge, which commands every given word. They live *in turn* the death of the other, for a time, the contretemps of their death. Both are in mourning—and both watch over the death of the other, upon the death of the other. Double death sentence. Romeo dies before Juliet, whom he has seen dead. They both live, outlive the death of the other.

17. The impossible—this theater of double survival—also tells, like every aphorism, the truth. Right from the pledge that binds together two desires, each is already in mourning for the other, entrusts death to the other as well: if you die before me, I will keep you, if I die before you, you will carry me in yourself, one will keep the other, will already have kept the other from the first declaration. This double interiorization would be possible neither in monadic interiority nor in the logic of "objective" time and space. It takes place nevertheless every time I love. Everything then begins with this survival. Each time that I love or each time that I hate, each time that a law *engages* me to the death of the other. And it is the same law, the same double law. A pledge that keeps (off) death can always invert itself.

18. A given series of aphorisms crosses over into another one, the same under different names, under the name of the name. Romeo and Juliet love each other across their name, despite their name, they die on account

of their name, they live on in their name. Since there is neither desire nor pledge nor sacred bond (*sacramentum*) without aphoristic separation, the greatest love springs from the greatest force of dissociation, here what opposes and divides the two families in their name. Romeo and Juliet bear these names. They bear them, support them even if they do not wish to assume them. From this name, which separates them but will at the same time have tightened their desire with all its aphoristic force, they would like to separate themselves. But the most vibrant declaration of their love still calls for the name that it denounces. One might be tempted to distinguish here, another aphorism, between the proper forename and the family name, which would only be a proper name in a general way or according to genealogical classification. One might be tempted to distinguish Romeo from Montague and Juliet from Capulet. Perhaps they are, both of them, tempted to do it. But they don't do it, and one should notice that in the denunciation of the name (act II, scene ii), they also attack their forenames, or at least that of Romeo, which seems to form part of the family name. The forename still bears the name of the father, it recalls the law of genealogy. Romeo *himself*, the bearer of the name is not the name, it is *Romeo*, the name that he bears. And is it necessary to call the bearer by the name that he bears? She calls him by it in order to tell him: I love you, free us from your name, Romeo, don't bear it any longer, Romeo, the name of Romeo:

JULIET:
O Romeo, Romeo, wherefore art thou Romeo?
Deny thy father and refuse thy name.
Or if thou wilt not, be but sworn my love
And I'll no longer be a Capulet. (II, ii, 33–36)

She is speaking, here, in the night, and there is nothing to assure her that she is addressing Romeo himself, present in person. In order to ask Romeo to refuse his name, she can only, in his absence, address his name or his shadow. Romeo—himself—is in the shadow and he wonders if it is time to take her at her word or if he should wait a little. Taking her at her word will mean committing himself to disowning his name, a little later on. For the moment, he decides to wait and to carry on listening:

ROMEO [*aside*]:
Shall I hear more, or shall I speak at this?

JULIET:
'Tis but thy name that is my enemy:
Thou art thyself, though not a Montague.
What's Montague? It is nor hand nor foot
Nor arm nor face nor any other part
Belonging to a man. O be some other name.
What's in a name? That which we call a rose
By any other word would smell as sweet;
So Romeo would, were he not Romeo call'd,
Retain that dear perfection which he owes
Without that title. Romeo, doff thy name,
And for thy name, which is no part of thee,
Take all myself.

ROMEO:
    I take thee at thy word.
Call me but love, and I'll be new baptis'd:
Henceforth I never will be Romeo.

JULIET:
What man art thou that thus bescreen'd in night
So stumblest on my counsel?

ROMEO:
        By a name
I know not how to tell thee who I am:
My name, dear saint, is hateful to myself
Because it is an enemy to thee.
Had I it written, I would tear the word.

JULIET:
My ears have yet not drunk a hundred words
Of thy tongue's uttering, yet I know the sound,
Art thou not Romeo, and a Montague?

ROMEO:
Neither, fair maid, if either thee dislike.
(II, ii, 37–61)

19. When she addresses Romeo in the night, when she asks him "O Romeo, Romeo, wherefore art thou Romeo? / Deny thy father and refuse thy name," she seems to be addressing *him, himself,* Romeo bearer of the name Romeo, the one who is not Romeo since he has been asked to disown his father and his name. She seems, then, to call him beyond his name. He is not present, she is not certain that he is there, *himself,*

beyond his name, it is night and this night screens the lack of distinction between the name and the bearer of the name. It is in his name that she continues to call him, and that she calls on him not to call himself Romeo any longer, and that she asks him, Romeo, to renounce his name. But it is, whatever she may say or deny, he whom she loves. Who, him? Romeo. The one who calls himself Romeo, the bearer of the name, who calls himself Romeo although he is not only the one who bears this name and although he exists, without being visible or present in the night, outside his name.

20. Night. Everything that happens at night, for Romeo and Juliet, is decided rather in the penumbra, between night and day. The indecision between Romeo and the bearer of this name, between "Romeo," the name of Romeo and Romeo himself. Theater, we say, is visibility, the stage [*la scène*]. This drama belongs to the night because it stages what is not seen, the name; it stages what one calls because one cannot see or because one is not certain of seeing what one calls. Theater of the name, theater of night. The name calls beyond presence, phenomenon, light, beyond the day, beyond the theater. It keeps—whence the mourning and survival—what is no longer present, the invisible: what from now on will no longer see the light of day.

21. She wants the death of Romeo. She will have it. The death of his name ("'Tis but thy name that is my enemy"), certainly the death of "Romeo," but they will not be able to get free from their name, they know this without knowing it. She declares war on "Romeo," on his name, in his name, she will win this war only on the death of Romeo himself. Himself? Who? Romeo. But "Romeo" is not Romeo. Precisely. She wants the death of "Romeo." Romeo dies, "Romeo" lives on. She keeps him dead in his name. Who? Juliet, Romeo.

22. Aphorism: separation in language and, in it, through the name that closes the horizon. Aphorism is at once necessary and impossible. Romeo is radically separated from his name. He, his living self, living and singular desire, he is not "Romeo," but the separation, the aphorism of the name remains impossible. He dies without his name but he dies also because he has not been able to set himself free from his name, or from his father, even less to renounce him, to respond to Juliet's request ("Deny thy father and refuse thy name").

23. When she says to him: my enemy is only your name, she does not think "my" enemy. Juliet, herself, has nothing against the name of Romeo. It is the name that she bears (Juliet and Capulet) that finds itself at war with the name of Romeo. The war takes place between the names. And when she says it, she is not sure, in the night, that she is making contact with Romeo himself. She speaks to him, she supposes him to be distinct from his name since she addresses him in order to say to him: "You are yourself, not a Montague." But he is not there. At least she cannot be sure of his presence. It is within herself, in her inner forum, that she is addressing him in the night, but still him in his name, and in the most exclamatory form of apostrophe: "O Romeo, Romeo, wherefore art thou Romeo?" She does not say to him: why are you called Romeo, why do you bear this name (like an article of clothing, an ornament, a detachable sign)? She says to him: Why *are you* Romeo? She knows it: detachable and dissociable, aphoristic though it be, his name is his essence. Inseparable from his being. And in asking him to abandon his name, she is no doubt asking him to live at last, and to live his love (for in order to live oneself truly, it is necessary to elude the law of the name, the familial law made for survival and constantly recalling me to death), but she is *just as much* asking him to die, since his life *is* his name. He exists in his name: "O Romeo, Romeo, wherefore art thou Romeo?" Romeo is Romeo, and Romeo is not Romeo. He is himself only in abandoning his name, he is himself only in his name. Romeo can (be) call(ed) himself only if he abandons his name, he calls himself only *from* [à partir de] his name. Sentence of death and of survival: twice rather than once.

24. Speaking to the one she loves within herself and outside herself, in the half-light, Juliet murmurs the most implacable analysis of the name. Of the name and the proper name. Implacable: she expresses the judgment, the death sentence [*l'arrêt de mort*], the fatal truth of the name. Pitilessly she analyzes, element by element. What's Montague? Nothing of yourself, you are yourself and not Montague, she tells him. Not only does this name say nothing about you as a totality but it doesn't say anything, it doesn't even name a part of you, neither your hand, nor your foot, neither your arm, nor your face, nothing that is human! This analysis is implacable, for it announces or denounces the inhumanity or the ahumanity of the name. A proper name does not name anything that is human, that belongs to a human body, a human spirit, an essence of man. And yet this

relation to the inhuman only befalls man, for him, to him, in the name of man. He alone gives himself this inhuman name. And Romeo would not be what he is, a stranger to his name, without this name. Juliet, then, pursues her analysis: the names of things do not belong to the things any more than the names of men belong to men, and yet they are quite differently separable. The example of the rose, once more. A rose remains what it is without its name; Romeo is no longer what he is without his name. But, for a while, Juliet makes out as if Romeo would lose nothing in losing his name: like the rose. But like a rose, she says to him in short, and without genealogy, "without why." (Supposing that the rose, all the roses of thought, of literature, of mysticism, this "formidable anthology," absent from every bouquet . . .)

25. She does not tell him to lose all names, rather just to change names: "O be some other name." But that can mean two things: take another proper name (a human name, this inhuman thing that belongs only to man); *or:* take another kind of name, a name that is not that of a man, take the name of a thing then, a common name that, like the name of the rose, does not have the inhumanity that consists in affecting the very being of the one who bears it even though it names nothing of himself. And, after the colon, there is the question:

> O be some other name:
> What's in a name? That which we call a rose
> By any other word would smell as sweet;
> So Romeo would, were he not Romeo call'd,
> Retain that dear perfection which he owes
> Without that title.[3]

26. The name is only a "title," and the title is not the thing that it names, any more than a title of nobility participates in the very thing, the family, the work, to which it is said to belong. *Romeo and Juliet* also remains the—surviving—title of an entire family of plays. We must apply what goes on in these plays also to the plays themselves, to their genealogy, their idiom, their singularity, their survival.

27. Juliet offers Romeo an infinite deal, what is apparently the most dissymmetrical of contracts: you can gain all without losing anything, it is just a matter of a name. In renouncing your name, you renounce noth-

ing, nothing of you, of yourself, nor anything human. In exchange, and without losing anything, you gain me, and not just a part of me, but the whole of myself: "Romeo, doff thy name, / And for thy name, which is no part of thee, / Take all myself." He will have gained everything, he will have lost everything: name and life, and Juliet.

28. The circle of all these names in *o*: *words, Romeo, rose, love.* He has accepted the deal, he *takes her at her word* ("I take thee at thy word") at the moment where she proposes that he *take* her in her entirety ("Take all myself"). Play of idiom: in taking you at your word, in taking up the challenge, in agreeing to this incredible, priceless exchange, I take the whole of you. And in exchange for nothing, for a word, my name, which is nothing, nothing human, nothing of myself, or else nothing for myself. I give nothing in taking you at your word, I abandon nothing and take absolutely all of you. In truth, and they both know the truth of the aphorism, he will lose everything. They will lose everything in this aporia, this double aporia of the proper name. And for having agreed to exchange the proper name of Romeo for a common name: not that of *rose*, but of *love*. For Romeo does not renounce all of his name, only the name of his father, that is to say his proper name, if one can still say that: "I take thee at thy word. / Call me but love, and I'll be new baptis'd: / Henceforth I never will be Romeo." He simultaneously gains himself and loses himself not only in the common name, but also in the common law of love: *Call me love.* Call me your love.

29. The dissymmetry remains infinite. It also hangs on this: Romeo does not make the same demand of her. He does not request that she who is secretly to be his wife renounce her name or disown her father. As if that were obvious and there was no call for any such rift [*déchirement*] (he will speak in a moment of tearing [*déchirer*] his name, the writing or the letter of his name, that is, if he had written it himself, which is just what is in principle and originarily excluded). Paradox, irony, reversal of the common law? Or a repetition that on the contrary confirms the truth of this law? Usually, in our cultures, the husband keeps his name, that of his father, and the wife renounces hers. When the husband gives his name to his wife, it is not, as here, in order to lose it, or to change it, but to impose it by keeping it. Here it is she who asks him to renounce his father and to change his name. But this inversion confirms the law: the name of the

father should be kept by the son, it is from him that there is some sense in tearing it away, and not at all from the daughter, into whose keeping it has never come. The terrible lucidity of Juliet. She knows the two bonds of the law, the *double bind* that ties a son to the name of his father. He can only live if he asserts himself in a singular fashion, without his inherited name. But the writing of this name, which he has not written himself ("Had I it written, I would tear the word"), constitutes him in his very being, without naming anything of him, and by denying it, he can only wipe himself out. In sum, at the very most he can deny it, renounce it, he can neither efface it nor tear it up. He is therefore lost in any case and she knows it. And she knows it because she loves him and she loves him because she knows it. And she demands his death from him by demanding that he hold onto his life because she loves him, because she knows, and because she knows that death will not come to him by accident. He is doomed [*voué*] to death, and she with him, by the double law of the name.

30. There would be no contretemps without the double law of the name. The contretemps presupposes this inhuman, too human, inadequation that always dislocates a proper name. The secret marriage, the pledge (*sacramentum*), the double survival that it involves, its constitutive anachrony, all of this obeys the same law. This law, the law of contretemps, is double since it is divided; it carries aphorism within itself, as its truth. Aphorism is the law.

31. Even if he wanted to, Romeo could not renounce his name and his father *of his own accord.* He cannot want to do so of his own accord, even though this emancipation is nevertheless being presented to him as the chance of at last being himself, of *inventing himself beyond the name*—the chance of at last living, for he bears the name as his death. He could not want it himself, in himself, because *he is not without* his name. He can only desire it from the call of the other, and *invent himself in the name of the other.* Moreover, he only hates his name starting from the moment Juliet, as it were, demands it from him:

My name, dear saint, is hateful to myself
Because it is an enemy to thee.
Had I it written, I would tear the word.

32. When she thinks she recognizes him in the shadow, by moonlight, the drama of the name is consummated (Juliet: "My ears have yet not drunk a hundred words / Of thy tongue's uttering, yet I know the sound. / Art thou not Romeo, and a Montague?" Romeo: "Neither, fair maid, if either thee dislike"). She recognizes him and calls him by his name (Are you not Romeo and a Montague?), she *identifies* him on the one hand by the timbre of his voice, that is to say by the words she hears without being able to see, and on the other hand at the moment when he has, obeying the injunction, renounced his name and his father. Survival and death are at work, in other words, the moon. But this power of death that appears by moonlight is called Juliet, and the sun that she comes to figure all of a sudden carries life *and* death *in the name of the father.* She kills the moon. What does Romeo say at the opening of the scene (which is not a scene since the name destines it to invisibility, but which is a theater since its light is artificial and figurative)? "But soft, what light through yonder window breaks? / It is the east, and Juliet is the sun! / Arise fair sun and kill the envious moon, / Who is already sick and pale with grief . . . " (II, ii, 2–5).

33. The lunar face of this shadow play, a certain coldness of *Romeo and Juliet.* Not all is of ice or glass, but the ice on it does not come only from death, from the marble to which everything seems doomed (*the tomb, the monument, the grave, the flowers on the lady's grave*), in this sepulchrally statuesque fate that entwines and separates these two lovers, starting from the fact of their names. No, the coldness that little by little takes over the body of the play and, as if in advance, cadaverizes it, is perhaps irony, the figure or rhetoric of irony, the contretemps of ironic consciousness. It always places itself disproportionately between the finite and the infinite, it makes use of inadequation, of aphorism, it *speculates*, it analyzes and analyzes, it analyzes the law of disidentification, the implacable necessity, the machine of the proper name that obliges me to live through precisely that, in other words, my name, of which I am dying.

34. Irony of the proper name, as analyzed by Juliet. Sentence of truth that carries death, aphorism separates, and in the first place separates me from my name. I am not my name. One might as well say that I should be able to survive it. But firstly it is destined to survive me. In this way it announces my death. Noncoincidence and contretemps between my

name and me, between the experience according to which I am named or hear myself named and my "living present." Rendezvous with my name. *Untimely*, bad timing, at the wrong moment.

35. Changing names: the dance, the substitution, the masks, the simulacrum, the rendezvous with death. Untimely. Never on time.

36. Speaking ironically, that is to say, in the rhetorical sense of the figure of irony: conveying the opposite of what one says. Here, the *impossible* then: (1) two lovers both outlive each other, each seeing the other die; (2) the name constitutes them but without being anything of themselves, condemning them to be what, beneath the mask, they are not, to being merged with the mask; (3) the two are united by that which separates them, and so on. And they state this clearly, they formalize it as even a philosophical speculation would not have dared to do. A vein, through the sharp tip of this analysis, receives the distilled potion. It does not wait, it does not allow any time, not even that of the drama, it comes at once to turn to ice the heart of their pledges. This potion would be the true poison, the poisoned truth of this drama.

37. Irony of the aphorism. In the *Aesthetics*, Hegel pokes fun at those who, quick to heap praises on ironists, show themselves not even capable of analyzing the analytical irony of *Romeo and Juliet*. He has a go at Tieck: "But when one thinks one has found the perfect opportunity to show what irony is, for example in *Romeo and Juliet*, one is disappointed, for it is no longer a question of irony."[4]

38. Another series, which cuts across all the others: the name, the law, the genealogy, the double survival, the contretemps, in short, the aphorism of *Romeo and Juliet*. Not of Romeo and of Juliet but of *Romeo and Juliet*, Shakespeare's play of that title. It belongs to a series, to the still-living palimpsest, to the open theater of narratives that bear this name. It survives them, but they also survive thanks to it. Would such a double survival have been possible "without that title," as Juliet put it? And would the names of Matteo Bandello or Luigi da Porto survive without that of Shakespeare, who survived them? And without the innumerable repetitions, each staked in its particular way, under the same name? Without the grafting of names? And of other plays? "O be some other name . . . "

39. The absolute aphorism: a proper name. Without genealogy, without the least copula. End of drama. Curtain. Tableau (*The Two Lovers United in Death* by Angelo dall'Oca Bianca). Tourism, December sun in Verona ("Verona by that name is known" [V, iii, 299]). A true sun, the other ("The sun for sorrow will not show his head" [V, iii, 305]).

—*Translated by Nicholas Royle*

§ 9   How to Avoid Speaking: Denials

I

Even before starting to prepare this lecture, I knew I wanted to speak of the "trace" in its relation to what one calls, sometimes abusively, "negative theology." More precisely, I knew I would *have* to do this in Jerusalem. But what about such a duty here? In saying I knew I would have to do it even before the first word of this lecture, I am already naming a singular anteriority of duty—a duty before the first word, is this possible?— that is difficult to situate and will perhaps be my theme today.

Under the very loose heading of "negative theology," as you know, one often designates a certain form of language, with its mise en scène, its rhetorical, grammatical, and logical modes, its demonstrative procedures—in short, a textual practice attested to or even situated "in history," although it does sometimes exceed the predicates that constitute this or that concept of history. Is there *one* negative theology, *the* (only) negative theology [la *théologie négative*]? In any case, the unity of its archive is difficult to determine. One might try to organize it around certain attempts that are taken to be exemplary or explicit, such as *The Divine Names* of Dionysius the Areopagite (Pseudo-Dionysius). But as we will see, for essential reasons, one is never certain of being able to attribute to anyone a project of negative theology *as such.*[1] Before Dionysius, one may look to a certain

"How to Avoid Speaking" was first given as a lecture in English in Jerusalem in June 1986 at the opening of a colloquium on "Absence and Negativity" organized by the Hebrew University and the Institute for Advanced Studies of Jerusalem.

Platonic or Neoplatonic tradition. After him, as far as the modernity of Wittgenstein and many others. More vaguely, in a less rigorous or informed way, then, "negative theology" has come to designate a type of attitude toward language and, within it, in the act of definition, attribution, semantic or conceptual determination. If one supposes, by provisional hypothesis, that negative theology consists in regarding every predicate, or even all predicative language, as inadequate to the essence, that is, to the hyperessentiality of God, and that, consequently, only a negative ("apophatic") attribution can claim to approach God, and to prepare us for a silent intuition of God, then, by a more or less tenable analogy, one will recognize some traits, the family resemblance of negative theology, in every discourse that seems to have recourse in a regular and insistent manner to this rhetoric of negative determination, endlessly multiplying the defenses and the apophatic warnings: this, which is called *X* (for example, the text, writing, the trace, differance, the hymen, the supplement, the *pharmakon*, the *parergon*, etc.), "is" neither this nor that, neither sensible nor intelligible, neither positive nor negative, neither inside nor outside, neither superior nor inferior, neither active nor passive, neither present nor absent, not even neutral, not even dialectizable in a third term, without any possible sublation (*Aufhebung*). Despite appearances, then, this *X* is neither a concept nor even a name. To be sure, it *lends itself* to a series of names, but it calls for another syntax and exceeds even the order and the structure of predicative discourse. It "is" not and does not say what "is." It is written completely otherwise.

I have deliberately chosen examples that are close to me and, as you might think, familiar. For two reasons. On the one hand, very early on, I was accused of—rather than congratulated for—repeating the procedures of negative theology in what was taken to be a well-known landscape. These procedures were then seen as simple rhetoric, even a rhetoric of failure, or worse, a rhetoric that renounces knowledge, conceptual determination, and analysis: for those who have nothing to say or who do not want to know anything, it is always easy to imitate the technique of negative theology. In fact, negative theology necessarily includes an apparatus of methodological rules. In a moment I will try to show how negative theology claims, at least, not to be assimilable to a technique that is exposed to simulacrum and to parody, to mechanical repetition. It escapes from these by means of the *prayer* that precedes apophatic utterances, and by the address to the other, to you, in a moment that is not only the preamble or the methodological threshold of experience. Naturally, prayer, invocation, and apostrophe can also be imitated, and can even lend themselves, as if despite themselves, to repetitive technique. In conclusion, I will come back to this risk, which, fortunately *and* unfortunately, is also a chance. But if the risk is inevitable, the accusation it incurs should not be limited to the apophatic moment of negative theology. It can be extended to all language, and even to all manifestation in general. This risk is inscribed in the structure of the mark.

There is also an automatic, ritualistic, and "doxic" exercise of suspicion brought against everything that resembles negative theology. It has interested me for a long time. Its matrix includes at least three types of objections:

(a) You prefer to negate; you affirm nothing; you are fundamentally a nihilist, or even an obscurantist; neither knowledge nor even theological science will progress in this way. Not to mention atheism, of which one has been able to say in an equally trivial fashion that it is the truth of negative theology.

(b) You abuse a simple technique; it suffices to repeat: "*X* is no more this, than that," "*X* seems to exceed all discourse or all predication," and so on. This comes down to speaking in order to say nothing. You speak only for the sake of speaking, in order to experience speech. Or, more seriously, you speak thus with an eye to writing, since what you write then does not even merit being said. This second critique already appears more interesting and more lucid than the first: to speak in order to speak, to experience what happens to speech through speech *itself*, in the trace of a sort of quasi-tautology, is not entirely to speak in vain and in order to say nothing. It is perhaps to experience a possibility of speech that the objector himself must presuppose at the moment when he addresses his criticism. To speak in order to say *nothing* is not not to speak. Above all, it is not to speak to no one.

(c) This critique does not, then, touch on the essential possibility of address or apostrophe. It also encompasses a third possibility, less evident but no doubt more interesting. Here the suspicion takes a form that can reverse the process of the accusation: once the apophatic discourse is analyzed in its logico-grammatical form, if it is not merely sterile, repetitive, obscurantist, mechanical, it may lead us to consider the becoming-theological of all discourse. From the moment a proposition takes a negative form, the negativity that manifests itself need only be pushed to the limit for it at least to resemble a theological apophatic. Every time I say: *X* is neither this nor that, nor the contrary of this or that, nor the simple neutralization of this or that with which it has *nothing in common*, being absolutely heterogeneous to or incommensurable with them, I would be beginning to speak of God, under this name or another. God's name would then be the hyperbolic effect of that negativity or any negativity that is consistent in its discourse. God's name would fit everything that cannot be broached, approached, or designated, except in an indirect and negative way. Every negative sentence would already be haunted by God or by the name of God, the distinction between God and God's name opening up the very space of this enigma. If there is a work of negativity in discourse and predication, it would produce divinity. It then suffices to change a sign (or rather to show, something easy and classical enough, that this inversion has *always already* taken place, that it is the very necessity of thought) in order to say that divinity is not produced but productive. Infinitely productive, Hegel, for example, would say. God is not merely the end, but the origin of this work of the negative. Not only would atheism not be the truth of negative theology, but, rather, God would be the truth of all negativity. One thus arrives at a kind of proof of God, not a proof of the *existence* of God, but a proof of God *by his effects*, or more precisely a proof of what one calls God, by the name of God, by effects without cause, by the *without cause.* The value of this word *without* [sans] will concern us in a moment. In the absolutely singular logic of this proof, "God" names *that without which* one would not know how to account for any negativity: grammatical or logical negation, illness, evil, and, finally, neurosis, which, far from permitting psychoanalysis to reduce religion to a symptom, would force it to recognize in the symptom the negative manifestation of God. Without saying that there must be at least as much "reality" in the cause as in the effect, and that the "existence" of God has no need of any proof other than religious symptomatics, one sees on the contrary—in the negation or suspension of the predicate, even of the thesis of "existence"—the first mark of respect for a divine cause that does not even need to "be." And those who would like to consider "deconstruction" a symptom of modern or postmodern nihilism could indeed, if they wished, recognize in it the last testimony, not to say the martyrdom, of faith in the present fin de siècle. This reading will always be possible. Who could prohibit it? In the name of what? But what has happened so that what is thus permitted is nonetheless never necessary? What must the writing of this deconstruction be—what must writing according to this deconstruction be—for this to be the case?

That was a first reason. But if I chose examples that were close to me it was for a second reason as well. I wanted to say a few words about a long-standing wish: to broach—directly and in itself—the network of questions that are gathered hastily under the heading of "negative theology." Until now, when faced with the question or the objection, my response has always been brief, elliptical, and dilatory.[2] Yet it was already articulated, it seems to me, in two moments [*temps*]:

1. No, what I write is not "negative theology." First of all, *insofar* as the latter belongs to the predicative or judicative space of discourse, to its strictly propositional form, and privileges not only the indestructible unity of the word but also the authority of the noun or the name [*nom*]— so many axioms that a "deconstruction" must start by reconsidering (and which I have tried to do since the first part of *Of Grammatology*). Next, insofar as "negative theology" seems to reserve, beyond all positive predication, beyond all negation, even beyond being, some superessentiality, a being beyond being. This is the word that Dionysius so often uses in *The Divine Names*: *hyperousios, -ōs, hyperousiotēs*. God as being beyond being or also God as without being.[3] This seems to exceed the alternative of a theism or an atheism that would only come to oppose each other around what one calls, sometimes ingenuously, the existence of God. Without being able to return to the syntax and semantics of the word "without [*sans*]," which I have tried to analyze elsewhere, I limit myself here to the first stage of this response. No, I would hesitate to inscribe what I put forward under the familiar heading of negative theology, precisely because of that ontological wager of hyperessentiality that one finds at work in both Dionysius and Meister Eckhart, for example, when the latter writes:

> Everything works in being [*Ein ieglich dinc würket in wesene*]; nothing works above its being [*über sîn wesen*]. Fire cannot work except in wood. God works above being [*Got würket über wesene*] in vastness, where he can roam. He works in nonbeing [*er würket in unwesene*]. Before being was, God worked [*ê denne wesen waere, dô worhte got*]. He worked being when there was no being. Unsophisticated teachers say that God is pure being [*ein lûter wesen*]. He is as high above being as the highest angel is above a gnat. I would be speaking as incorrectly in calling God a being as if I called the sun pale or

black. God is neither this nor that [*Got enist weder diz noch daz*]. A master says: "Whoever imagines that he has understood God, if he knows anything, it is not God that he knows." However, in saying that God is not being and is above being [*über wesen*], I have not denied being to God [*ich im niht wesen abegesprochen*]; rather, I have elevated it in him [*ich hân ez in im gehoehet*].[4]

In the movement of the same paragraph, a quotation from St. Augustine recalls the simultaneously negative and hyperaffirmative meaning of the "without": "St. Augustine says: God is wise without wisdom [*wîse âne wîsheit*], good without goodness [*guot âne güete*], powerful without power [*gewaltic âne gewalt*]." The "without" does not merely dissociate the singular attribution from the essential generality: wisdom as *being*-wise in general, goodness as *being*-good in general, power as *being*-powerful in general. It does not only avoid the abstraction tied to every noun and to the being implied in every essential generality. In the same word and in the same syntax, it transmutes into affirmation its purely phenomenal negativity, which ordinary language, riveted to finitude, gives us to hear in a word such as "without," or in other analogous words. It deconstructs grammatical anthropomorphism.

To go no further than the first moment of my response, it was because of this movement of hyperessentiality that I thought I had to refrain from writing in the register of "negative theology." What "differance," "trace," and so on, "mean-to-say"—which consequently *does not mean to say anything*—would be "something" "before" the concept, the name, the word, that would be nothing, that would no longer pertain to being, to presence or to the presence of the present, or even to absence, and even less to some hyperessentiality. Yet the ontotheological reappropriation always remains possible—and doubtless *inevitable* insofar as one is speaking, precisely, in the element of ontotheological logic and grammar. One can always say: hyperessentiality is exactly that, a supreme being that remains incommensurable with the being of all that is, that *is* nothing, neither present nor absent, and so on. If in fact the movement of this reappropriation appears irrepressible, its ultimate failure is no less necessary. But I concede that this question remains at the heart of a thinking of differance or of a writing of writing. It remains a question, and this is why I return to it again. Following the same "logic," and I am still holding to the first moment of this response, my uneasiness was nevertheless also directed toward the promise of that presence given to intuition or vision. The promise of such a presence often accompanies the apophatic crossing. It is doubtless the vision of a dark light, no doubt an intuition in the "brilliant darkness [*hyperphoton*],"[5] but still it is the immediacy of a presence. Leading to a union with God. After the indispensable moment of prayer (of which I will speak again later), Dionysius thus exhorts Timothy to the *mystika theamata*:

> For this I pray; and, Timothy, my friend, my advice to you as you look for a sight of the mysterious things, is to leave behind you everything perceived and understood, everything perceptible and understandable, all that is not and all that is [*panta ouk onta kai onta*], and, with your understanding laid aside [*agnōstos*], to strive upward as much as you can toward union with him who is beyond all being and knowledge [*tou hyper pasan ousian kai gnōsin*]. By an undivided and absolute abandonment of yourself and everything, shedding all and freed from all, you will be uplifted in a pure ecstasy [*ekstasei*] to the ray of the divine shadow which is above everything that is [*pros tēn hyperousion tou theiou*]. (*MT* 1: 998b–1000a)

This mystic union, this act of *un*knowing, is also truly "to see and to know [*to ontōs idein kai gnōsai*]" (*MT* 2 1025a). It knows unknowing itself in its truth, a truth that is not an adequation but an unveiling. Praising "the Superessential One in a superessential way [*ton hyperousion hyperousiōs hymnēsai*]," this union aims "unhiddenly [to] know [*aperikalyptōs*: in an open, unhidden manner] that unknowing [*agnōsian*] which itself is hidden from all those possessed of knowing amid all beings" (*MT* 2: 1025b–c). The revelation is called forth by an elevation: toward that contact or vision, that pure intuition of the ineffable, that silent union with what remains inaccessible to speech. This ascent corresponds to a rarefaction of signs, figures, symbols—and also of fictions, as well as myths and poetry. Dionysius treats this *economy* of signs as such. *The Symbolic Theology* is more voluble and more voluminous than *The Mystical Theology*. For it treats "analogies of God drawn from what we perceive [*hai apo tōn aisthētōn epi ta theia metōnumiai*]" (*MT* 3: 1033a); it describes the meaning of forms (*morphai*) and figures (*skhēmata*) in God; it measures its discourse against "symbols" that demand more words than the rest, since "*The Theological Representations* and a discussion of the names appropriate to God are inevitably briefer than what can be said in *The Symbolic Theology*." With the ascent beyond the sensible, one gains in conciseness, for "the more we take flight upward, the more our words are confined to the ideas we are capable of forming" (*MT* 3: 1033b). But there is also something beyond this economical conciseness. By passing beyond the intelligible itself, the *apophatikai theologai* aim toward absolute rarefaction, toward silent union with the ineffable:

> [S]o that now as we plunge into that darkness which is beyond intellect, we shall find ourselves not simply running short of words [*brakhylogian*] but actually speechless [*alogian*] and unknowing [*anoēsian*]. In the earlier books my argument traveled downward from the most exalted to the humblest categories, taking in on this downward path an ever-increasing number of ideas which multiplied with every stage of the descent. But my argument now rises from what is below up to the transcendent, and the more it climbs, the more language falters, and when it has passed up and beyond the ascent, it will turn silent completely, since it will finally be at one with him who is indescribable [*aphthenktōi*]. (*MT* 3: 1033b–c)

This economy is paradoxical. By right and in principle, the apophatic movement of discourse would have negatively to re-traverse all the stages of symbolic theology and positive predication. It would thus be coextensive with it, confined to the same quantity of discourse. In itself interminable, the apophatic movement cannot contain within itself the principle of its interruption. It can only indefinitely postpone the encounter with its own limit.

Alien, heterogeneous, in any case irreducible to the intuitive *telos*—to the experience of the ineffable and the mute vision that seems to orient this apophatic, including the prayer and the praise that prepare its way—the thinking of differance would thus have little affinity, for an analogous reason, with the current interpretation of certain well-known statements of the early Wittgenstein. I recall these words often quoted from the *Tractatus*, for example, "6.522—The inexpressible, indeed, exists [*Es gibt allerdings Unaussprechliches*]. It *shows itself*, it is the mystical." And "7.—What we cannot speak of we must pass over in silence."

It is the nature of this "we must [*il faut*]" that is significant here: it inscribes the injunction of silence in the order or the promise of a "one must speak," "it is necessary [*il faut*]—not to avoid speaking"—or rather "it is necessary that there be some trace." No, "it is necessary that there *have been* some trace," a sentence that one must simultaneously turn toward a past *and* toward a future that are still unpresentable. It is (now) necessary that there *have been* some trace (in an immemorial past, and it is because of this amnesia that the "it is necessary" of the trace is necessary). But also, it is necessary (as of now, it will be necessary, the "it is necessary" always also holds for the future) that in the future there will have been some trace.

But let us not be too hasty. In a moment it will be necessary to differentiate between these modalities of the "it is necessary."

2. For—and this was often the second moment of my improvised responses—the general title of "negative theology" perhaps conceals confusions and often gives rise to simplistic interpretations. Perhaps there is within it, hidden, restless, diverse, and itself heterogeneous, a massive and indistinct multiplicity of possibles for which the single expression "negative theology" still remains inadequate. In order to engage oneself seriously in this debate, I have often said in response, it would be necessary to clarify this designation by considering quite dissimilar corpuses, scenes, proceedings, and languages. As I have always been fascinated by the movements said to be those of negative theology (which, no doubt, are themselves not strangers to the experience of fascination in general), I objected in vain to the assimilation of the thinking of the trace or of differance to some negative theology, and my response amounted to a promise: one day I will stop deferring, one day I will try to explain myself directly on this subject, and at last speak of "negative theology" *itself*, assuming that some such thing exists.

Has this day come?

In other words: how to avoid speaking about negative theology? But how to resolve this question, and decide between its *two* meanings? 1. How to avoid speaking of it henceforth? This seems impossible. How could I remain silent on this subject? 2. How, if one speaks of it, to avoid speaking of it? How *not to* speak of it? How must one not speak of it? How to avoid speaking of it badly? What precautions must be taken to avoid errors, that is, inadequate, insufficient, or simplistic assertions?

I return to my very first sentence. I knew, then, what I would *have* to do. I had implicitly promised that I would, one day, speak directly of negative theology. Even before speaking, I knew that I was committed to doing it. Such a situation leaves room for two possible interpretations, at least. 1. Even before speech, in any case before a discursive event as such, there is necessarily an engagement or a promise. The discursive event presupposes the open space of the promise. 2. This engagement, this given word, already belongs to the time of speech (*la parole*) by which I keep my word, "je tiens parole," as one says in French. In fact, at the moment of promising to speak one day of negative theology, I already started to do so. But this is only a confused hint of the structure I would like to analyze later.

Having already promised, *as if in spite of myself,* I did not know *how* I could keep this promise. How to speak appropriately of negative theology? Is there a negative theology? A single one? A regulative model for all the others? Can one adjust a discourse to it? Is there some discourse that measures up to it? Is one not compelled to speak of negative theology according to the modes of negative theology, in a way that is at once impotent, exhausting, and inexhaustible? Is there ever anything other than a "negative theology" of "negative theology"?

Above all, I did not know when and where I would do it. Next year in Jerusalem, I told myself, in order perhaps to defer indefinitely the fulfillment of this promise. But also to let myself know—and I did indeed receive the message—that on the day when I would in fact go to Jerusalem, it would no longer be possible to delay. It will then be necessary to do it.

Will I do it? Am I in Jerusalem? This is a question to which one will never respond in the present tense, only in the future or in the past anterior.

Why insist on this postponement? Because it appears to me neither avoidable nor insignificant. One can never decide whether it does not give rise, as postponement, to the very thing it defers. It is not certain that I will keep my promise today, but nor is it certain that in further delaying its fulfillment, I have not, nevertheless, already kept it.

In other words: am I in Jerusalem or elsewhere, very far from the Holy City? Under what conditions does one find oneself in Jerusalem? Is it enough to be there physically, as one says, and to live in places that bear this name, as I am now doing? What is it to live in Jerusalem? This is not easy to decide. Allow me to quote Meister Eckhart again. Like that of Dionysius, Meister Eckhart's work sometimes resembles an endless meditation on the meaning and symbolism of the Holy City: a logic, rhetoric, topology, and tropology of Jerusalem. Here is one example among so many others:

> Where I sat yesterday I said something [*dâ sprach ich ein wort*] that sounds incredible—I said Jerusalem is as near my soul as the ground I stand on now

[*mîner sêle als nâhe als diu stat, dâ ich nû stan*]. Yes, in holy truth! whatever is a thousand miles further off than Jerusalem is as close to my soul as my own body is. I am as sure of this as that I am a man.[6]

Thus I will speak of a promise but also within the promise. The experience of negative theology perhaps holds *to* a promise, that of the other, which I must keep because it commits me to speak where negativity ought to lead discourse to its absolute rarefaction. Indeed, why must I speak *in view* of explaining, teaching, leading—on the paths of a psychagogy or of a pedagogy—in the direction of silence, of union with the ineffable, mute vision? Why can I not avoid speaking, if not because a promise has committed me even before I begin the briefest speech? If I therefore speak of the promise, I will not be able to keep any metalinguistic distance in regard to it. Discourse on the promise is a promise in advance: *within* the promise. I will thus not speak of this or that promise, but of that which, as necessary as it is impossible, inscribes us with its trace in language—before language. From the moment I open my mouth, I have already promised; or rather [*plutôt*], and earlier [*plus tôt*], the promise has seized the *I* that promises to speak to the other, to say something, to affirm or to confirm by speech at least this, at the extreme limit: that it is necessary to be silent and to be silent about what one cannot speak of. One might have known this in advance. This promise is older than I am. Here is something that appears impossible, the theoreticians of speech acts would say: like every authentic performative, a promise must be made in the present, in the first person (singular or plural) by one who is capable of saying *I* or *we*, here and now, for example in Jerusalem, "the place where I am now" and where I can therefore be held responsible for this speech act.

The promise of which I will speak will have always escaped this demand for presence. It is older than I am or than we are. On the contrary, it renders possible every present discourse on presence. Even if I decide to be silent, even if I decide to promise nothing, not to commit myself to saying anything that would confirm once again the destination *of* speech, and the destination *to* speech, this silence still remains a modality of speech: a memory of promise and a promise of memory.

So I knew it: I will not be able to avoid speaking of it. But how and under what title will I do so? One day, at Yale, I received a telephone message: it was necessary for me to give a title on the spot.[7] I had to improvise in two minutes, which I first did in my language: "Comment ne pas dire [How not to say] . . . ?" The use of the word *dire* allows for a certain suspension. "Comment ne pas dire?" can mean: how to be silent, how not to speak in general, how to say nothing, how to avoid speaking; but it can also mean: how, in speaking, not to say this or that, in such and such a way, which is both transitive and modalized? In other words: how, in saying and speaking, to avoid this or that discursive, logical, rhetorical mode? How to avoid an unjust, erroneous, aberrant, abusive form? How to avoid a particular predicate, and even predication itself? For example: how to avoid a negative form, or how not to be negative? How to say something finally? Which comes back to the apparently reverse question: how to say, how to speak? Between the two interpretations of "Comment ne pas dire?" the meaning of the uneasiness thus seems to get reversed: from "How to be silent?" (How to avoid speaking at all?) one passes— moreover, in a completely necessary way and as if from within—to the question, which can always become the prescriptive heading of a recom- mendation: How not to speak, what words to avoid, in order to speak *well? How to avoid speaking* is thus at once or successively: how is it neces- sary not to speak? how is it necessary to speak? (here is) how it is necessary not to speak, and so on. The "how" always shelters a "why," and the "it is necessary" has the double value of a "should" or "ought" and a "must."

I therefore improvised this title on the telephone. Letting it be dictated to me by I do not know what unconscious order—in a situation of abso- lute urgency—I thus also translated my desire still to defer. This reaction of flight reproduces itself on the occasion of every lecture: how to avoid speaking, and first of all how to avoid committing oneself by giving a title even before writing one's text? But also, in the economy of the same gesture: how to speak and do it *as it should be done* [comme il se doit], *as it must be done* [comme il faut], in order to assume the responsibility for a promise? Not only for the archi-originary promise that establishes us a priori as responsible for speech, but for this promise in particular: to give a lecture on "absence and negation," on the not [*ne-pas*] (how not to, ought not, should not, must not, etc.), on the "how" and the "why" (of the) *not* [ne pas], the step [*le pas*], negation and denial, and so on, and thus to commit oneself to giving a title *in advance*. Every title has the value of a promise; a title given in advance is the promise of a promise.

It was thus necessary for me to respond, but I assumed responsibility by deferring it. Before or rather within a *double bind*: *how to avoid speak- ing* since I have already begun to speak and have always already begun to promise to speak. That I have already begun to speak, or rather that at least the trace of a speech will have preceded this speech, this is what cannot be denied. Translate: *one can only deny it.* There can only be denial of this undeniable. What, then, to do with negations and denials? What to do with them before God, that is the question, if there is a question. For the sudden appearance [*surgissement*] of every question is perhaps secondary; it perhaps follows as a first, reactive response, the undeniable *provocation*, the unavoidable denial of the undeniable provocation.

In order to avoid speaking, to delay the moment when one will have to say something and perhaps avow, surrender, impart a secret, one multiplies the digressions. I will attempt a brief digression here on the secret itself. Under this title, "How to avoid speaking?" it is necessary to speak of the secret. In certain situations, one asks oneself, "How to avoid speaking?" either because one has promised not to speak and to keep a secret or because one has an interest, sometimes vital, in keeping silent, be it under torture. This situation again presupposes the possibility of speaking. Some would say, perhaps imprudently, that only man is capable of speaking, because only he can *not* manifest what he might manifest. Of course, an animal may inhibit a movement, abstain from a dangerous gesture, for example, in a defensive or offensive predatory strategy, or even in the delimitation of a sexual territory or in a seduction maneuver. One might say that an animal can, then, not respond to the inquisition or requisition of a stimulus or of a complex of stimuli. According to this same and somewhat naïve philosophy of animality, one might nevertheless observe that an animal is incapable of keeping or even having a secret, because it could not *represent to itself as such*, as an *object* before consciousness, something that it would have to forbid itself from manifesting. One would thus link the secret to an objective representation (*Vorstellung*) placed before consciousness and expressible in the form of words. The essence of a secret would remain rigorously alien to every other nonmanifestation, and first of all, that of which the animal might be capable. The manifestation or nonmanifestation of *this* secret, in short its possibility, would never be of the order of the symptom. An animal could neither choose to keep *itself* silent [se *taire*]—nor to keep a secret silent.

I will not take up this enormous problem here. To treat it, one would have to take account of numerous mediations, and then to question in particular the possibility of a preverbal or simply nonverbal secret— linked, for example, to gesture or to mimicry, and even to other codes and more generally to the unconscious. One would have to study the structures of denial before and outside of the possibility of judgment and of predicative language. Above all, one would have to reelaborate a problematic of consciousness, that thing that, more and more, one avoids speaking of, as if one knew what it was or as if its riddle had been exhausted. And yet is any problem more novel today than that of consciousness? Here one is tempted to designate, if not to define, consciousness as that place in which is retained the singular power not to *say* what one knows, to keep a secret in the form of representation. A conscious being is a being capable of lying, of not presenting in a discourse what it nonetheless has an articulated representation of: a being that can avoid speaking. But to be able to lie, a second and already modalized possibility, one must first—a more essential possibility—be able to keep for oneself, by saying to oneself, what one already knows. To keep for oneself is the most incredible and thought-provoking power. But this keeping-for-oneself, this dissimulation for which it is already necessary to be several and to differ from oneself, also presupposes the space of a promised speech, that is to say, a trace whose affirmation is not symmetrical. How to ascertain absolute dissimulation? Does one ever dispose of sufficient criteria or an apodictic certainty that would allow one to conclude: the secret has been kept, dissimulation has taken place, one has avoided speaking? Without even thinking of the secret that is wrested away by physical or mental torture, certain uncontrolled manifestations, whether direct or symbolic, somatic or figurative, may leave in reserve a possible betrayal or avowal. Not that everything manifests itself. It's just that nonmanifestation is never assured. According to this hypothesis, it would be necessary to reconsider all the boundaries between consciousness and the unconscious, as well as those between man and animal, that is, an enormous system of oppositions.

But I will avoid speaking of the secret as such. These brief allusions to the negativity of the secret and to the secret of denial seemed necessary to me in order to situate another problem. Again I will only touch on it. It's a question of what has always associated, in a way that is not fortuitous, "negative theologies" and everything that resembles a form of esoteric sociality with the phenomena of secret societies, as if access to the most rigorous apophatic discourse demanded the sharing of a "secret"—that is, of a power-to-keep-silent that would always be something more than a logical or rhetorical technique that could be easily imitated—and of a reserved content, of a place or wealth that had to be withheld from just anyone. It is as if divulgence imperiled a revelation promised to apophasis, to this decrypting that, to make the thing appear in a manifest fashion (*aperikalyptōs*), had first to find it hidden. A recurrence and a regulated analogy: those who, still today, denounce "deconstruction," for example, with its thinking of differance or the writing of writing as a bastardized resurgence of negative theology, are also those who readily suspect those they call *deconstructionists* of forming a sect, a brotherhood, an esoteric corporation, or more vulgarly, a clique, a gang, or, I quote, a "mafia." Since there is a law of recurrence here, the logic of suspicion can be formalized up to a certain point. Those who lead the investigation or the trial say or tell themselves, successively or alternatively:

1. Those people, adepts of negative theology or deconstruction (the difference matters little to the accusers), must indeed have a secret. They must be hiding something since they say nothing, speak in a negative way, answer "no, it's not that, it's not so simple" to all questions, and say, in sum, that what they are speaking about is neither this, nor that, nor a third term, neither a concept nor a name, in short *is* not, and thus is nothing.

2. But since this secret obviously cannot be determined and is nothing, as these people themselves recognize, they have no secret. They pretend to have one in order to organize themselves around a social power founded on the magic of a speech that is skilled at speaking in order to say nothing. These obscurantists are terrorists who remind one of Sophists. A Plato would be of use in combating them. They wield a real power, which may be situated inside or outside the Academy: they contrive to blur even this boundary. Their alleged secret belongs to sham, mystification, or at best to a politics of grammar. Because for them there is only writing and language, nothing beyond, even if they claim to "deconstruct" "logocentrism" and even start there.

3. If you know how to question them, they will end up admitting: "The secret is that there is no secret, but there are at least two ways of thinking or proving this proposition," and so on. Experts in the art of evasion, they know better how to negate or deny than how to say anything. They always agree to avoid speaking while speaking a lot and "splitting hairs." Some of them seem "Greek," others "Christian"; they have recourse to many languages at once, and one knows some who resemble Talmudists. They are perverse enough to make their esotericism popular and "fashionable." End of a familiar indictment.

One finds hints of this esotericism in the Platonism and Neoplatonism that remain so present at the heart of Dionysius's negative theology. But in the works of Dionysius, and in another way in those of Meister Eckhart, no mystery is made of the necessity of the secret—to be kept silent, preserved, shared. It is necessary to stand apart, to find the proper *place* [lieu] for the experience of the secret. This detour through the secret will lead, in a moment, to the question of *place* that will henceforth orient my talk. Following the prayer that opens his *Mystical Theology*, Dionysius names the secret of the superessential divinity several times, the (cryphio-mystical) "secrets" of the "darkness beyond light of . . . silence." The "secret" of this revelation gives access to the unknowing beyond knowledge. Dionysius exhorts Timothy to divulge the secret neither to those who know, believe they know, or believe they can know by way of knowledge, nor a fortiori to the ignorant and profane. Avoid speaking, he advises him in short. It is thus necessary to separate oneself twice: both from those who know—one could say here, from the philosophers or the experts in ontology—and from the vulgar profane who manipulate predicative language as naïve idolaters. One is not far from insinuating [*sous-entendre*] that ontology itself is a subtle or perverse idolatry; one will hear this [*entendra*], in an analogous and different way, through the voice of Levinas or Jean-Luc Marion.

The paragraph I am going to read is interesting, moreover, in that it defines a beyond that exceeds the opposition between affirmation and negation. In truth, as Dionysius expressly says, it exceeds *position* (*thesis*) itself, and not merely curtailment, subtraction (*aphairesis*). At the same time, it exceeds privation. The *without* of which I spoke a moment ago marks neither a privation nor a lack nor an absence. As for the *hyper* of the superessential (*hyperousios*), it has the double and ambiguous value of what is above in a hierarchy, thus both beyond and more. God (is) beyond being but as such is more (being) than being: *no more being and being more than being: being more*. The French expression "plus d'être [more being, no more being]" formulates this equivocation in a fairly economical manner. Here is the call to the initiatory secret, and the warning:

> § 2. But see to it that none of this comes to the hearing of the uninformed [*tōn amuētōn*], that is to say, to those [among the profane: this passage of the manuscript is lost] caught up with the things of the world [*tois ousin*], who imagine that there is nothing that could exist superessentially [*hyperousiōs*] and who think that by their own intellectual resources they can have a direct knowledge of him who has made the shadows his hiding place [Ps. 18:12].

And if revelation of the divine mystery is beyond such people, what is to be said of those others ["those other profane," ms.], still more uninformed, who describe the transcendent Cause [*hyperkeimenēn aitian*] of all things in terms derived from the lowest orders of being, and who claim that it is in no way superior to the godless, multiformed shapes [*polyeidōn morphōmatōn*] they themselves have made? What has actually to be said about the Cause of everything is this. Since it is the Cause of all beings, we should posit and ascribe to it all the affirmations we make in regard to beings, and, more appropriately, we should negate all these affirmations since it surpasses all being. Now we should not conclude that the negations are simply the opposites of the affirmations, but rather that the cause of all is considerably prior to this, which is itself *situated beyond* all position, whether negative or affirmative [*hyper pasan kai aphairesin kai thesin*]—beyond privation [*tas sterēsis*]. (*MT* 1: 1000a–b; emphasis added—JD)

It is *situated*, therefore. It situates itself *beyond* all position. What is this place? Between this place and the place of the secret, between this secret place and the topography of the social bond that must protect the nondivulgence, there must be a certain homology. The latter must govern some—secret—relation between the topology of what stands beyond being, without being [*sans être*]—without being it [*sans l'être*], and the topology, the initiatory politopology that both organizes the mystical community and makes possible this address to the other, this quasi-pedagogical and mystagogical speech that Dionysius singularly directs to Timothy (*pros Timotheon*: the dedication of *The Mystical Theology*).

In this hierarchy,[8] where does the speaker stand? And the one who listens and receives? And the one who speaks while *receiving* from the Cause that is also the Cause for this community? Where do Dionysius and Timothy stand, both they and all those who are potentially reading the text addressed by the one to the other? Where do they stand with regard to God, to the Cause? God resides in a place, Dionysius says, but he is not this place. To gain access to it is not yet to contemplate God. Even Moses must retreat. He receives this order from a place that is not a place, even if one of the names of God can sometimes designate place itself. Like all the initiated, he must purify himself, move away from the impure, separate himself from the many, join "the chosen priests." But access to this divine place does not yet grant him passage to the mystical Darkness where profane vision ceases and where it is necessary to be silent. There he is finally *permitted* and *prescribed* to be silent by closing his eyes:

It [the universal and good cause] is on a plane above all this, and it is made manifest only to those who travel through foul and fair, who pass beyond the summit of every holy ascent, who leave behind them every divine light, every voice, every word from heaven, and who plunge into the darkness. . . . It is not for nothing that the blessed Moses is *commanded to submit first to purification* and then *to depart from* those who have not undergone this. When every purification is complete, he hears the many-voiced trumpets. He sees the many lights, pure and with rays streaming abundantly. Then, *standing apart* from the crowds and accompanied by chosen priests [*tōn ekkritōn hiereōn*], he pushes ahead to the summit of the divine ascents. And yet he does not meet God himself, but contemplates, *not him who is invisible* [*atheatos gar*], but rather *where he dwells* [*topon*]. This means, I presume, that the holiest and highest *of the things perceived with the eye of the body or the mind* are but the rationale which presupposes all that lies below the Transcendent One. Through them, however, his unimaginable presence [*parousia*] is shown, walking the heights of those holy places [*tōn hagiōtatōn autou topōn*] to which the mind at least can rise. But then he [Moses] breaks free of them, away from what sees and is seen, and he plunges into the really mysterious darkness of unknowing [*tēs agnōsias*]. Here, renouncing all that the mind may conceive ("closing his eyes" [MS]), wrapped entirely in the intangible and the invisible, he belongs completely to him who is beyond everything. Here, being neither oneself nor someone else, one is supremely united by a completely unknowing inactivity of all knowledge, and knows beyond the mind by knowing. (*MT* 1: 1000c–d; emphases added—JD)

I will take up three motifs from this passage.

1. To separate oneself, to move away, to withdraw with the chosen, from the start this topolitology of the secret obeys an order. Moses "is commanded to submit first to purification and then to depart from those who have not undergone this." This order cannot be distinguished from a promise. It is the promise itself. The knowledge of the High Priest who intercedes, so to speak, between God and the holy institution, is the knowledge of the promise. Dionysius makes this clearer still, in *The Ecclesiastical Hierarchy*, on the subject of the prayer for the dead. *Epangelia* means both the commandment and the promise: "He knows that the promises of God will surely be realized [*tas apseudeis epangelias*] and in this way he teaches all those present that the gifts for which he duly pleads [*kata thesmon hieron*] will be granted to all those who live a perfect

life in God."[9] Earlier, it was said that "[t]he hierarch knows well what the true scriptures have promised" (*EH* 561d).

2. In this topolitology of the secret, the figures or *places* of rhetoric are also political stratagems. The "sacred symbols," the compositions (*synthēmata*), the signs and figures of the sacred discourse, the "mysteries," and the "contrived symbols" are so many "shields" invented against the many. All of the anthropomorphic emotions that one attributes to God, the grief, the anger, the repentances, the curses, so many negative feelings, and even the "sophistries" (*sophismata*) he uses in the Scriptures "to evade his promises," are nothing but "sacred pictures [*hiera synthēmata*] boldly used to represent God, so that what is hidden may be brought out into the open and multiplied, what is unique and undivided may be divided up, and multiple shapes and forms be given to what has neither shape nor form [*kai typōtika, kai polymorpha tōn amorphōtōn kai atypōtōn*]. All this is to enable the one capable of seeing the beauty hidden within these images to find that they are truly mysterious, appropriate to God, and filled with a great theological light" (Letter 9 to Titus [*L* 1105b ff.]). Without the divine promise that is also an injunction, the power of these *synthēmata* would be merely conventional rhetoric, poetry, fine arts, perhaps literature. It would be enough to doubt this promise or disregard this injunction to see an opening—and also a closing upon itself—of the field of rhetoricity or even of literariness, the lawless law of fiction.

Since the promise is also an order, the rhetorical veil becomes a political shield, the solid barrier of a social division, a *shibboleth*. One invents it to protect access to a knowledge that remains *in itself* inaccessible, untransmissible, unteachable. We will see that what is unteachable is nevertheless taught in another mode. To have recourse to the use Lacan makes of this word in a domain that is certainly not without relation to the present one, this nonmatheme can and must become a matheme. One must not think, Dionysius specifies, that rhetorical compositions are sufficient unto themselves in their simple phenomenon. They are instruments, technical mediations, weapons, at least defensive weapons, "shields [*probeblēsthai*] of the understanding of what is ineffable ['intransmissible' (ms.)] and invisible to the common multitude. This is so in order that the most sacred things are not readily handled by the profane but are revealed instead to the real lovers of holiness. Only these latter know how to put away the workings of childish imagination regarding the sacred symbols" (*L* 1105c).

Here is another political and pedagogical consequence, another institutional trait: the theologian must practice, not a double language, but the double inscription of his knowledge. Dionysius evokes a dual tradition, a dual mode of transmission (*dittēn paradosin*); on the one hand ineffable, secret, prohibited, reserved, inaccessible (*aporrhēton*) or mysterious (*mystikēn*), symbolic and initiatory; on the other hand, philosophical, demonstrative (*apodeiktikēn*), exposable. The critical question obviously becomes the following: how do these two modes relate to each other? What is the law of their reciprocal translation or of their hierarchy? What would be its institutional or political figure? Dionysius recognizes that each of these two modes "intersects" with the other. The "inexpressible" (*arrhēton*) is interwoven or intersects (*sympeplektai*) with "the expressible" (*tōi rhētoi*).

To what mode does this discourse belong, then, that of Dionysius but also my own about him? Must it not necessarily stand in the place, which cannot be an indivisible point, where the two modes cross each other—such that the crossing itself, or the *symplokē*, belongs properly to neither of the two modes and no doubt even precedes their distribution? At the crossing of the secret and the nonsecret, what is the secret?

At the place of crossing of these two languages, each of which *conveys* the silence of the other, a secret must and must not allow itself to be divulged. It can and it cannot do this. One must not divulge, but it is also necessary to make known or rather allow to be known this "it is necessary," "one must not," or "it is necessary not to."

How not to divulge a secret? How to avoid saying? How to avoid speaking? Contradictory and unstable meanings give such a question its endless oscillation: what must one do so that the secret remain secret? How to make it known, so that the secret of the secret—as such—not remain secret? How to avoid this divulgence? These slight disturbances underlie the same sentence. At the same time stable and unstable, this sentence allows itself to be carried by the movements of what I am calling "denial" (*dénégation*), a word that I would like to hear prior even to its elaboration in a Freudian context (this is perhaps not easy and assumes at least two preconditions: that the chosen examples extend beyond both the predicative structure and the ontotheological or metaphysical presuppositions that still underlie psychoanalytic theorems).

There is a secret of denial and a denial of the secret. The secret as such, *as secret*, separates and already institutes a negativity; it is a negation that denies itself. It de-negates itself. This de-negation does not happen to it by accident; it is essential and originary. And in the *as such* of the secret that denies itself because it appears to itself in order to be what it is, this de-negation does not give dialectic a chance. The enigma of which I am speaking here—in a way that is too elliptical, too "brief," as Dionysius would say, but also too verbose—is the *sharing out* [partage] *of the secret.* Not only the sharing of the secret with the other, my partner in a sect or in a secret society, my accomplice, my witness, my ally. But first of all the secret shared out, divided *in itself,* its "proper" partition, that which divides the essence of a secret that cannot even appear, even to a single person, except by losing itself, by divulging itself, hence dissimulating itself, as secret, by showing itself: by dissimulating its dissimulation. There is no secret *as such,* I deny it. And this is what I confide in secret to whoever allies himself with me. This is the secret of the alliance. If the theological necessarily insinuates itself here, this does not mean that the secret itself is theo-logical. But does something like the secret *itself,* properly speaking, ever exist? The name of God (I do not say God, but how to avoid saying God here, from the moment that I say the name of God?) can only be *said* in the modality of this secret denial: above all, I do not want to say that.

3. My third remark also concerns place. *The Mystical Theology* distinguishes, as we've seen, between access to the contemplation of God and access to the place where God resides. Contrary to what certain acts of naming may allow one to think, God is not simply his place, not even in his most holy of places. He is not and he has no place, he does not take place [*n'a pas lieu*], or rather he is and has/takes place [*a lieu*] but without being and without place, without being his place. What is the place, what takes place or gives place to thought, henceforth, in this word? We will have to follow this thread in order to ask ourselves what an event can be, what *takes place* in this *atopic* of God. I say *atopic,* hardly playing at all: *atopos* is the senseless, the absurd, the extravagant, the mad. Dionysius often speaks of God's madness. When he cites Scripture ("the foolishness of God is wiser than men"), he evokes the theologians' practice of overturning and denying "the usual sense of a deprivation" with respect to God (*DN* 7: 865b). A single clarification for the moment: if God's place, which is not God, does not communicate with the divine superessence, it is not only because this place remains either perceptible or visible. It is also insofar as it is an intelligible place. Whatever may be the ambiguity of the passage and the difficulty of knowing whether the place "where [God] dwells"—and which is not God himself—does or does not belong to the

order of the sensible, the conclusion seems unambiguous: "The presence" (*parousia*) of God is situated at the "heights of those holy places [*tais noētais akrotēsi tōn hagiōtatōn autou topōn*]" (*MT* 1: 1000d).

II

We are still on the threshold.

How to avoid speaking? And why lead this question now toward the question of place? Was it not already there? And isn't to lead always to go from one place to another? A question about place does not stand outside of place; it is properly *concerned* with place.

In the *three stages* that now await us, I thought it necessary to privilege the experience of place. But already the word "experience" seems risky. The relation to place about which I am going to speak will perhaps no longer have the form of experience, at least if experience still assumes the encounter with or crossing of a presence.

Why this privileging of place? Its justifications will appear, I hope, along the way. Here are nevertheless a few preliminary and schematic indications.

Since such is the topos of our colloquium in Jerusalem, it is first of all a matter of poetry, literature, literary criticism, poetics, hermeneutics, and rhetoric: everything that can make speech or writing, in the ordinary sense, communicate with what I am calling here a trace. Each time it is impossible to avoid, *on the one hand*, the immense problem of figural spatialization (both *in* speech or writing in the ordinary sense and in the space *between* the ordinary sense and the other, of which the ordinary sense is only a figure); and, *on the other hand*, that of meaning and reference, and *finally*, that of the event insofar as it takes place.

As we have already begun to see, figurality and the places [*lieux-dits*] of rhetoric are the very concern of apophatic procedures. As for meaning and reference, we also need to recall this—in truth, the recall of the other, the call of the other as *recall*: At the moment when the question "how to avoid speaking?" is raised and articulated in all its modalities, whether it is a matter of the rhetorical or logical forms of speech [*du dire*], or of the simple fact of speaking, it is already, so to speak, *too late*. It is no longer a question of not speaking. Even if one speaks so as not to say anything, even if an apophatic discourse deprives itself of meaning or of an object, it takes place. What initiated or made it possible *has taken place*. The possible absence of referent still signals, if not toward the thing one is speaking of (like God, who is nothing because he takes place, *without place, beyond being*), at least toward the other (other than being) that/who calls or to which/whom this speech is addressed, even if it speaks to the other only in order to speak, or to say nothing. This call of the other, having always already preceded the speech to which it has therefore never been present a first time, announces itself in advance as a *recall* [rappel]. Such a reference to the other will always have taken place. Before any statement and even before all discourse in general, promise, prayer, praise, celebration. The most negative discourse, beyond even nihilisms and negative dialectics, keeps a trace of it. A trace of an event older than it *or* of a "taking-place" to come, one *and* the other: there is here neither alternative nor contradiction.

Translated into the *Christian* apophatics of Dionysius (although other translations of the same necessity are possible), this means that the power to speak and to speak *well of* God already proceeds from God. This is the case even if to do this one must avoid speaking in some way or other in order to speak *rightly* or *truly*, even if one must avoid speaking entirely. This power is a gift and an effect of God. The cause is a kind of absolute referent but, first of all, an order and a promise. The cause, the gift of the gift, the order and the promise are the same, the *very thing* to which or rather to Whom responds the responsibility of whoever speaks and "speaks well." At the end of *The Divine Names*, the very possibility of speaking of the divine names and of speaking of them correctly comes back to God, "the cause of all goods for having given me the words to speak and the power to use them well [*kai to legein kai to eu legein*]" (*DN* 13: 981c). Following the implicit rule of this utterance, one may say that it is always possible to call God, to call this assumed origin of all speech, its required cause, by the name of God. The exigency of its cause, the responsibility before what is responsible for it, demands what is demanded. It is for speech, or better yet for silence, a demand, the exigency or the desire, as you wish, for what is also called meaning, referent, truth. This is what God's name always names, before or beyond other names: the trace of the singular event that will have made speech possible even before speech turns back toward—in order to respond to it—this first or last reference. This is why an apophatic discourse must also open with a prayer that recognizes, assigns, or ensures its destination: the Other as Referent of a *legein* that is none other than its Cause.

The event that is always presupposed, this singular having-taken place, is also for every reading, every interpretation, every poetics, every literary criticism, what is commonly called the *oeuvre*: at least the already-there [*dejà-là*] of a phrase, the trace of a phrase whose singularity would have to remain irreducible and whose reference indispensable in a given idiom. A trace has taken place. Even if the idiomaticity must necessarily be lost or let itself be contaminated by the repetition that confers on it a code and intelligibility, even if it *comes only to erase itself* [n'arrive qu'à s'effacer], if it arrives only by *erasing itself*, the erasure will have taken place, be it in ashes. *Il y a là cendre.*[10]

What I have just evoked seems to concern only the finite experience of finite works [*œuvres*]. But since the structure of the trace is *in general* the very possibility of an experience of finitude, the distinction between a finite cause and an infinite cause of the trace appears—let us venture to say—secondary here. The distinction is itself an effect of trace or difference, which does not mean that the trace or differance (I have tried to show elsewhere that differance is finite, insofar as it is infinite)[11] has a cause or origin.

Thus, the moment that the question "How to avoid speaking?" arises, it is already too late. It was no longer a question of not speaking. Language has begun without us, in us, before us. This is what theology calls God, and it is necessary, it will have been necessary, to speak. This "it is necessary" is *at once* the trace of an undeniable necessity (which is another way of saying that one cannot avoid denying it: one can only deny it) *and* of a past injunction. Always already past, hence without a past present. It was indeed necessary to be able to speak in order to allow the question "How to avoid speaking?" to come about. Having come from the past, a language before language, a past that was never present and remains thus immemorial, this "it is necessary" seems then to signal the event of an order or a promise that does not belong to what is commonly called history, the discourse of history or the history of discourse. Order or promise, this injunction commits (me), in a way that is rigorously asymmetrical, even before I myself have been able to say *I*, and to sign—in order to reappropriate it for myself, to restore the symmetry—such a *provocation*. This in no way mitigates my responsibility, on the contrary. There would be no responsibility without this *forecoming* [prévenance] of the trace, and if autonomy were first or absolute. Autonomy itself would not be possible, nor would respect for the law (the sole "cause" of this respect) in the strictly Kantian sense of these words. To elude this responsibility, to deny it, to try to erase it by an absolute backward turn, I still or already have to countersign it. When Jeremiah curses the day he was born,[12] he must still or already *affirm*. Or rather, he must confirm, in a movement that is no more positive than negative, according to the words of Dionysius, for it does not belong to position (*thesis*) or to de-position (privation, subtraction, negation).

Why three stages? Why should I now proceed in three stages? I am certainly not intent on acquitting myself of some dialectical obligation. Despite some convincing appearances, what is at issue here is a thinking that is essentially alien to dialectic, even if Christian negative theologies owe much to the Platonic or Neoplatonic dialectic, and even if it is difficult to read Hegel without taking account of an apophatic tradition that was not foreign to him (at least through the mediation of Bruno, thus of Nicholas of Cusa and of Meister Eckhart, etc.).

The three "moments [*temps*]" or the three "signs" that I will now connect, as if in a fabulous narrative, do not form the moments or signs of a history. They will not reveal the order of a teleology. Rather they involve deconstructive questions on the subject of such a teleology.

Three stages or, in any case, three places to avoid speaking of a question that I will be unable to discuss, so as to deny it in some way, or so as to speak of it without speaking of it, in a negative mode: what of negative theology and its ghosts in a tradition of thought that is neither Greek nor Christian? In other words, what of Jewish and Arab thought in this regard?[13] For example—and in everything I will say—a certain void, the place of an internal desert, will perhaps allow this question to resonate. The three paradigms, which I will situate very quickly (and a paradigm is often a model of construction), will surround a resonating space about which nothing, or almost nothing, will ever be said.

A. The first paradigm is Greek. I will quickly give it names, proper or not: Plato and the Neoplatonisms, the *epekeina tēs ousias* of the *Republic*, and the *khōra* of the *Timaeus*. In the *Republic*, the movement that leads *epekeina tēs ousias*, beyond Being (or beyond beings, a serious question of translation on which I cannot dwell here), no doubt inaugurates an immense tradition. One may follow its pathways, detours, and overdeterminations until arriving at what in a moment will be the second paradigm, the Christian apophases, and those of Dionysius in particular. Much has been written about this filiation and its limits; this is not my aim here. In the few minutes that I have at my disposal, since it cannot be a question of indulging in a micrological study, or even of summarizing what I am attempting to do elsewhere, at this moment, in seminars or texts in preparation, I will content myself with a few schematic traits. I choose them from the perspective that is ours here, that of the question "How to avoid speaking?" as I have started to define it: the question of place as place of writing, of inscription, of the trace. For lack of time, I will have to streamline my remarks: neither long quotations nor "secondary" literature. But this will not, as we will see, render the hypothesis of a "naked" text any less problematic.

In the Platonic text and in the tradition it marks, it seems to me that one should distinguish between *two* movements or *two* tropics of negativity. These two structures are radically heterogeneous.

1. One of them finds both its rule and its example in the *Republic* (509b et seq.). The idea of the Good (*idea tou agathou*) has its place beyond being or essence. Thus the Good is not, nor is its place. But this not-being is not a nonbeing; it stands, so to speak, beyond presence or essence, *epekeina tēs ousias*, beyond the beingness of Being [*l'étantité de l'être*]. From beyond the presence of all that is, the Good gives birth to being or to the essence of what is, *to einai* and *tēn ousian*, but without itself being. Whence the homology between the Good and the sun, between the intelligible sun and the sensible sun. The former gives to beings their visibility, their genesis (growth and nourishment). But it is not itself becoming; it is not visible, and it does not belong to the order of what proceeds from it, either according to knowledge or according to being.

Without being able to enter into the readings that this immense text demands and has already provoked, I will note two points that matter to me in this context.

On the one hand, whatever may be the discontinuity marked by this beyond (*epekeina*) in relation to being, in relation to the Being of being or to beingness [*étantité*] (three distinct hypotheses nonetheless), this singular limit does not give rise [*lieu*] to determinations that are simply neutral or negative but to a *hyperbolization* of that beyond which the Good gives one to think, to know, and to be. Negativity serves the *hyper* movement that produces, attracts, or guides it. To be sure, the Good is not, in the sense that it is not Being or a being, and every ontological grammar must take on a negative form as regards it. But this negative form is not neutral. It does not oscillate between the *neither this–nor that.* First of all, it obeys the logic of the *super,* of the *hyper,* that heralds all the superessentialisms of Christian apophases and all the debates that develop around them (for example, the critique of Dionysius by St. Thomas, who reproaches him for having placed *Bonum* before or above *Ens* or *Esse* in the hierarchy of divine names). This maintains a sufficiently homogeneous, homologous, or analogous relation between Being and (what is) beyond Being, so that what exceeds the limit can be compared to Being, albeit through the figure of hyperbole; but most of all, so that what is or is known *owes* its being and its being-known to this Good. This analogical continuity allows for translation; it allows one to compare the Good to the intelligible sun, and the latter to the visible sun. The excess of this Good that (is) *hyperekhon,* is situated by its transcendence at the origin of being and knowledge. It allows one to *give an account,* to speak both of what is and of what the Good is. Knowable things draw from the Good not only the faculty of being known, but also being (*einai*), existence or essence (*ousia*), even if the Good does not belong to *ousia* (*ouk ousias ontos tou agathou*) but to something that far surpasses (*hyperekhontos*) being in dignity, antiquity (*presbeia*), and power (*all'eti epekeina tēs ousias presbeiai kai dynamei hyperekhontos* [*Republic* 509b]). The excellence is not so foreign to being or to light that the excess itself cannot be described in the terms of what it exceeds. When, a little earlier, an allusion is made to a third kind [*genre*] (*triton genos*) that seems to disorient the discourse, because it would be neither the visible nor sight—or vision—it is precisely a matter of light (507e), itself produced by the sun, and offspring of the Good (*ton tou agathou ekgonon*) that the Good has engendered as its own likeness (*hon tagathon egennēsen analogon* [508b–c]). This analogy between the visible sun and the intelligible sun allows one to have confidence in the resemblance between the Good (*epekeina tēs ousias*) and that to which it gives birth, being and knowledge. The negative discourse regarding what stands beyond Being, and apparently no longer tolerates ontological predicates, does not interrupt this analogical continuity. In truth, it presupposes it; it even lets itself be guided by it. Ontology remains possible and necessary. The effects of this analogical continuity can be perceived in the rhetoric, the grammar, and the logic of all discourses on the Good and the beyond Being.

On the other hand, immediately following the passage on what (*is*) *epekeina tēs ousias* and *hyperekhon*, Glaucon addresses himself or pretends to address himself to God, to the god of the sun, Apollo: "By Apollo, what divine hyperbole [*daimonias hyperbolēs*: what daemonic or supernatural excess]!" We should not give too much weight to this invocation or this address to God when speaking of that which exceeds Being. It seems to be made lightly, in a somewhat humorous manner (*geloiōs*), as if to punctuate the scene with a breath. I note it for reasons that will become clear in a moment, when the necessity for every apophatic theology to begin with an address to God becomes something quite other than dramatic rhetoric: it will have the seriousness of a prayer.

Why have I just pointed out the allusion to "third kind" that is destined to play a role of analogical mediation, the role of light between sight and the visible? Because in the *Sophist* (243b), this schema of the *third* also concerns being. Of all the pairs of opposites, one may say that each term *is*. The being (*einai*) of this *is* figures as a third that is beyond the two others (*triton para ta duo ekeina*). It is indispensable to the interweaving (*symplokē*) or to the dialectical intercrossing of the forms or the ideas in a *logos* capable of taking in the other. After having raised the question of nonbeing, which would in itself be unthinkable (*adianoēton*), ineffable (*arrhēton*), unpronounceable (*aphtenkton*), foreign to discourse and to reason (*alogon*) (238c), one comes to the presentation of the dialectic itself. Passing by way of parricide and the murder of Parmenides, this dialectic admits the thinking of nonbeing as *other* and not as absolute nothingness or the simple opposite of being (256b, 259c). This to confirm that there cannot be an absolutely negative discourse: a *logos* necessarily speaks of something; it cannot avoid speaking of something; it is impossible for it to refer to nothing (*logon anankaion, hotanper ēi, tinos einai logon, mē de tinos adunaton* [262e]).

2. I will distinguish the tropic of negativity, which I have just outlined very schematically, from another tropic, also in Plato's works, another way of treating the beyond (*epekeina*) of the limit, the third kind and place. This place is here called *khōra*; I am, of course, alluding to the *Timaeus*. When I say that this can be found "in Plato's works," I leave aside, for lack of time, the question of knowing whether or not it belongs within the Platonic text, and what "within" means here. These are questions that I will discuss at length elsewhere in a forthcoming text. From this work in progress,[14] I will permit myself to lift a few of the elements that are

indispensable in the formulation of a hypothesis that relates to the present context.

Khōra also constitutes a third kind (*triton genos* [*Timaeus* 48e, 49a, 52a]). This place is not the intelligible model that inspires the demiurge. Nor does it belong to the order of copies or sensible mimemes that it impresses in the *khōra*. It is difficult to speak of this absolutely necessary place, this place "in which" the mimemes of the eternal beings originate by imprinting themselves (*typōthenta*) on it, this impression-bearer (*ekmageion*) of all types and schemas. It is difficult to adapt a true or firm *logos* to it. We glimpse it only "when we dream" and one can only describe it by a "bastard reasoning" (*logismōi tini nothōi*). This spacing neither dies nor is it ever born (52b). Its "eternity" is not, however, that of the intelligible models. At the moment, so to speak, when the demiurge organizes the cosmos by cutting, introducing, and impressing the images of the models "in" the *khōra*, the latter must already have been there, as the "there" itself, outside of time or in any case outside of becoming, in an outside-time without common measure with the eternity of ideas and the becoming of sensible things. How does Plato deal with this disproportion and heterogeneity? There are, it seems to me, *two concurrent languages* in these pages of the *Timaeus*.

Indeed, one of these languages multiplies the negations, the warnings, the evasions, the detours, the tropes, but *with a view* to reappropriating the thinking of the *khōra* for ontology and for the Platonic dialectic in its most dominant schemas. If the *khōra*, place, spacing, recipient (*hypodokhē*) is neither sensible nor intelligible, it seems to *participate* in the intelligible in an enigmatic way (51a). Since it is "all-receptive," it makes possible the formation of the cosmos. As it is neither this nor that (neither intelligible nor sensible), one may speak *as if* it were a mixed participant in both. *Neither-nor* easily becomes *both*, both this and that. Whence the rhetoric of the passage, the multiplication of figures that are traditionally read as metaphors: gold, mother, wet nurse, sieve, recipient, molding stuff, and so on. Aristotle provided the matrix for many of the readings of the *Timaeus*, and since his *Physics* (bk. 4), one has always interpreted this passage on the *khōra within* philosophy, in a consistently anachronistic way, as if it prefigured, on the one hand, the philosophies of space as *extensio* (Descartes) or as pure sensible form (Kant); or on the other hand, the materialist philosophies of a substratum or substance that stands, like the *hypodokhē*, beneath the qualities or the phenomena. These readings, the wealth and complexity of which cannot be touched on here, are still possible and, up to a certain point, justifiable. As for their anachronistic character, it seems to me not only obvious but structurally inevitable. The *khōra* is the very anachrony of spacing; it anachronizes, it calls forth anachrony, provokes it without fail from the pretemporal *already* that gives rise [*lieu*] to every inscription. But this is another story that we cannot get into here.

The other language and the other interpretive decision interest me more, without ceasing to be anachronistic in their own way. The synchrony of a reading does not have a chance here and would no doubt miss the very thing it claims to fit. This other gesture would inscribe an irreducible spacing within (but therefore also outside, once the inside is placed outside) Platonism, or even within ontology, dialectics, and perhaps philosophy in general. Under the name of *khōra*, the place belongs neither to the sensible nor to the intelligible, neither to becoming nor to nonbeing (the *khōra* is never described as a void), nor to being: according to Plato, the quantity or the quality of being are measured against its intelligibility. All the aporias, which Plato does not dissimulate, would signify that there *is there* [*il* y a là] something that is neither a being nor a nothingness; something that no dialectic, participationist schema, or analogy would allow one to rearticulate with any philosopheme whatsoever: neither "in" Plato's works nor in the history that Platonism inaugurates and dominates. The *neither-nor* can no longer be reconverted into *both-and.* Hence the so-called metaphors are not only inadequate, in that they borrow from the sensible forms inscribed in the *khōra* figures that are without pertinence for designating the *khōra* itself, they are also no longer metaphors. Like all the rhetoric that forms its systematic network, the concept of metaphor stems from this Platonic metaphysics, from the distinction between the sensible and the intelligible, and from the dialectic and analogicism that we inherit along with it. When the interpreters of Plato discuss these metaphors, whatever the complexity of their debates and analyses may be, we never see them question the concept of metaphor itself.[15]

But to say that Plato does not use metaphor or sensible figures to designate the place does not imply that he speaks properly of the literal [*propre*] and properly intelligible meaning of *khōra*. The value of receptivity or of the receptacle that forms the elementary invariant of this determination seems to me to stand beyond this opposition between figurative meaning and literal meaning. The spacing of *khōra* introduces a dissociation or a differance in the literal meaning that it makes possible, thus forcing one to take tropic detours that are no longer rhetorical figures. The typography and the tropic to which the *khōra* gives rise [*lieu*], *without giving anything*, are moreover explicitly marked in the *Timaeus* (50b–c). Plato says this in his way: it is necessary to avoid speaking of *khōra* as "something" that is or is not, that would be present or absent, intelligible, sensible, or both at once, active or passive, Good (*epekeina tēs ousias*) or Evil, God or man, living or nonliving. Every theomorphic or anthropomorphic schema should thus be avoided. If the *khōra* receives everything, it does not do this in the manner of a medium [*milieu*] or a container, or even a receptacle, because the receptacle is still a figure inscribed in it. It is not an intelligible extension, in the Cartesian sense, a receptive subject, in the Kantian sense of *intuitus derivativus*, or a pure sensible space as a form of receptivity. Radically anhuman and atheological, one cannot even say that it *gives* place or that there *is* [*il* y a] the *khōra*. The *es gibt*, thus translated, still announces or recalls too much the dispensation of God, of man, or even that of Being of which certain of Heidegger's texts speak (*es gibt Sein*). *Khōra* is not even the *ça*, the *es* of the giving [*le donner*] before all subjectivity. It does not give rise [*lieu*] as one would give something, whatever it might be; it does not create or produce anything, not even an event insofar as the event takes place. It gives no order and makes no promise. It is radically ahistorical, because nothing happens through it and nothing happens to it. Plato insists on its necessary indifference: to receive all things and let itself be marked or affected by what is inscribed in it, the *khōra* must remain without form and without proper determination. But if it is amorphous (*amorphon* [50d]), this signifies neither lack nor privation. Nothing negative and nothing positive. *Khōra* is impassive, but it is neither passive nor active.

How to speak of it? How not to speak of it? A singularity that interests us in this context, the impossibility of speaking of it and of giving it a proper name, far from reducing one to silence, still dictates an obligation, because of or in spite of this very impossibility: *it is necessary* to speak of it and there is a rule for this. What is it? If one wishes to respect the absolute singularity of the *khōra* (there is only one *khōra*, even if it can be the pure multiplicity of places), *it is necessary always to refer to it in the same way.* Not to give it the same name, as one French translation suggests, but to call it, to address oneself to it, in the same way (*tauton autēn aei prosrēteon* [50b]). This is not a question of a proper name, but rather of appellation, a way of addressing oneself. *Prosērō*: I address myself, I address my speech to someone, and sometimes: I adore the divinity; *prosrēma* is the speech addressed to someone; *prosrēsis* is the salutation that calls. One will respect the absolute uniqueness of the *khōra* by always calling it in the same way—and this is not limited to the noun or the name, a sentence is necessary. To obey this injunction without order or promise, an injunction that has always already taken place, one must think that which—standing beyond all given philosophemes—will have nevertheless left a trace in language, for example, the word *khōra* in the Greek language, insofar as it is caught up in the network of its usual meanings. Plato had no other. Along with the word, there are also grammatical, rhetorical, logical, and hence also philosophical possibilities. However insufficient they may be, they are given, already marked by this unheard-of trace, promised to the trace that has promised nothing. This trace and this promise are always inscribed in the body of a language, in its lexicon and its syntax, but one must be able to rediscover the trace, still unique, in other languages, in other bodies, in other negativities as well.

B. The question now becomes the following: what happens between, *on the one hand*, an "experience" such as this one, the experience of the *khōra* that is above all not an experience, if what one understands by this word is a certain relation to presence, whether sensible or intelligible, or even a relation to the presence of the present in general, and, *on the other hand*, what one calls the *via negativa* in its Christian moment?

The passage by way of negativity of the discourse on the *khōra* is neither a last word nor a mediation in the service of a dialectic, an elevation toward a positive or true meaning, a Good or a God. It is not a matter here of negative theology; there is reference to neither an event nor a gift, nor an order, nor a promise, even if, as I have just underlined, the absence of promise or order, the barren, radically anhuman and atheological nature of this "place" obliges us to speak and to refer to it in a certain unique way, as to the wholly other that would not even be transcendent, absolutely remote, nor immanent or close. Not that we are obliged to speak of it, but if, moved by a duty that does not come from it, we think it and speak of it, then it is necessary to respect the singularity of this reference. Although it is nothing, this referent appears irreducible and irreducibly other: one cannot invent it. But since it remains foreign to the order of presence and absence, everything seems to suggest that it could only be invented in its very alterity, at the moment of address.

But this unique address is not a prayer, a celebration, or praise. It does not speak to You.

Above all, this "third kind" that the *khōra* would also be does not belong to a *group of three*. "Third kind" is *here* only a *philosophical* way of naming an *X* that is not included in a group, a family, a triad, or a trinity. Even when Plato likens it to a "mother" or to a "wet nurse," this always virginal *khōra* does not in truth form a couple with the "father" to whom Plato "likens" the model; the *khōra* does *not engender* the sensible forms that are inscribed in it, which Plato "likens" to a child (50d).

To ask what *happens* between this type of experience (or the experience of the *typos*) and the Christian apophases is not necessarily or solely to think of histories, of events, of influences. Indeed, the question that arises here concerns historicity or eventness [*événementialité*], that is, significations foreign to the *khōra*. Even if one wanted to describe "what happens" in terms of structures and relations, it would be necessary to recognize that what happens between the two is, perhaps, precisely the event of the event, history, the thinking of an essential "having-taken-place," of a revelation, of an order and a promise, of an anthropo-theologicalization that—despite the extreme rigor of the negative hyperbole—seems to take command once again, closer still to the *agathon* than to the *khōra*. And the trinitarian schema seems absolutely indispensable, for Dionysius, for example, to ensuring the passage or crossing between the discourses on the divine names, symbolic theology, and mystical theology. The affirmative theologemes celebrate God as the Good, the intelligible Light, even the Good "above all light" (God is the "authority of all illuminating power, being indeed the source of light and actually transcending light" [*DN* 4: 701a–b]). Even if this Good is called formless (like the *khōra*), this time it is what gives form: "Given that the Good transcends everything, as indeed it does, its nature, unconfined by form, is the creator of all form. In it is nonbeing really an excess of being. It is not a life, but is, rather, superabundant Life. . . . " (*DN* 4: 697a). This Good inspires an entire erotics, but Dionysius warns us: one must avoid using the word *erōs* without first clarifying the meaning, the intention. One must always start from the intentional meaning and not from the mere words (*DN* 4: 708b–c): "Let no one imagine that in giving status to the term 'yearning [*erōs*]' I am running counter to scripture. . . . Indeed some of our writers on sacred matters have thought the title 'yearning [*erōs*]' to be more divine than 'love [*agapē*].' The divine Ignatius writes: 'He for whom I yearn has been crucified'" (*DN* 4: 708c–709b). The holy theologians attribute the same value, the same power of unification and gathering, to *erōs* and to *agapē*, which the multitude has trouble comprehending because it assigns yearning to the body, to the division, to the partitioning (ibid.). In God, yearning is at once ecstatic, jealous, and subordinate (*DN* 4: 712a et seq.). This erotics leads and thus leads back to the Good, circularly, that is, toward what "is established far beyond and before simple being and non-being" (*DN* 4: 716d). As for Evil, it "is not among the things that have being nor is it among what is not being. It has a greater nonexistence and otherness from the Good than nonbeing has" (ibid.). What is the more of this less with regard to what is already without essence? Evil is even more without essence than the Good. One should draw out, if possible, all that follows from this singular axiomatic. This is not my aim at the moment.

Between the theological movement that speaks and is inspired by the Good beyond being or by the light and the apophatic path that exceeds the Good, there must be a passage, a transfer, a translation. An experience must still guide the apophasis toward excellence, not allow it to say just anything, and prevent it from manipulating its negations like empty and purely mechanical phrases. This experience is that of prayer. Here prayer is not a preamble, an accessory mode of access. It constitutes an essential moment, it regulates discursive asceticism, the passage through the desert of discourse, the apparent referential vacuity that avoids empty delirium and prattle only by beginning by addressing itself to the other, to you. But to you as "Trinity!! Higher than any being, any divinity."

I will distinguish at least two traits in the very numerous experiences and determinations of what is called prayer. I isolate them here, at the risk of neglecting all the rest, in order to clarify my remarks. 1. In every prayer there must be an address to the other as other, and I will say, at the risk of shocking you, *God, for example.* In the act of addressing oneself to the other as other one must, of course, pray, that is, ask, implore, summon. It does not matter what one is asking for; pure prayer asks only that the other hear the prayer, receive it, be present to it, be the other as such, gift, call, and the very cause of the prayer. This first trait characterizes a discourse (an act of language even if the prayer is silent) that, as such, is not predicative, theoretical (theo*logical*), or constative. 2. But I will distinguish this trait from another with which it is most often associated, in particular by Dionysius and his interpreters, namely, praise or celebration (*hymnein*). That the association of these two traits is essential for Dionysius does not signify that one trait is identical to the other, nor even in general indissociable from it. To be sure, neither prayer nor praise is an act of constative predication. Both have a performative dimension, the analysis of which would require long and difficult developments, especially as to the origin and validation of these performatives. I will restrict myself to one distinction: although prayer in itself, if one can say that, does not imply anything but the address asking the other—perhaps beyond request [*demande*] and gift—to give the promise of its presence as other, and finally the transcendence of its very alterity, without any other determination, praise, though not a simple attributive speech, nevertheless preserves an irreducible relation to attribution. As Urs von Balthasar rightly says, "When it is a question of God and the divine, the word *hymnein* nearly replaces the word 'to say.'"[16] Nearly, in fact, but not entirely, and how can one deny that praise qualifies God and *determines* prayer, *determines* the other, the One to whom it addresses itself, refers itself, invoking the other even *as* the source of prayer? And how can one deny that, in this movement of determination (which is no longer the pure address of the prayer to the other), the naming of the *trinitary* and superessential God distinguishes Dionysius's *Christian* prayer from all other prayer? To refuse this no doubt subtle distinction, inadmissible for Dionysius and perhaps for Christians in general, is to refuse the essential quality of prayer to every invocation that would not be Christian. As Jean-Luc Marion rightly remarks, praise is "neither true nor false, nor even contradictory" (192), although it says something *about* thearchy, about the Good and about analogy; and if its attributions or namings do not belong to the ordinary value of truth, but rather to a supertruth ruled by superessentiality, praise nonetheless does not merge with the movement of prayer itself, which does not speak *about* but *to*. Even if this address is immediately determined by the discourse of praise and if the prayer addresses itself to God by speaking (to him) about him, the apostrophe of prayer and the determination of praise are not the same but two different structures: "Trinity!! Higher than any being, any divinity. . . . Guide of Christians in the wisdom of heaven!" In a moment I will quote more extensively from this prayer, which opens *The Mystical Theology* and prepares the definition of apophatic theologemes. For "that is why we must begin with a prayer" (*eukhēs aparkhesthai khreōn* [*DN* 3: 680d]), says Dionysius. Why? To attain union with God no doubt; but to speak of this *union*, it is still necessary to speak of *places*, of height, of distance and proximity. Dionysius proposes to his addressee or the immediate dedicatee of his work, Timothy, to examine the name "Good," which expresses divinity, *after* having invoked the Trinity, that principle of Good that transcends all goods. One must pray in order to *approach* it as close as possible, that is, to raise oneself toward it—and receive from it the initiation of its gifts:

> [W]e should be uplifted to it and be shaped by it so as to learn of those good gifts which are gathered together around it. For the Trinity is present in all things, though all things are not present to it.
>
> But if we invoke it with prayers that are holy, with untroubled mind, with a suitability for union with God, then we are surely present to it. For the Trinity is not in any one location in such a manner as to be "away from" one place or moving "from one spot to another." Even to speak of it as "present in everything" is inaccurate since this does not convey the fact that it infinitely transcends everything and yet gathers everything within it. (*DN* 3: 680b)

By a series of analogies, Dionysius then explains that, in approaching and elevating ourselves thus, we do not traverse the distance that separates us from a place (since the residence of the Trinity is not local: it is "everywhere and yet nowhere"). What is more, the Trinity draws us toward it, while it remains immobile, like the height of the sky or the depths of the sea from which we would pull on a rope in order to draw near it, not bring it to us: "That is why we must begin with a prayer before everything we do, but especially when we are about to talk about God. We will not pull down to ourselves that power which is both everywhere and yet nowhere, but by divine reminders and invocations we may commend ourselves to it and be joined to it" (*DN* 3: 680d).

The principle of the good is beyond being, but it also transcends the good (*DN* 3: 680b). God is the good that transcends the good and the being that transcends being. This "logic" is also that of the "without" that I evoked earlier in the quotations from Meister Eckhart quoting St. Augustine ("God is wise *without wisdom*, good *without* goodness, powerful *without* power") or St. Bernard ("To love God is a manner *without* manner"). In the negativity without negativity of these utterances about a transcendence that is nothing other than (and wholly other from) what it transcends, we might recognize a principle of demultiplication of voices and discourses, of disappropriation and reappropriation of utterances, with the most distant appearing closest, and vice versa. A predicate can always conceal another predicate, or even the nakedness of an absence of predicate, the way the veil of a garment—sometimes indispensable—may both dissimulate and make visible the very thing that it dissimulates—and render it attractive at the same time. Hence the voice of an utterance can conceal another, which it then appears to quote without quoting it, presenting itself as another form, namely, as a quotation of the other. Whence the subtlety, but also the conflicts, the relations of force, even the aporias of a politics of doctrine, I mean the politics of initiation or teaching in general, and an institutional politics of interpretation. Meister Eckhart, for example (but what an example!) knew something about this. Not to mention the arguments he had to deploy against his inquisitorial judges ("They regard as error whatever they fail to understand"), the strategy of his sermons put to work a multiplicity of voices and of veils that he superimposed or removed like peels [*pelures*] or furs [*pelages*], thematizing and exploring a quasi-metaphor to the point of extreme bareness; and one is never sure whether this bareness allows one to see the nakedness of God or to hear the voice of Meister Eckhart himself. "Quasi stella matutina," which gave the Cologne judges so many excuses, stages the drama of twenty-four philosophers (*Liber 24 philosophorum* of Pseudo–Hermes Trismegistus) who have come together to speak of God. Eckhart chooses one of their assertions: "God is something that is of necessity above being [*got etwaz ist, daz von nôt über wesene sîn muoz*]" (*Q* 142; 256). Speaking thus of what one of his masters says, he *comments* in a voice that no longer permits one to decide whether it is or is not his own. And in the same movement, he cites other masters, Christians or pagans, great or subordinate masters (*kleine meister*). One of them seems to say, "God is neither being nor goodness [*Got enist niht wesen noch güete*]. Goodness adheres to being and is not more extensive [*breiter*]. If there were no being, neither would there be goodness. Yet being is purer than goodness. God is neither good nor better nor best of all. Whoever would say that God is good would be treating him as injustly as though he were calling the sun black" (*Q* 148; 257). (The Bull of Condemnation mentions this passage only in an appendix, without concluding that Eckhart truly taught it.) The theory of archetypes that forms the context of this argument attenuates its provocative character: God does not share any of the modes of being with other beings (divided into ten categories by these masters), but "neither does he lack any of them [*er entbirt ir ouch keiner*]" (*Q* 148; 257).

But here is what "a pagan master" says: the soul that loves God "perceives him under the coat of goodness [*nimet in under dem velle der güete*]," but reason or rationality (*Vernünfticheit*) pulls off this coat and grasps God bare (*in blôz*). Then he is undressed (*entkleidet*), stripped "of goodness and of being and of all names" (*Q* 152; 258). Eckhart does not contradict the pagan master; nor does he agree with him. He remarks that, unlike the "holy masters," the pagan speaks in accordance with "natural light." Then, in a voice that appears to be his own, he differentiates—I dare not say that he dialectizes—the preceding statement. In the lines I am preparing to quote, a certain value of unveiling, of laying bare, of truth as what is beyond clothing appears to orient, at the end of ends and in the final analysis, the entire axiomatic of this apophasis. One cannot, of course, speak rigorously here of value and axiomatic, given that what orders and rules the apophatic procedure precisely exceeds the good or goodness. But there is indeed a rule or a law: one must go beyond the veil or the clothing. Is it arbitrary still to call this unveiling truth or supertruth, an unveiling that is perhaps no longer an unveiling of being? Or light, that is no longer the clearing of being? I don't think so. Consider the following:

> I said in a lecture that the intellect [*vernünfticheit*] is nobler than the will, and yet they both belong in this light. A professor in another school said that the will was nobler than the intellect because the will grasps things as they are in themselves, while the intellect grasps things as they are in it. This is true. An eye is nobler in itself than an eye that is painted on a wall. Nevertheless, I say that the understanding is nobler than will. The will perceives God in the garment [*under dem kleide*] of goodness. The understanding perceives God bare, as he is stripped of goodness and being [*Vernünfticheit nimet got blôz, als er entkleidet ist von güete and von wesene*]. Goodness is a garment [*kleit*] by which God is hidden, and the will perceives God in this garment of goodness. If there were no goodness in God, my will would want nothing of him. (*Q* 152–53; 258)

Light and truth, these are Meister Eckhart's words. "Quasi stella matutina" is this as well, and it is also a topology (height and proximity) of our relation to God. Like the adverb *quasi*, we are *beside* the verb that is the truth:

> "As [*als*] the morning star through the mist." I would now like to focus on the little word *quasi* which means "as" [*als*]. Children in school call this

an adverb [*ein bîwort*]. This is what I focus on in all my sermons. What one can most properly [*eigenlîcheste*] say about God [these last words are omitted in the French translation] is that he is word and truth [*wort and wârheit*]. God called himself a word [*ein wort*]. St. John said: "In the beginning was the Word" (Jn. 1:1). He means that one should be an ad-verb to the Word [*wort*]. The planet Venus [*der vrîe sterne*], after which Friday [*vrîtac*] is named, has many names. . . . In contrast to the other stars it is always equally near the sun. It never departs farther from, nor approaches nearer to [*niemer verrer noch naeher*], the sun. It stands for [*meinet*] a man who wants always to be near to and present [*gegenwertic*] to God in such a way that nothing can separate him from God, neither happiness nor unhappiness, nor any creature. . . . The more the soul is raised [*erhaben*] above earthly things, the more powerful [*kreftiger*] it is. Whoever knows but one creature would not need to ponder any sermon, for every creature is full of God and is a book [*buoch*]. (Q 154–56; 259)

In its pedagogical necessity and initiatory virtue, the sermon supplements, not so much the Word, which has no need for it, as the inability to read the authentic "book" that we are, as creatures, and the adverbiality we should be as a result. This supplement of adverbiality, the sermon, must fulfill and orient itself (as one orients oneself by the morning star) by prayer or the invocation of the trinitary God. This is both the orient and end of the sermon: "the soul should be an ad-verb and work one work with God [*mit gote würken ein werk*] in order to receive its happiness in the same inwardly hovering knowledge where God is happy. That we may be forever an ad-verb to this Word, for this may we receive the help of the Father and the same Word and the Holy Spirit. Amen" (Q 158; 260).

This is the end of the Sermon; the prayer does not directly address itself, in the form of apostrophe, to God himself. However, at the opening and from the very first words of *The Mystical Theology*, Dionysius addresses himself directly to You, to God, already determined as "Trinity!! Higher than any being" in the prayer that prepares the theologemes of the *via negativa*:

Trinity!! Higher than any being [*Trias hyperousie*], any divinity [*hyperthee*], any goodness [*hyperagathē*]! Guide of Christians in the wisdom of heaven [*theosophias*]! Lead us up beyond unknowning and light, up to the farthest, highest peak of mystic scripture, where the mysteries of God's Word lie simple, absolute and unchangeable in the brilliant darkness of a hidden silence. Amid the deepest shadow they pour overwhelming light on what is most manifest.

Amid the wholly unsensed and unseen they completely fill our sightless minds
[*tous anommatous noas*] with treasures beyond all beauty.

For this I pray; and, Timothy, my friend . . . look for a sight of the mysterious things. (*MT* 1: 998a)

What is happening here?

After having prayed (he writes, we read), he presents his prayer. He
quotes it and I have just quoted his quotation. He quotes it in what is
properly an *apostrophe* to its addressee, Timothy. *The Mystical Theology* is
dedicated to him; in order to initiate him, it must *lead* him on the paths
to which Dionysius himself has prayed to God to lead him, or more literally to *direct* him in a straight (*ithunon*) line. A ped*agogy*, thus, that is
also a myst*agogy* and a psych*agogy*: the gesture of leading or directing the
psychē of the other passes here through apostrophe. The one who asks to
be led by God turns for an instant to another addressee, in order to lead
him in turn. He does not simply turn away from his first addressee, who
is *in truth* the first Cause of his prayer and who already guides it. It is in
fact because he does not turn away from God that he can turn toward
Timothy and *pass from one address to the other without changing direction*.

The writing of Dionysius—which at present we believe we are reading
or are reading in order to believe—stands in the spacing of the *apostrophe*
that *turns* the discourse *away* in the *same* direction, between the prayer
itself, the quotation of the prayer, and the address to the disciple, in other
words, the best reader, to the reader who should let himself be led to
become better, to us who at present believe we are reading this text. Not
to us such as we are, at present, but such as we should be, in our souls,
if we read this text as it should be read, rightly, in the proper direction,
correctly: according to its prayer and its promise. It also beseeches us to
read correctly, according to its prayer. And none of this would be possible
without the possibility of quotation (of iteration more generally)—and
of an apostrophe that allows one to speak to several people at once. To
more than one other. Thus the prayer, the quotation of the prayer, and
the apostrophe, from one you to the other, are all weaving the *same* text,
however heterogeneous they may appear. There is text because there is
this iteration.[17] Where then does this text take place? Does it have a place,
at present? And why can't one separate there the prayer, the quotation of
the prayer, and the address to the reader?

The identity of *this* place, and thus of *this* text, and of *its* reader, is instituted from the future of what is promised by the promise. The coming of this future [*la venue de cet avenir*] has a provenance, it is the event of this promise. Unlike what seemed to happen in the "experience" of the place called *khōra*, the apophasis puts itself in motion, it *initiates itself*, in the sense of initiative and initiation, from the event of a revelation that is also a promise. The latter belongs to a history; or rather, it opens a history and an anthropo-theological dimension. The hyphen [*trait d*'union] unites the new writings, which are adjoined to the "divinely anointed scriptures themselves" (*DN* 3: 681b); it marks the very place of this adjunction. This place is itself assigned by the event of the promise and the revelation of scripture. It is this place only from what will have taken place—according to the time and history of this future perfect. The place is an event. Under what conditions does one find oneself in Jerusalem, we asked earlier, and where is the place thus named? How can one measure the distance that separates us from it or draws us closer to it? Here is the answer of Dionysius, who cites scripture in *The Ecclesiastical Hierarchy*: "Do not depart from Jerusalem but wait for the promise of the Father which you heard from me . . . you shall be baptized with the Holy Spirit" (*EH* 512c). Situation of this speech that situates a place: he who transmitted the promise (Jesus, "divine founder of our own hierarchy") speaks of Jerusalem as the place that takes place from the event of the promise. But the place thus revealed remains the place of waiting [*le lieu de l'attente*], waiting for the fulfillment of the promise. Then it will take place fully. It will be fully a place.

Thus an event prescribes to us the good and right apophasis: how to avoid speaking. This prescription is at once a revelation and a teaching of the Holy Scripture, the architext before all supplementary "adjunction":

> [*W*]e must not dare to apply words or conceptions [*ou tolmēteon eipein, oute mēn ennoēsai*] to this hidden trancendent God. We can use only what scripture has disclosed [*para ta theoeidōs hēmin ek tōn hierōn logiōn ekpephasmena*]. In the scriptures the Deity has itself benevolently taught us what belonged to his Goodness. (*DN* 1: 588c; my emphasis—JD)

This superessential goodness is not entirely incommunicable; it can manifest *itself*, but it remains separated by its superessentiality. As for those theologians who have "celebrated" its inaccessibility and penetrated the "hidden depths of [its] infinity," they have left no "trace" (*ikhnous*).

A *secret manifestation*, then, if such a thing is possible. Even before demanding the extreme negativity of the apophasis, this manifestation is communicated to us as a "secret gift" by our inspired leaders. We learn thus to decipher symbols, we grasp how the love of God toward humanity "cover[s] the truths of the mind with things derived from the realm of the senses. And so it is that the Superessential is clothed in terms of being, with shape and form on things which have neither, and numerous symbols are employed to convey the varied attributes of what is an imageless and supra-natural" (*DN* 1: 592b). In short, we learn to read, to decipher the rhetoric without rhetoric of God—and finally to be silent.

Among all of these figures of the unfigurable, there is *here* [*il y a* là] the figure of the seal. This is not one figure among others; it figures the figuration of the unfigurable itself, and the discourse on the imprint seems to displace the Platonic typography of the *khōra*. The latter gave rise to inscriptions, to *typoi*, for the imitations of models. Here the figure of the seal, which also seals a promise, is valid for the entire text of creation. It carries over a Platonic argument, one of the two schemas that I tried to distinguish earlier, into another order. God is both participable and nonparticipable. The text of creation would be like the typographic inscription of the nonparticipable in the participable:

> It is rather like the case of the circle. The center point of the circle is shared by the surrounding radii. Or take the example of a seal. There are numerous impressions [*ektypōmata*] of the seal [*sphragidos*] and these all have a share in the original prototype; it is the same whole seal in each of the impressions and none participates in only a part.
>
> However, the nonparticipation [*amethexia*] of the all-creative Godhead rises far beyond all these figures [*paradeigmata*]. (*DN* 2: 644a–b)

For unlike what happens with the seal, here there is no contact, no community, no synthesis. The next part of the demonstration recalls again, while displacing it, the need for the *khōra* to be formless and virginal. Otherwise it could not lend itself to the writing of the imprints in it:

> Maybe someone will say that the seal is not totally identical in all the reproductions of it [*en holois tois ekmageiois*]. My answer is that this is not because of the seal itself, which gives itself completely and identically to each. The substances which receive a share of the seal are different. Hence the impressions of the one entire identical archetype [*arkhetypias*] are different. (*DN* 2: 644b)

Thus everything will depend on the material or the wax (*kēros*) that receives the imprint. It must be receptive, soft, easily shaped, smooth, and virginal, so that the imprint will be pure, clear, and long-lasting (*DN* 2: 644b).

If we recall that the *khōra* was also described as a receptacle (*dekhomenon*), we can follow another displacement of this figure, the figure of figures, the place of other figures. Henceforth the "receptacle" is both *psychical* and *created*. It was neither in Plato. Later, St. Augustine once again provides the mediation, and Meister Eckhart cites him in his sermon "Renovamini spiritu": "Augustine says that in the highest part of the soul, which he calls *mens* or *gemüte*, God created together with the soul's being, a power [*craft*], which the authorities call a store [*sloz*] or a coffer [*schrin*] of spiritual forms or formal images."[18] The creation of the place, which is also a power, grounds the resemblance of the soul with the Father. But beyond the Trinity, if one can say this, beyond the multiplicity of images, beyond the created place, the *impassivity without form* that the *Timaeus* attributed, if one can still say this, to the *khōra*, is here found to suit God alone: "if all the images are detached from the soul, and it contemplates only the Simple One [*das einig ein*], then the soul's naked being finds the naked, formless being [*das blose formlose wesen*] of the divine unity, which is there a being over being, accepting and reposing in itself [*ein uberwesende wesen, lidende ligende in ime selben*]" (*MEP* 3: 437–38; 206). This impassivity of the formless is the unique and wondrous source of our emotion [*passibilité*], of our passion, of our noblest suffering. We can suffer only God, then, and nothing other than him: "Ah! marvel of marvels [*wunder uber wunder*], how noble is that acceptance, when the soul's being can accept nothing else than the naked unity of God!" (ibid.).

Named in this way, "God is nameless [*namloz*]," and "no one can say anything or understand anything about him." Of this "transcending being [*uber swebende wesen*]" who is also a "transcending nothingness [*ein uber wesende nitheit*]" (*MEP* 3: 441–42; 207), one must avoid speaking. Eckhart lets St. Augustine speak: "The best that one can say about God is for one to keep silent [*swigen*] out of the wisdom of one's inward [divine] riches." Eckhart adds: "So be silent" (*MEP* 3:442; 207). Otherwise you lie and sin. This duty is a duty of love; the apostrophe commands love, but it speaks out of love and implores the aid of God in a prayer: "You should love him as he is a non-God, a nonspirit, a nonperson, a nonimage, but as he is a pure, unmixed, bright 'One,' separated from all duality; and in that One we should eternally sink down, out of 'something' into 'noth-ing.' May God help us to that. Amen" (*MEP* 3:448; 208).

To speak so as to order one not to speak, to say what God is not and that he *is* a non-God. How is one to hear the copula of being that articu-lates this singular speech and this order to be silent? Where does it have its place? Where does it take place? It is the place, the place of this writ-ing, this trace (left in being) of what is not, and the writing of this place. This place is only a place of passage, and more precisely, a threshold. But a threshold, this time, to give access to what is no longer a place. A sub-ordination, a relativization of place, with an extraordinary consequence: place is being. What finds itself reduced to the condition of threshold is being itself, being as place. Only a threshold, but a sacred place, the an-techamber [*parvis*] of the temple: "When we grasp God in being, we ap-prehend him in his antechamber [*vorbürge*], for being is the antechamber in which he dwells [*wonet*]. Where is he then in his temple, in which he shines as holy [*heilic*]? Intellect [*vernünfticheit*: rationality] is the temple of God" (*Q* 150; 257).

The soul, which exercises its power in the eye, allows one to see what is not, what is not present; it "works in nonbeing and so follows God who works in nonbeing." Guided by this *psychē*, the eye thus passes the thresh-old of being toward nonbeing in order to see what does not present itself. Eckhart compares the eye to a sieve. Things must be "sifted [*gebiutelt*]." This sieve is not one figure among others; it tells the difference between being and nonbeing, it discerns this difference, it allows one to see it, but as the eye itself. There is no text, above all no sermon, no preaching [*prédication*] is possible, without the invention of such a filter.

C. I had therefore decided *not to speak* of negativity or apophatic move-ments in the Jewish or Arab traditions. For example. To leave this im-mense place empty, and above everything that might connect the name of God with the name of the Place, to remain thus on the threshold—is this not the most consistent apophasis possible? What one cannot speak of, is it not best to pass it over in silence? I will let you answer this question. It is always entrusted to the other.

My first paradigm was Greek, the second was Christian, without yet ceasing to be Greek. The last will be neither Greek nor Christian. Were I not afraid of trying your patience, I would remind you of what in Hei-degger's thought might resemble the most questioning legacy, both the boldest and most liberated repetition of the traditions I have just evoked. I will have to limit myself to a few reference points here.

One could read *What Is Metaphysics?* as a treatise on negativity.[19] It grounds negative discourse and negation in the experience of the nothing that itself nihilates (*das Nichts selbst nichtet*). The experience of anxiety puts us in relation to a nihilation (*Nichtung*) that is neither an annihilation (*Vernichtung*) nor a negation or a denial (*Verneinung*). It reveals to us the strangeness (*Befremdlichkeit*) of what is (being, *das Seiende*) as what is wholly other (*das schlechthin Andere*). It thus opens up the possibility of the question of Being for *Dasein* whose structure is characterized precisely by what Heidegger then calls transcendence. This transcendence, "Vom Wesen des Grundes" says, is "specifically expressed [*eigens ausgesprochen*]" by the Platonic expression *epekeina tēs ousias*. Without being able to engage in the interpretation of the *agathon* that is then proposed by Heidegger, I just wanted to mark this passage beyond Being, or rather beyond beings, and the reinterpretation of negativity that accompanies it. Heidegger immediately specifies that Plato could not elaborate the original content of *epekeina tēs ousias* as the transcendence of *Dasein* ("der ursprüngliche Gehalt des *epekeina* als Transzendenz des Daseins"). He makes an analogous gesture with regard to the *khōra*: in the *Einführung in die Metaphysik*, a brief parenthesis suggests that Plato fell short of thinking the place (*Ort*), a thinking that nonetheless suggested itself to him. Plato would, in truth, have only prepared (*vorbereitet*) the way for the Cartesian interpretation of space as *extensio* (*Ausdehnung*).[20] Elsewhere I have tried to show what is problematic and reductive about this perspective. Seventeen years later, the last page of *Was heisst Denken?* again mentions *khōra* and *khōrismos*, without any explicit reference to the *Timaeus*. Plato, who is supposed to have given the most decisive *Deutung* for Western thought, situates the *khōrismos*, the interval or separation, the spacing, between beings and Being. And yet "[*hē khōra*] heisst der Ort," "[*hē khōra*] is the *locus*, the site, place." For Plato, beings and Being are thus "differently located [*verschieden geortet*]." "Thus when Plato gives thought to the different location [*die verschiedene Ortung*] of beings and Being, he is asking for the wholly other place [*nach dem ganz anderen Ort*] of Being, as against the place of beings."[21] That Plato is afterward suspected of having fallen short of this wholly other place, and that one must lead the difference (*Verschiedenheit*) of places back to the distinction (*Unterschied*) and the fold of a duality (*Zwiefalt*) that must be given beforehand so that it does not receive "specific attention"—this is a movement I cannot follow either at the end of *Was heisst Denken?* or elsewhere. I merely underscore this movement toward a *wholly other* place, as the place of Being or the *place of the wholly other*: in and beyond a Platonic or Neoplatonic tradition. But also in and beyond a Christian tradition about which Heidegger always claimed—while being immersed in it, as he was in the Greek tradition—denial or no, that it could in no case accommodate a philosophy. "A Christian philosophy," he often says, "is a squared circle and a misconception [*Missverständnis*]." It is necessary to distinguish between ontotheology, or theiology, on the one hand, and theology, on the other.[22] The former concerns the supreme being, the being par excellence, the ultimate foundation or *causa sui* in its divinity. The latter is a science of faith or of divine speech, such as it manifests itself in revelation (*Offenbarung*). Heidegger again seems to distinguish between, on the one hand, manifestation or the possibility of Being's revealing itself (*Offenbarkeit*), and, on the other hand, the revelation (*Offenbarung*) of the God of theology.[23]

Enormous problems lie behind these distinctions. One may follow in Heidegger the threads we have already identified: revelation, the promise, or the gift (*das Geben, die Gabe,* the *es gibt,* that progressively and profoundly displace the question of Being and the transcendental horizon that belonged to it in *Sein und Zeit,* that of time),[24] or even what is sometimes translated, so problematically, by event, *Ereignis.* I will limit myself to the question that my title imposes: How to avoid speaking? Or more precisely: How to avoid speaking *of Being?* In this question I will stress no less the significance of avoidance (*avoiding*) than that of Being, as if to grant them equal dignity, a sort of common essentiality, which will bring with it some consequences. It is the consequences that interest me.

What does avoidance mean here? Is its mode or mood, still with respect to Being or the word "Being," the same one we've recognized in apophatic theologies? Would these be examples of aberration or of a "squared circle," namely, Christian philosophies or shameful ontotheologies, for Heidegger? Does avoidance belong to the category or to the diagnosis of denial or denegation (*Verneinung*), in a sense determined this time by a Freudian problematic ("I am not saying that at all")? Or again: is Heidegger in a relation of avoidance with regard to the traditions and texts that I have just evoked, in particular, those of Dionysius and Meister Eckhart?[25] What abyss might this simple word "avoidance" then designate?

(*To say nothing*, once again, of the mystics or theologies of the Jewish, Arab, or other traditions.)

Twice, in two apparently different contexts and senses, Heidegger *explicitly proposes* to avoid (is there denial, in this case?) the word "Being." To be precise: not *to avoid* speaking of Being but to avoid *using* the word "Being." To be more precise still: not to avoid *mentioning* it, as certain speech act theorists who distinguish between mention and use would say, but to avoid using it. He explicitly proposes, thus, neither to avoid speaking of Being nor in some way to avoid mentioning the word "Being," but to refrain from using it normally, if one can say that, without placing it in quotation marks or under erasure. And in both cases, we may suspect, the stakes are serious, even if they seem to depend on the subtle fragility of a terminological, typographical, or more broadly, "pragmatic" artifice. But in both cases, what is at issue is *place*, and this is why I am privileging them.

1. First, in *Zur Seinsfrage* (1952), when it is a matter of thinking the essence of modern nihilism, Heidegger reminds Ernst Jünger of the necessity of a topology of Being and nothingness. He distinguishes this topology from a simple topography, after he has just proposed a reinterpretation of the seal, the *typos*, of Platonic typography and modern typography. It is at this point, then, that Heidegger proposes to write "Being," the word "Being," under erasure, an erasure in the form of a crossing out (*kreuzweise Durchstreichung*). The word "Being" is not avoided; it remains legible. But this legibility indicates that the word can only be read, deciphered; it cannot or should not be pronounced, used normally, one might say, as an utterance in ordinary language. It must be deciphered under a typography that is spatialized, spaced or spacing, printed over. This typography should, if not avoid, at least prevent, warn, dismiss while designating, the normal recourse (if such a thing exists) to this strange word. But Heidegger also warns us against the simply *negative* use of this *Durchstreichung*. The essential function of this erasure is not to *avoid*. No doubt, Being is no being, and it can be reduced to its turns, turnings, historical tropes (*Zuwendungen*); one must therefore avoid representing it (*vorzustellen*) as something, an object that stands *face-to-face* (*gegenüber*) with man and then comes toward him. To avoid this objectifying representation (*Vorstellung*), the word "Being" will thus be written under erasure. The word henceforth cannot be heard, but it can be read

in a certain way. In what way? If this *Durchstreichung* is not a sign, or a merely negative sign (*kein bloss negatives Zeichen*), it is because it does not erase "Being" under conventional and abstract marks. Heidegger makes it point to (*zeigen*) the four regions (*Gegenden*) of what he here and elsewhere calls the fourfold (*Geviert*): earth and sky, mortals and divinities. Why does this written cross, according to Heidegger, not have a negative meaning at all? 1. By withdrawing Being from the subject/object relation, it allows Being to be read, both the word and the meaning of Being. 2. It also "shows" the *Geviert*. 3. But above all it *gathers*. This gathering takes place. It has its *place* (*Ort*) at the crossing through of the *Durchkreuzung*.[26] The gathering of the *Geviert*, their gathering in a place of crossing (*Versammlung im Ort der Durchkreuzung*), gives itself to be read and written in an indivisible topos, in the simplicity (*die Einfalt*) of this point, of this *Ort* whose name appears so difficult to translate. Heidegger tells us elsewhere that this name "originally suggests" "the point of the spear," that toward which everything converges and comes together. This indivisible point always assures the possibility of the *Versammlung*. It gives place to it; it is always the gathering, das *Versammelnde*. "The site gathers unto itself, supremely and in the extreme [*Der Ort versammelt zu sich ins Hochste and Äusserste*]."[27]

However, to think the negative appearance of this erasure, to gain access to the origin of negativity, of negation and nihilism, and perhaps also of avoidance, one would have to think the place of the nothing. "What is the locale of the nothing [*der Ort des Nichts*]?"[28] Heidegger had just asked himself. Now he continues: *the nothing should also be written, and that means thought.* Like Being, it would also have to be written and read under erasure: "Wie das Sein, so müsste auch das Nichts geschrieben und d.h. gedacht werden."

2. Elsewhere, in an apparently different context, Heidegger explains the sense in which he would *avoid* speaking of Being, this time without crossing it out. More precisely, the sense in which he would avoid *writing* the word "Being." More precisely still (always in the conditional, and this mood is very important here), the sense in which "the word 'Being' [*das Wort 'Sein*]" should not take place, happen, arrive (*vorkommen*) in his text. It is not a matter of "remaining silent," as one would prefer to do, he says elsewhere,[29] when the "thinking of God" (on the subject of God) is in

question. No, the point is, rather, not to allow the word "Being" to occur [*venir*], on the subject of God.

The text is presented as a *transcription*. Responding to students at the University of Zurich in 1951, Heidegger recalls that Being and God are not identical, and that he would always avoid thinking God's essence on the basis of Being. He makes this clearer still in a sentence in which I emphasize the words *were, would,* and *write*: "If I *were* yet *to write* a theology—to which I sometimes feel inclined—the word 'Being' *would* not occur in it [find its place in it, take place in it, figure or happen in it] [*Wenn ich noch eine Theologie* schreiben würde, *wozu es mich manchmal reizt, dann* dürfte *in ihr das Wort 'Sein' nicht vorkommen*]."[30]

How is one to analyze the folds of denial in this conditional writing during an oral improvisation? Can one recognize its modalities without first departing from the content and the thing itself: that of Being and God? Heidegger speaks in order to say what *would happen if he were to write* one day. But he knows that what he says is already being written. If he were to write a theology, the word "Being" would not be crossed out; it would not even appear. For the moment, speaking and writing about what he *would* or *could* write regarding theology, Heidegger allows the word "Being" to appear; he does not use it, but mentions it without erasure when he is indeed speaking of theology, the very theology he is tempted to write. Where does this, then, take place? Does it take place? What would take place?

Heidegger continues, "Faith does not need the thought of Being." And, as he often recalls, Christians should let themselves be inspired by Luther's lucidity on this subject. And yet, even if Being is not "the ground and essence of God [*Grund und Wesen von Gott*]," the experience of God (*die Erfahrung Gottes*)—that is, the experience of revelation—occurs "in the dimension of Being [*in der Dimension des Seins sich ereignet*]." This revelation is not the one (*Offenbarung*) that religions speak of, but the possibility of this revelation, the opening for this manifestation, this *Offenbarkeit* that I spoke of earlier and in which an *Offenbarung* can take place and man can encounter God. Although God is not and need not be thought on the basis of Being as his essence or ground, *the dimension of Being* gives access to the advent, the experience, the encounter with this God who nevertheless is not. And the word "dimension"—which is also difference—gives a measure here by giving place. One could outline a singular chiasmus. The anxious experience of the nothing would open us to Being. Here, the dimension of Being opens to the experience of God who is not or whose being is neither essence nor ground.

How not to think of this? This dimension of opening, this place that gives place without being either essence or ground—is this step or passage, this entryway that gives access to God, not the "antechamber [*vorbürge*]" that Meister Eckhart speaks of? "When we grasp God in being, we apprehend him in his antechamber, for being is the antechamber in which he dwells." Is this a theological, an ontotheological, tradition? Or a theological tradition? Would Heidegger accept it? Would he disown it? Would he deny it?

I do not intend to answer these questions, or even to conclude with them. More modestly, in a more hurried but also more programmatic way, I will return to the enigma of avoidance, of negation, or denegation, or denial in a scene of writing. Heidegger *says* (then allows it to be written in his name) that if he *should write* a theology, he would avoid the word "Being." He would avoid writing it, and the word would not figure in his text, or rather should not be present in it. What does he mean? That the word would still figure in it under erasure, appearing without appearing, quoted but not used? No, it should not figure in it at all. Heidegger knows perfectly well that this is not possible, and perhaps it is for this fundamental reason that he did not write this theology. But did he not write it? And did he avoid writing the word "Being" in it? In fact since Being is not (a being) and in truth is nothing (that is), what difference is there between writing "Being," this being that is not, and writing "God," this God of whom Heidegger also says that he is not? Of course, Heidegger does not simply say that God is not a being; he makes it clear that he has nothing to do with Being ("Mit dem Sein, ist hier nichts anzusichten"). But since he recognizes that God announces himself to experience in the "dimension of Being," what difference is there between writing a theology and writing on Being, of Being, as Heidegger never stopped doing? Most of all, when he writes the word "Being" under and in the place (*Ort*) of the deletion [*biffure*] in the form of a cross? Did Heidegger not write what he says he would have liked to write, a theology *without* the word "Being"? But did he not also write what he says should not be written, what should not have been written, namely a theology that is opened, governed, taken over by the word "Being"?

He wrote, with and without the word "Being," a theology with and without God. He did what he said one must avoid doing. He said, wrote, and allowed to be written exactly what he said he wanted to avoid. He was not without leaving a trace of all these folds. He was not without allowing a trace to appear, a trace that is, perhaps, no longer his own, but that remains *quasiment* [as if] his own. *Not, without, quasiment* are three adverbs. *Quasiment.* Fiction or fable, everything happens as if I wanted to ask, on the threshold of this lecture, what these three adverbs mean and where they come from.

P.S. One more word to conclude, I beg you to forgive me for it. I am not sure that only rhetoric is at stake. But this concerns again the strange discursive modality, or rather this *no (step of) writing* [ce pas d'écriture], this pass or dodge of Heidegger's. What does he do? Essentially, he says to these students: if I had to write a theology (I have always dreamed of this, but I have not done it and I know that I will never do it), I would not let the word "Being" occur (*vorkommen*). It would not find a place, it would not have the right to a place in such a text. I mention this word here, but I have let it occur and it could figure in all of my work only *by not doing so*—since I have always said that Being *is not* (a being, that is) and that *it should always have been* written *under erasure*, a rule that I did not in fact always observe, but which I should have respected in principle and by rights, starting from the first word, from the first verb. Understand me: an erasure that would, above all, have nothing negative about it! And even less any hint of denegation! And so on.

What is the discursive modality of this *no (step of) writing* and of this abyss of denial? Is it, first of all, a modality, a simple modality among other possible ones, or is it rather a quasi-transcendental recourse of writing? We should not forget that we are dealing first of all with an oral declaration, later consigned to writing from memory by Beda Allemann. Heidegger certainly approved the protocol, although he remarked that it did not render present the atmosphere of the interview, nor would a "complete stenogram" have done so: no writing could have rendered what had been said *there*.

What was said *there* was addressed to colleagues and students, to disciples, in the very broad sense of this word. Like the address of Dionysius, in his apostrophe to Timothy, this text has a pedagogical or psychagogical virtue. It remains, as text (written or oral, it does not matter), only to this extent: repetition or iterability on an *agogic* path.

But there is never a prayer, not even an apostrophe, in Heidegger's rhetoric. Unlike Dionysius, he never says "you": either to God or to a disciple or to a reader. There is no place, or in any case, there is no regularly assigned place, for these "neither true nor false" utterances that prayers are, according to Aristotle. This can be interpreted in at least two ways, and they seem contradictory.

1. This absence means that theology (in the sense in which Heidegger links it to faith and distinguishes it from theiology and from metaphysical ontotheology) is rigorously excluded from his texts. Theology is well defined in them but excluded, at least insofar as what should *direct* it, namely the movement of faith. And in fact, although he thinks that only the truth of Being can open one to the essence of the divinity and to what the word "god" means (we know the famous passage in the "Letter on 'Humanism'"), Heidegger says the following: "Within thought, nothing could be accomplished that could prepare for or contribute to determining what happens in faith and in grace. If faith summoned me in this way, I would close down shop.—Of course, within the dimension of faith, one still continues to think; but thinking as such no longer has a task."[31] In short, neither faith nor science, as such, thinks or has thinking as its task.

This absence of prayer, or of apostrophe in general, also confirms the predominance of the theoretical, "constative," even propositional form (in the third-person present indicative: *S* is *P*) at least in the rhetoric of a text that nevertheless powerfully challenges the determination of truth linked to this theoreticism and to this judicative form.

2. But at the same time, on the contrary, one can read in it a sign of respect for prayer. For the formidable questions called up by the essence of prayer: can a prayer, must a prayer let itself be mentioned, quoted, and taken up [*entraîner*] in a compelling [*entraînante*] agogic proof? Perhaps it should not. Perhaps it must not do this. Perhaps, on the contrary, it must do this. Are there criteria external to the event itself that would allow one to decide whether Dionysius, for example, distorted or rather accomplished the essence of prayer by quoting it, and first of all by writing it for Timothy? Does one have the right to think that, as pure address, on the edge of silence, foreign to every code and to every rite, hence to every repetition, prayer should never be turned away from its present by a notation or by the movement of apostrophe, by a multiplication of addresses? That each time it takes place only once and should never be recorded? But perhaps the contrary is the case. Perhaps there would be no prayer,

no pure possibility of prayer, without what we make out as a threat or a contamination: writing, the code, repetition, analogy or the (at least apparent) multiplicity of addresses, initiation. If there were a purely pure experience of prayer, would one need religion and affirmative or negative theologies? Would one need a supplement of prayer? But if there were no supplement, if quotation did not bend [*pliait*] prayer, if prayer did not bend [*pliait*], if it did not submit [*se pliait*] to writing, would a theiology be possible? Would a theology be possible?

—Translated by Ken Frieden and Elizabeth Rottenberg

§ 10 Désistance

PARENTHESES

(Parenthetically: How are they going to translate *désister*? I wonder. They will have to take into account the place this word occupies in Philippe Lacoue-Labarthe's work. It seems discreet, and yet so many paths cross there! Then they will have to manage, in another, and a non-Latin language, the relations between an entire family of words. Words that in our tradition bear a strong philosophical tenor. Verbs such as to exist [*exister*], to subsist [*subsister*], to consist [*consister*], to persist [*persister*], to insist [*insister*], to resist [*résister*], to assist [*assister*]—and undoubtedly others I am forgetting; then, too, nouns without corresponding verbs: substance, constancy [*constance*], instance, instant, distance.

Désister [to desist], which is much rarer, announces perhaps something other than another term in this series. Perhaps it does not mark anything negative. Perhaps the *dé-* does not determine the *-ister*, or rather, as we will see, the *-ester*. Perhaps the *dé-* dislodges it radically, in an uprooting that would gradually dislocate the whole series, which seemed merely to be modifying a common stem and assigning complementary attributes to it. A powerful meditation on the root, on the a-radicality of *ist, est, -ister, -ester*: here is what we might follow, among other paths, across Lacoue-Labarthe's texts. Lacoue-Labarthe, for his part, occasionally employs the

---

Preface to Philippe Lacoue-Labarthe, *Typography: Mimesis, Philosophy, Politics,* ed. and trans. Christopher Fynsk (Cambridge, Mass.: Harvard University Press, 1989; reprint, Stanford: Stanford University Press, 1998).

verb *désister*, or the noun *désistement*. For reasons that I will have to explain, I propose *désistance*, which for the moment is not French.

Désistance is the ineluctable.

There are, to begin with, at least two experiences of the ineluctable. I might say offhand, to formalize things a little: two *typical* experiences.

The first type: this has to happen, *il faut que cela arrive* [How are they going to translate *il faut*? "Has to," "is to," "ought to," "must," "should"?], this cannot and must not be eluded. This has to begin sometime, someday, in accordance with the necessity of what will have been announced in the future tense. I, the one who says it, precede and anticipate in this way the event of what happens to me, which comes upon me or to which I come. I am then like the [free] subject or the [aleatory] accident of the ineluctable. The latter does not constitute me. I am constituted without it.

Second type: what announces itself as ineluctable seems in some way to have already happened, to have happened before happening, to be always past, in advance of the event. Something began before me, the one who undergoes the experience. I am late. If I insist upon remaining the subject of this experience, it would have to be as a prescribed, pre-inscribed subject, marked in advance by the imprint of the ineluctable that constitutes this subject without belonging to it, and that this subject cannot appropriate even if the imprint appears to be properly its own. We can begin to see here the outlines of what we will be analyzing a little further on: a certain constitutive *desistance* of the subject. A [de]constitution rather than a destitution. But how could a desistance be constitutive or essential? It distances [from itself] any constitution and any essence. The imprint of the ineluctable is not one imprint among others. It does not contain a multiplicity of characters, determinations, or predicates—including the ineluctable, among others. No, the imprint, the *typos*, of this preinscription is the ineluctable itself. Ineluctability is pre-impression, and this marks the desistance of the subject. I am not simply the subject or the supporting basis of the imprint or of "my" impressions. But this still does not imply that the ineluctable might be conceived of as a genetic program or a historical predestination; rather, the latter are supplemental and late determinations of it. Let us not be too quick to draw a conclusion from this preliminary exercise. Its purpose, in parentheses, is only to strike the keynote for what follows and to lay out the terms of the ineluctable.

Why begin this way? For at least two reasons. First of all, Lacoue-Labarthe's work, his oeuvre, resembles, for me, the very *trial* of the ineluctable: insistent, patient, thinking—the experience of a very *singular* thought of the ineluctable. The word "singularity" might lead us to think of novelty. And in fact the reader will have to recognize something quite obvious: following unprecedented schemas, a very new configuration here joins the question of Being and the question of the subject in its philosophical, political, ethical, poetic, literary, theatrical, and musical dimensions, in the reasons and the madness of its autobiography. A different thought of mimesis and of the *typos* gives access today to these figures and to this configuration. But the idea of novelty still remains too bound up with that of a periodization, or, in the best of cases, with an epochal structure of the Heideggerian type. And, as we will see, certain questions addressed to Heidegger, notably on the subject of the subject, of the *Gestell* and of mimesis, would seem to prompt some reservations in relation to a history of Being and its epochs. As for the word "configuration," it already presupposes too much in the way of *consistency* and identifiable collectedness in the *figure*—two of the richest problematics in this book—for us to be able to rely on it. A new configuration, yes, very new, but this novelty disturbs the very possibility of the *configurable*; it qualifies neither a period nor an epoch, even less a fashion. Perhaps not even a history. What, then? One must be patient; I will try to explain why. One must learn to read Lacoue-Labarthe, to listen to him, and to do so at his rhythm [learn to follow his rhythm and what he means by "rhythm"], that of his voice, I would almost say his breath, the sentence that is not even interrupted when it multiplies caesuras, asides, parenthetical remarks, cautions, hesitations, warnings, signs of circumspection, parentheses, quotation marks, italics—and above all dashes—or all of these at once [for example, he writes "I" and "me" in quotation marks, not even excepting his own name at the end of "Typography" at the moment when he exposes himself the most on the subject of the subject and exposition—or presentation {*Darstellung*}]. One must learn the necessity of a scansion that comes to fold and unfold a thought. This is nothing other than the necessity of a rhythm, rhythm itself.

I had a second reason for beginning this way, in parentheses: I was unable, for my part, to avoid trying to follow the thread of a word, *désistement*, which I believe to be untranslatable—this, at the very moment of introducing a translation. And I could not avoid asking myself why I did it. Is it a law? These words never manage to avoid me. I jump right in, and I would be hard put to choose between two hypotheses: choice or compulsion. This preface will serve to remove the alternative. It will tie a thinking of the untranslatable idiom to the "logic" of a double constraint [double bind, double obligation: one must {*il faut*}: one must not {*il ne faut pas*}: avoid. One must avoid avoiding, but one cannot avoid avoiding and one must not].

I have not really begun this preface, but here it is in parentheses already well along, ineluctably. In certain languages—ours—a few words articulate a syntactic formation that lends itself to redoubling the movement of negation: "ne pas ne pas [not not]," not do something that already consists in not doing—not avoiding or not eluding. The ineluctable thus belongs to this family, as does the unavoidable. One designates in this manner what cannot or must not be eluded, or avoided. The undeniable appears to be part of the same series, but it says something more, or less. It names negation or de-negation, even supernegation {*sur-négation*}, the supplemental *ne pas* one finds at work in the other terms of the group. This supplementary redoubling of negation is not necessarily reducible to the work of dialectic or to an unconscious denegation. Lacoue-Labarthe will help us, perhaps, to step back from a Hegelian, Marxist, or Freudian interpretation of such a possibility. And *désistement* might be one of its names.

In the prehistory of this preface—to carry on with my fable—I was troubled even before beginning: How are they going to translate the word *désistement*, its discreet and at the same time insistent recurrence in Lacoue-Labarthe's work? How have they already translated it? I don't want to know yet; it is better that I not know. I write this even as Chris Fynsk, in Strasbourg, puts the final touches on the translation of *Typography*, now finished. But I have not read it. One can imagine a few solutions. The word exists in English: "to desist." The codes of jurisprudence generally predominate here, as in French. But the term does not allow for a reflexive construction, which is always obligatory in French: *se désister*, to renounce a suit or some legal action, a responsibility. What is more, in English it always designates, it seems to me, an interruption in time [to cease, to stop, to leave off]. Hence a certain divergence and very different syntactic possibilities. It is true that the word *désistance*, at least if one domesticated it in French, naturalized it, repatriated it to the point that it lost its common meaning of cessation, would be closer to what Lacoue-Labarthe seems to want to mark. But the difficulty, precisely, lies elsewhere, and this is why the word *désistance*, in French, a word that

Lacoue-Labarthe never uses and that moreover does not yet exist, could prove useful. On the condition that it not be simply transcribed in English, without further precautions, as "desistance"! This does not simplify the task, I admit, but is that the point? Lacoue-Labarthe's own use of *désistement* already marks a departure from the French idiom. The word can barely be translated in ordinary French. The *désistement*—henceforth I will speak of the *désistance*—of the subject does not carry the *juridical* sense that initially imposes itself in normal usage,[1] even though one can decipher in it a certain relation to the law. Nor does it let itself be determined reflexively [as in *se désister*, the only accepted form in "normal" French]. But if the *désistance* of the subject does not first signify a *self*-desistance, we should not conclude as to some passivity of the said subject. Nor as to its activity. *Désistance* better marks this middle voice. Before any decision, before any *desition* [as one might also say in English to designate a cessation of being], the subject is desisted without being passive; it desists without desisting itself, even before being the subject of a reflection, a decision, an action, or a passion. Should one then say that subjectivity *consists* in such a *désistance*? No, that is just the point—what is involved here is the impossibility of *consisting*, a singular impossibility: something entirely different from a lack of consistency. Something more in the way of a "[de]-constitution" [174]. I will attempt to analyze it, but let us already recognize the following: the great task of the translator, his madness, his agony, his aporias, always proceed from some initial strangeness, from the gap already opened in the idiom of the original text.

Indeed [to further tangle the threads of this prehistory], I almost began this preface—precisely—with the problem of translation. But did I avoid doing so? Have I not already done it? Lacoue-Labarthe's work might also be read as a thought constantly at grips with the most serious thing at stake in translation, as a thinking that is prey to translation, a thinking *of* translation; an experience of thinking for which translation is not a problem among others, an object, something that would satisfy an obligation, or what a conscience or a conscientious subject would face up to—but rather the experience of thinking itself, its most essential and most risky passage, in those places where the experience of thinking is also a poetic experience. The privileged examples: *Gestell*, mimesis, *rhuthmos*, and so many other words—in truth, other phrases—that take these words into their web. And then there are the translations Lacoue-Labarthe has published elsewhere [signs of which appear in this book] that bear witness to the same experience: his translation of the translation of Sophocles by Hölderlin [a madness upon madness], and his translation of Celan, an incomparable poet-translator one never reads alone—I mean without taking into account the genealogy of so many other poets. For however impressive the coherence of the texts gathered in this collection might be, it should not make us forget the extensive and highly differentiated range of fields traversed by so many of Lacoue-Labarthe's other texts [written sometimes in other modes, both poetic and philosophical], which the English-speaking reader will find available, I hope, before too long. This coherence does not take the form of what in philosophy is called a system—for essential and explicit reasons that all lead back to *désistance*, and to the disarticulation or the dehiscence that it inscribes in every totality. The insistent return of this motif traces out merely the silhouette of a unity, and more of a rhythm than an organic configuration.

So I have just reread these texts. A joy to rediscover, to discover in another way, the force and the exigency, the uncompromising vigilance, of a faithful thought. *Justly* faithful, and precisely to the ineluctable. It is as though this thinking of *désistance* never desisted. For almost twenty years now—if I may be allowed to say this, and the American reader ought to know it—this thought has remained for me a strange measure, the precise inordinacy {*juste démesure*}, so to speak, of what will inevitably have to be thought tomorrow: its resource, its task, its chance. In saying this, I am not in any way yielding to the conventions of the preface, or to an evaluation it cannot not prescribe. No doubt because he was sensitive to what I have shared with Lacoue-Labarthe and to what he has given me, our friend Eugenio Donato, who originally had the idea of putting together this collection, was the first to hope I would write its preface. What I share with Lacoue-Labarthe, we also both share, though differently, with Jean-Luc Nancy. But I hasten immediately to reiterate that despite so many common paths and so much work done in common, between the two of them and among the three of us, the *experience* of each remains, in its singular proximity, absolutely different; and this, despite its inevitable impurity, is the secret of the idiom. The secret: that is to say, first of all, the *separation*, the without-relation, the interruption. The most urgent thing—I will try to work on this—would be to break here with the family resemblance, to avoid genealogical temptations, projections, assimilations, or identifications. And it is not because they are impossible that the temptation becomes more avoidable. On the contrary. Assimilation or specular projection: these are what Lacoue-Labarthe constantly puts us on guard against. He uncovers their fatal character, the *political* trap even in Heidegger's "unacknowledged" and "fundamental" mimetology,[2] in an interpretation of originary mimesis as imitation. Whether one accepts or refuses imitation, then, the result remains the same: a failure to recognize originary mimesis as *désistance*. A first point of reference for taking an altogether preliminary measure of the path followed: once the consequences of the Heideggerian *Destruktion* or the Nietzschean demolition have been followed out as far as possible [and not without laying bare the irreducibility of the one to the other], once the irrecusable necessity of these moments has been assumed, the way in which they are *incontournable* {impossible to get around} [this is Lacoue-Labarthe's word,[3] and along with the irrecusable {*l'irrécusable*}, let us add it to the series of supernegations], the stubborn permanence in these two thinkings of a still Platonic apprehension of mimesis, an ontomimetology, will be brought out. An equivocal and troubling repetition. Lacoue-Labarthe does not oppose it and does not criticize it; he is not even sure that he is deconstructing it, or that "deconstruct" is the best word for describing what he does with it by reinscribing it in another structure: *abîme, Unheimlichkeit,* double bind, *hyperbology.* He opens on an entirely different thinking of mimesis, of *typos* and of *rhuthmos,* a thinking that, while borne by the impetus of Nietzschean-Heideggerian deconstruction, nevertheless impresses upon it, as we will see, a supplementary torsion, reorganizes the entire landscape, and brings out, or brings into play, new questions: on another dimension of the subject, of politics, of literary or theatrical fiction, of poetic experience, of auto- or hetero-biography.

Imprint and caesura, the sharp-edged signature of this work interrupts the most powerful of filiations. Ineluctably, at the most necessary moment, when that tradition can no longer think or secure what it repeats as its own traditionality [exemplarity, identification, imitation, repetition]. The signature interrupts, or rather marks with an incision, the fold along which metaphysical ontomimetology is destined to divide or desist, the ontomimetology that runs from Plato to Aristotle, from Hegel to Heidegger, but also the one that continues in a more surreptitious manner in Nietzsche, Freud, and Lacan. The idiom of this signature [but let us not forget, there is also a *désistance* of the idiom] remains atypical in relation to what is identified, too quickly and too often, above all in the United States, with the name "poststructuralism." And its caesura is all the more marking in that the signature avoids avoidance or denegation; it never flees explication [*Auseinandersetzung*] and the most redoubtable proximity to the thinking that it overtaxes with constantly renewed questions. Exemplary probity, both prudent and adventurous—a superior probity that, without giving in to dogmatic moralism, submits the ethical demand to the trial of thought.

Hence, of course, the need for these multiple dissociations, which should be enumerated and respected: this belongs neither to metaphysical ontotheology nor to ontomimetology [a concept forged by Lacoue-Labarthe and which no longer corresponds to a historial or epochal unity of a Heideggerian type, since the delimitation of ontotheology in the history of Being still belongs to the whole without whole of ontomimetology]; and while not strictly speaking Nietzschean or Heideggerian, neither is it Marxist, Freudian, Lacanian, poststructuralist, or postmodern. And yet, despite these dissociations, these distancings that are neither critiques nor oppositions, one never has the feeling of isolation or insularity. Another figure imposes itself on me, but it is only a figure: that of a besieged power. Besieged because it exposes itself on all sides, even to the question: What is obsidionality?[4] What is obsessionality when an ineluctable double bind makes it so that one cannot close a front, or a parenthesis, except by opening another on another side? And what would the question "What is . . . ?" with its epochs [and the suspension of an *epochē* is also a setting in parentheses, or even, as we will see shortly, a setting in parentheses of the thesis or the thetic in general], have to do, or not have to do, with madness? The besieged power remains impregnable because it has no figurable site, a single site, a single figure; it has no proper identity, properly proper. Unstable and destabilizing, it harasses out of its *désistance* all the others in turn, without letting up, without granting them the least respite. Hence the "style," the *ethos*, the "character" [and here I refer to the problematic that begins and complicates itself as it unfolds in "The Echo of the Subject," in the section titled "The Novel Is a Mirror"], the rhythm of the warnings. Lacoue-Labarthe multiplies parentheses in order to caution us at every instant against omissions, avoidances, simplifications: from all sides, overdetermination can return to surprise us, one might miss a twist or a fold, traps are everywhere, the double bind leaves no way out, nor does the hyperbologic—one has to know this in order to begin to think. And the warning is not finally meant to protect anyone. It stands watch so that one will not fail to expose oneself: do not forget that you are exposed, that you must expose yourself on this side and then again on that side—do not avoid exposure, which in any case will not miss you, or me.

This presupposes a moment of contract, alliance, fidelity. One must read, and to do this one must come to terms, negotiate, compromise. Fidelity to what, finally, or to whom? Well, perhaps to the very thing that you, who besiege me in such a necessary fashion, who are already there before me, did not avoid, or could not not avoid [does this come down to the same thing?], and that therefore takes the form of the ineluctable. This form is terrifying, for it lends itself to all figures, all schemas—it is unstable and amorphous. A singular fidelity to what finally no longer even demands fidelity. But would there ever be a fidelity without the faith called for by such dissymmetry?

It would have been best not to multiply the preliminary, preambulatory precautions for this preface and to jump immediately outside the parenthesis. But how? There was also the temptation to begin, by way of exergue, with yet another long parenthesis on the subject of a very brief parenthesis I would have quoted, only seven words. I would have masked a name, thus pretending to replace the most irreplaceable, a name, by another: figure, fiction, simulacrum of synonymy. In Lacoue-Labarthe's essay titled "Typography," one encounters the following, in parentheses: "(in any case, Heidegger never avoids anything)" [62].

Oh, really? How so? Is that possible?

On first reflection, my impulse was to respond: It is difficult to know whether this is true of Heidegger or of anyone; but if it were true of someone, it would be true of he who dared write this, "Heidegger never avoids anything"! Unless this is the one thing he should have avoided saying or thinking. For after all, how does one dare write such a sentence? By what right? And is there any sense in advancing such a statement about someone, anyone? What is the meaning of this provocation?

Let us not rush. In one sense, indeed, it is possible not to avoid anything: never pass by a question, a possibility, a truth, and a truth about truth, a necessity. Never miss a fold or a twist. But one can also, in a second sense, not avoid anything, even the worst: mistakes, weaknesses, misapprehensions, inhibitions, omissions, compromises—also avoidances and denials. Compulsively. As is said in colloquial French: "ne pas en manquer une {never to miss one}." When Lacoue-Labarthe says of Heidegger that "he never avoids anything," he clearly means this in the first sense: the good sense of the expression. Heidegger stands up to things, never avoids anything: this is why there is no "getting around him." And yet, Lacoue-Labarthe's abyssal irony inscribes this incredible parenthesis in an analysis devoted entirely to describing the way in which Heidegger passes by, circumvents [more or less] deliberately, the very thing that he, Lacoue-Labarthe, wants not to avoid. For he is concerned with "tracking down {*dépister*}" [this is his word] the tortuous strategy Heidegger employs to avoid what he does not avoid, to avoid without avoiding. Heidegger's denial? Lacoue-Labarthe's denial regarding Heidegger's denial, which he would like to point out and yet at the same time [double bind] not point out? If not, then what does "avoid" mean? And what about denial? Especially when it is a matter, as we will verify in a moment, of a "vast movement" by Heidegger, his "maneuver" [I am quoting Lacoue-Labarthe], in a thinking concerned with thinking, over and above the meaning of an ontotheology without which the very concept of denial could not have been formed, the *unthought* itself. Concerned with thinking not just this or that unthought, but the structure, the possibility, and the necessity of the unthought in general, its quasi-negativity [the *un*-thought is un-*thought*, he reminds us] that whatever Heidegger says about it, and I have my doubts here, gathers each time in the unity of a single site, as if there were only *one* unthought in which each "great" thought—and herein would lie its greatness—would find its secret law. But I will return to this shortly.

What are we to understand by "avoid" or "deny" when this unthought of unthinking {*cet impensé de l'impenser*} itself, that of Heidegger, involves motifs such as those of writing, of poetic or fictional *Darstellung*, the subject of enunciation, the madness or politics of this subject, the unity of the text, and so on, so many signifying terms without which philosophy and psychoanalysis, logic and pragmatics, would have difficulty defining these figures that are blithely called "avoiding," "denying," "eluding," and so on? These common determinations can no longer suffice, and it is at the site of this limit that Lacoue-Labarthe's gesture seems to operate a far-reaching strategic displacement. For one of the most daring and unprecedented analyses in "Typography," the very one in which it is indicated that "in any case, Heidegger never avoids anything," multiplies around these questions a series of troubling diagnoses on the matter of a Heideggerian "maneuver." For the moment, I find no word more appropriate than "diagnosis," though I mean it in the sense of Nietzschean genealogy,

whatever reservations one might have, with Lacoue-Labarthe, in this regard. These diagnoses are all the more serious in that they neither accuse
nor criticize anyone: they merely indicate a certain fate that one will never
escape simply by de-limiting it. And these diagnoses are all the more interesting, in each of their formulations, in that they concern movements
by which Heidegger will have appeared to avoid this or that [we will see
why in a moment], and open, in their very act of delimitation, the space
of Lacoue-Labarthe's singular problematic, truly without precedent. What
are these formulations? Let me first quote them, as such—indeed, in their
simple *form*—before coming, outside parentheses, to the thing itself. First
of all, Lacoue-Labarthe tells us, Heidegger "'eliminates {*évacue*}' (or *sublimates*). . . ." Note, as always, the signs of prudence, the vigilant circumspection, the insurance taken against all the risks to which he does not
fail to expose himself at every instant: quotation marks around "eliminates," as if immediately to withdraw an unsatisfactory word [Heidegger
never eliminates anything—any more than Lacoue-Labarthe does]; then
sublimates is in italics. And in parentheses. For the word might seem to
be borrowed from a foreign and very problematic context [the Freudian
aporetics of sublimation]. But a necessary point of passage is maintained
by the word itself, which leads back to the question of the sublime, present elsewhere in the confrontation with Heidegger and with regard to a
certain unpresentability of the entirely other. Heidegger, then, "'eliminates'" or "*sublimates*" *three* questions that, according to Lacoue-Labarthe,
are moreover *the same*. On this unity or this unicity, I would myself have
a question, but this too will be for later. One single question, then, one
question in three, the same question "always in view and always thrust
aside" [62] in such a way that Heidegger could fail to attend to it, simply
pass right by it—or even pretend not to "pay attention to it."

It would therefore not be impossible to pretend not to pay attention.
More precisely: to do so in a thoughtful reading or a meditation, for in
"everyday life" we know that nothing is easier. As always, Lacoue-Labarthe gives generous credit to the thought he examines, or "tracks down
[*dépiste*]." He credits it with the greatest strength, the greatest cunning,
the most lucid *knowledge*—one that can never be taken unawares by the
questions one might put to it:

> It is no doubt possible to *track down* in the whole of the procedure Heidegger
> follows when dealing with *Zarathustra*, and already in the very positing of the
> question that governs it ("Who is Nietzsche's Zarathustra?"), a kind of vast

movement turning around a question that Heidegger *knows full well* cannot be avoided or eluded (in any case, Heidegger never avoids anything), but which he judges to be indispensable, in order to *neutralize its power*, to "cut off its support," and take it from behind. [62; emphases added—JD]

One can therefore neutralize the *power* and thus avoid in a certain way what one cannot avoid *seeing* or *knowing*. A whole strategy, a whole war in relation to this power can therefore be employed, can deploy its "maneuvers" or manipulations. The essential question here bears less on the fact of the maneuver than on the course chosen:

But why does Heidegger's maneuver here go by way of *Gestalt*? Why does it even go beyond *Gestalt* in search of *Ge-stell*?
Once again, what happens with (the word) *Ge-stell*? [Ibid.].

Here we are, then, here is the content, if one may say so, of the question: *Ge-stell*, or the word *Ge-stell*, for the division between the word and the thing is difficult to make, for essential reasons. What is at stake in the thing is also the affair of language. But this "content," as we will see, retains in fact a necessary relation to what one commonly calls form: *Gestalt*, presentation [*Darstellung*], exposition, fiction, everything that *Darstellung* implies in the network of meanings in -*stellen*, an entire hive that it disorganizes perhaps by putting it to work, perhaps also because it does not belong to it quite as simply as it might appear to. Heidegger, in any case, is said to have avoided it, knowing "full well {*pertinemment*}" that he was thus circumventing, at least provisionally, the ineluctable.[5]

And yet, further on, the tracking, the following of traces, becomes more relentless. Hemmed in, Heidegger "cannot avoid falling." Can that be said? It is true—this is a man who never avoids anything. To follow a trail, this is also *nachstellen*, and Lacoue-Labarthe proposes a translation: "to track or be after; to avenge." Where is it that Heidegger cannot avoid falling? It is still a matter of *Darstellung* and of the Platonic paradigm of the mirror. This latter

is therefore—in fact—a paradigm of *Darstellung*. But it is fixed, a trick paradigm—a trap consisting of an artfully camouflaged hole into which Heidegger, in a certain way, cannot avoid falling. And it is a mimetic fall—if there ever was one—since he falls for the trap while trying to outdo Plato. This can be "seen." I ("I") mean that all of this is perfectly legible: there are signs, and the "accident" does not occur without leaving traces. [89]

You saw them—no, you *read* the quotation marks, the quotation marks in parentheses. This accident was not an accident—the fall was inevitable; but we are no longer dealing here with the subject [I] of a perception or of a science, of a seeing or a knowing. What happened to Heidegger, or with him, under his name, is serious in another sense, and his nonavoidance no longer comes under these categories. A moment ago, we were told that Heidegger never avoids anything. Almost thirty pages later, we hear that "he could not avoid falling" into a carefully camouflaged "hole." If this ineluctable no longer comes under the categories of seeing and knowing, the logic or psychoanalysis of denial, one may have an inkling of the singular nature of what is at stake when Lacoue-Labarthe sets out after the traces left by this fatal accident [which one might almost call necessary or essential]. The deciphering, whose stages I cannot try to reconstitute here, is neither a matter of *seeing* nor of *knowing*, nor of any established discipline, hermeneutics or psychoanalysis. Nor do I think one can speak here of a philosophical method or of a philosophical reading.

Is it absolutely necessary to give it a name? Lacoue-Labarthe seems to describe a strategy: "turning movement," "cut off from its support," "taken from behind," "maneuver." But also the failure, the expiration, the fall, the great slip of a thought. What must Lacoue-Labarthe's strategy be, this strategy without war, for tracking down traces, upsetting or taking Heidegger's grand maneuver by surprise—itself not a simple maneuver among others [military, methodical, scientific, logical, psychoanalytic, hermeneutic, philosophical]? In fact, it is a maneuver that concerns the most constraining Platonic tradition, and finally the entire ontotheology that follows from it, up to the very concepts of ontotheology, the history of metaphysics, even *Ge-stell.* And within these, the determination, thought to be derived and secondary, of the subject or of subjectity.

This, in short, was one of the questions I was asking myself when I came up against this short parenthesis ["(in any case, Heidegger never avoids anything)"], the only phrase, undoubtedly, against which I could not help reacting initially in protest. This is why, spontaneously, I almost began there. Resistance—for this was a resistance on my part—often indicates the sensitive point in a reading, the point of incomprehension that organizes it. "How can he write this?" I asked myself. And about anyone? How could someone, a finite thinker, and a thinker of finitude, never avoid anything, even while knowing, "full well," what he avoids when he avoids it? Above all, when this thinker of finitude takes seriously the necessity of the unthought, to the point of recognizing in it the essential condition, almost the source of thought—something entirely different from a lack: "What is *un*thought is such in each case only as the un-*thought*," Heidegger says [quoted in note 22, 61], as Lacoue-Labarthe reminds us.

When Paul de Man dared to say that Rousseau's text had no "blind spot," I felt the same impatience. Impatience is never justified. It should incite one to take one's time and to submit oneself to what is not self-evident—without avoiding it. Hence I offer, if I may, a first piece of advice, at the point of closing this long parenthesis: work at reading and rereading these difficult texts [with their incidental phrases, quotation marks, and parentheses], themselves and those they examine; submit to their strategy, made up of audacity, cunning, and prudence, and to the intractable necessity that constrains them, to their rhythm, above all, their breath—ample periods and the deep respiration of thought. Their time is that of a long distance run during which you follow someone who continually addresses you; he turns to you, describes the ups and downs of a terrain he knows well, interrupts himself, and then starts right in again, warns you of the risks involved, of pitfalls and traps waiting ahead, jumps you'll have to take, of the stretch you can't see yet, of the necessity of a detour, of a new punctuation, inventing another scansion in order to cross the finish line or clear a new path. If sometimes you have the feeling that you are dealing with a thinker who is panting or harried, disabuse yourself: you are reading someone who on the contrary is tracking—*polemos* without polemics—the most powerful thoughts of our tradition. I close the parenthesis. Is this possible?)

Gestell

So let us begin, here, with this example. Because it announces Lacoue-Labarthe's *manner* and *maneuver*, the hand or the rhythm of his surgery, and because I cannot do more in a preface. Accepting the risks of this limitation and hoping above all that the reader will turn to Lacoue-Labarthe himself, I will restrict myself to *three examples*, each time following a single thread: *désistance*. Each of the examples will bear the signature of a foreign word (*Gestell, mimesis, rhuthmos*), foreign first of all to the language to which it seems to belong. It will correspond to a kind of madness in translation, as in the tradition: obsession and splitting [*schize*], siege and caesura, double bind, fate and impossibility of reappropriation, hyperbology, ineluctable disidentification. Another rule of limitation and another risk: to introduce one only to those places where Lacoue-Labarthe sharpens his thinking of *désistance* by testing it against works that are both the most foreign and the closest, thus the most resistant: for example, those of Nietzsche, Heidegger, Freud, Lacan.

Beyond anthropological pathos and that of the so-called positive forms of knowledge, Lacoue-Labarthe has always granted madness the dignity of a major question for thought. Without "demagoguery" and without "psychagogy."[6] Before asking whether insanity must be excluded or mastered, that is to say, domesticated by philosophy, one must try to think this obsessive fear [*hantise*], that is, the way in which philosophy is regularly visited, haunted, inhabited by madness. There is a domesticity of "philosophical madness." At its beginning and at its end, "Typography" opens on this predestination of philosophy to madness. The examples (they are only examples) are Rousseau (his "and this is how we become mad," from the "Preface" to the *New Heloise*), Nietzsche ("The Significance of Madness in the History of Morality," in *Daybreak*), but also Kant, Comte, and Hegel. Among all the paths of these extraordinary and profuse analyses, one should isolate the thread that links madness to a new "question of the subject." Lacoue-Labarthe takes it up, taking up again even the title, and sends it off again in an unprecedented way. He has been doing this now for almost fifteen years,[7] with discretion, patience, and rigor, in a kind of solitude, and without engaging in the "return to the subject" that has recently been animating Parisian conversations, and that (and this is in *the best of cases*, no doubt the least dogmatic and the most refined) certain authors believe they find in Foucault's very last works. Nevertheless, *in every case*, a rigorous reading of Heidegger, an effective working-across [*traversée*] of his texts on the subject of subjectity, has been carefully omitted.[8] Lacoue-Labarthe does something entirely different. He does not propose to restore, rehabilitate, or reinstall "the subject"; rather, he proposes to think its *désistance* by taking into account *both* a deconstruction of the Heideggerian type *and* that about which Heidegger would have remained silent.

What silence? The word appears at least twice. What it designates is not without some relation to the ineluctable. Even if he "never avoids anything," Heidegger remains silent on something about *Darstellung* that is not easily domesticated, ordered, classified in the great family of *Ge-stell* (*bestellen, vorstellen, herstellen, nachstellen*). It introduces a disorder to which Heidegger does not attend, or, as is said somewhere, to which he pretends not to pay attention. Heidegger's "silence" on the subject of *Darstellung* can be deciphered in two ways: either he neglects the fact that *Darstellung* belongs to *Ge-stell*, and thus neglects everything that it would oblige him to take into account (Lacoue-Labarthe recalls all of this); or else he inscribes *Darstellung* in a homogeneous series and thus reduces it to being merely a mode among others. In his delimitation of an "onto-typology," Heidegger remains "elliptical" (this word also appears twice: see 56 and 59) as to the relation between, on the one hand, work and suffering (at issue is Ernst Jünger, *Der Arbeiter, Über den Schmerz*), and, on the other, (re)presentation by figure (*gestalthafte Darstellung*). And in his "relatively elliptical treatment of Jünger's relation to Hegel," Heidegger also observes a "certain silence" (259) on the relation between the metaphysics of *Gestalt*, or the representation of Being as figure, and *Darstellung*, namely, "literary presentation."[9] And what holds for Jünger would hold also for those other "writers," Nietzsche and Rilke. Ellipsis and silence signal a "loss" that is something other than the "disappearance of a word" and that concerns the derivation *stellen-darstellen*.[10] In examining "what happens" with "(the word) *Ge-stell*" and its impossible translation, Lacoue-Labarthe defines the site of a new "question of the subject." Here is its "content"—it is the passage I cited a moment ago for its "form":

I ("I") will not return here to the way in which Heidegger, in a single move, "eliminates" (or *sublimates*), for the sake of a primary *destination* of the unthought [*l'impensé(e)*] in Nietzsche (i.e., in "Nietzsche"), at one and the same time the question of the "poetic" or "fictional" ("literary") character of *Zarathustra*, the question of a certain dispersion or breaking up of the Nietzschean "text" (more difficult to get around, however, than "the absence of the work"—a capital work—wherein the un-*thought* itself *would organize itself* with the essential "articulation" of a few fundamental words), and, finally, the question of Nietzsche's "madness." Elsewhere, it seemed to me possible to show—but to be honest, it was a bit obvious—that these three questions are really only one, or more exactly, that they all gravitate around a single, central question, at the same time always in view and always thrust aside (constantly proposed, moreover, in terms unacceptable to *thought*: metaphysically marked, and therefore constantly condemned—without "appeal"), and this

is the question of the *subject*. The question of the "subject of enunciation,"
let us say, or of "writing"—nothing, in any case that might be simply, that is,
immediately, assimilated or *identified* with the subject of the "metaphysics of
subjectivity," under any form whatsoever. (61–62)

Typography, or what is now brought together under this title, takes its
force in large measure from the impressive articulation in "a single central
question" of this question of the subject, which Lacoue-Labarthe removes
from the Heideggerian deconstruction—that is to say, from the delimitation of an onto-typo-logy or a metaphysics of subjectivity. He removes
it by showing how Heidegger removes himself from it; and, most important, he leads back to its unicity, which is also a center of gravity, a
great number of questions. Among them, "a certain breaking apart of the
'text'"—the Nietzschean text in this case, but with regard to which I wonder (actually this is only an uneasiness) whether Lacoue-Labarthe does not
also risk being reductive in turn. He does this with the best justification
in the world, since this gathering in the reelaboration is the best possible
strategic lever for a deconstructive reading of Heidegger—but it is not
without confirming in passing the fundamental axiom according to which
the un-*thought* of a thought is always single, always unique,[11] constituting
in a certain way the very site out of which a thought gives or gives itself to
be thought. Lacoue-Labarthe proceeds as though the way in which Heidegger defines the un-*thought* of Nietzsche, or the un-*thought* in general,
implied in its turn only one and unique un-*thought*: that around which or
out of which Heidegger's thought organizes itself. But is this not to repeat,
on the subject of Heidegger, what Lacoue-Labarthe himself accused Heidegger of, namely, of privileging a "primary *destination* of the un-thought
[*l'impensé(e)*]"—that of Nietzsche for Heidegger, that of Heidegger for
Lacoue-Labarthe? What if Heidegger's unthought (for example) was not
one, but plural? What if his *un*thought was believing in the unicity or
the unity of the un*thought*? I will not turn my uneasiness into a critique,
because I do not believe that this gesture of gathering is avoidable. It is
always productive, and philosophically necessary. But I will continue to
wonder whether the very "logic" of *désistance*, as we will continue to follow it, should not lead to some irreducible dispersion of this "unique central question," as question of the subject—to its disidentification, in some
sense, its disinstallation. And I will continue to ask whether the "subject"
in question, even if it exceeds the limits of the "metaphysics of subjectity"

or onto-typology, does not continue to reflect, or to collect in its gathering force, in the unicity of its question, something of the Heideggerian "unthought." In a word, whether it is not necessary to separate the two questions that have been brought together here: that of the "subject of enunciation" and that of "writing." But no doubt Lacoue-Labarthe does so, and this is even what he calls "typography," beyond the formulation and the strategic moment I have just isolated somewhat artificially.

The strategy of "Typography" has a subtlety I could not hope to account for here. At the risk of magnifying its basic traits in an exaggerated way, I will read in it first a kind of general destabilization or disinstallation. General, first of all, because redoubled. This redoubling has to do with the essence without essence of mimesis, with the fact that it *is* not, that it does not *exist*, but *desists*, and that this involves nothing negative. To think it, one must not install oneself (upside down) in Plato's mimetology as it is finally confirmed by Heidegger. One must not *rehabilitate*, reclaim, save a mimesis defined as a "declension," "instability," accidental "disinstallation," or "fall" that has happened to truth—to that *alētheia* interpreted by Heidegger in his reading of book 10 of the *Republic* in a curious fashion as *Unverstelltheit*: installation, non-disinstallation, stele. If the abyssal redoubling must be thought as destabilizing truth or the stele from its origin, as one might say, one must still not give in to the almost irresistible temptation to generalize the mimesis condemned by Plato or to rehabilitate it by conferring on it the noble status of an originary mimesis.[12] The line to be crossed, for such a temptation, seems so subtle that no one—I would say not even Lacoue-Labarthe—can constantly avoid doing so. The difference can be marked simply with visible or invisible quotation marks around the word "originary." And when one wants to underscore that mimesis does not have the (destitute) status of a fall or an accidental derivation, one is indeed tempted to call it, "against" Plato, "originary," "'originary'"—while making it clear that the quality of being originary is incompatible with that of mimesis, and so on.

The fold or abyssal redoubling that we are attempting to talk about does not, therefore, come to destabilize a truth that would already be— *déjà serait, esterait*, as it is sometimes translated. *Désistance* is first of all the *désistance* of truth. This truth never resembles itself. Whence its resemblance to mimesis. But how is it possible to resemble mimesis without already being contaminated by it? And how can one think this originary contamination in a nonnegative and nonoriginary way in order to keep one's utterances from being dictated by the dominant mimetologism? Truth, then, never resembles itself. It withdraws, masks itself, and never ceases, says Lacoue-Labarthe, who this time uses the reflexive construction of "desist": to desist itself, *se désister* (118).

Before coming to this result, let us note what in the lexicon justifies the privilege given to this word, *désister*, and above all what it is that, in relating it to the quasi-radical *ist*, or rather *stare*, in French *ester*, uproots it so as to remove *désister*, *désistement*, *désistance* from the series of stances to which they seem to belong (subsistence, substance, resistance, constancy, consistency, insistence, instance, assistance, persistence, existence, etc.). As it is put to work by Lacoue-Labarthe, *désistance* is not a modification, above all not a negative one, of *ester*. The *dé-* supermarks precisely this: its nonbelonging to the family of *ester*. I have already suggested this, and I return to the point now in order to further complicate what is at stake in the translation. One should know that *ester* is not only a kind of root. The word exists in French, even if it is rare. It has a meaning that is specifically juridical, like *se désister*, and signifies "to present oneself," "to appear" [*paraître*, *comparaître*] in a court of law. *Ester en jugement* [to appear in court, to plead], *ester en justice* [to go to law], is to present oneself before the law as plaintiff or defendant. Now, it happens that as a result of this semantics of presentation or appearance, this act of presence, if one can say this, it has sometimes been thought that one might translate *wesen*, in its Heideggerian usage, by *ester* or *estance*.[13] Let me then risk the following suggestion: if *beyond* its juridical code, and *in* its "typographical" implementation, *désistance* does not modify *estance*, and does not belong to it as one of its determinations, but rather marks a rupture, or a departure, or a heterogeneity with respect to *estance* or *Wesen*; if it says neither absence nor disorder or inessentiality, neither *Abwesen* nor *Unwesen*, nor even some *Entwesen* (this latter removed from its trivial connotation), then it would be quite difficult to re-translate it into the code, the problematic, or even the question of the meaning or truth of Being—or, if you prefer, into the language of "Heidegger." This does not mean that nothing more passes, or happens, between the two languages, but the passage is offered by another abyss, the one Heidegger speaks of and *also* another. I do not know whether Lacoue-Labarthe will accept my hypothesis, or even whether it will interest him. Perhaps he will refuse it outright; perhaps, on the contrary, it will appear to him to go without saying—he who once wrote: "I have a lot of trouble not seeing in Heidegger's 'Being,' if it is still Being and if it is the Being *of* Heidegger, the same thing as (if not the very possibility of) Levinas's 'otherwise than being.'"[14] Perhaps. Perhaps (and here is the opening I am attempting, perhaps in vain) *désistance*, as I read it in Lacoue-Labarthe, calls for an "otherwise than being" (otherwise than *ester*), other still, and that would be neither "Heideggerian" nor "Levinasian" (these attributes impose a stupid economy on us), without ceasing to clear, between these two thoughts, so close to one another and so heterogeneous, the way [*le passage*] for a thinking translation.

Estance, the meaning *estance*, would thus find itself destabilized in itself, without this being able to appear as a negativity. *Désistance*, that of truth first of all, would condition all the positions and all the stances that it nevertheless ruins and throws into a panic [*affole*] from within. A question of translation, again, and a passage between the Greek (*alētheia*, translated or interpreted by Heidegger as *Unverstelltheit*), the German (*Ge-stell* and the words in *stellen*, whose resources are deployed in the section entitled "The Stele"), and the Latin (*sto, stare*, etc.). We should pause for some time around this point of passage, the privilege of which, for those of us who write more in Latin, is found described in a note. Lacoue-Labarthe does not seek in this note (nor will I) to dissimulate the abyss opened beneath what is here called a *Witz*. Abyss, hiatus, or chaos:

> Heidegger in fact plays constantly on the drawing together (if not the pure and simple "assimilation") of *stehen* and *stellen*, even while maintaining a certain difference between them. It is as if he identified the *stal* of *stellein* (which means to equip, but also, in the middle voice, to send word, to send for) with the *sta* of *stele*, the column or *stele* (cf. *istemi*, or, in Latin, *sto, stare*)—thus proceeding (as is so often the case in Heidegger) finally more by philological *Witz* than by any true etymologism . . . even though in a text very close to the one that concerns us primarily here . . . Heidegger notes, in passing, that the Greek word *thesis* (which derives from the—simple—Indo-European root *dhe*) can in German be translated at the same time by *Setzung, Stellung,* and *Lage.* (66–67, note 31)

Désistance perhaps brings to light the insanity or unreason, the *anoia* against which Platonic onto-ideology, or even Heidegger's interpretation of it (101ff.), is established, installed, stabilized. But just as it is not reducible to a negative mode of the stance, it is not to be confused with madness—though in doubling or disinstalling everything that secures reason, it can resemble insanity. Madness against madness. The double bind oscillates between two madnesses, for there can also be a madness of reason, of the defensive stiffening in *assistance*, imitation, identification. Double bind between the double bind and its other. I am jumping here, by ellipsis, to Hölderlin and "The Caesura of the Speculative," but I will come back to this point:

> [For now] the historical scheme and the mimetology it presupposes begin slowly, vertiginously, to vacillate, to distort, and to hollow out in an abyssal manner. And if you also consider that the structure of supplementation, defining in sum the mimetic relation in general, the relation between art and nature, is in Hölderlin's eyes fundamentally a structure of *assistance*, that it is necessary if man is to be *prevented* from [*pour* éviter *que l'homme*] "taking flame in contact with the element," then you will not only understand what the stakes were for him in Greek art (it was a matter, finally, of dealing with a "madness" brought about by excessive imitation of the divine and speculation), but you also will understand why in the modern epoch—even though this epoch *reverses, in principle*, the Greek relation between art and nature— one must indeed repeat what is most Greek in the Greeks. Begin the Greeks again. That is to say, no longer be Greek at all. (My emphases—JD)[15]

Désistance: mimesis or its double. *Désistance, that is to say*, and *in other words*, what it doubles and engulfs [*abîme*], *alētheia*. As a consequence, the new "question of the subject" calls for another experience of truth. Another engagement of Heideggerian deconstruction: one that involves *playing* (mimesis plays, there is some play in it, it allows some play and forces one to play), playing (at) the return of a truth determined as *homoiōsis*, adequation, similitude, or resemblance, but that is also removed, through this return that is played at and played out, from the Heideggerian interpretation (accuracy, exactitude, e-vidence) which finds itself destabilized in its turn. *De*stabilized not only through a movement of destabilization, but through this movement of *désistance* that dislodges it from any relation to a possible stance.

It will indeed be necessary to take a detour and a return path—or, rather, to follow the trajectory of a *supplementary loop*. Both *inside* and *outside* the path of epochality. I am tempted to call such a loop a ring, or even a band. A certain *circulation*, as we will see, takes on the value of a prescription: (double) obligation, injunction, bond [*alliance*].

Mimesis

A *critical* question—the question of critique, in other words, of *decision*: one cannot avoid missing mimesis as soon as one identifies it and wants to decide on its truth value. One would not find it if one had not already missed it in looking for it; that is, if one did not have faith in its identity, its existence, or its consistency. This is what Plato, Heidegger, and Girard do in very different, but finally analogous ways. In the extraordinary bidding scene that he stages between them, Lacoue-Labarthe sets the latter two, so to speak, back to back, though not without playing (to keep to this code of games and strategies), Heidegger against Girard. Girard would like to "appropriate" or "identify" mimesis. Thus, he fails to seize it; or rather, "infallibly," says Lacoue-Labarthe—the ineluctable as always—he betrays its essence precisely by conferring on it an essence or a property. A truth to be revealed. Here the ineluctable comes down to missing the lack, or—still more paradoxical—missing this lack whose structure, finally, is not negative: it is to appropriate (for oneself) or decide on what is proper where there is only the im-proper or the non-proper. The latter remains all the more ungraspable in that it is not negative; it defies all those dialectics that, literally, it lets loose, liberates, induces. Such is, without being (it), mimesis as *désistance*.

> [The act of differentiating, appropriating, identifying, *verifying* mimesis] would without fail betray the essence or property of mimesis, if there were an essence of mimesis or if what is "proper" to mimesis did not lie precisely in the fact that mimesis has no "proper" to it, ever (so that mimesis does not consist in the improper, either, or in who knows what "negative" essence, but *ek-sists*, or better yet, "de-sists" in this appropriation of everything supposedly proper that necessarily jeopardizes property "itself"). Which would betray its essence, in other words, if the "essence" of mimesis were not precisely absolute vicariousness, carried to the limit (but inexhaustible), endless and groundless—something like an infinity of substitution and *circulation* (already we must again think of Nietzsche): the very lapse "itself" of essence. (116)

We are far from any mimetologism, from the interpretation of mimesis as imitation, or even as representation, even though the re- of re-petition, at the origin of all re-presentation, has to do with *désistance* (112). *Désistance* of the "same," therefore, and of the "essence"; like "proper" one can do no more than write these words in quotation marks, insofar as one must leave them in their own language.

From the passage I have just cited, let us retain for a moment the word *circulation.* It is emphasized; and it will lead us toward this feigned but necessary rehabilitation of truth as *homoiōsis,* which no longer belongs to Heidegger's epochal interpretation. If Girard, referring mimesis to the subject of desire, interprets it as assimilation, indifferent reciprocity, and thus finally as a general instability or disinstallation, he nevertheless maintains the hope of a *revelation* of mimesis. Lacoue-Labarthe seems first of all to set Heidegger against this, not the interpreter of the *Republic* for whom mimesis is also disinstallation as fall, decline, diminution of truth (of truth as *Unverstelltheit*), but the one for whom the aletheic withdrawal remains inadequate—"inadequation" itself—to any opposition of the adequate and the inadequate, of presence and absence, and thus to any revelation (for example, religious or anthropological). I quote the word "inadequation" because it carries the whole weight of this movement. This inadequation does not belong to the couple "adequate/inadequate" of truth as *homoiōsis,* as it is circumscribed and decidably situated by Heidegger. Nevertheless, it is necessary that this lexicon, this simulacrum or this fiction, reassume its "right" (precisely that of mimesis) in disturbing the order of a history of truth as Heidegger recounts it to us. The *désistance* or de-stabilization of *alētheia,* in it (by or as mimesis), reintroduces an inadequation or an instability of *homoiōsis* that resembles what it nevertheless displaces. Hence the vertigo, the unease, the *Unheimlichkeit.* Mimesis "precedes" truth in a certain sense; by destabilizing it in advance, it introduces a desire for *homoiōsis* and makes it possible, perhaps, to account for it, as for everything that might be its effect, up to and including what is called the subject. All of this

> is not unrelated, strange as it may seem, to that determination of truth that Heidegger always endeavored to consider as secondary and derived (the determination of truth as *homoiōsis,* as adequation, similitude, or, resemblance), but that would in its turn be *displaced,* in any case removed from the horizon of accuracy and of exactitude (of e-vidence), never being rigorously where one expects to see it or precisely what one wants to know. In other words, an unstable *homoiōsis* that *circulates* endlessly between inadequate resemblance and resembling inadequation, confounding memory as well as sight, upsetting the play of *alētheia* and indeed carrying its breakdown right up to the very means of signifying its difference—so inapprehensible (imperceptible) is the agitation that this unstable *homoiōsis* imparts to the Same. (121)

Along with the Same, there is the economy, the law of the *oikos* that finds itself radically destabilized by the *désistance* of mimesis: "any historic or historial economy," any guarantee of critical, theoretical, or hermeneutic reappropriation. Finally, all discourse, be it that of a certain deconstruction, to the extent that the discourses of Girard or Heidegger could be said to belong, however "unequally" (123), to deconstruction. Lacoue-Labarthe calls for a "(de)construction" "more positive than critical, something, as it were, *not very negative*. Credit should be given, in other words, to the philosophical even in its very lapsing, in its exposure and failure, in the default of its so-called (or rather self-proclaimed) infallibility. Indeed, one should *sustain* to the end the philosophical thesis itself, the thesis according to which—always—truth and knowledge *are necessary* [il faut *la vérité et le savoir*]" (123).[16]

What has just happened? From one deconstruction to the other. By re-accentuating, *remarking* the truth of adequation, by holding it no longer simply for a secondary, inscribable, classified, decidable determination, Lacoue-Labarthe dislocates the epochal history scanned by the Heideggerian deconstruction. Not that he rehabilitates, as such, the truth of adequation or *homoiōsis*. On the contrary, he makes an abyss appear in it, a disturbing and destabilizing power that it draws from a pre-originary mimesis. This "truth" is now no longer simply derived from an other, more originary truth. Haunted by mimesis, it now plays a much more determinant role than the one to which Heidegger seemed to confine it. Hence the sort of loop or supplementary torsion, the *ring* [anneau] that is both one more and one less in the epochal chain. This more-and-less dissimulates itself, but its effect is not simply local. It disorganizes the essential schemas—I would not venture to say the axiomatic or regulative principle—of the Heideggerian deconstruction. Thus, in a certain way, the deconstruction signed by Lacoue-Labarthe, if the word "deconstruction" still fits, would no longer bear a relation of filiation to that of Heidegger. Not only does it no longer resemble it, if only thereby in its style, but it ceases to pursue, develop, continue, prolong it. It interrupts it. It no longer resembles it? Certainly it does, but it merely resembles it. In truth, it interrupts it. And so far as truth is concerned, the resemblance remains troubling. Obviously, one must think together the two propositions that I have advanced here and which describe another double bind, one that might be uncovered in Lacoue-Labarthe's very writing: (1) he cannot and should not be read without Heidegger, since he never writes without pursuing an interminable reading of Heidegger; (2) and yet, what he does remains entirely different. But aside from the double bind that holds him, by this supplementary link [*anneau*], to the "uncircumventable [*incontournable*]" necessity of the Heideggerian questions, another consequence imprints itself on all of these texts. What consequence? Beyond the fundamental ontology that ordered and unified all fields and that Heidegger himself suspended at a given moment, beyond the power of gathering that continued to exert itself over an epochal history of Being, a diversity is liberated that can no longer be called a multiplicity of regions or ontological fields. The latter offer themselves to Lacoue-Labarthe's typography, a typography that is no longer *fundamental:* philosophy, theater, poetics, painting, music, "auto-biography," politics. These are no longer regional instances, and one can no longer speak glibly of the essence of the poetic, of the political, the theatrical, and so on. There is no longer *one* central question that is always the same.

For example: as it will later develop, particularly in "Transcendence Ends in Politics," "Poétique et politique," "Histoire et mimesis," "L'Antagonisme,"[17] and almost everywhere in *Typography* and *L'Imitation des modernes,* the second title of which is *Typographie* II, the political dimension of this link appears clearly. Between, on the one hand, a thought of mimesis that dislocates the Heideggerian deconstruction or disturbs the possibility of the epochal delimitations it implements (for example, the space of an ontotypology) and, on the other hand, the strictly, literally political interpretation of the Nietzschean or Heideggerian *text* (in the latter case, I mean by "text" Heidegger's acts and works), one can recognize at every step the differentiated coherence. I cannot demonstrate this here. But if the genre of the preface—why deny it?—calls for peremptory evaluations, then let us say that regarding these serious and formidable problems, I know no judgment more sure than Lacoue-Labarthe's, none more rigorous and prudent, more attentive both to the discreet folds and to the great amplitude, the breadth without measure of what one cannot easily continue to call a scene, a sequence, a period, or a history—a terrifying deportation, in any case, whose measurelessness [*démesure*] still seems to defy the very hope of a judgment and a justice. And yet there is the instance of the *il faut* I have just cited; there is philosophy and its law. This thinking of *désistance* is one of the most demanding thoughts of *responsibility.* The fact that the traditional categories of responsibility no longer suffice places irresponsibility *rather* on the side of these categories.

How can one assume a responsibility in *désistance*, the responsibility *of désistance* itself? One can vary or deconstruct all the predicates of responsibility in general, yet one cannot completely reduce the *delay*: an event, a law, a call, an other are *already* there; others are there—for whom and before whom one must answer. However "free" it is supposed to be, the *response* inaugurates nothing if it does not come *after*. Prescription, typography, *ethos*, ethics, character, delay.

The (de)constitutive disappropriation of the subject, that destabilization to which mimesis *submits* the subject from the "beginning"—this is what gives *désistance* the phenomenal form of "delay [*retard*]." In "Typography" the word appears twice: "delay in coming to speak," "belatedness [*retard*] (impossible to overcome) with respect to its [the child's] 'own' birth" (127)[18]—that kind of pre-maturation that philosophical anti-*mimesis* has always wanted to erase. But *Bildung* and *paideia* could finally only confirm, by this "supplemental birth," the irreducibility of a typo-graphical structure, of a "character" (*ethos* or *typos*) already in subjection. One might invoke here the subject's preinscription in a symbolic order that always precedes it. But the *désistance* of which Lacoue-Labarthe speaks disturbs even the order with and in which Lacan defines this situation: a logic of opposition and of splitting, an identification of the Other, in short the very thing that mimesis—as close as can be to resemblance—ruins, destabilizes, (de)constructs:

> Traversed from the very beginning by a multiple and anonymous discourse (by the discourse of the others and not necessarily by that of *an* Other), the "subject" is not so much (de)constituted in a splitting or a simple *Spaltung*—that is, in a *Spaltung* articulated simply in terms of the opposition between the negative and presence (between absence and position, or even between death and identity)—as it is splintered or dispersed according to the disquieting instability of the improper. Whence the obsession with appropriation that dominates through and through the entire analysis of mimesis, of mimetism, and that works to create—well before a concern is shown for the problematic of the lie—its full economic (and consequently political) bearing. (128)

All of the traits isolated here seem pertinent, and we are given, it seems to me, the rule governing their selection, both for Platonic discourse (see the analysis that directly follows this passage) and for Lacanian discourse, including its "concern . . . shown for the problematic of the lie" (129). And who will think that Platonism is out of date when it denounces in mimesis—in other words, in désistance—madness, feminization, hysteria?[19]

RHUTHMOS

In the beginning was rhythm, said von Bülow. Another way of marking the fact that there is no simple beginning: no rhythm without repetition, spacing, caesura, the "repeated difference-from-itself of the Same," says Lacoue-Labarthe (196)—and thus repercussion, resonance, echo, reverberation.[20] We are constituted by this rhythm, in other words (*de-*)*constituted* by the marks of this "caesuraed" stamp, by this rhythmotypy that is nothing other than the divided idiom in us of *désistance*. A rhythm gathers us and divides us in the prescription of a character. There is no subject without the signature of this rhythm, in us before us, before any image, any discourse, before music itself. "Rhythm would also be the condition of possibility for the subject" (195). We are "rhythmed" (202, 206) in such a way that rhythm no longer comes to us as a predicate. The "character" it imprints or prescribes is not the attribute of the being we are, namely, our existence. No, before the stance of our being-present, before its consistency, its existence, and its essence, there is rhythmic *désistance*.

To treat rhythm is thus not to add a chapter to the new typography of the subject. It is to think *désistance* as it is *written*. "Before" the specular reflexivity of the *psyche*, before any "image" and even before any autographical (autobiographical or autothanatographical) "discourse." Nevertheless, the question of the *autos* and its self-relation as rhythm, traversing all of Lacoue-Labarthe's work, finds its most impressive unfolding in "The Echo of the Subject." Point of departure: the relation between autobiography and music, a reminder concerning *désistement* and above all of the necessity for "deconstruction" to take on "the site of greatest resistance." Which are the proper names [*noms propres*] that are best suited [*propres*] to designate this site? Heidegger, of course, and Lacoue-Labarthe immediately makes this clear. But it will be necessary to add Freud and Lacan, and this debate will be fiercer, more specific as well. And Reik, although his case seems more complicated still, as we will see, in this extraordinary dramaturgy where no place is ever won: an implacable fidelity, an exemplary probity pushes Lacoue-Labarthe to respect every fold, every overdetermination of the scene, *recalling one to another, both for and against*. A Lacanian quadrangulation against the Oedipal theory and thus against Freud; a thematics of voice and rhythm in Reik against specular or optical theoreticism, or even Freud's verbocentrism—which we also find in Lacan, whose division between the imaginary and the symbolic is blurred by this thematics. And finally Reik's relapse and his "theoretical failure," his subjection to Freud and the triumph of the Oedipal, and so on.

Why does the motif of rhythm, when articulated in this way with that of typographical inscription, possess such effective deconstructive power?

Because it ties together several possibilities. It makes it possible to open a new problematic of the subject (of its "character," of what prescribes or preinscribes it, also divides it according to the cut and the repetition of a *désistance*) by turning the Heideggerian deconstruction away from a metaphysics of subjectity—that is to say, by removing the subject from its determination by the notions of the self, consciousness, representation, and optical or discursive objectivity, and by thus assuming in it a psychoanalytic dimension. But simultaneously, the motif of rhythm makes it possible to deconstruct, in a certain philosophy of psychoanalysis, *both* the hegemony of the visual, of the image or of the specular, *and* the hegemony of discursivity—for example, that of the verbal text in music. These two hegemonies have never been incompatible; on the contrary, they are coordinated in the history of metaphysics, which still commands these psychoanalytic theories, from Freud to Lacan. Rhythm—the spaced repetition of a percussion, the inscriptive force of a spacing—belongs neither to the visible nor to the audible, neither to spectacular figuration nor to the verbal representation of music, nor to music, even if it structures them *insensibly*. The structuration that I called rhythmotypical or typorhythmic a moment ago must remain insensible. It belongs to no sense. This is also why, despite appearances, "The Echo of the Subject" is less concerned with music than with rhythm in music or in dance. But to speak of the insensibility of rhythm is not to declare it intelligible. Cadence and caesura, rhythmotypy opens the possibility of an intelligible sense or meaning; it does not belong to it. (Nietzsche, in passing, *laterally*: "to mistake the rhythm of a sentence is to mistake the very meaning of the sentence" [161].) I say *laterally* because this thought of rhythm has always *haunted* our tradition, without ever reaching the center of its concerns. And "The Echo of the Subject" is also a text on the musical ghost, haunting, obsession, or rather the reverberation, the return of rhythm. This is a very ancient war. It is "normal" that rhythm be repressed, if one can say this, and even by the *theories* of repression. The pressure it exerts, and the pressure exerted on it, form a compression, a *compulsion*, one could say, which is scanned regularly by traces: all of them signaling that rhythmotypical compulsion constitutes (translation: deconstitutes), desists the "subject" in the knot that lies at its core, in its "soul," in its ineluctable destiny—whatever name one chooses for the dis-location of this destinal site. An ineluctable laterality, then, in the margins of a philosophy entirely preoccupied with avoiding rhythm: Hölderlin ("All is rhythm [*Rhythmus*], the entire destiny of man is a single celestial rhythm, just as the work of art is one unique rhythm" [139]), Mallarmé ("because every soul is a rhythmic knot" [140]). In the margins of philosophy, before it: I am thinking of the work, which is now well known, in particular that of Benveniste, on the use of the word *rhuthmos* (by Leucippus, for example) to designate a graphic configuration. Heidegger, indeed, recalled that Georgiades had translated *rhuthmos* by *Gepräge* (imprint, seal, type, character [200]). This is no doubt true, but it did not prevent him from bringing the problematic of the *typos* back to the ontotypology that I mentioned earlier, and that of the subject back to the epoch of subjectity: a double reason, at a different degree of generality, for reading "The Echo of the Subject" as a new inflection in the displacement of Heideggerian deconstruction—another knot in the supplemental loop I defined above. But Heidegger does not occupy center stage in this scene, a scene whose turbulence is, properly speaking, unimaginable (for it is also a matter of what goes beyond the image, the imaginary, the spectacular and the specular—or renders them indeterminable). Were it not for this unimaginable, I would say that "The Echo of the Subject" can be read as a resonating *theater*, a series of dramatic reversals, a great tragic mythology sweeping along with it philosophers, musicians, and psychoanalysts in an excess of filiations, denials of filiation or paternity, dramas of specularity, mimetic rivalries, linked knots of double binds, transgressions and re-Oedipalizations of the law, triangulations and retriangulations: Mahler, von Bülow and Beethoven, Reik, Abraham, and Freud. But also Heidegger and Lacan, Rousseau, Hegel, Nietzsche, and Girard. And Groddeck and Thomas Mann and Leucippus. And Wallace Stevens. I am forgetting more than one. And Lacoue-Labarthe. For we must never forget: what he *says* of the double bind—of which he speaks more and more in his texts and that happens to be named here at the very moment when it is a question of a subject "that 'desists' because it must always confront at least two figures (or one figure that is *at least* double)" (175) and when, in passing, he is destabilizing the Lacanian distinction between the imaginary and the symbolic—what Lacoue-Labarthe *undergoes* [fait], in saying this, of the double bind, is the experience of the ineluctable. This is an experience that there can be no question of my—("I"), Lacoue-Labarthe—escaping. I write myself in writing about how things are written [*comment ça s'écrit*] in this auto-biographical, allo- and thanatographical theater. If I pose or propose anything at all in it, it is not only a theory, or even a practice of the double bind on the scale of an immense tradition—a tradition scanned, continued, interrupted, by what all these names appear to sign. I present myself, or rather *write myself*, sign my own *désistance*, the impossible itself, as an experience of the double bind, the poetic experience of the double bind. Double constraint, double law, knot and caesura of a divided law, the law of the double. The knot and the caesura, the obligation and the cut—that is rhythm. And is rhythm not the double law—and vice versa? The task would be to think this. And the supplementary ring [*anneau*] of *this* deconstruction would be nothing other, would have no other modality than this double constraint that no dialectic could ever overcome.

Unless—unless the double bind as such is still too linked to opposition, contradiction, dialectic; unless it still belongs to *that kind* of undecidable that always derives from dialectical calculation and contraction. In which case, it would be necessary to think another undecidable, to interrupt *this* double bind with a gap or a hiatus—and recognize in an *arrhythmic* caesura the respiration of rhythm. This necessity still awaits us.

But as you can see, a preface cannot measure up to a text like this. I am leaving the substance [*fond*] of things, the *background* of the scene, to meticulous readings and rereadings. As I committed myself to do, I am following only the threads of the debate Lacoue-Labarthe openly conducts with those who represent the strategic site of greatest resistance. As concerns Heidegger, we have begun to measure its dimensions. There remain Freud, Lacan, and Reik.

Freud: he admits to not having "experience" with music and musicians. When he privileges the text to the detriment of music, he prudently limits the scope of his assertions to those individuals who are not "really musicians." Even if it is formulated with some uneasiness, this limitation was frequently emphasized by Reik. It confirms the general organization of the theory, a certain logocentric theoreticism. Freud orders all interpretation around the articulation of discourse and figuration (*Darstellbarkeit*), a semiotics of verbal signifiers and visual forms.

Lacan: the least one can say is that he does not break with this theoretical structure. Lacoue-Labarthe does not propose a "critique" of his text. As always, he proceeds "with and against Lacan" (174). This was already the case in *The Title of the Letter*.[21] But he demonstrates that what appears *theoretically* accurate and even insuperable is a certain theoreticism. The latter is inscribed in the ontology of the figure (a figural and fictional ontology); it is always a matter of delimiting this ontology, which submits the Lacanian recasting of Freud to the gaze, to the theoretical, to the specular, and to the speculative. And therefore to an ontomimetological interpretation of *mimesis*. The demonstration bears principally upon the conditions under which the Oedipal triangle is open to the mythic quartet or to the "quaternary system," not to mention the theory of fictional figurality in "The Mirror Stage."[22] The theory of narcissism (and the notion of an "imaginary death") brings "back into vigor the eidetic transcendence of Platonism whose logic Heidegger brought forth . . . [and the mediation of this 'fourth element,' the imaginary death, would be constitutive] of the 'giving of meaning' itself, or of what establishes, in its unverifiable truth, as Lacan said, 'the measure of man.'. . . In which case, and this is indeed what Lacan stated in conclusion, the theory of narcissism is nothing other than the truth of *The Phenomenology of Mind*" (171–72).

But if this quaternity remains "very Hegelian, perfectly dialectical," the entire discourse on the splitting, the alienation, the *Spaltung* of the subject remains a dialectical ontology of the lack and of negativity, a logic of opposition: the very logic, one will remember, that a thinking of mimesis comes to double, disturb, and destabilize. The "loss of the subject," in the Lacanian sense, its very ek-sistence, has as its paradoxical effect a suturing, or let us say rather, an obliterating, of *désistance*. Here again, the experience of *désistance* is prey to the double bind:

> Thus, because it takes into account this discord that no speculation can dialectize because it is inscribed in the specular relation itself, it is very likely that we are dealing here with a *loss of the subject*, undermining in advance any constitution, any functional assumption, and any possibility of appropriation or reappropriation. This loss of the subject is imperceptible, however, and not because it is equivalent to a secret failing or hidden lack, but because it is strictly indissociable from, and doubles, the process of constitution or appropriation. For this reason, I have already proposed [in "Obliteration"] to speak of (de)constitution. But this is makeshift. What should be noted here, with and against Lacan, and going back from Lacan to Reik, is that there is a constant though muffled breakdown of the imaginary, of the resources of the imaginary. The imaginary destroys at least as much as it helps to construct. More precisely, it continually alters what it constructs. This explains,

perhaps, why the subject in the mirror is first of all a subject in "desistance [*désistement*]" (and why, for example, it will never recover from the mortal insufficiency to which, according to Lacan, its prematuration has condemned it). It explains also the delay, the inhibition, the *après-coup* effects, the deterioration—in short, everything belonging to the deadly repetition at work in more than just so-called obsessional neurosis. We are dealing here not with a pure rupture of the economic in general, but with the slow erosion of appropriation. . . . The dialectic of recognition itself does not perhaps function so well, not only because every subject is on its way to death, or even because it is irremediably separated from itself (as "subject"), but simply because it comes to itself only in losing itself.

The "theoretical" consequence (though at the limit of the theorizable): the figure is never *one*. Not only is it the Other, but there is no unity or stability of the figural; the imago has no fixity or proper being. There is no "proper image" with which to identify totally, no essence of the imaginary. (174–75)

I want to interrupt this quotation for a moment in order to emphasize the coherence of these words in their political dimension, even if the latter is less marked in "The Echo of the Subject" than, for example, in more recent texts devoted to Nietzsche or to Heidegger. Less marked does not mean absent: when the stakes identified are none other than the psychoanalytic institution or identification in general, they are obviously, and immediately, political: "Why would the problem of identification not be, in general, the essential problem of the political?" This is the conclusion of "Transcendence Ends in Politics" (300), and the analysis leading up to it follows paths analogous to the one I have been tracing: ek-sistence (not *désistance*) defined by Heidegger in a still ontotypological fashion in the Rectoral Address, an "unavowed numerology" that would be "overdetermining politically Heidegger's thought," a certain double bind in national identification (imitation and refusal of imitation), and so on. It is still a matter of an interpretation of mimesis, and of a *désistance* prey to the double bind inasmuch as there is no "essence of the imaginary." Lacoue-Labarthe continues immediately as follows:

What Reik invites us to think, in other words, is that the subject "desists" because it must always confront *at least* two figures (or one figure that is *at least* double), and that its only chance of "grasping itself" lies in introducing itself and oscillating *between* figure and figure (between the artist and the scientist, between Mahler and Abraham, between Freud and Freud). And this perhaps accounts for the logic of the double bind, the "double constraint." . . . Everything seems to point to the fact that this destabilizing division of the figural (which muddles, certainly, the distinction between the imaginary and the symbolic, and broaches at the same time the negativity or absolute alterity of the "real") is precisely what is involved in the "musical obsession," connecting it, as a result, with the auto-graphical compulsion itself. (174–75)

Here is "what Reik invites us to think [*ce qu'engage à penser Reik*]." Beyond Freud, beyond Lacan, already, but with them, and falling back regularly under the law they represent, submitting to it anew each time he threatens to transgress it. He falls back and submits. The words "failure" and "submission" recur on almost every page of this magnificent text.[23] For what Reik invites us to think is what Lacoue-Labarthe thinks and what Reik could deliver only by not knowing how to deliver himself from it. Not that it is a matter here of a simple liberating transgression—and the conclusion of "The Echo of the Subject," once the thinking has been delivered, has nothing triumphant about it. In truth, it does not conclude, except with a "perhaps": "Perhaps it is impossible to get beyond the closure of narcissism, even by shaking its specular model" (205). That is to say, the optical, theatrical, theoretical, and Oedipal model, the psyche that forces Reik's relapse and the "theoretical failure" that is nothing other than the failure in theory, because of theory, of a theorization of this very thing, which, as experienced in thought cannot be theorized, and which is rhythm, even more than music. This latter experience does not go beyond theory in the direction of some occult region where affect would have to be put before knowledge. On the contrary, it makes it possible to think the law of the theoretical—as such. Lacoue-Labarthe analyzes patiently, with a kind of rigorous compassion, the return of this law in Reik's text, in its theoretico-auto-analytic adventure. He recognizes in it all its daring moves, the "suspicions" about Freud,[24] the intimations of what he "invites us to think" without thinking it himself—namely, the closure in which remains, and will remain, a psychoanalysis still too Greek, in any case too Platonic (ontotypological, ontoeidetic, mimetological, etc.),[25] and into which he falls back, submitting himself to it. He subjects himself. The movement by which he institutes himself as a subject, in the course of an analytic autobiography "haunted" by the return of music and rhythm, is also the movement by which he *subjects himself* to the law represented by Freud. He subjects himself as a defense, inhibition,[26] resistance before the very thing that engages his thinking and in which he engages our thought:

a certain *désistance* of the subject in the experience of the double bind and its rhythmic (de)constitution. He cannot not avoid the unavoidable. He resists *désistance*, consolidates his subjectity in this subjection, in this very failure, in this renunciation, of which, as several signs clearly show, he was well aware. One might say that in surrendering to this resistance, he had to abdicate in the face of the responsibility of thinking, of thinking that which he invites us to think. He, Reik, desisted in the face of the task that seemed incumbent upon him: to think ineluctable *désistance*. This is not a moral offense, of course, but how is it possible? Read "The Echo of the Subject." In a labyrinth that I will not try to reconstitute, and that no commentary could "double" (for its course is *unique*, and all along it a logic of resonance is substituted for that of the mirror: Echo undoes Narcissus, if not Psyche, transforming the whole space of this logic, its whole temporality, in this way), I will propose merely a supplementary thread. Not in order to dramatize a reading that has strictly no need of it—or to play Ariadne. But in order to approach somewhat the signature of Lacoue-Labarthe when he says "I" (in quotation marks, here and there throughout his work), when he speaks of madness, of style, of autobiography or allobiography, of death or of music, of Reik—or of an other, for he who is named Reik in this text is also anyone who has linked, at the edge of madness (what is that exactly, the edge [*le bord*]?), the autobiographical adventure, and its doubles, and the other, and death, to the musical obsession (Rousseau, Nietzsche), to the concern with rhythm (Hölderlin, Mallarmé, Nietzsche again). Reik, and all of them—these are Lacoue-Labarthe, you will say, rushing to identify the identifications; and if that is the case, I wish you luck if some day you want to put a stop to this genealogical chain. But no, Lacoue-Labarthe could not *read* Reik as he does except insofar as he has broken the identification, or knew how to follow him while always removing the barriers to which the other's resistance was clinging. And each time he removes one of these limits, he explains its source and its mechanism, and then its ineluctable return. In this gesture, and by this rhythm—you will be able to verify this—Lacoue-Labarthe is at every instant as close and as far from Reik as he could possibly be. And he tells you everything you need to know to think the law of this paradox.

He even has a name for the law of the paradox: it is the hyperbologic.[27] At this point, when I have to cut things short, too late and too early, I will take up only one example: the *caesura*. There is no rhythm without caesura. And yet, as Hölderlin reminds us, the caesura "itself" must be "antirhythmic" (234), even arrythmic. This interruption does not have the dialectical cadence of a relation between rhythm and nonrhythm, the continuous and the discontinuous, and so on. It interrupts alternation, "the constraint of *opposition* in general" (212), the dialectic and the speculative, even the double bind (236ff.) when it maintains an oppositional form. It is ineluctable—and it does not avoid avoidance:

> It prevents [*éviter*] (a protective gesture, which does not necessarily mean a "ritualistic" one) the racing oscillation, *panic*, and an orientation toward this or that pole. It represents the active neutrality of the interval between [*l'entre-deux*]. This is undoubtedly why it is not by chance that the caesura is, on each occasion, the empty moment—the absence of any "moment"—of Tiresias's intervention: that is to say, of the intrusion of the prophetic word. (235)

When the caesura, gap, or hiatus marks the withdrawal of the divine and the turning back of man toward the earth in Sophoclean tragedy, it plays at and undoes mourning. A *Trauerspiel* plays at mourning. It doubles the *work* of mourning: the speculative, the dialectic, the opposition, the identification, the nostalgic interiorization, even the double bind of imitation. But it does not avoid it. Gap or hiatus: the open mouth. To give, to receive. The caesura at times takes one's breath away. When chance has it, it gives one speech.

—Translated by Christopher Fynsk

§ 11 A Number of Yes

Oui, à l'étranger.

Yes, to the stranger. Yes, in foreign parts. We will have crossed paths most often abroad. These encounters retain an emblematic value for me. Perhaps because they took place elsewhere, far away, but more surely because we never parted—I haven't forgotten—without a promise. Any more than I have forgotten what Michel de Certeau writes about writing in the mystical text: it is also a promise, through and through.

To me, it is as if these encounters in the other's country—by which I also mean the interruption intimately marking them, the separation that tears apart their very event—described in their own way the paths taken by thought when it merges with the word given in writing: at the heart of the same time, of a single time, the opening *and* the cut. Already a citation from *La Fable mystique*:

> Angelus Silesius . . . identified the written expression of the Separated (*Jah, or Jahvè*) with the limitlessness of the "yes" (*Ja*) . . . . The same phoneme (*Ja*) brings together separation and openness, the *No-Name* of the Other and the *Yes* of the Volition, absolute separation and infinite acceptance.
>
> *Gott Spricht nur immer Ja*
> God always says only Yes [or: I am].[1]

Chance encounter in the singularity of a "graph," the coincidence of

---

The first version of this essay appeared in the issue "Michel de Certeau" of *Cahiers pour un temps*, edited by Luce Giard (1987).

the cut and the opening. We will have to come back to this again and again.

Of these encounters, which immediately became separations, I shall say nothing, nothing directly. Let me just murmur a few place names to myself. I remember the California sun, in San Diego and in Irvine. I remember Cornell, Binghamton, New York, and, finally, I remember Venice, in the snow, in December 1983. How can I gather all this memory together in a figure where it is no longer distinguished from what I have learned and am still learning to read in Michel de Certeau? If memory here could inhabit a single word, and one that resembled him, it would perhaps be *yes*.

What he has said to us *on the subject* of the *yes* was not simply a discourse on a particular element of language, a theoretical metalanguage bearing on one possibility of utterance, on one scene of utterance among others. For essential reasons, it is always risky to say "*the* 'yes,'" to make the adverb "yes" just another name or word, an object *on the subject* of which constative statements might pronounce the truth. Because a *yes* no longer suffers any metalanguage; it engages the "performative" of an originary affirmation and remains thus presupposed by every utterance *on the subject* of the *yes*. Moreover—to put it aphoristically—for Michel de Certeau, there is no subject of any kind that does not arise from the scene of the *yes*. The two *yesses* we have just discerned (but why are there always two? We will ask ourselves this question again) are not homogeneous, and yet they are deceptively similar. That a *yes* should be presupposed each time, not only by every statement on the subject of the *yes,* but also by every negation and every opposition, dialectical or not, between the *yes* and the *no,* this is perhaps what immediately gives the affirmation its essential, irreducible *infinity.* Michel de Certeau insists on this infinity. He sees in it the "mystic postulate." The latter "advances a limitless 'yes.'" The admirable analysis he then proposes seems to me to be traversed by at least four questions. Before asking them—as if to prolong an interrupted colloquy—and sketching out a kind of *quasi*-transcendental or ontological analytic of *yes,* let me quote a long passage from "The 'Performance' of the Subject" in *The Mystic Fable*:

> In a more discreet but insistent tradition, the "performance" of the subject is also taken to be marked by the *yes*—a "yes" as absolute as the *volo,* without objects, without goals. Whereas knowledge delimits its content through a procedure that is essentially a "no," a labor of making distinctions ("this is

not that"), the mystic postulate advances a limitless "yes." Naturally, this is a postulate of principle, as independent of circumstances as the intention aimed at "all," "nothing" or God. Its model is in a surprising statement of St. Paul about Christ: "In Him there has been only Yes (*nai*)." This paradox of a "yes" without limit in the compass of a singular (Jesus) outlines a contradictory and placeless theory of the (Christic) Subject. An infinite yes pierces the field of separations and distinctions practiced by the entire Hebraic epistemology. This "yes" is repeated later. The same historical lapsus (the same forgetting) recurs. In the seventeenth century, Angelus Silesius went even further. He identified the written expression of the Separated (*Ja*, or *Jahvé*) with the limitlessness of the "yes" (*Ja*). In the very place of the sole proper Name (a Name that distances all beings) he installs disappropriation (by a consent to all). The same phoneme (*Ja*) brings together separation and the openness, the *No-Name* of the Other and the *Yes* of the Volition, absolute separation and infinite acceptance.

> *Gott Spricht nur immer Ja*
> God always says only Yes [or: I am].

There is identity between Christ's "yes" and the "I am (the Other)" of the burning bush. The Separated is reversed, becoming the exclusion of exclusion. Such is the cipher of the mystic subject. The "yes," a figure of "abandonment" or "detachment," is, ultimately, "interiority." In that land, a whole population of intention cries out on all sides "yes, yes," like Silesius's God. Is that space divine or Nietzschean? The speaking word [*Wort*], originator of this place [*Ort*], participates in the "essence," which, according to Evagrius, "has no opposite." (174–75)

I will leave the four questions open or suspended. The answers will not come, not from me in any case, but that hardly matters. That is what I would like to show. Not that the answer here matters less than the question. It is the question that matters less than a certain *yes,* the *yes* that resounds in it always in order to come *before* it. What is of interest here is a *yes* that opens the question and always lets itself be presupposed by it, a *yes* that affirms prior to, before or beyond any possible question.

First question. Why does repetition belong to the destiny of the *yes?* Michel de Certeau makes two allusions to two repetitions that apparently do not have the same meaning in his eyes. He does not reduce one to the other and does not dwell on them. There is first "this 'yes'" that, he says, "is repeated later. The same historical lapsus (the same forgetting) recurs." This reproduction seems not to have the same value or the same meaning as the "yes, yes" of Silesius's God. No doubt. But what is the common root of these two repetitions or reproductions? And what if, curiously, they repeated or implicated each other? Does the *quasi-*transcendental or ontological structure of the *yes* not prescribe this double destiny, which is also a destiny of duplicity?

Second question. Why is it necessary to choose between a "divine" and a "Nietzschean" space? Michel de Certeau is no doubt alluding to numerous texts by Nietzsche, for example "The Seven Seals (Or: The Yes and Amen Song)" in *Also sprach Zarathustra.* And in fact Nietzsche himself opposes the light, dancing, ethereal *Ja* of the innocent affirmation to the *Ja, Ja* of the Christian ass suffering or sighing beneath the burden of a gravely assumed responsibility ("Der Esel aber schrie dazu I-A" ["Die Erweckung"]). Repetition and memory (*Ja, Ja*) seem to be assigned to the Christian *yes,* which would also be a *yes* of finitude. In its very innocence, the infinite *yes* is excessive in the face of this finitude, and it is probably for this reason that Michel de Certeau poses his question in the form of an alternative ("divine or Nietzschean"), thus perhaps referring to "das ungeheure unbegrenzte Ja—und Amen—sagen" of *Also sprach Zarathustra* ("Vor Sonnen-Aufgang"). But once again, is there not in the *quasi-*transcendental or ontological experience of the *yes* a common root which, without annulling the alternative, nonetheless prescribes that we derive it from a more "ancient" possibility?

Third question. Concerning this boundless *yes,* Michel de Certeau says *both* that it "pierces the field of separations and distinctions practiced by the entire Hebraic epistemology" and that it reminds us of "identity between Christ's 'yes' and the 'I am (the Other)' of the burning bush." These two propositions do not contradict each other, of course. A "Hebraic epistemology" of separation is not necessarily attuned to or homogeneous with the infinite affirmation. Furthermore, the boundless *yes* does not exclude separation, on the contrary. Between the Judaic affirmation and the Christian affirmation we will certainly not speak of affinity, even less of affiliation. But does the "identity between Christ's 'yes' and the 'I am (the Other)' of the burning bush" not open, once again, on an event or an advent of the *yes* that would be *neither* Jewish *nor* Christian, not yet or no longer simply one or the other? And rather than to the abstract structure of some ontological or transcendental condition of possibility, doesn't this "neither . . . nor" refer us back to the "quasi" that I have been hinting at above ("quasi-transcendental" or "quasi-ontological") and that would harmonize [*accorderait*] the originary eventness of the event with the fabulous narrative or with the fable inscribed in the *yes* as the origin of all speech (*fari*)? One might wonder, for example, whether Franz Rosenzweig is still speaking as a Jew, or if he speaks as the already over-Christianized Jew that some accused him of being, when he recalls us to the originary *yes* in certain texts whose status remains essentially uncertain, like everything that says (the) *yes*, between the theological, the philosophical (transcendental or ontological), and the song of praise or the hymn. Let us not forget that the Hebrew *yes* (*ken*) can always inscribe itself in the Shekinah whose tradition is often invoked in *The Mystic Fable*.[2] Since Michel de Certeau does not, to my knowledge, quote Rosenzweig (whose *Star of Redemption* had not yet been translated when he published *The Mystic Fable*), perhaps it is best to extract first these few lines of Rosenzweig's:

> Yea is the beginning. Nay cannot be the beginning; for it could only be a Nay of the Nought. This, however, would presuppose a negatable Nought, a Nay, therefore, that had already decided on a Yea. . . . This non-Nought is, however, not independently given, for nothing at all is given except for the Nought. Therefore the affirmation of the non-Nought circumscribes as inner limit the infinity of all that is not Nought. An infinity is affirmed: God's infinite essence, his infinite actuality, his Physis. . . . Such is the power of Yea that it adheres everywhere. . . . It is the arche-word [*Urwort*] of language, one of those which first makes possible, not sentences, but any kind of sentence-forming words at all, words as parts of the sentence. Yea is not a part of a sentence, but neither is it a shorthand symbol for a sentence, although it can be employed as such. Rather it is the silent accompanist of all parts of a sentence, the confirmation, the "sic!" the "Amen" behind every word. It gives every word in the sentence its right to exist, it supplies the seat on which it may take its place, it "posits." The first Yea in God establishes the divine essence for all infinity. And this first Yea is "in the beginning."[3]

As originary word (*Urwort*), the *yes* undoubtedly belongs to language. It is definitely a word. It can always be a word, and translatable. And yet, implicated by all the other words whose source it figures, it also remains silent, the "silent accompanist" (a little like the "I think" in Kant that "accompanies" all our representations), and thus in a certain way foreign to language, heterogeneous to the set of terms [*vocables*] thus defined [*cernés*] and concerned [*concernés*] by its power. It is therefore a kind of inaudible term, inaudible even in the utterance of a determined *yes,* in one language or another, in a given sentence valid as affirmation. Language without language, it belongs without belonging to the whole that it simultaneously institutes and opens. It exceeds and punctures the language to which it nonetheless remains immanent: like language's first inhabitant, the first to step out of its home. It *causes* to be and *lets* be everything that can be said. But one can already see its intrinsic double nature announcing itself, or more precisely, confirming itself. It is without being language; it merges without merging with its utterance in a natural language. For if it is "before" language, it marks the essential exigency, the engagement, the promise to come to language, in a given language. Such an event is required by the very force of the *yes*. Insofar as it approves or confirms every possible language, says Rosenzweig, the *sic* or the "amen" that it institutes doubles the archi-originary *yes* that gives the first breath to every utterance with an acquiescence. The "first" is already, always, a confirmation: *yes, yes*, a *yes* that goes from *yes to yes* or that comes from *yes to yes*. Something of this acquiescence also bespeaks a certain cruel rest, a "cruel repose" (*immanem quietem*), to which I will refer again later (139, 142).[4] Can one take account of, give an account of, attempt the enumeration of this redoubling of the *yes*? Why is its analytic only "quasi" transcendental or ontological?

Fourth question. Michel de Certeau analyzes the performance of the *yes* in the course of an interpretation of the *volo* ("a 'yes' as absolute as the *volo*, without objects, without goal" [174]), in the particularly beautiful pages devoted to "A Preliminary: The *Volo* (from Meister Eckhart to Madame Guyon)" (164ff.). Is the thinking of this *yes* coextensive with that of a *volo*? Does the originary consent that thus lets itself be uttered or heard in this wordless word belong to the "absolute volitive" that, as Michel de Certeau suggests, is "the equivalent of what Jacob Böhme posits at the origin of all existence: the violence, the furor even, of a Will" (169)? Must it be said, then, that this determination of the *yes* is still dominated by what Heidegger calls a metaphysics of the will, in other words by the interpretation of Being as the unconditional will of a subjectivity whose hegemony marks all modernity, at least from Descartes to Hegel and to Nietzsche? And if this is so, would it not be necessary to detach the experience and the description of the *yes* from those of a *volo*? At issue, of course, would be an experience without experience, a description without description: no determinable presence, no object, no possible theme. Because I cannot enter into this immense and daunting problematic here, I will situate three possible points of reference.

A. Having upheld the irreducible privilege of the questioning attitude, throughout an almost thirty-year course of inquiry, having written that questioning (*Fragen*) was the piety (*Frömmigkeit*) of thinking, Heidegger had at least to complicate this axiom. First by recalling that piety should from the start have been understood as the docility of listening, the question being thus, before anything else, a receptive modality, an attentiveness that relies on what gives itself to be heard rather than, prior to, the enterprising, inquisitorial activity of a request or an inquest. Secondly by insisting henceforth on a more originary dimension of thought, the *Zusage*, this confident acceptance, this assent to the proffered word (*Zuspruch*) without which no question is possible, a *yes* in short, a sort of pre-engagement presupposed by every language and by every speech (*Sprache*). This dimension of "experience" clearly resonates, in his later texts, with that of *Gelassenheit*. I bring up the word not only because of the major role it plays in these texts of Heidegger's but also to evoke Meister Eckhart, of whom Heidegger was, no doubt to an even greater extent than he says, an assiduous reader. Michel de Certeau names Heidegger from the first page of the introduction to *The Mystic Fable*,[5] and he alludes to Meister Eckhart's *Gelâzenheit* in the chapter with which we are concerned. What he says of it brings me to my second point of reference.

B. This *Gelâzenheit* bespeaks the non-willing [*non-vouloir*] in the most unconditional willing. Such that the very unconditionality of a willing without end and without object turns the will into a-will [*a-volonté*]. Once again, it is necessary to quote *The Mystic Fable* at length:

> Finally, this *volo*, because it has no particular object and "clings" to *nothing*, changes into its opposite—not to want anything—and thus takes up the entire range, both negative and positive, of wanting. The will is stabilized (in affirmation or negation) only if it is attached to a particular object ("I want" or "I do not want" *that*) and, consequently, if there is a distinction between a particular subject ("I") and a particular object ("that"). Once this link to a particular has been removed, the will turns back upon itself and identifies itself with its opposite. "To want all" and "to want nothing" coincide. The same is true of "to want nothing" and "not to want anything." Once it is no longer the wanting *of* something and no longer moves in the orbits formed by the constellations of distinct subjects and objects, the *volo* is also the act of "renunciation of one's will." It is *not-wanting* as well, for example, in the

"giving up" [*Gelâzenheit*] and "detachment" [*Abegescheidenheit*] of Meister Eckhart. The suppression of the object (I want *nothing*) will, moreover, have repercussions on the subject. *Who*, after all, wants? What is the "I" that wants? There remains, dislocated, the act of wanting, a force that is born. The verb is "tied to nothing" and not to be appropriated by anyone. It passes through times and places. In the beginning is the verb to will. It posits from the very beginning what will be repeated in mystic discourse by many other verbs (to wound, to seek, to pray, to die, etc.), itinerant acts among actors who may be positioned at one moment as subjects, at another as objects. Who loves whom? Who wounds whom? Who prays to whom? Sometimes God, some-times the faithful. . . . (169–70)

C. The consequence of this is without measure. Particularly for every-thing in the Heideggerian discourse that distinguishes *epochs* within the history of Being. It is the very thought of a history of Being that finds it-self affected by this internal *epochē*, which thus splits, divides, or suspends the *yes*. If the very unconditionality of willing turns it into non-willing, and this according to a necessity that is internal, essential, and itself un-conditional, then no "metaphysics of will" remains rigorously *identifiable*. Will is not identical to itself. Nor is everything that Heidegger constantly associates with it: subjectity, objectness, the *cogito*, absolute knowledge, the *principle of reason* ("Principium reddendae rationis: nihil est sine rati-one"), calculability, and so on. And among so many other things, the one that interests us most here: the "giving reason," the "giving an account," the countability and the computability, even the imputability of the in-numerable *yesses*. The *yes* gives or promises *that very thing* [cela même], it gives it right from the promise: the incalculable itself.

One begins to get a sense of it now: a transcendental or ontological an-alytic of the *yes* can only be fictive or fabulous, entirely given over to the adverbial dimension of a "quasi." Let us take things up again naïvely. The archi-originary *yes resembles* an absolute performative. It does not describe or state anything but engages one in a kind of archi-engagement, alliance, consent, or promise that merges with the acquiescence given to the ut-terance it always accompanies, albeit silently, and even if this utterance is radically negative. Given that this performative is presupposed as the condition of any determinable performative, it is not simply one perfor-mative among others. One could even say that, as a *quasi*-transcendental and silent performative, it is removed from any science of utterance, just as it is from any speech act theory. It is not, strictly speaking, an act; it is not assignable to any subject or to any object. If it opens the eventness of every event, it is not itself an event. It is never *present* as such. What translates this nonpresence into a present *yes* in the act of an utterance or in any act at the same time dissimulates the archi-originary *yes* by revealing it. The reason that thus withdraws it from any linguistic theory (but not from any theory of its linguistic effects) likewise wrests it from any knowledge, in particular from any history. Precisely because it is implied in all writing of history.

That being the case, the analytic of an unpronounceable "yes" that is neither present nor object nor subject could no more be ontological (a discourse on the being of a presence) than transcendental (a discourse on the conditions of an object—theoretical, practical, esthetic—for a subject). Any ontological or transcendental statement presupposes the *yes* or the *Zusage*. Thus it can only fail to make it its theme. And yet, *it is necessary*—yes—to maintain the ontological-transcendental exigency in order to uncover the dimensions of a *yes* that is neither empirical nor ontic, which does not fall within a science, an ontology or regional phenomenology, or, finally, any predicative discourse. Presupposed by every proposition, it cannot be confused with the position, thesis, or theme of any discourse. It is through and through the fable that, *almost* [quasiment] before the act and before the *logos*, remains *almost* [quasiment] at the beginning: "Par le mot *par* commence donc ce texte [With the word *with* begins then this text]" (Francis Ponge, "Fable").[6]

Why *almost* [quasiment] at the origin? And why a transcendental-ontological *quasi-analytic*? We have just seen why the quasi- bears on the ontological-transcendental pretension. Let me add one more word as well: a *quasi-analytic*. An analytic must return to structures, principles, or simple elements. But the *yes* never lets itself be reduced to any ultimate simplicity. Here we rediscover the fatality of *repetition*, and of repetition as an *incisive opening*.[7] Let us suppose a first *yes*, the archi-originary *yes* that engages, promises and acquiesces before all else. On the one hand, it is originarily, in its very structure, a response. It is *first second*, coming after a demand, a question, or another *yes*. On the other hand, as engagement or promise, it must *at least* and in advance be tied to a confirmation in another [*prochain*] *yes*. *Yes* to the other [*au prochain*], that is, to the other *yes* that is already there but nonetheless remains to come. The "I" does not preexist this movement, nor does the subject; they are instituted in it. I ("I") can say *yes* ("yes-I") only by promising to keep the memory of the *yes* and to confirm it immediately. Promise of memory and memory of promise. This "second" *yes* is a priori enveloped in the "first." The "first" would not take place without the project, the wager [*la mise*] or the promise, the mission or emission, the send-off [*envoi*] of the second that is already there in it. This last, the first, is doubled in advance: *yes, yes,* assigned in advance to its repetition. Since the second *yes* inhabits the first, the repetition augments and divides, splits in advance the archi-originary *yes.* This repetition, which figures the condition of an opening of the *yes,* threatens it as well: mechanical repetition, mimicry, thus forgetting, simulacrum, fiction, fable. Between the two repetitions, the "good" and the "bad," there is both cut and contamination. "Cruel tranquility," cruel acquiescence. The criterion of conscience or subjective intention has no pertinence here; it is itself derived, instituted, constituted.

Promise of memory, memory of promise in a place of eventness that precedes all presence, all being, all psychology of the *psychē,* as well as all morality. But memory itself must forget in order to be what it is its mission to be since and from [*depuis*] the *yes.* Promised from the "first," the "second" *yes* must come as an absolute renewal, once again absolutely inaugural and "free," failing which it would only be a natural, psychological, or logical consequence. It must act *as if* the "first" had been forgotten, past enough to require a new, initial *yes.* This "forgetting" is not *psychological* or accidental, it is structural, the very condition of fidelity. Of both the possibility and impossibility of a signature. The divisibility against which a signature strains [*se tend*]. Volontarily and involontarily, the in-volontary [*in-volonté*] of unconditional willing, the second first *yes* breaks with the first *yes* (which was already double), it *cuts itself off* from it in order to be what it must be, "first," unique, uniquely unique, opening *in its turn, in vicem, vice versa,* in its day, each time the first *time* (*vices, ves, volta, fois, Mal,* etc.). Thanks, if this can be said, to the threat of this oblivion, the memory of the promise, the promise itself can take its first step, namely, the second. Is it not in the experience of this danger—to which a *yes* always *renders thanks* [rend grâce]—that, as Michel de Certeau says, the same *yes* "is repeated later" in "the same historical lapsus (the same forgetting)" and that "the same phoneme (*Ja*) brings together separation and the openness"?

Already but always a faithful countersignature, a *yes* cannot be counted. Promise, mission, emission, it always sends itself off in number.

—*Translated by Brian Holmes*

§ 12 Interpretations at War:
Kant, the Jew, the German

As will soon become easily apparent, the choices I have made for this paper bear a *necessary* relation to *this very place:* the university, an Israeli institution in Jerusalem. They bear a necessary relation to *this very moment:* the terrible violence marking once again the history of this land

This text was first published in *Phénoménologie et politique: Mélanges offerts à Jacques Taminiaux* (Bruxelles: Ousia, 1990). To testify to my gratitude and admiration, I thought this text might be less inappropriate than another. All the philosophers (beginning with Hermann Cohen), all the themes or problems touched on in this paper are among those that Jacques Taminiaux has addressed in his thinking, his writing, and his teaching. This essay is also cut out, somewhat brutally, from the fabric of the work of a seminar that I have pursued for some years on "Philosophical Nationality and Nationalism." Among the many premises or contextual elements that I have had artificially to neglect, let me at least signal the "Kritisches Nachwort als Vorwort" that Cohen added to a later edition of his *Deutschtum und Judentum.* I will doubtless return to it elsewhere. I also wanted to pay homage to Jacques Taminiaux for what remains for me a singular political experience. Two years ago, during an international conference in Jerusalem (see "How to Avoid Speaking" in this volume), I had proposed that our next meeting, projected for the following year, have as its theme "The Institutions of Interpretation." This title was retained and the meeting took place in Jerusalem on June 5–11, 1988. The preamble to my paper, the English title of which, difficult to translate, I have kept, describes the spirit in which I participated in this meeting—as well as in others, simultaneously, in the occupied territories, with Palestinian colleagues, outside of their universities which were then, and still are, closed by administrative decision (on July 15, 1988).

and pitting against each other all those who believe they have the right to inhabit it.

Why is this relation a *necessary* one?

Like other papers, mine will consist of a set of interpretive hypotheses on the subject, precisely, of the institutions of interpretation. Consequently, it will stand, certainly and de facto, in a relation to an *institutional context*, the one which is determined today, here, now, by a university, a state, an army, a police force, religious authorities, languages, peoples, and nations. But this de facto situation also calls for interpretation and responsibility. I therefore did not think I should accept the fact of this situation passively. I have chosen to treat a subject that would allow me, while touching directly on the themes stated in the agenda of this conference ("The Institutions of Interpretation"), to ask at least indirectly, and as carefully as possible, some questions about what is going on here now. Although the mediations required between the talk I am about to give and the current violence, here and now, are numerous, complicated, and difficult to interpret, although these mediations call for as much patience as caution on our part, I shall not use them as a pretext to wait and remain silent before that which demands *immediate* response and responsibility.

I had already communicated my anxiety to the organizers of this meeting. I had expressed to them my wish to participate in a conference where Arab and Palestinian colleagues would be officially invited and actively involved. The organizers of this meeting, Professors Sanford Budick and Wolfgang Iser, shared my concern. I thank them for the understanding they have shown in this regard. With all the gravity this requires, I wish to state right now my solidarity with all those, in this land, who demand an end to violence, those who condemn the crimes of terrorism, of military and police repression, and those who advocate the withdrawal of Israeli troops from the occupied territories as well as the recognition of the Palestinians' right to choose their own representatives for negotiations that are now more indispensable than ever. This cannot be accomplished without ceaseless, well-informed, courageous reflection. This reflection should lead to new, or not so new, interpretations of what—two years ago, while this conference was being planned here—I had proposed to call the "institutions of interpretation." But that same reflection should also lead us to interpret the dominant institution that is the state, here the Israeli state (whose existence, it goes without saying, must henceforth be recognized by all and definitively guaranteed), along with its prehistory, the conditions of its recent founding, and the constitutional, legal, political foundations of its present functioning, the forms and limits of its self-interpretation, and so forth.

As is evident from my presence here, this declaration is inspired not only by my concern for justice and by my friendship for both the Palestinians and the Israelis. It is meant also as an expression of respect for a certain image of Israel and as an expression of hope for its future.

I am not saying this, of course, in order to tailor my remarks artificially to some external circumstance. The call for such historical reflection, anxiety-laden as it might appear, courageous as it must be, seems to me to be inscribed in the most strictly determining context of our meeting. It constitutes in my view its very meaning—and its urgency.

I

Taking for granted a certain familiarity with the text that was distributed in advance and that defined the most general horizon of this paper,[1] let me state without further introduction the reasons that lead me to compare and contrast, in a manner still partial and preliminary, two German Jewish thinkers, in a highly determined politico-institutional context.

1. Hermann Cohen and Franz Rosenzweig both assumed their Jewishness radically, although in opposite ways.

2. Neither one of them was a Zionist, and Rosenzweig was even frankly hostile, so it seems, to the project of an Israeli state.

3. Both having privileged the reference to Kant, both took a certain distance from Kant—a different sort of distance in each case.

4. Although they belonged to different generations, their lives did cross. Rosenzweig followed Cohen's teaching. He declared his admiration for the grand master of neo-Kantianism in a text that I will quote shortly. He then moved away from Cohen, even turned against him, at least as far as his thinking about and relation to Judaism were concerned. He produced a critical reading of Cohen's *Deutschtum und Judentum*, which we will begin to analyze in a moment.

5. Two different generations, two different situations, indeed; and yet the two texts by which we will be guided are more or less contemporane-

ous. Both date, as to the publication of the one and the preparation and "composition" of the other, back to the 1914–18 war. Both are caught up and rooted in that war: in a war, one might say, that neither of the two thinkers survived—not, in any case, to the extent of reaching the next stage alive, the next stage being the moment when Nazism casts over that whole adventure, over what I would call the German-Jewish psyche of the 1914–18 war, a revealing and at the same time deforming light. The risk is all the more serious in that it remains ambiguous: the future anterior can lead to retrospective distortions, and it can also tear down veils. Cohen died at the end of the war, in 1918, three years after the publication of *Deutschtum und Judentum.* Rosenzweig became aphasic and was then totally paralyzed in 1922 by a disease that would cause his death seven years later, in December 1929.

By way of introduction to this context, let us first read a tribute by Rosenzweig to Cohen upon the latter's death in 1918. Noticeable at once is a certain distrust of this great, highly respected academic, this master of neo-Kantianism, who left such a deep mark on German philosophy over a half-century, the half-century spanned by the two Franco-German wars (1870–1920). It is too often forgotten, when one is interested in Husserl and Heidegger, that this neo-Kantian sequence largely determined the context *in* which, that is to say also *against* which, Husserl's phenomenology, later the phenomenological ontology of the early Heidegger (who, moreover, succeeded Cohen in his Marburg chair—and this also marks an institutional context in the strictest sense) arose: against neo-Kantianism and in another relation to Kant.

Rosenzweig recalls his initial distrust of this great academic philosopher whose authority, in Jewish and non-Jewish circles, stemmed from a respectable professorial image, which, having radiated its light from the University of Marburg, continued to do so from Berlin, where Cohen taught, in 1913, at another institution, the Institute of Judaism. The work published by Cohen during those years bears a very Kantian title (in fact it is like the book of a Jewish Kant on religion within the limits of reason alone: *Religion der Vernunft aus den Quellen des Judentums*) and was to have a certain influence on Rosenzweig. Rosenzweig had begun attending Cohen's lectures in 1913 with a limited, or rather a distrustful, interest. This distrust is directed first at a sort of institutional entity, "the fairgrounds of German university philosophy":

I attended Hermann Cohen's lecture courses only during his Berlin years. Nor had I read practically anything by him, except for a few occasional works on Jewish theology. Both what I had read, which left me cold and made a dull impression on me, and a gradually emerging fundamental distrust of anything that, on the fairgrounds of German university philosophy, found its little group of admirers, had kept me from attempting a closer acquaintance with it. Thus I was not prepared for anything when, in November 1913, driven by an upsurge, not of interest, but only of curiosity, I sought out his lectures at the Lehranstalt.[2]

Distrust gave way to delighted astonishment. Certain points of the encomium recall or anticipate the experience that some have described of their encounter with Heidegger's teaching during the years immediately following the war. All of this tells us something of the cultural context and Rosenzweig's relation to academic philosophy. It is then a typical reaction, whose typicality appears interesting here, for it amounts to saying: at last, here is a philosopher who is not a professional academic; he thinks in front of us; he speaks to us of what is at stake in existence; he reminds us of the abyssal risk of thought or existence. Rosenzweig speaks of the feeling of the abyss (*Abgrund*) to describe this experience. One expected a professor, and here is a man walking on the edge of a precipice, a flesh-and-blood man, a man who does not forget his body. This aura also surrounds the teaching of his successor, Heidegger, from its beginnings in the lectures of his early years. In those lectures, he speaks of the university, he calls for a thinking, within the university, that would be a thought of existence and not an abstract, comfortable, ultimately irresponsible exercise. And this is exactly Rosenzweig's language: where he expected to see a professor lecturing from on high [*en chaire*], he discovers a man, a singular man attentive to the singularity of each existence, a man and a body over the abyss:

Here I experienced an unprecedented surprise. Being accustomed to finding smart people speaking from philosophical lecterns—people of fine, sharp, elevated, profound mind . . . I found a philosopher. Instead of tightrope walkers, who, more or less daringly, more or less skillfully, execute their jumps on the high wire of thought, I saw a human being. The desperate emptiness or indifference of content from which almost all philosophizing from today's lecterns seemed to me to suffer—this indifference that continually made one wonder why in the world this man who was standing there before one had chosen to philosophize, of all things, instead of doing something else—here nothing of all that was in evidence. Here that question fell completely silent; here one had the indestructible feeling: this human being must philosophize, he carries the treasure within himself that is forced upward by the powerful word. What I, despairing of the present, had long since come to seek only in the writings of the great dead—the strict scientific spirit brooding over the abyss of an undivided world of chaotically pressing realities—here I saw it all at once in living speech, face to face. ("Ein Gedenkblatt")

What is thus being revealed to Rosenzweig? A Jew, nothing less than the essence of the Jew, but also of the German Jew. And one cannot very well say whether he is more purely Jewish because he is a German Jew or essentially Jewish and on top of that, by some accident or otherwise, also a German Jew. The ambiguity is remarkable; for it is with this German Jew, with a particular way of being a German Jew, *Jewish* and German (I will return to one of Rosenzweig's letters that says: "Let us then be Germans and Jews. Both, without worrying about the 'and,' and without talking about it a great deal—but really *both*"),[3] that Rosenzweig, like Scholem and Buber in a different way, will eventually break, despite the respect that Cohen always inspired, with this great figure of rationalist German Judaism, liberal and non-Zionist if not assimilationist, this Jewish *and* German thinker.

For the moment, we can be attentive to the most salient features of this encomium of a German Jew by Rosenzweig. Let us distinguish at least three of them.

A. As Scholem was to do later in a now famous letter addressed to him,[4] Rosenzweig associates rather strangely and also in a biblical manner the figure of the abyss with that of volcanic fire. Boiling over, eruption, gushing forth out of untold depths, a mixture of water and fire, but especially the convulsive rhythm of the flow of lava—such is Cohen's speech.

B. Convulsion, the convulsive tremor that marks the rhythm of volcanic production and scans the jet or projection of lava, the jaculation of liquid fire, is also the tempo of discontinuous rhetoric, and this too is Cohen's speech. Rosenzweig recognizes in it the caesura in rhetorical composition, the aphoristic quality of a speech that cares nothing for composition or is composed of an irregular series of aphoristic interruptions. But he recognizes it primarily as a property of *Jewish* speech—an interpretation for which I leave him, as I always do, the responsibility.

This interruption, this interruptivity in which Rosenzweig sees something essentially Jewish, calls for at least *three* remarks:

(1) It ought to mark, as a circuit breaker would, the essence of the conjunction "and," which not only defines the relation of the Jew to the German ("Let us be Jewish *and* German") but also determines the Jewish in the German: ruptivity, a dissociative and irruptive power. The volcano is irruption, but irruption is what the coming of an event initiates, rupture and hence interruption in the totalizing synthesis. We know that Rosenzweig's thought is characterized first and foremost *both* by this thought of the "and" *and* by what within it dislocates any totalizing synthesis. It does not forbid all gathering [*rassemblement*], but it interrupts the gathering in the "syn-" of the *synthesis* or the *system*, especially in the form of the state. The "and" of "Jewish *and* German" is perhaps a "syn-" or a "with," but without an identifying or a totalizing synthesis. It conveys disjunction as much as conjunction. It is this "lack of transition" that Rosenzweig thinks he sees in Cohen and of which he will say that "nothing is more Jewish." This has to do primarily with Cohen's manner of speaking and teaching: lack of transition also, he notes, thus of mediation between thought and feeling, the coldest thought and the most passionate feeling. This "logic" is just as paradoxical as that of the "and." The lack of transition signifies an omission of the middle term and of everything that plays the role of mediation in a dialectic, whether by this one means the process of being and absolute knowledge or the art of language. But this non-mediation can translate into two apparently contradictory effects: on the one hand, discontinuity, the abrupt juxtaposition of two heterogeneous elements, the relation without relation between two terms without continuity, without analogy, without resemblance, terms that are not susceptible to any genealogical or deductive derivation; but, on the other hand, and for the very same reason, the lack of transition produces a sort of immediate continuity that joins one to the other, the same to the same and to the non-same, the other to the other.

(2) This disjunctive conjunction, this "lack of transition," is also a way of connecting without connecting in rhetoric and in argumentation, for instance, philosophical argumentation: "a single word or a very short sentence of five or six words," he says. An aphoristic seriality, in short. And yet is it not almost at the same time he writes this about Cohen that Rosenzweig himself, in an eruptive manner, like a series of brief volcanic tremors, writes *The Star of Redemption* on postcards, so it is said, while serving at the front? In any case, the conjunctive-disjunctive texture of the book clearly exhibits this rhythm: lack of transition, continuity and discontinuity, a style that is rather alien to that of the classic presentation

of the system or of the philosophical treatise, an argumentation, a rhetoric and connecting devices unlike those that dominate the history of Western philosophy. This history, this philosophy, these canons, are familiar to Rosenzweig. He will have confronted them and broken with them to a certain extent, and not only to the extent that he was not an academic.

(3) The homage is not given to the writing but to the speech. It is addressed not to an author of books but to a man, to an existence in which thought and feeling are one. The author left Rosenzweig cold and distrustful; the living speech surprises and excites him. This speech is enchanted as well as enchanting, and the rhythm-inflected motion of the body involves the hands as much as the voice. We know what attention Rosenzweig paid to phonic rhythm, especially Rosenzweig the translator, and not only the translator of the Bible.

> What kind of magic was it that inhabited the spoken word of this man? In his spoken word more than in his written word, which could easily take on a certain color of the distant. In his speech there was something like a volcano under smooth ground. When for a time it had spun on in rigorous objectivity and the listener saw the flow of thoughts pass calmly under the mighty head, there would suddenly erupt at some point, completely unannounced, impossible to calculate or anticipate in advance, the firestream of the personality. It would be at times only a gesture, a movement of the hand—although he usually spoke almost without movement, one actually always had to keep one's eyes on him—a single word, a brief sentence of five, six words: and the flowing river would have expanded into an overflowing sea; through the web of thoughts there shone the world reborn in the human heart. It was just this perfectly unexpected quality of these eruptions that gave them their compelling force. The boiling up of pathos from its subterranean sources, wholly unprepared for; the close proximity of the coolest thought and of the most passionate feeling—perhaps *there is nothing more Jewish than this lack of transition* [my emphasis—JD]. Just as this German, this German Jew with the highest, freest, and best-grounded consciousness, was a Jewish and onlyjewish [*nurjüdisch*] Jew in perhaps deeper attachments of his soul than the many who today, with the clearest longing and desire, clamor to be Onlyjews [*Nurjuden*]. ("Ein Gedenkblatt")

The last paragraph will seem strange. I stress its allusion to the system. The encomium first emphasizes Cohen's *singularity* and *solitude*: he is *the only one* today, *the only one* of his generation to do this or that. He stands apart from the "crowd" and from "the crowd of his contemporaries."

What is he the only one to do? First of all, not to dissociate feeling and intellect. Thus he confronts the great problems of concrete humanity, of life and death. But because he never dissociates—this is his greatness and his singularity—he is the only one to propose a system. What does this mean? To propose a system is not merely to promise one, as has so often been done in the history of philosophy; it is to provide it. Cohen has a system, Rosenzweig seems to be saying. Not only does he have it, he gives it, he delivers what he promised, what others have promised without keeping their promise, or what others have given without having. Cohen gives what he has, he has what he gives, and this is the system. The system is his generosity, the sign of the overabundance he was not content to promise or have but that he was able to produce, to give, in this case, to teach.

Now, let us not forget, the author of *The Star of Redemption* directed his entire thought against or rather beyond the system, in any case, against or beyond systemic totality, especially in its Hegelian form. He cannot, therefore, simply praise a thinker for having promised, produced, or given a system. The system is perhaps that which cannot be given, that which forbids or reappropriates the gift in advance and in a circular manner. The highest praise that he himself can confer, the most generous gift, is to have thought, to have given one to think *beyond* the system. Whether it is true or false, this at any rate is what he offers to Cohen's memory. But also to the Jew. For in this passage beyond the system, Rosenzweig thinks he recognizes the Jew, someone who is not just the rationalist philosopher, the neo-Kantian of the Jewish religion of the Enlightenment, of the (Jewish) religion within the limits of reason alone, but the man of piety.

> The peculiarity of his scientific personality within the whole crowd of his contemporaries was also likely rooted exactly here. He was after all perhaps the only one of his entire generation, and even still of the subsequent generation, who did not, with pseudo-scientific high-mindedness, push aside the eternal fundamental questions of humanity, the questions that concern life and death, or wrap them up in a meager tangle of feeling and intellect, but who seized such questions in their grand and pure meaning. It therefore could not possibly have been a coincidence that he, again as *the only one* among those who in those decades still trusted at all in philosophy's autonomous scientific power, *not only promised the system, but actually gave it* [my emphasis—JD]. It was the very fact that he did not evade the essential that kept him from evading the most essential, the question concerning the whole. He had an originary,

and not a merely acquired relationship to the ultimate questions. This drove him beyond the system and finally to the immediate eye-to-eye confrontation with these questions in his final theological period. Perhaps only here, in the septuagenarian, did the profoundly childlike nature of this great soul break fully into the light, "childlike" in the sense of the line from the Marienbad Elegy—"so bist du alles, bist unüberwindlich [So you'll be everything, defeated never]." The thing is that he was basically altogether simple. He was a pious man. ("Ein Gedenkblatt")

This posthumous homage allows us to glimpse the relation without relation (but in so many respects exemplary for what interests us here) between these two German Jews, neither of whom ever knew Nazism, neither of whom was a Zionist, but both of whom had undoubtedly so much to say and still give us so much to think, whether they knew it or not, about what was to follow after their deaths.

II

A few years before his death, in the middle of the war, the man whom Rosenzweig describes as a "child-like septuagenarian" writes a text titled *Deutschtum und Judentum*.[5] Following its publication in 1915, this essay was reprinted three times within a year. It became a sort of bestseller in its class (ten thousand copies) and in 1924, in Berlin, it was reedited, with a preface by Rosenzweig, in volume 2 of the *Jüdische Schriften*. Another text by Cohen bears the same title and took up the same arguments in a less polemical and a less political manner in 1916. As has often been pointed out, and the fact is well known, the concern with defining the relation between Germanness and Judeity did not originate in this period. An enormous literature, which also dealt with the problems of emancipation, assimilation, conversion, and Zionism, had been devoted to it.

This text has been described as "cursed [*maudit*]"; this is the word that the French translator, Marc B. de Launay, risks within quotation marks at the outset of his presentation. Professing a sort of German hypernationalism, alleging a German-Jewish symbiosis at times defined in terms that clash with common sense, it is addressed first and foremost to American Jews. Once convinced, American Jews should exercise the strongest pressure to prevent the United States from entering the war in support of England and especially of France, countries that, by allying themselves with tzarist barbarism, have betrayed the ideals of the French Revolution.

These ideals would be better represented by Kantianism and by German socialism (and let us not forget that Cohen is a socialist). This text may well have been *maudit*, condemned by Rosenzweig, Scholem, Buber, and many Zionists, but it nevertheless represented, in a form both learned and at times extravagant, excessive but carefully elaborated, something then typical of a certain German-Jewish intelligentsia, the very class that would end up either in exile (often precisely in America) or in the camps some twenty-five years later—as was the case of Martha Cohen, Hermann's wife, who died in Theresienstadt at the age of eighty-two. This text seemed to me to deserve special attention, a strategically motivated attention, in our context because it represents, in a manner so remarkably worked out, a certain type of militant patriotism in the German-Jewish community, and also because to this end, it mobilizes the Kantian reference, indeed, the socialist, national, and neo-Kantian reference. At that period, during World War I and probably the years immediately following it, the militant patriotism of Scheler or Husserl, for instance, belongs, despite so many differences, to the same configuration. Such at least is my hypothesis.

This strategy also dictates to us a principle of selective reading in a text that addresses the entire history of the Greek, Jewish, and Christian West, the entire history of philosophy, literature, and the arts, Jewish and German culture, politics, law, morality, religion, the categorical imperative and messianism, the state and the nation, the army and secondary or university education. By granting a privilege to the Kantian core of this text, we will gravitate around several Kantian or neo-Kantian cells. Neo-Kantianism in this case can mean two things: sometimes a Kantianism that is adopted and adapted, adjusted or appropriated, sometimes a critique of the Kantian critique in Kant's name, a Kantianism of right or inspiration that claims to be opposed to a Kantianism of fact or to go beyond it. Kant against Kant, or Kant without Kant.

Let us go directly, in order to begin, to the clearest proposition, the firmest and, for us, the most interesting one: the close, deep internal kinship (*die innerste Verwandtschaft*) between Judaism and Kantianism. That is to say also between Judaism and the historical culmination (*geschichtliche Höhepunkt*) of idealism as the essence of German philosophy, namely, the Kantian moment, the holy of holies (*innerstes Heiligtum*) that is Kantianism with its fundamental concepts (the autonomy of universal law, freedom, and duty). It is the same Kant who, Adorno says, is the star witness of the German tradition or the German mind.[6] How then is this proposition supported (especially *DJ,*§§ 6–12)? What is the placing-in-perspective, in other words, the historical contextualization that claims to justify such an interpretation?

It is, first of all, within a comparative logic that has its own history and its own institutions, the argument of the *tertium comparationis.* In hazarding a comparison (*Vergleichung*) between different peoples or the spirits of different peoples (*Volksgeister*), one must avoid abuses and provide a legitimation for such a science of the spirit (*Geisteswissenschaft*). To this end one must make sure that the two terms have maintained an intimate relation, an intrinsic association (*innerliche Verbindung*) with a third term (*tertium comparationis*). The third term, in this case, is nothing other than Hellenism, particularly Greek philosophy. Both Jewish and German idiosyncrasies have had fruitful internal relations with Greek philosophy. Far from being placed in opposition to the Jewish, as has long been the custom, the Greek is seen on the contrary as consubstantial with the Jewish idiom, which presumably received from the Greek a new force and a new imprint (*Aufprägung*). This is not merely a relation of mixture, identity, or reciprocity (the *Jewgreek is Greekjew* of *Ulysses*). Cohen invokes here the great figure of Philo Judaeus. The exile of Judaism to Alexandria brought the destiny of Israel to a world level. It universalized it, cosmopolitanized it to a certain extent in its world mission (*Weltmission*) without calling its foundations into question. This cosmopolitical moment has become essential to Judaism. Philo would have been Plato's Jewish heir, who prepared the way for Christianity through the *logos,* the new "holy spirit" (*heilige Geist*). Plato (and Philo), as Pascal might have said, in order to prepare for Christianity. The *logos,* which in fact acts as a mediator in Philo's philosophy, becomes the mediator (*Mittler*) between God and man, between God and the world. Undoubtedly, Philo is not Jewish insofar as he is a Platonist. But this disciple of Plato's (and discipline here has an institutional character) dominates a Judeo-Alexandrian current that reconciles Hellenism and Judaism through the mediation of *logos* and the holy spirit. This influence was not only speculative, but also institutional. It marked the entire social life of the Jews. With respect to Alexandrian Judaism, Philo will have been not just a member, much less a "mentor" (as de Launay, reluctant to overburden the text, translates it with discretion), but a *Mitglied,* a member, and especially a *Führer,* a guide. To translate *Führer* by "mentor" is to seek to spare this German hypernationalist text a disturbing connotation (might the Jews, too, have a *Führer*?), but it is also to neglect how the use of the word *Führer* can be altogether common in the German language.

The Neoplatonic *logos* thus seals the Judeo-Hellenic alliance. It is also that without which the Church, the institution of Christianity, if not Christianity itself, is unthinkable. At the same time, within the element of *logos* and Christianity, Greece becomes the fundamental source (*Grundquelle*) of Germanness. Whether they know it or not, whether they like it or not, the Germans are Jews. At any rate, Judaism cannot be eradicated from their genealogy. Whatever the violence or the artificiality of the syllogism, it tends to whisper the following, which Cohen obviously does not say, at least not in these terms: there is in the German unconscious, that is to say, deep within the German spirit, an ineradicable, indestructible, undeniable proposition, a German cogito: ". . . *ergo sumus* all German Jews." Cohen, for his part, assumes quite literally the middle term of the syllogism, the Christian *logos* that serves as mediator between Judaism and Germanness, between the Jewish spirit and the German spirit.

Again this may be conscious or unconscious. Even though he does not use the word "unconscious," one cannot say that Cohen excludes the hypothesis, which we would need to evoke a psyche that must have been at work, going as far as genocide, the ultimate, murderous denial of origin or resemblance and the dark history of a crucified father or mediator. The word matters little here, since Cohen names a fundamental historical force (*Grundkraft*) that can never "run out or be used up" and something that, "throughout the course of national history, continually lets the natural force that is its source [*Quellkraft*] come alive." This is, says Cohen (*DJ*, § 2), "what must have occurred [*sich ereignen*] in the relationship between Germanness and Judaism, mediated through Christianity, perhaps several times *at internal turning points in the history of the German spirit*." Cohen underlines this last part of the sentence: "so dürfte es sich . . . vielleicht mehrmals an *inneren Wendepunkten in der Geschichte des deutschen Geistes* ereignen." A strong sentence and an odd one: it says that there is a German spirit, that this spirit has, that it *is* a history marked by events, decisive events, which constitute turns or turning points. At each turning point, each curve, each bend of the curve, at every turn or cast of the German mind, an originary "force," namely, the Jewish genealogy or lineage, must have played a marking role. The German comes to terms with the Jew at each decisive turn of his history, in history as history of spirit, and, in an exemplary manner, as history of the German spirit. In coming to terms with the Jew, the German comes to terms with himself, since he carries and reflects Judaism within himself: not in his blood but in his soul. Or in his spirit. Not in his blood, for this genealogy is not a natural but an institutional, cultural, spiritual, and psychic one. If we may assume that, in this argument, race is reducible to biologico-naturalist schemas (let us keep in mind Rosenzweig's enigmatic thinking of blood), the question of racism is neither raised nor is it necessary. On the other hand, at least in this moment of the syllogism, Cohen seems already to appeal to a theory of the German-Jewish psyche. Psyche, because the genealogy— which joins so to speak the Jew and the German to culminate in Kant—is not at all a natural, physical, genetic genealogy. Rather, it passes by way of the alliance of the religious and the philosophical, the contract between languages that consigns the Judeo-Hellenic heritage, according to the essential mediation of the *logos,* to the form of an absolute logocentrism. What is in question is indeed a psyche, since the alliance is not natural but sealed within the whole semantic family of the *logos*: reason, discourse or speech, gathering, and so forth. What is in question is also a psyche, not only a mirror, but also a soul that holds the spirit, the holy spirit, without necessarily implying consciousness or representative knowledge. Cohen speaks of a force that acts at the great turning points of the history of the German spirit, but a force of which the Jewish or German "subjects" are not necessarily conscious. Hence the need for pedagogy, for a didactic analysis concerning that which at times sleeps and at times awakens in this logocentered psyche.

We have only begun to read this strange document. And one already has the sense of a text pervaded by intuitions or by symptoms, by a sensitivity to critical symptoms that are later rationalized, interpreted in a way that is sometimes forced, artificial, naïvely ingenious, but still according to schemas or gestures whose extravagance, indeed delirium, may well be saying something essential. One question might then be the following: in order to *give an account* (*logon didonai,* a Greek and Platonic formula invoked by Cohen on the next page) of the German-Jewish phenomenon (and who will deny the existence of such a "phenomenon"?) in its often delirious forms, is it possible not to involve logic, *logos,* in this delirium? Can one avoid entering into it in order to give an account of it? How can one not slip into this psyche and its phantasmatic life so as to explain it, describe it, and speak of it? Isn't everything artificial or in any case non-natural in what we are here calling psyche?

Let us try to make this series of questions more accessible by means of two distinct propositions at different levels.

FIRST PROPOSITION

Perhaps it is unimportant to decide whether Cohen takes what he says seriously or not, whether he believes it or not. No doubt he did seriously believe it, but the question may lie elsewhere entirely, as long as we do not go further than the trivial determination of what such belief or such seriousness might be. If one were to prove to Cohen that all this is delirious, he might say: but, after all, who told you that this was the "objective" truth or that I believe it as in something objectifiable? I am explaining the German spirit, in the German-Jewish psyche that constitutes it. If this psyche, and the entire Judeo-Greco-Christian underpinning that structures it, seems delirious to you, if it gives rise to some delirium, to all types of violence, to the highs (*Höhepunkten*) and the lows, the depressions, the crises, the historical turning points, the expulsions, the murders or the suicides, the reappropriations by emancipation or by genocide, well, then, I am just telling you what this thing you call delirium is made of. And my discourse must appear delirious because it reflects a psyche that is itself a reflexive delirium. Whether I, a German Jew, believe it or not, is an uninteresting or irrelevant question. Whether or not my discourse is implicated in its object is a (positive or negative) sign that does not affect the interest of its content. Since we are dealing with something like the German spirit or the Judeo-Greco-Christian psyche, we are not dealing with a simple example of the scientific "subject-object" relation; it is not as if my own discourse (which is also a discourse on the origin of the value of objectivity and a history of reason) had to submit to the requirements of objectivity. You have every right to consider my discourse a symptom of the madness it describes—this does not affect its value, its relevance as a *true symptom*, in a sense. If it is a symptom of what it describes, it is perhaps all the more revealing of the unconscious truth of which it speaks or—and this amounts to the same thing—that speaks through it. In this realm, the symptom is knowledge, knowledge is symptom. Between the two there is no longer the limit that an objectivist, positivist, or scientistic rationalism [would like to impose, with as much artificiality as violence.

And the artificiality]⁷of this violence cannot come about except through institutions. There is nothing natural in it, by definition. This kind of rationalism has no understanding of the spirit or the psyche; it does not see that these cannot be made into an object. The object itself is caught in a structure of interpretation and institution, of "artificial" reflection, what we also call a psyche. Most notably, this form of rationalism (which we will not confuse with reason itself, or reason in general, but which we still interpret in the name of reason and not to the benefit of some irrationalism) is amnesia itself, with regard to its own genealogy, that very same genealogy, Cohen might say, that we are describing here: all of philosophy, reason, or *logos* in its demand to give an account (*logon didonaï*), indeed the principle of reason itself. Far from becoming the object of rational knowledge, as the symptom of an alleged delirium, Cohen might have added, it is my discourse that gives an account of so-called objective knowledge. That is why a symptom may be true, true according to a truth that it speaks and that is no longer of the order of positive objectivity. A little further on, in an even more hallucinated or hallucinating moment of his interpretation, Cohen writes: "Maimonides is the symptom of Protestantism in medieval Judaism" (*DJ*, § 9). What is translated here by de Launay as "symptom" is precisely *Wahrzeichen.*

SECOND PROPOSITION

This realm [*région*], in which the symptom has a chance of being the truth, of speaking as the truth, is not to be considered just one realm among others. It is the one I am talking about, Cohen might say, and properly speaking, both for me and for those to whom I address myself, it is not a realm. It is nothing less than *logos*, that which is in the beginning and which holds together speech and reason. *Logos* speaks of *and by itself* [de lui-même]. *By itself*, that is to say, spontaneously, on its own account, principially; for one need not give an account of that which is a principle and answers for itself. *Of itself*, for, through my mouth, *logos* in fact speaks of *logos*, of itself. Any claim to objective knowledge that one might want to place in opposition to it is still nothing but its "logical" manifestation.

This "logic," then, remains rather strong. For it is less a "logic" than the ambition to speak about logic, to say what is true about the origin of logic, namely the *logos*. There is perhaps a "meta-logic," but there is no meta-*logos*.

III

We have deliberately stayed with the initial *syllogism* of this discourse. It is indeed a sort of syllogism: the being by [*auprès de*] itself, the being with (*syn-*) itself of *logos*, which gathers and gathers itself [*rassemble et se rassemble*] to speak of itself. The originary syllogism of the *logos* itself when it produces its own logic. How and through what mediations can one be led to conclude from this originary syllogism as to the greatness of the German army, the necessity of mandatory military service, the duty of the Jews throughout the world to recognize Germany as their true homeland and to prevent America from allying itself with England, with Russia, and with France, which betrayed its own revolution? We are only at the beginning. And we begin, as one must, with *logos*. But before going any further, and in order to understand the necessity of going further, we must perhaps concern ourselves with what, at first glance, looks like a flaw in this deduction of the Judeo-German psyche. If the starting point for its constitution is the Greek *logos*, if *logos* is its principal mediator and is allied to both Alexandrian Judaism and Christianity, a Christianity that has as much need of the Greek as of the Jew, then where has the German gone in this story? What happens with the German? Does it add anything essential to this plot? With this kind of logic, why not speak of the *same* psyche wherever Hellenism, Judaism, and Christianity existed? Given the wealth of Spanish culture, but also the historical violences to which it gave rise, why not be interested in a Judeo-Spanish psyche? Why not accord it a decisive role in the history of the West? I am not even speaking of a Judeo-Arab psyche, which seems to be excluded from the very principle of this powerful fable.

Although Cohen does not ask this question as such and in these terms, one can say that his argument does implicitly address it. The point is to prove that not only is the German moment of this syllogism essential and necessary, but that there is no other Judeo-*X* psyche (Spanish, Italian, French, and still less Arab, that is, non-Christian). There is no other psyche that measures up to this syllogism. In a word, there can be no Judeo-Muslim or Judeo-Catholic (Spanish, French, or Italian) psyche. The psyche we are talking about is not even Judeo-Christian in general; it is strictly Judeo-Protestant, that is to say, thanks to Luther, Judeo-German.

This, for at least two reasons.

The first is easy to formulate; it concerns a German tradition that sur-

vived up until Heidegger: the German holds an absolutely privileged relation with the Greek: descendance, mimesis, and rivalry, with all the
consequent paradoxes. I have tried to approach one of these paradoxes in
my reading of Heidegger.[8] No other European people supposedly has this
competitive affinity with Greece. If the Greek tradition is safeguarded in
a privileged manner within German culture and more specifically within
German philosophy, then the syllogism implies the German spirit. Cohen
emphasizes this from the end of the first paragraph: "But Christianity is
unthinkable without the *logos*. And thus Hellenism is also a fundamental
source of Christianity. *With this, however, Hellenism prepares itself to be no
less a fundamental source* [Grundquelle] *of Germanness*" (*DJ*, § 1).

The second reason concerns the deep and specific mainspring of this
text, its rhetoric, the mechanics of demonstration and persuasion that
are at work in it, those that we are analyzing here while emphasizing the
privileged reference to Kant. What is at stake is nothing less than an interpretation of the meaning of Being. At a level and in a style that are not
Heidegger's—far from it—but that might call for some prudent analogies,
Cohen tries to answer the question of Being. *He, too* (for the same may
be said of Heidegger) does so through an interpretation of Platonism,
an interpretation of the instituted interpretations of Platonism, of the
Platonic *logos, eidos*, and especially *hypotheton*. This history of interpretations gives a double privilege to the German spirit in its becoming, in the
concatenation of its spiritual events, both philosophical and religious. On
the one hand, it is the privilege of German idealism, as a philosophy, or,
rather, as the moral consciousness of philosophy and science. It constitutes the ideal interpretation of Platonic idealism. On the other hand, and
primarily, it is the Lutheran Reformation. The latter must be recognized
as the religious form of rationality that opposes *logos, eidos*, and especially
hypotheton to the dogma of the ecclesial institution. One might consider
the Reformation from this point of view as a critique of instituted truth,
of the institutional dogmatism that freezes the interpretation of Scripture.
This critique, in turn, can only give rise to institutions, and we could
follow the progress of the Protestant motif in modern hermeneutics. But
this German Reformation would then align itself with, be on the side of,
the Aufklärung, not facing off against it. The French Lumières, which
should be distinguished from the Aufklärung in this respect, could only
oppose the Catholic Church. By allying itself with critical science, with
hypothesis, with doubt, with the history of knowledge, with the calling

into question of institutional authorities, and so on, "with the Reformation the German spirit steps into the center of world history [*Mit der Reformation tritt der deutsche Geist in den Mittelpunkt der Weltgeschichte*]" (*DJ*, § 7).

How does Cohen intend to demonstrate this? The comparative method, when it comes to determining national spirits, appeals not only to the *tertium comparationis*. It is necessary for it to be interested also in the essential depth of each national spirit (*Nationalgeist*), beyond extrinsic properties such as its political, social, and moral determinations (in the sense of "mores": *sittliche Eigenschaften*). This depth manifests itself in spiritual culture: religion, art, philosophy. Pure science—for example, mathematics—is excluded from it, since it is universal by essence. The reciprocal "influence" (*Einwirkung*) and "interaction" (*Wechselwirkung*) between Judaism and Germanness are analyzed in the element of this spiritual culture. Cohen begins neither with religion nor with art but with philosophy, which is "the most graspable scientifically [*wissenschaftlich fassbarsten*]." The question "Was ist deutsch?" [What is German?], which runs from Wagner to Nietzsche, Adorno, Gehlen, and so on, amounts here essentially to the question "What is German philosophy?" The simple, straightforward, unequivocal answer: the essence of German philosophy is idealism. "*Was bedeutet aber Idealismus?*" [But what does "idealism" mean?] The answer, as one may suspect, is more complicated than the question. It is this answer that assumes a historical displacement within what can safely be called an institution of interpretation, namely, the dominant interpretation of Platonism. Idealism is not a theory of ideas as opposed to the sensible or to matter; it is not an anti-sensualism or an anti-materialism. Despite his maturity and his didactic precision, Plato did not determine the idea (*eidos*) with complete clarity. If he asked the question of Being, of substance, of the eternal being, he did so with terms among which those that referred to vision (*Schauen*) or to intuition (*Anschauung*) were mistakenly privileged in accordance with the etymology of the word *eidos*. The most fundamental determination, however, one that is to be found in Plato but that has nevertheless been covered over and neglected in spite of all the resurgences of Neoplatonism and the Renaissance, the one that founded idealism as a scientific project and a method, is *hypotheton*, the concept of hypothesis. Without expanding on Plato's complicated discourse on the subject of hypothesis and the anhypothetic, Cohen assumes rather bluntly the hypothesis of an affiliation between the Platonic concept of hypothesis and Kepler's astronomy or physics. Through Kepler, after Kepler, German thought is authentically supposed to have given scientific idealism (which Platonism had not yet been) its full effectiveness.

The property of the German spirit is played out in the interpretation of the meaning of Being *or* the meaning of the idea. Heidegger also linked (for example, in his *Nietzsche*) the destiny of the German people to the responsibility of this type of question. But one of the many radical differences between Cohen and Heidegger (Cohen's successor, let us not forget, in the institution that is the University of Marburg), is that in the eyes of the former, *the interpretation of the idea as Being is not German*, it is less German in any case than the interpretation of the idea as hypothesis. This latter interpretation is more "critical"; it suspends the naïve ontology of the idea in favor of its methodologico-scientific interpretation. For philosophical (that is, German) idealism must be a project of scientific philosophy: not science itself but philosophy as scientific (*wissenschaftlich*). Such is the answer to the question: "What significance [*welche Bedeutung*] does it have for the characteristics of the German spirit whether the idea is known only as Being or whether it is known as hypothesis?" (*DJ*, § 4).

It is a subtle twist. What is German is not science or hypothesis. These, as we have seen, are universal. But the inaugural philosophical interpretation, the determination of the idea as hypothesis, opening the problematic of scientific knowledge, this is what is supposed to be Platonic-German; this is the historical event that properly institutes and constitutes the German spirit in its exemplary mission, hence in its responsibility. If, as Cohen recognizes, science is universal in its methodological and hypothetical procedures, if it is the "condition of . . . all natural thought in human life, as in the historical conduct of peoples" (*DJ*, § 5), the specificity of the German spirit and of the philosophical idealism that it has in some sense signed is to have *borne within itself* this universal possibility, to have made it come about by testifying to it. Here again lies its exemplarity.

> It is with this concept [the Platonic concept of the hypothesis] that Kepler developed his astronomy and his mechanics. . . . And in Kepler German thought made scientifically effective true *scientific idealism*, that of the idea, as hypothesis. . . .
>
> The methodical sense of this beginning with the hypothesis thus becomes clear. *Being* is not taken to be *immediately given*—a prejudice assumed by sensualism—but rather it is thought as a universal *pro-ject*, as a *task* that is to

be solved and proven by way of scientific treatment. The idea, thought as hypothesis, is consequently by no means the solution to the task, but rather only the precise determination of the task itself. (*DJ*, §§ 4–5; Cohen's emphases)

What we have here, then, under the name of hypothesis, is indeed a determination of the idea: an opening to the infinite, an infinite task for "philosophy as a rigorous science" (this had already long been the title of a famous text by Husserl), or else, Idea in the Kantian sense, an expression that would also guide Husserl as he was diagnosing the crisis of European sciences and defining the infinite task, but also in many other contexts, including the most "teleologist" of his discourses.

> For this reason it [the idea thought as hypothesis] is not somehow true from the outset and in itself, let alone the final truth in general; rather it must stand up to the *test* of its truth, and only this test decides about its truth.
>
> This is why Plato also used another term for this method of the idea, namely *rendering account* (Rechenschaftsablegung) (*logon didonai*).
>
> Thus the idea (*idea*) is so far from being identical with the concept (*eidos = logos*) that the concept (*logos*) is itself verified only through the idea and its rendering of accounts.
>
> It may now be understood what depths are excavated and established for the *conscientiousness* of scientific thinking by means of this documented, authentic meaning of *idealism*. . . . This insight is the fundamental precondition of all genuine science and thus of all philosophy, of all scientific fecundity, but it is *no less the condition of all natural thought in human life*, just as in the historical conduct of peoples.
>
> § 6. This sobriety is the clear and profound meaning of *German* idealism; it is what always characterizes its science and its philosophy in their classic productions. And beginning from this fundamental feature of the scientific spirit, we must now draw and test the conclusion for all historical, and especially also *political*, behavior of the German people. (*DJ*, §5–6)

This movement then leads to Kant. Who is Kant? He is the holy of holies of the German spirit, the deepest, innermost sanctum of the German spirit (*in diesem innersten Heiligtum des deutschen Geistes*), but he is also the one who represents the most intimate affinity (*die innerste Verwandschaft*) with Judaism (*DJ*, § 12). This kinship is sealed in the most intimate depth and the most essential interiority. This seal is sacred, sacredness itself, the historical sacredness of the spirit. But if it is necessary here to insist on *das Innerste*, the innermost and most intimate, it is precisely because underlying this sacred alliance is interiority itself. This alliance is not simply internal like the spirit; it is concluded in the name of moral conscience (*Gewissen*) as absolute interiority. It was certainly made possible by the Greek third term or by the logocentric triangle of Greco-Judeo-Christianity; but it is at the moment of the Reformation that this Judeo-German kinship is born by being reborn. It then experiences one of its many births, which, like German idealism, scan this teleological process, from Kepler to Nicholas of Cusa to Leibniz and finally to Kant. The Reformation, something irreducibly German in Cohen's eyes, places the German spirit "at the center of world history [*in den Mittelpunkt der Weltgeschichte*]." A rather indisputable proposition, if we accept a certain number of protocols that we will not analyze here. In its spirit, this Reformation is the faithful heir of Platonic hypotheticism: the respect for hypothesis, the cult of doubt, the suspicion regarding dogma (or if one prefers, regarding *doxa*) and institutions founded on dogma, the culture of interpretation—that is, of interpretation that is *free* and that, in its spirit at least, tends to free itself from all institutional authority. The Reformation wants to give an account and justify (*logon didonai*). It holds nothing as established; it submits everything to examination. To give an account and to justify—reason-giving (*Rechenschaft*) and justification (*Rechtfertigung*)—this is the slogan (*Schlagwort*) of the Reformation. It is the exercise of *logos*, of *logon didonai*, or, in Latin, of *ratio*, of *rationem reddere*. We might compare this schema with that of Heidegger concerning a Principle of Reason that, after a period of incubation, finds the event of its formulation in Leibniz in order then to dominate all of modernity. It so happens that Heidegger's text (*Der Satz vom Grund*) is also, among other things, a meditation on the institution of the modern university in the context [*mouvance*] of the Principle of Reason. But Heidegger does not seem to be interested in Protestantism from this point of view, and even less so in some Judeo-German affinity around the Principle of Reason.

What does Cohen say when he names the event of Protestantism? He speaks cautiously of the "historical spirit of Protestantism [*der geschichtliche Geist des Protestantismus*]." This spirit is not to be confused with the empirical history of factual events; it is a current, a force, a *telos*. It is so strong, internal, and undeniable that even non-Protestants, Catholics and Jews, must recognize it. It is as if Cohen were saying to the latter: become Protestant enough to recognize, beyond the institutional dogma, scientifically, rationally, philosophically, by consulting nothing but your conscience, the very essence of Protestantism, of this Protestant spirit that already inhabits you. The hidden axiom of this provocation is not only the paradox of some logico-speculative perversity. It is also like a grand maneuver: that of philosophy, of the conversion to Protestantism, of conversion in general. If you recognize that Protestantism is the truth, the very demand for truth beyond instituted dogma, the demand for knowledge and freedom of interpretation without institution, then you are already Protestant in submitting to this demand for truth; you are Protestant whatever the religious and dogmatic institution to which you think you otherwise belong. It is because you were *already* Protestant (and this temporal modality is the entire question of truth) that you converted. And you converted secretly, even if ostensibly, dogmatically, institutionally, you are Catholic, Jewish, Muslim, Buddhist, or even atheist. Likewise, you are Kantian but also Jewish, Jewish and German, the Jew himself being, as we will see, a Protestant and the Protestant a Platonic Jew, if only you are a philosopher and have in you, as a matter of conscience [*en conscience*], the demand for hypothesis, for truth, for science.

Before proceeding further, let us try to formalize one of the laws of this "logic," such as it is at work in Cohen's interpretation. Cohen analyzes not only alliances, genealogies, marriages, minglings of spiritual blood, graftings, cuttings, derivations. He is not analyzing some chemico-spiritual composition of the German, the Jew, or the Christian. No, he has a thesis, which is also a hypothesis, an underlying and substantial thesis, the hypothesis of any possible thesis on the subject of any spiritual genealogy of peoples, of any possible alliance among the spirits of peoples. What is this absolute hypothesis, which may ultimately resemble Cohen's anhypothetic, all the more so as it involves morality and the Good, that is to say, the *agathon* in which Plato located the anhypothetic? It is that the general possibility of spiritual kinships, of this general *economy* of the spirit, hence of spiritual families (*oikonomia* here names the law, the law of the family *oikos* as *the law* itself), the possibility of this genealogy *without limit* does not merely find an example or an application in the Judeo-German or rather in the Judeo-Protestant case. Judeo-Protestant Platonism or logocentrism is the very event that makes possible this general economy, this spiritual hybridization as world genealogy. I am indeed saying *world logocentrism*. "Logocentrism" is not Cohen's word, but I believe I have justified its use. "World" because spiritual globalization [*mondialisation*] would have its origin in this Judeo-Protestant psyche that, in the name of *logos*, of spirit, of philosophy as idealism, hence of knowledge and scientificity, as "[moral] conscience of philosophy and science [*Gewissen der Philosophie und der Wissenschaft*]," has become the "center of the world."

The abstract form of these propositions should not mislead us. This is an economic formalization, of course, and Cohen's language, too, is a composite one: very concrete notations together with the boldest metaphysical shortcuts. But some may be tempted, as I am, to translate or theatricalize these theorems.

This might perhaps produce the following scenario, and some would say: "Yes indeed, this is what is going on: if globalization [*mondialisation*], if the homogenization of planetary culture involves technoscience, rationality, the principle of reason (and who can seriously contest this?), if the great family of *anthropos* is being gathered together by means of this general hybridization—through the greatest violence, no doubt, but irresistibly—and if it becomes unified and begins to gather itself and gather not as a genetic family but as a "spiritual" family, trusting in this whole called science and the discourse of human rights, in the unity of technoscience and the ethico-juridico-political discourse of human rights, namely, in its common, official, and dominant axiomatic, then humanity does indeed unify itself around a Platonico-Judeo-Protestant axis (and the Catholics are already Protestant, as we have seen, just like the Jews: they are all Neoplatonic Kantians). The Platonico-Judeo-Protestant axis is also the one around which the German-Jewish psyche revolves—heir, guardian, responsible for the Platonic hypothesis, itself relayed by the principle of reason. This unification of *anthropos* passes in fact by way of what is called European culture, now represented, in its indivisible unity, by the economic-technical-scientific-military power of the United States. Now if one considers the United States to be a society essentially dominated, in its spirit, by Judeo-Protestantism—without even mentioning an American-Israeli axis—and if one continues with the same hypothesis, then Cohen's hypothesis concerning the Platonic hypothesis and its lineage does not seem quite so mad. If it is mad, this is because it translates the 'real' madness, the truth of a real madness, this logocentric psychosis that would have taken hold of humanity over twenty-five centuries ago, confusing or articulating science, technology, philosophy, religion, art, and politics all together within the same whole." End of fable—or truth of truth.

But from what external location can one claim to deliver a verdict on this truth of truth? This logocentrico-Judeo-Protestant truth? This is the whole question of what some call deconstruction: a seism that *happens* to truth, without one being able to decide whether it comes from the outside or from the inside, if it is happening now or has always been happening, or in what sense and to what extent the label "deconstruction in America," currently so widespread, is a fable, a rhetorical convenience, a metonymy, or an allegory. Is history, in its harshest reality, also in its most murderous aspect, not made up of these displacements of figures?

You can see the other reason I had for putting an allusion to the United States of America in the mouth of my imaginary interlocutor, this man both so sensible and so mad, this man without place who still inhabits, and already no longer inhabits: neither the old world nor the new world. This is because the hypothesis about hypothesis, Cohen's anhypothetical hypothesis, is surely addressed, as an open letter, to all of humanity—and it is as such that it reaches us now, right here (and what is our here-and-now made up of? How can we keep it in parentheses?). But the anhypothetical hypothesis was first intended for America, for the American Jews at a certain moment, during a real war inside Europe, but only a possible war between Germany and the United States. Cohen wants to prevent this war. He wants to intervene to avert the confrontation between two brothers, or at least between two members of the great Judeo-Protestant family. He even has two other hypotheses on this subject, perhaps a hypothesis and a certainty, perhaps even two certainties: (1) If the United States enters the war, Germany will lose (and indeed this is what happened twice). (2) Pressure exerted by the American Jews can determine the American decision: they are powerful in the United States and their link to Judaism remains very strong. It all seems as though the First so-called World War, up until 1917, and then the Second so-called World War, up until 1941, remained secondary, local wars so long as the United States did not take part in them. Why is this? Not for quantitative or geographical reasons, but because they had not yet divided the spiritual world; they had not yet pitted one against the other the two great sons or brothers of the family, the two major members of the great Judeo-Protestant body in the world, the two lobes of the German-Jewish psyche or of its powerful Judeo-Americano-German prosthesis. This psyche, as a *psyché* always does, keeps watch over [*garde*] the spirit. When war breaks out between the United States and Germany, it is an enormous family feud, a dissension, a war of secession: not between *two* opposite blocks, *X* and *X*, nor between Jews and Protestants, but between Judeo-Protestants and Judeo-Protestants. Cohen's rhetoric is being raised like a white flag: stop this fratricidal war. Would this Jewish, socialist, German, pacifist, nationalist, internationalist, and neo-Kantian philosopher have said that World War II finally brought about what he feared and which happened right before his death in 1918, namely, a war within the spirit? Within the spirit as the spirit of philosophy, the consciousness and moral conscience of science, the Judeo-Protestant *logos* under the watch of the Judeo-German psyche?

IV

We have spoken of the soul—or psyche. We have spoken of the spirit—the German spirit, the holy spirit, the spirit of Judaism. But we have only alluded to conscience, specifically, to *Gewissen*, to that moral conscience that would situate the becoming-German of philosophy in history. As the authentic, completed form of Platonic idealism, German idealism arises with Protestantism, that is, with the tendency to recognize no authority other than the authority of *Gewissen*.

On the one hand, idealism is conscience, the *Gewissen* of philosophy and science. On the other hand, Protestantism commands us not to put our trust in the Church and its works, that is, in the institution, or in its priests, but "only in the work of one's own conscience [*allein die eigene Arbeit des Gewissens*]."

But to put one's trust only in the incessant "work" of conscience is a double and equivocal gesture in the eyes of "religious thought [*das religiöse Denken*]." And this partly explains how the German Reformation could have been at the source of an Aufklärung that, unlike the French Lumières and *Encyclopédie*, does not oppose faith. This is because the work of conscience both liberates and burdens religious thought. Emancipation and oppression at the same time. *Befreien* and *belasten*, because in delivering it from dogmatico-ecclesial authority and the external weight of the institution, it charges conscience with taking on itself, all alone, a purely internal responsibility. Conscience must *institute* itself, stand up and hold itself up all by itself, assume a faith exposed to the blows and objections of knowledge. Faith is like a self-instituting decision whose authenticity seeks no external guarantee, at least not in institutions of this world. Whence the double sense (*Doppelsinn*) of this faith (*Glaube*) to which Luther appeals against the Church: a faith that is anti-institutional and archi-institutional. We should never forget, let it be said in passing, the enormous respect that Luther always inspired in the German Jewish intelligentsia. Rosenzweig and Buber, for example, when they came to translate the Bible from Hebrew to German, consider Luther to be the great ancestor, the formidable rival, the unequaled master. Rosenzweig speaks of him at times in a tone of overwhelmed fervor.

In its double sense, such a faith constitutes idealism insofar as it is opposed to the instituted givens of the Church. But the Church is reluctant to part with the force of idealism. Thus, at least as a polemical pretext, it too internalizes what contests it, both from without and from within, from an outside that precisely claims the authority of the inside, of the most intimate *Gewissen*. Having consecrated the Reformation to a certain extent, the Church assigns itself a duty (*Pflicht*) of justification (*Rechtfertigung*, which refers back to *logon didonai*). This duty of justification is the only source of felicity, of salvation (*Seligkeit*). It confers on religion a new authenticity, a new truth, a new truthful truth, a truthfulness (*Wahrhaftigkeit*). This is a historical event, since this truthfulness or this authenticity is new. Such an event institutes a new relation of religion to truth as truthfulness, as authenticity rather than as truth of correspondence in the sense of science or objective knowledge. This instituting event, whose scope cannot be overestimated, makes faith (*Glauben*) come alive to its authenticity. At the same time, it assigns a "new determination [*eine neue Bestimmung*]" to the German spirit.

The concept of *Wahrhaftigkeit* is clearly an ambiguous one. It gestures simultaneously toward the true and toward the truthful, both toward the truth of knowledge and toward the authenticity of a certain existence, here an existence in faith. The Reformation exposes [*met à vif*], it brings to life [*rend vivante*] two types of certainty (*Gewissheit*) in modern man (indeed, Cohen raises the question of modernity; one might say that he claims to define the advent of modern times). (Let us not forget that for Heidegger, who instead suspected it, the value of certainty, which he associates more with the idealism of the Cartesian *cogito*, also marks the advent of a certain modernity.) It is better to retain here the German word *Gewissheit*. Unlike "certainty," it maintains communication between knowledge (*Wissen*), science (*Wissenschaft*), moral conscience (*Gewissen*), self-consciousness (*Selbstbewusstsein*), and certainty (*Gewissheit*). There is *Gewissheit*, the certainty of scientific knowledge, and there is *Gewissheit* in the realm of faith. As soon as questions of faith are no longer exposed to skepticism, as they were when they were only guaranteed by the dogmatism of the ecclesial institution, they are gathered together and held fast (*zusammengefasst und festgehalten*) in a doctrine of morality, as that very doctrine (*als Lehre der Sittlichkeit*). Henceforth morality stands on the side of religion, at its side, right up against religion, inseparable from a sort of "religion within the limits of reason alone," as Kant the *Aufklärer* might say. Morality is no longer the rival but the ally of religion. Religion is no longer the *infâme* that the French Lumières (still too Catholic, because anti-Catholic, and, I might add, too French in 1915!), with Voltaire, wanted to get rid of. The ideal of Protestantism structures and founds the cultural and scientific conscience of modern peoples on these two types of *Gewissheit*. Consequently, the development of ethics, like that of religion, becomes conditioned by this idealism of modern culture. Without it there is no rectitude or justice (*Aufrichtigkeit*), no honesty, no personal conscience for the man of modernity.

What becomes of Judaism in all this?

If it is not prepared in a scientific manner, if it does not stem from positive science itself, idealism tends naturally toward philosophical speculation. That is to say also toward ontology and the thinking of Being itself. Now, Judaism begins with the self-presentation of God in the burning bush. God said: "Ich bin der Ich bin [I am that I am]." In translating the Hebrew formula into German, Cohen notes that the temporal form of the original version is marked by the future. God names *himself*, he calls himself *Being*. But he calls himself (into) being in the future, a future that is not simply the modification of a present, another present to come. And this being to come is unique. Cohen immediately translates the "Ich bin der Ich bin" without any further precaution, into the Platonic idiom: God is Being, God is one; there is no being outside him; any other being, "as Plato would say [*wie Platon sagen würde*] is but pure appearance, a mere phenomenon [*Erscheinung*]." God is Being; it is in him that the world and humanity have their foundation, that which guards and maintains them. Judaism would thus merge with Platonism, Yahweh with the *agathon* or *anhypotheton*. Like the Good, God escapes all image, all comparison, all perception. He remains unrepresentable. The purely intuitive thought relating to him is not a thought of knowledge (*Denken der Wissenschaft*), but a thought of love (*Denken der Liebe*): "The knowledge of God is love," says Cohen. "Love" would be the authentic word for faith in reformed biblical language. This is the Greco-Platonic Eros, at the source of knowledge and aesthetic feeling. This is also the vocabulary of so many Christian texts and above all evangelical ones.

Hence the initial kinship of Judaism with idealism. This kinship is explored and developed, from Philo to the twelfth century with Maimonides, the source of the great scholastics, of Nicholas of Cusa in his doctrine of divine attributes, and of Leibniz, who also quotes him when he speaks of the divine being. Hence this odd formula: Maimonides is the "symptom" (the revealing sign, the mark, *Wahrzeichen*) of a medieval Jewish Protestantism. There would have been a Jewish Reformation before the letter of the Christian Reformation. Maimonides is its proper name; he is the emblem or seal of the alliance between these two Reformations. Between them, he signs the alliance or contract for the first time. He is the figure of the first signatory or the first delegate to the signing of this alliance, an alliance that forms the German-Jewish psyche, the mirror or the reflexive conscience of modernity. All of this goes in the direction of an "authentic [*echten*] Platonic idealism."

If Maimonides had only known, if he had only seen himself in advance carried away by this fantastic cavalcade, by the gallop of a German-Jewish historian of philosophy, running through all of Western history in a single breath without stopping for a single moment, before an American public! If he had only known—he who considered himself more Judeo-Maghrebian, Judeo-Arab, or Judeo-Spanish—that one day he would see himself recruited for this strange struggle, having unwittingly signed an alliance with post-Lutheran Germany, having consigned the great Jewish alliance to this alliance between the two alleged Reformations, would his soul rest in peace, I mean, would his psyche? And if Plato had only known? If all of them had known?

Their protest against Cohen, that is to say, against Protestantism, would perhaps not have been unjust. But who can say that it would have been true for all that? For ultimately what is the truth in this case? Is it not precisely an interpretation of the truth of truth itself in the origin of its institution?

How does Cohen rationalize this recruitment of Maimonides for the German-Jewish cause? He does not rationalize; he does not think he has to rationalize. He speaks of reason itself—and of the historical institution of rationalism. Although he does not challenge the religious institutions, as Luther might have, Maimonides still seeks the foundations of religion.

He founds religion on a great and rigorous rationalism. It is in the name of reason that he founds the Jewish Reformation.

When it comes to Maimonides, Cohen's silence in one particular regard may seem astonishing. In this text that overflows with learning and cites just about every canonized philosopher (provided he not be French, with the exception of Rousseau, of whom we will speak later), one philosopher is never named. No significant place is recognized for him. He is, however, a great rationalist philosopher, Jewish in his own way, and precisely a critic of Maimonides: Spinoza. Cohen knows him well, he had written a lot about him. Why does he not grant him any place here? This is something he has in common with Heidegger, in what is for both a meditation on the *logon didonai* and on the Principle of Reason. There would be a great deal to say about this shared silence. All the more so since Cohen talks abundantly about Mendelssohn. This is particularly difficult to do without mentioning the man who for Mendelssohn was a master, certainly a disputed one, but nonetheless a master. The last lines of the article seem to take aim at a certain Spinozism, without naming Spinoza, as if to excommunicate him from the German-Jewish psyche, along with mysticism and pantheism. At the moment of celebrating the unity of the God who is one, Cohen writes: "The future of German culture [*Gesittung*] rests on the force of the national spirit to resist all the charms of mysticism, but also the pantheistic illusions of monism: to grasp nature and morality, 'the starry sky above me and the moral law within me' in their cognitive difference from one another, and to strive for their unification [*Vereinigung*] only in the thought of the One God" (*DJ*, § 50).

The absence of Spinoza seems all the more glaring in that Cohen speaks of a religion and a morality founded on the love of God and on Pauline law: these are also the essential motifs of Spinoza's *Tractatus Theologico-politicus*. Cohen often speaks of *spirit:* the German spirit and the holy spirit. I, for my part, have often spoken of a German-Jewish *psyche,* of symbiosis or spiritual alliance. But did Cohen say nothing of the soul, of the Jewish or the German soul, of the Jewish psyche or the German psyche? We are getting to it.

According to Cohen, there are two principles of Judaism. One is God's oneness; the other is the "purity of the soul [*Reinheit der Seele*]." The Jewish morning prayer says: "My Lord, the soul you gave me is pure. You created it, you formed it inside me, you breathed it into me [and the psyche is breath], you preserve it inside of me and it is you who will take it back again some day in order to return it to me in the life to come." The purity of the soul, says Cohen, is the "foundation pillar [*Grundpfeiler*]" of Jewish piety. Hence the immediacy of the relation to God, without intercessor, without mediator. After Maimonides, Cohen cites another Jew, Ibn Ezra, the earliest and the most important among the critics of the Bible. The authority of this Ibn Ezra, let me note in passing in order to recall Spinoza once more, is invoked at length in the *Tractatus Theologico-politicus*, particularly in chapter 8, where the issue is the authorship of the Holy Scripture, especially of the Pentateuch. Everyone thought Moses was the author, especially the Pharisees, who resorted to an accusation of heresy against anyone who doubted this. Ibn Ezra, however, "a man of enlightened intelligence, and no small learning," says Spinoza, "was the first, so far as I know, to treat of this prejudice."[9] But he dared not say it openly, and so to outsmart what was also the authority of an institution, he said it cryptically. Spinoza intended to lift this self-censorship and disclose his true intentions.

But what does Ibn Ezra say, the one whom Cohen now cites? One of his maxims states that there is no mediator between God and man other than human reason. The holy spirit is just as much man's spirit as it is God's spirit. Man's spirit is holy because the holy God deposited it in him. What passes through the spirit is both the reconciliation (*Versöhnung*) between God and man and the redemption of sins: purity of soul and holiness of spirit. Quoting one of David's psalms, Cohen wants to show (*DJ*, § 11) that in Judaism redemption presupposes a concept of the human psyche.

This Jewish concept of the soul implies an immediate relation to one God. No mediator is necessary. But if it permits an understanding of freedom and of what morality presupposes of freedom, how can this philosophy of immediacy account for duty, obligation, commandment? What is to be done with the law, which is so essential to Judaism? The way in which Cohen poses and resolves the problem in three lines (it's wartime) is marvelous. A marvel of elliptical simplification, not to say distressing simplism, especially when one knows that this sparseness conceals enormous exegetical problems and hermeneutic debates that remain open despite the libraries and institutions that are enriched by them every day. Cohen knows them well; he inhabits them, teaches in them, and occasionally writes about them.

What does he say? The following: I have just shown a "point of support

[*Stützpunkt*]" of idealism, but there is another fundamental conception (*Grundgedanke*) of Judaism. Since Paul, it has been opposed to the first conception by way of the concept of the law. This is a single sentence, at the beginning of § 12. It is true that in very well known and extremely complex texts (which, moreover, Spinoza interprets in his way around the problem of circumcision in chapter 3 of the *Tractatus*), Paul says some rather negative things about obedience to the law in Judaism, at least to the external and transcendent law that is supposed to be at the origin of sin, and to which Paul opposes love and internal law.

The fundamental thought of Judaism, if there is one and if one interprets it along Cohen's lines, is thus stretched between two poles: freedom of the soul in the immediate relation to God, and respect for transcendent law, duty, and commandment. Despite their contradictory appearance, one must think the unity of movement between these two poles. But who has done this? Who has thought, all in one piece, as a single revolution, that which revolves about these two poles, freedom and duty, autonomy and universal law? Kant, and this thinker penetrated to the depths of Judaism, into its spirit or its soul. Since he is the holy of holies of the German spirit, it is in "this innermost sanctum of the German spirit [*in diesem innersten Heiligtum des deutschen Geistes*]" that we find "the innermost kinship [*die innerste Verwandtschaft*]" or affinity of the German spirit with Judaism. "Duty is God's commandment, and in Jewish piety it must grow together with awe [here not *Achtung*, Kant's word, but *Ehrfurcht*] to become the free service of love: love of God in the love of human beings." The spiritual consanguinity, the psycho-spiritual symbiosis is sealed in the *Critique of Practical Reason* and in everything that accords with it in Kant's work and elsewhere.

The gesture is not new. Kant's thought, whose Protestant filiation is so evident, was very quickly interpreted as a profound Judaism. Let us recall that he was immediately greeted as a kind of Moses, and that Hegel saw in him an ashamed Jew.[10] This philosophical antisemitism, or, rather, this anti-Judaism, will reappear, with scarcely different motivations, in Nietzsche's *contra* Kant. On the other hand, *Religion within the Limits of Reason Alone* does resemble that Judeo-Reformationist Aufklärung of which Cohen speaks. The *Critique of the Faculty of Judgment* describes the exemplarity of the Jewish experience in its relation to the sublimity of the moral law. The fact that *Anthropology from a Pragmatic Point of View* includes at least one properly antisemitic note (literally, anti-Palestinian)

is not incompatible with Kant's quasi-Judaism. Besides, with what is antisemitism not compatible? This is a terrible question, for it is directed as
much at Jews, at those who call themselves Jews, as it is at non-Jews, at
antisemites and at those who are not Jews, and still more perhaps at the
philosemites. Without being able to formalize here the strange logic of
this question, or to demonstrate that one cannot expect any positive and
determinate answer, I would say only that the essential measurelessness
[*démesure*] of this thing called antisemitism is heralded there. It does and
does not have a form. Its form consists in de-forming and de-limiting
itself ceaselessly in order to make contracts with everything that is opposed to it. Instead of deploying this logic, which we cannot do here, let
us make do with an image and a fact: the tribute of a bouquet of flowers
that, during a public demonstration in Nice, the Jewish militants of the
Front National thought fit to present to Jean-Marie Le Pen (the man who
dared to speak of the Shoah as a "detail" and who won 14 percent of the
vote in the first round of the last presidential election [in 1988]). One can
explore all the possible combinations in the positions thus taken, and the
matrix of strategies gathered in this bouquet.

Cohen, whether he likes it or not, presents at every moment a bouquet
to all the Le Pens who lie dormant or rather who never sleep, and do not
concern themselves with details. Concerning details and antisemitism in
its most visible empirico-political manifestations, Cohen was well aware
that at the very moment he was writing to celebrate its sense of sublime
sacredness and moral law, this German culture or society practiced, officially and institutionally, a form of legal antisemitism. This antisemitism
touched Cohen quite closely in his own institution: it took the form of
excluding Jewish students from corporative student associations. Cohen
devotes no more than a brief allusion to it, and this in no way disorganizes his discourse, which would like to remain "spiritual," not factual.
He claims not to be able to broach this question in detail (*wir hier keine
Einzelforderungen aufstellen*) (*DJ*, § 42). It is a time of war and thus not
the right moment to open fronts at home, national and German-Jewish
solidarity above all; we will see later that there is still progress to be made,
and our American Jewish coreligionists are well aware of this (it is true
that a *numerus clausus* was applied to Jews in a quasi-official manner for
a long time in the United States, and was in fact still being applied after
World War II to full professors in Ivy League universities). Cohen was
aware, then, as a university professor (and, let me recall once more that he

was the first Jewish professor of this rank in Germany), of the existence of
this embarrassing detail, the exclusion of Jewish students from the corporative community. He defers the analysis: "We live in the supreme hope of
German patriotism that the unity between Germanness and Judaism that
paved the way for the history of German Judaism up until now, will from
now on finally shine forth as a *cultural-historical truth* [my emphases—
JD] in German politics and in the life of the German people, as well as
in the feeling of the German people [*im deutschen Volksgefühl*: we shall
return to *Gefühl* shortly]" (*DJ*, § 41). This already amounts to recognizing
that the psycho-spiritual truth, like the truth of cultural history, is not yet
incarnated in historical effectivity: the truth has not yet been recognized.
Cohen goes on:

> In what way the conditions of national cohesion [rather than a consensus,
> as one might say: *nationale Einmütigkeit*] will infuse social life, about this
> complicated question we do not wish to examine in detail here. But for the
> great national educational institutions that are the universities there ought to
> be an unconditional obligation [*unbedingte Verpflichtung*] regarding the pro-
> priety and the preservation of the sense of national honor: that the exclusion
> of Jewish students from student corporations and fraternities [*Verbindungen*]
> simply disappear, "as going against good manners [*als gegen die guten Sitten
> verstoßend*]." This exclusion also goes against the respect [*Achtung* this time]
> that is due to the Jewish professor. Whoever does not hold me worthy of his
> social academic community [and here, in an exemplary manner, the professor
> uses the first person], ought also to shun my lectures and scorn my teaching.
> This demand is thus directed as incisively to the academic authorities as it is
> to the students with their academic freedom. (*DJ*, § 42)

Logically Cohen could not but appeal to academic freedom. In a way
that is as formal as it is perverse, it is in the name of this freedom that the
exclusion was practiced: one has the right freely to set the conditions of
association. Cohen's appeal is both very dignified and a little humiliating:
first for himself, but also for the Jewish students, whose rights would have
to be protected and guaranteed by the prestige or the authority of the
important Jewish professors.

But for Cohen this is only a contextual and an institutional question.
It remains relatively minor; one can put off treating it "in detail" until
later. What counts, in the relative scale of urgency in wartime, is the most
fundamental thing, namely, Judeo-Kantian law and its correlation with

the freedom, the autonomy of the subject as spirit, soul, and conscience. The choice here is not between an institutional context and a fundamental authority but between two orders of interpretation and institutionality, for what I am calling the Judeo-Kantian also belongs to the order of historical events. These do not go without instituting moments and are always incarnated, if we follow Cohen, in peoples, nations, languages, and even in juridico-political structures. We are getting to this. As the deepest foundation of all morality, God's law is also the foundation of right and the state. The Mosaic code [*le droit mosaïque*] has always been recognized, even if, when Grotius's jurisnaturalism first arose, it was rejected on account of its formal justifications. In fact, this divine law and this Mosaic code were, according to Cohen, at the living source of right [*du droit*]. They made possible the institution, the just establishment of rights [*du droit*], and first of all the juridical feeling. The latter presents an analogy, at a level which is not that of moral law, with the feeling of respect defined by Kant. It commands the universal conscience of what is just, even beyond the Judeo-Christian cultures, for example, in Islam (here Cohen cites Friedrich Adolf Trendelenburg, author of *Das Naturrecht aufdem Grunde der Ethik* [1860]). By uniting freedom and duty in "personality," Kant simultaneously states both the difference and the intimate link, a new *Verbindungslinie* between ethics and religion. In religion, this new "line of alliance" gathers together "soul and spirit [*die Seele und der Geist*]."

V

"Kant, the Jew, the German." In this title, none of the attributes is secondary, none is more essential than the others. What is at issue is a co-substantial reciprocity rather than a co-attribution. This fundamental identification or this substantial alliance might be called *subjectal*. It is in the very subjectity of the Kantian subject, of man as subject of morality and right [*droit*], free and autonomous, that the Jew and the German are associated. Their *socius* (alliance, spiritual symbiosis, psyche, etc.) is the very *socius* that makes of the *subjectum* a moral being and a being of rights [*un être de droit*], a freedom, a person.

At this point, a leap seems to be required in the reading. It is necessary to bring out the strategy and the pragmatics of this text, the contextual and institutional aim of its rhetoric, at a moment when a new line of alliance between soul and spirit has just been named. This will also allow us to recall that German, if not Jewish, is also German as a language, German as it is spoken.

Cohen's strategy aims at demonstrating to all the Jews of the world, primarily but not only to American Jews, that the universality of the moral subject is rooted in an event: the history of the German spirit and of the German soul. Such that Germany is the true homeland of every Jew in the world, "the motherland of his soul [*das Mutterland seiner Seele*]." If religion is his soul, the homeland of his soul is Germany. The old accusation against Jewish internationalism or cosmopolitanism rests on an obscure prejudice. We should not take it into account when we want to elucidate questions of principle. If there is a Jewish internationalism, it is insofar as all the Jews of the world have a common homeland for their psyche (*Seele*). This homeland, however, is not Israel but Germany: "I believe that, apart from the question of naturalization [*Naturalisierung*], the Jew in France, in England, and in Russia also has duties of piety [*Pflichten der Pietät*] toward Germany; for it is the *motherland of his soul*, just as religion is his soul."

Cohen does not want to avoid the contradiction in which he confines these poor non-German Jews in wartime, for analogous discourses might well be held at the same time, for example in France or in America. He goes on to develop an argument that I will not try to paraphrase—it remains too inimitable. Before quoting a paragraph, let me briefly note that, in the name of what is claimed to be "the finest political tact" (*Freilich bedarf es des feinsten politischen Taktes*), it comes down to demanding of all the Jews of the world that they recognize Germany as the motherland of their soul, without betraying their other homeland, while still working toward universal peace, that is, toward the end of a war that will be won by Germany—a war in which the sacred obligation to love one's neighbor, even if he is one's enemy, should be upheld.

> Naturally it requires the finest political tact so as not to let this piety damage or encumber the higher duty of love of one's fatherland. However this difficulty in wartime is fundamentally contained in the following one: that every war should be fought by everyone with a *long view to peace, in profound humanity*. Wars of annihilation of the peoples are a disgrace to humanity. Is the duty of piety on the part of one who is naturalized (even only in part) to his homeland so distant from this universal international duty?
> It is perhaps the most concrete meaning of *love of the enemy* that there

always remains preserved in the enemy people its share not only in humanity as such, but in the complicated offshoots of this idea. And it is by no means a new beginning, let alone a leap, from this universal duty of humanity to the piety toward one's own, spiritual-psychic [*geistig-seelisch*], even bodily motherland, which is the obligation of anyone who has the fate of joining a foreign state-union, or even of being born into one.

Only beginning from this principle will the *international peace efforts* attain a core, unambiguous point of departure, and from there an effectiveness that would be incontestable by all parties. The humanity of one's home can become the native soil [*Mutterboden*] of a veritable internationality, for the firm foundation of a spirit of peace. (*DJ*, § 40)

The last sentence says that humanity (*Humanität*: and Fichte reminds us that, in its abstraction, this Latin word is not equivalent to *Menschheit*, which is an immediately sensible and intelligible essence for a German) can become the maternal ground (*Mutterboden*) of a true internationality in view of founding, establishing, or justifying, of firmly instituting by right [*en droit*] (*Begründung*) a spirit of peace, a sense of peace (*Friedensgesinnung*).

The statement is rather odd, precisely in terms of its language. Why should the American Jews, who are Cohen's primary addressees and who came by the thousands from Germany or Russia, still have a pious duty toward Germany, even though they are American citizens? Why should they piously (*pietätsvoll*) respect (*achten* this time) their psycho-spiritual motherland (*als ihr seelisch-geistiges Mutterland*)? Because of language, more precisely and even more significantly, because of the so-called *Jargon*, the Yiddish language. Even if it maims, mutilates, truncates (*verstümmelt*) the mother tongue, it still signals back to the language to which it owes the originary force of reason (*Urkraft der Vernunft*) as originary force of spirit (*Urkraft der Geistes*). It is through the mediation of this language, German, that man (and here, in an exemplary manner, the German Jew) has been able to spiritualize his thoughts and ennoble his religious habits. He must not refuse his loyalty to the people who gave him such a rebirth (*Wiedergeburt*).

Addressing himself thus to the American Jews, Cohen indicts the attitude of certain French or English Jews (those who, for their part, indulged in analogous—and for essential reasons, only analogous—rhetoric). These Jews showed themselves to be weak in the face of a Russia that annexed their brethren and ungrateful with regard to Germany. Such for example is the case of "Herr Bergson," who put his talent and his credit in the service of France. This perjurer [*parjure*] loses his soul because he forgets that he is the son of a Polish Jew (not even a German!) and especially that his parents spoke Yiddish (not even pure German, which Cohen, like every self-respecting member of a certain German-Jewish intelligentsia, puts way above that degraded [*verstümmelt*] form of the noble German idiom):

> But in this context we must also expose the invectives of the French philosopher who, using all the means of virtuosity and advertising [*der Virtuosität und der Reklame*], which unfortunately have worked only too well for him also in Germany [one hears analogous things today from certain German philosophers], has played himself up as an original philosopher: He is the son of a Polish Jew who spoke Yiddish. What might be happening in the soul of this Mr. Bergson when he remembers his father and denies "ideas" to Germany! [*Er ist der Sohn eines polnischen Juden, der den Jargon sprach. Was mag in der Seele dieses Herrn Bergson vorgehen, wenn er seines Vaters gedenkt und Deutschland die "Ideen" abspricht!*]

Our analysis must become more refined to draw closer still to the most pointed specificity of *this* interpretation, in *this typical* contextual and institutional situation (*this* war, *this* German-Jewish Professor, *this* neo-Kantian philosopher, etc.), and to better determine the articulation between the "external" and the "internal" institution *of* these interpretations. There are several ways to do this. Having chosen to privilege the reference to *Kant, the Jew, the German,* we will underscore first the ambivalence that continues to mark this reference despite the hyperbolic tribute. This ambivalence also corresponds to a general type. It is not specific to neo-Kantianism, to Cohen, or to German-Jewish thinkers of the period. We do not have enough time and space to better situate Rosenzweig's thought in this respect, in its double relation to Kant and to Cohen. In the course of a brief detour, we will try to invoke not only Rosenzweig's ambivalence toward Kant, but also—which is more interesting at this point—his awareness of it and his interpretation, even his diagnosis of it.

In 1923, Buber had just published his lectures on Judaism (*Reden über das Judentum* [Frankfurt a/M, 1923]). Rosenzweig wrote to thank him for the book. From this long letter, dealing mainly with Jewish law, I will quote first a tribute to Buber that announces a kind of double bind in filiation or rather in *discipline.* Just as, for "our spiritual Judaism," it is both possible and impossible to inherit from Kant, both possible and impossible to be Kant's *disciple*, so it will be both possible and impossible to follow Buber (and a fortiori Cohen). Rosenzweig writes: "If you have thus redeemed the teaching for us, from out of the genteel poverty of a few fundamental concepts to which the nineteenth century wanted to restrict it (it was not the first to do so, but the first to do so with practical and consequential seriousness), and have thereby freed us from the already imminent danger of having to believe our spiritual Judaism dependent on the question of whether we were capable of being Kantians or not . . ."[11]

Possibility and impossibility: we could and could not be Kant's heirs. This translates perhaps into "we could but we should not" or "we should not have." Or else: "With regard to Kant, to the one who gave its categorical formulation to the law and to the imperative of the same name, we have contradictory attitudes, perhaps contradictory duties. Kant was and should not have been the institutor and the law of our relation to the law. And from this Moses to whom Kant has so often been compared, from this idol or effigy of Moses and from the necessarily troubled and ambiguous link that we have had to him, you, Buber, have freed us."

Actually, you have and you have not freed us. For the same ambivalence is in turn expressed with regard to Buber's teaching. According to Rosenzweig, Buber confined the relation to the law to a pedagogical space, that is to say, to a theoretical or an epistemological space. The law, however, is not only an object of knowledge, any more than it is a text that one should be content to read or study:

> . . . it is thus all the more curious that after liberating us and pointing the way to the new teaching, when you seek to answer the other side of the question "What should we do?"—the question of the law—that you allow this law, and us with it, to remain wholly bound in the shackles that the nineteenth century had put on it, as well as on the teaching.[12] For what you here acknowledge as the legitimate representative of the law, in order to come to terms with it and, after this attempt, which, as was to be expected, proved fruitless, to turn your back to it and refer yourself and us questioners to a reverent, but practically indifferent and personally abstinent, taking-note of the law as our sole task— is that really Jewish law, the law of millennia, studied and lived, analyzed and rhapsodized, the law of everyday and of the day of death, petty and sublime, sober and yet woven in legend; a law that knows both the fire of the Sabbath candle and that of the martyr's stake? (702; 77)

Where is the place in this letter that the double bind becomes tied to the question of the nation? The "unheard of" singularity of the Jewish nation in its relation to the law is that its birth belongs not to nature but precisely to the Law. Rosenzweig dissociates nature and nation, birth according to nature and birth according to law. This distinction actually remains a Kantian one. All nations, he says, are born at the heart of nature, in the bowels of mother nature. This is why they need a historical development. At the moment of their birth, of course, they do not yet have a history, they do not even have a face. The Jewish nation has a history, so to speak, *before* being born. It is not born naturally but is instead torn from another nation, for having been known, called by God's Law even before its birth. It is born of this calling in a nonnatural way. Its face was already formed, its birth already inscribed in a history that had begun before it, even though it was already its own. That is why the history of this nation is in some sense supernatural, transhistorical or, if one prefers, prehistoric. Its path remains unique. Like Heidegger, Rosenzweig thinks this in the form of the *path* [chemin] and as a new thinking of the path, thought as path. He links the path to the Law. This passage of the letter is a passage, on the path of which we are and that we are. It is a passage on the path and on the leap: "Law and teachings—the path leads us to both only if we know ourselves to be merely at its beginning and that we must take each step ourselves. But for the law, what is the path?" (704–5; 80)

This is Kafka's question in *Vor dem Gesetz* (written a few years earlier): How to gain access to the Law? How to touch it? What is the step leading to the Law? Rosenzweig questions this path toward the Law as a path toward the inaccessible. He does so using words and accents that are very close to Kafka's. The "trail" is "open" to the one who, having traveled the "whole length" of the path, would not even have "the right to say that he had now arrived at the goal." "Such a one could only ever say: now he has traversed the entire path [*Weg*], but the goal still lies, even for him, a step beyond, in the path-less [*im Weglosen*]. Why, then, nonetheless the path? Does it lead, does any path lead into the path-less?" Does it still deserve to be called a "path"? A "laborious and aimless detour through knowable Judaism gives us the certainty that the ultimate leap, from that which is knowable for me to that which we need to know at any price, the leap into the teachings, leads us to *Jewish* teachings." What is the need for this ultimate leap? The answer says the "unheard of" singularity of the Jewish nation. Its relation to the Law is but is not the one determined by Kant:

This need is not present in this way for other peoples. When a member of one of these peoples teaches, he teaches within his people and toward his people, even if he has not learned. All he teaches becomes the possession of his people. For the peoples have a face only in the process of becoming—each has its own. None of them knows at birth just what it is to be; their faces are not molded while they are still in nature's lap. . . . But to our people, the only one that did not arise from the womb of nation-bearing nature, but—unheard of!—was led forth "a nation from the midst of another nation" [Deut. 4:34], to our people was decreed a different fate. Here its very birth became the great moment of its life, its mere existence already joined it with its destiny. Before it was formed, it was, like its prophet [Jeremiah], already known. Thus belongs to it only he who reflects upon this determining origin; and he who is no longer able or willing to say the new word that he speaks "in the name of his speaker" and thus to link it, and himself along with it, to the golden chain, breaks away from the people. And that is why for this people learning the knowable is the sole condition under which the teaching of the unknown can become *its* teaching. (705; 81)

Let us return to Cohen after this detour. There are several points of reference in his equivocal relation to Kant. As we have seen in his way of recounting history, Cohen regularly assigns a multiplicity of origins to what he calls the German spirit or German idealism: the Platonic hypothesis, its adoption or anticipation by Judaism—by Philo in particular—the Christian *logos*, the Reformation, Kepler, Nicholas of Cusa, Leibniz, Kant. Each time its birth only announces another birth. At a given moment, the peak, the high point (*Höhepunkt*) in this chain of births or mountains, is Kant ("until it [German idealism] reached its historical high point [*seinen geschichtlichen Höhepunkt*] with Kant" (*DJ*, § 6). Here, then, is the ambiguity: it now seems (§ 44) that the real high point is not Kant. It is Fichte: Fichte discovered that the social Self is a national Self ("*Das soziale Ich hat er als das nationale Ich entdeckt*" is emphasized by Cohen). By searching and finding in the "national Self" the "supra-empirical foundation of the Self," he thus constituted "in fact [*in der Tat*] a peak of German philosophy (*So bildet Fichte in der Tat einen Höhepunkt der deutschen Philosophie*).

How is this possible? What does it mean? Let us first note that, as for Rosenzweig, it is the thinking of the national that makes it possible to go beyond the Kantian peak. But this time it is in view of a summit that identifies the national with the essence of the German or of the Judeo-German couple. Its representative figure is a thinker of the German nation, the one who saw the German nation as a chosen nation and who occasionally used the reference to Jewish prophecy to intimate what he wanted to intimate of the German nation to the German nation. In his *Addresses to the German Nation*, Fichte also speaks of a path of human history. He even specifies the "midway" point at which the second half of human history must begin:

> The real destiny of the human race on earth . . . is in freedom to make itself what it really is originally. Now this making of itself deliberately, and according to rule, must have a beginning somewhere and at some moment in space and time. Thereby a second great period, one of free and deliberate development of the human race, would appear in place of the first period, one of development that is not free. We are of the opinion that, in regard to time, this is the very time, and that now the race is exactly midway between the two great epochs of its life on earth. But in regard to space, we believe that it is first of all the Germans who are called upon to begin the new era as pioneers and models for the rest of mankind.[13]

It is not insignificant that this *Address* (the third) ends with "the vision of an ancient prophet":

> Thus says the prophet by the river of Chebar, the comforter of those in captivity, not in their own, but in a foreign land. "The hand of the Lord was upon me, and carried me out in the spirit of the Lord, and set me down in the midst of the valley which was full of bones, and caused me to pass by them round about: and, behold, there were very many in the open valley; and, lo, they were very dry. And He said unto me, Son of man, can these bones live? And I answered, O Lord God, thou knowest. Again He said unto me, Prophesy upon these bones, and say unto them O ye dry bones, hear the word of the Lord. Thus saith the Lord God unto these bones, Behold, I will cause breath to enter into you, and ye shall live: and I will lay sinews upon you, and will bring up the flesh upon you, and cover you with skin, and put breath in you, and ye shall live: and ye shall know that I am the Lord." . . . Though the elements of our higher spiritual life may be just as dried up, and though the bonds of our national unity may lie just as torn asunder and as scattered in wild disorder as the bones of the slain in the prophecy, though they may have whitened and dried for centuries in tempests, rainstorms, and burning sunshine, the quickening breath of the spiritual world has not yet ceased to blow. It will take hold, too, of the dead bones of our national body, and join them together, that they may stand glorious in new and radiant life. (Ibid., 43–44)

How does Cohen analyze Fichte's relation to Kant? And how does he account for this duality of peaks? (1) By dissociating the theoretical from the practical; (2) by recalling the social point of view that is latent in Kantian ethics; (3) by showing that the manifestation of the latent unites the national and the social, nationalism with socialism (*DJ*, § 44).

Cohen recognizes that from a theoretical point of view, Kant remains unsurpassed. Fichte's philosophy of the Self (*die Ich-Philosophie Fichtes*) is a theoretical regression. It would be superficial or inconsistent to mis-recognize this, says Cohen. He opposes himself here to those academics who, in the name of purely patriotic considerations, out of concern for "patriotic merit," are prepared, in this context, to prefer the nationalist Fichte at any price. Cohen's complex gesture consists in recognizing the national question as an essential and an essentially philosophical question, but at the same time in emphasizing that from a theoretical point of view, Fichte's philosophy of the Self is a regression. Cohen also admits that philosophy is a "national matter [*eine nationale Sache*]" and one must be grateful to Fichte, in spite of his "theoretical regression," for having made some progress (*Fortschritt*): he brought the latent socialism of Kantian ethics into its "explicit development." Let us not forget that this national-ist discourse of 1915 is also a socialist discourse. Fichte's great "discovery" is that the Self is social, but also that the social Self is in its origin and essence a national Self.

In other words, the "I" of "I think," the *cogito*, is not formal, as Kant thought. It appears to itself in its relation to the other, and this *socius*, far from being abstract, manifests itself to itself originally in its national determination, as belonging to a spirit, a history, a language. I—the Self—signs first in its spiritual language. The nationality of the ego is not a characteristic or an attribute that supervenes to a subject who was not national-social to begin with. The subject is originally and through and through, substantially, subjectally national. The *ego cogito* discovered by Fichte is national. It has a universal form, but this universality does not come to its truth except as nationality. This "new truth [*neue Wahrheit*] completes" in fact (*in der Tat*) what was latent in the *Ich* of the Kantian *Ich denke* because it is a "new realization [*Verwirklichung*] of the I." It goes beyond the ethical abstraction of humanity and provides the *Lebensgrund* of Fichte's idealism.

These statements revolve around themselves—like that mirror called a *psyché*. If the essence of egological effectivity is nationality, if this is the truth of idealism, that is, of philosophy itself of which German idealism is also the actualization [*effectuation*], then one must say, conversely, that the nation is an *ego*. It relates to itself in the form of egological subjectivity. The truth of nationality asserts itself as idealism. And because the truth of philosophical idealism, that is, of philosophy in general, is German idealism, the truth of nationality *in general* is German idealism. When one says "in general" one must think that the actualization (*Verwirklichung*) of this generality is—German—nationality. The truth of the *I* inasmuch as it *posits itself* is German. If in the act of positing itself as nationality one finds something of *reflection* and thus of the narcissistic structure in which a "new truth" "discovers" (*entdeckt*) itself, if this new truth posits itself in unveiling itself, then the mirror of a certain *psyché* is to be found in the revolving center of the relation to itself of the ego as national ego. There is room for a self as other in this self-relation of the national self. Not only for another self that would be as close as possible but for any other self. Hence the literally cosmopolitan proposition that is deduced, according to good Fichtean logic, from this national-socialist German idealism. This is the exemplary superiority of German idealism as of German nationality. The German spirit is the spirit of humanity: "The spirit of humanity is the originary spirit of our ethics. In this ethical determinacy, the German spirit is the spirit of the cosmopolitanism and of the humanity [*der Geist des Weltbürgertums und der Humanität*] of our classical age" (*DJ*, § 45), that is to say, of the eighteenth century.

At the peak of the Fichtean peak, Cohen fears, to be sure, the narcissistic effects of this exaltation of the German spirit and of the national *ego*. This fear and its formulation belong moreover to the program or the typology of all nationalisms. There is always a moment at which one must issue a warning, as Cohen does, against a national enthusiasm or excitation (*nationale Begeisterung*) that shows every sign of narcissistic infatuation (*Eigendünkel*) and sentimental complacency regarding what is properly one's own. Cohen remains Kantian enough to suspect this *Begeisterung*. He wants to balance enthusiasm with a consciousness of the law, the severity of obligation, a sense of responsibility. Privilege also assigns a mission; it even consists in this mission. The national Self is, of course, also a "We," and, first of all, a subject of rights, especially of duties. With no other transition, Cohen moves on to a list of consequences that seem to follow, in a quasi-analytical way, from this German idealism: mandatory military service, the right to vote, compulsory education.

While taking care not to give in to misleading analogies, one might be tempted to recall here the three "services" that Heidegger derives, in his Rectoral Address (1933)—another war discourse, postwar and prewar— from the self-affirmation, or the self-positing of the German university. To be sure, the content of these two times three duties is not exactly the same, although both knowledge and the army are there. Heidegger does not mention the right to vote, which moreover is not a duty, but in both cases, all of these obligations or services (*Aufgabe, Dienste*) are derived from national self-affirmation. And even if the democratic theme is absent from Heidegger's text, the socialist, even populist theme permeates both texts.

Let us not imprudently bring these two gestures together. The differences between them are considerable. But they make their mark within the common web of a tradition that should never be forgotten. All the more so since Cohen's text is also, in many respects, a text about the academic institution. This can be recognized by the crucial role that the German university plays in the argument. First, because German idealism has no meaning, no *effectivity*, precisely, outside the effectivity of the German university and its history during the nineteenth century (which is also, let us never forget, the century of the emancipation of the Jews; and Cohen is still a man of the nineteenth century). Secondly, because, as Cohen literally says, the university must become the thing of the people, a true people's school: "*Die Universität muss die wahrhafte Volksschule werden*" (*DJ*, § 44, Cohen's emphasis). The self-positing of the German spirit, the reflexive psyche that ensures its guard and tradition, only finds its effective truth in the people's university. Let us attempt still another prudent and limited analogy. Just as for Heidegger in 1933, among the three obligations (*Bindungen*) or services (*Arbeits-, Wehr-, Wissensdienste*) that are equally originary and of equal dignity, the service of knowledge maintains a privilege inasmuch as it molds the guardians and the guides of the German people in its university, likewise it is to the "higher institutions of education [*höheren Bildungsstätten*]" that Cohen wants to entrust this pedagogical function. It must be accessible to the popular classes and ensure social justice and national unity.

These three duties bind the consciousness of the national subject. They limit the risks of the exaltation into which one might be drawn by a dangerous interpretation of Fichte's thought. From one peak to another. One before the other, and Cohen returns regularly from one to the other. In defining the three duties and this cohesion of the national consciousness (*Einheitlichkeit des Nationalbewusstseins*) that forms the living core of the "national feeling," he emphasizes the word "feeling" (*Gefühl*) but insists on the necessity of understanding Kant's thought, which is not merely a sentimental thought about duty and responsibility. (It is true that it is also this: respect for the law must remain a feeling): "Every German must know, with an intimacy such as love offers, his Schiller and his Goethe, and must carry them in his mind and his heart. But this intimacy presupposes that he has also acquired from his Kant a popular-scientific insight and an understanding" (*DJ*, § 44).

Here the question of military service, that is, the first of the three obligations mentioned earlier, deserves special attention. For three reasons. First, of course, because this text is being written and published in the middle of a war by a socialist who wants to remain pacifist and cosmopolitan in spite of everything. Secondly, because Cohen links this question specifically to Kant. Finally, because its relation to the Jewish question is at the time rather peculiar in Germany. Let us follow these three threads.

There is no exaggerating the importance of music in this problematic of the German nation—and no doubt of any other nation. We thus see the military thematic appear at the very heart of what we are being told about the soul, about the national psyche, and about music. The latter is first the rule of breath and pneumatic structures (*Lufthauch, Luftgebilde*), that is to say, psychic structures as well. Music is the place of the "spiritual sublime [*geistige Erhabenheit*]" (*DJ*, § 15). Now the fusion of spirit and soul (*Verschmelzung von Geist und Seele*) does not achieve its ultimate fulfillment (*Vollendung*) except in German music (*einzig in der deutschen Musik*). This must be demonstrated in order to answer the question of the particularity of German music and the question of knowing why it should have such an impact on what is proper (*die Eigenart*) to the German spirit. Music is the most ideal of the arts (*die idealste der Künste*). This hierarchy of the arts, according to their respective ideality, is presupposed by the entire discourse. It calls for a comparative analysis of the classifications of art, from Hegel to Heidegger at least. Here this higher ideality of music puts it in tune with the whole idealistic intention of this discourse on German idealism. If music is the most ideal art, it is precisely because of its psychic character. The structure, the architecture or the edification (*Gebäude*) of music is pure breath (*reiner Hauch*), respiration, *spiritus* and psyche. As attentive as he is to rhythm, Cohen is also mindful of the vast empire of mathematical forms that organize music. Rosenzweig pays Cohen the tribute of having been, perhaps unwittingly, a great mathematical thinker:

> Hermann Cohen, contrary to his own conception of himself and contrary to the appearance of his works, was something quite different from a mere epigone to the movement [that begins with Plato], which had truly run its course. And it remained for him to discover in mathematics an organon of thinking, for the very reason that it generates its elements not out of the empty Nothing of the one and universal Zero, but out of the determinate Nothing of the differential, which is each time assigned to the sought-after element.[14]

In the same development, Rosenzweig speaks of Cohen as a "master." A master because he truly broke with the "idealism" to which he nevertheless laid claim, broke with Hegel, precisely, by his return to Kant. Rosenzweig wants to introduce into the heart of the idealist tradition ruptures to which Cohen did not pay enough attention. The same development involves nothing less than a thought of nothingness that would also call for a debate with Heidegger:

> Mathematics is the guide for the sake of these two paths. It teaches us to know the origin of the Something in the Nothing. And thus, even if the master would strongly object, we are here building upon the great scientific achievement of his logic of origin the new concept of the Nothing. May he otherwise have been more of a Hegelian than he admitted—and thereby as much of an "idealist" as he wished to be—here, in this fundamental idea, he broke decisively with idealist tradition. In place of the one and universal Nothing, which, like the Zero, was permitted to be really nothing more than "nothing," in place of this veritable "non-thing" [*Unding*], he posited the particular Nothing, which burst fruitfully into the realities. It was precisely Hegel's foundation of logic upon the concept of being that he there decidedly opposed [I would say that Heidegger did so too in his own way in *Was ist Metaphysik?*], and with it the entire philosophy into whose inheritance Hegel had come. For here for the first time a philosopher who himself still considered himself an "idealist" (one more indication of the force of what happened to him) recognized and acknowledged: that what confronted thought, when it set forth in order to "purely generate," was not Being, but Nothing.
>
> For the first time. Even if it remains true that here as everywhere, among all the thinkers of the past, Kant alone—indeed, as always, in those remarks that he made without drawing their systematic consequences—showed the way we shall now go. (Ibid.)

Need we point out again the institutional dimension of these very overdetermined interpretations? They concern the system, the unity of the corpus, the way in which interpretive, auto- or hereto- interpretive traditions, hence academic institutions, evaluate, manage, conceal, rank, canonize—founding themselves in these operations. And let us not forget that what we have here, in appearance, is a nonacademic who is speaking of the academy. And yet it is not enough to be a stranger to the university by profession to be simply outside of it. Neither as a civilian nor as a military man, to use convenient yet problematic distinctions, especially during wartime. But what is wartime? Nothing that is military is foreign to knowledge, to the matheme and to mathematics. Especially not military music. The greatness of German music appeals to the sublimity of spiritual forms (*Erhabenheit der geistigen Formen*). This whole discourse about nationalism is also a discourse on the sublime. This sublime edifice (*dieser erhabene Formenbau*) plunges its rays into the deepest sources of originary feeling. This sublimity of spiritual forms goes hand in hand with the mathematization of rhythms. It links up with the sources of feeling and thus makes for the originality of German music. But with what must this structuring of feeling be compared? Cohen's answer: with that of a *Heerzug*, a military array, a military train, procession, or parade (*DJ*, § 15).

Here we must recall the history that Cohen places in perspective: not only that of the emancipation of the German Jews, but also that of a world Jewry interpreted on the basis of German Jewry and what links it to the Aufklärung and to Kant. Cohen has no doubt about this, as he says (*DJ*, § 33): Mendelssohn's influence and Kant's influence were simultaneous and of the same nature. This influence reaches beyond Germany, to Judaism in all its depth "as well as to the entire cultural life of the Jews, at least of all Occidental Jews of the modern world." (This last restriction seems very important, especially if one considers the essentially European character of early Zionism.) Having noted this influence, Cohen emphasizes once more the "very internal or very profound moral affinity" between Germanness and Judaism. At issue is political socialism. Political socialism corresponds both to the generalization of the priesthood, which is both a Lutheran and a Jewish motif, and to messianism. In sum, in its modernity, the German state is priestly and messianic. This is recognizable in its social policy, and more precisely in the fact that social policy is recognized by it as a duty: an ethical duty prior to being a political one, a duty already prescribed by natural law. Socialism is not one policy among others, and it is the German policy par excellence, by essence. Socialism is national, and it is German. There may be different political or politicizing modalities, different strategies in the implementation of socialism, but as to its end there can be no doubt whatsoever. This socialist policy, this morality inspired by a universal priesthood, serves a fundamental messianism: Judeo-German messianism.

To illustrate this truth (certain indications of which are undeniable in any case), Cohen gives some examples. First of all, Bismarck made universal suffrage a right written into the constitution. (Let me recall here a remark by Blanchot who wonders whether Heidegger did not mistake Hitler for Bismarck in 1933, in connection with the alliance between nationalism and socialism, in connection with National Socialism.)[15] Bismarck, according to Cohen, draws a logical conclusion that is inscribed in the very idea of a German Reich. The second example is the one toward which we have been heading for some time. The same logic led the disciples of Kant to make compulsory military service a major institution, one that deserved to be inscribed in the German constitution. And if Cohen emphasizes that these were disciples of Kant, it is to remind us that they were pacifists in principle. Because of the war for Schleswig-Holstein and the war against Napoleon, they had to give in to its necessity. This necessity is still marked by democracy, by social democracy rather than by militarism. The compulsory character of military service corresponds to a democratization of the military institution. The founding of social democracy is moreover an essential property (*Eigenart*) of the German spirit in Cohen's eyes; he recalls furthermore that the Jews proved their military patriotism in the wars of liberation, whereas, at the time of Frederick II, they had been barred from military service. This patriotic zeal would thus have lucidly anticipated and prepared, in spirit, the letter of the legal apparatus. As for the fact of social democracy, as an ethical phenomenon (once purged of its "material scoria"), that is, the essence of the German spirit in its alliance with Judaism, Cohen sees many signs of it, such as, for example, Marx's Jewish origin or the religious orientation of Ferdinand Lassalle in his youth (*DJ*, § 34).

VI

Interpretations at war, we were saying. The status, the date, and the purpose of Cohen's *Deutschtum und Judentum* justify the attention paid to what in it concerns the philosophy of the army as well as the philosophy of war. Cohen seeks to reconcile at least three apparently incompatible things: (1) He wants—and does not hide it—Germany's victory. (2) He wants it as a German Jew and so must interpret this victory as a victory for Judaism, knowing full well that the majority of Jews in the world are not German. (3) As a good Kantian, he is committed not only to cosmopolitanism but also to pacifism. How does he manage this?

1. He clearly wants a military victory, "the heroes' victory of our fatherland" [*den Heldensieg unseres Vaterlandes*]." When he says "our," he is addressing himself to the Germans, to the German Jews, but also to all the Jews of the world who should recognize, let us remember, their being [*être*] or their duty to be [*devoir-être*] German. This "we" carries with it, in this usage—in its pragmatics, its rhetoric—the teleological force of the "we" in Fichte's *Addresses to the German Nation*. This "we" is both invoked as that which remains to be constituted and presupposed as that which is most originary. The hoped-for victory definitely includes the actual military triumph of German arms ("Wir hoffen auch den Triumph der deutschen Waffen" [*DJ*, § 41]). But Cohen's discourse gets more entangled when it comes to justifying this war. Is it "just"? As a socialist pacifist Cohen begins by asking himself: Was it necessary? Is war in general necessary? His apparently calm reply: we shall not discuss these questions here. They reflect historical judgment and a philosophy of history. As to the causes of (the) war, the question is left to the historians and to the disciplines that simultaneously treat history, economics, and the state. A strange move, but one based, in any case, on the division of labor as a division of problematic regions, of disciplines of knowledge, and of academic departments. All of which are presuppositions and, furthermore, institutional presuppositions.

How can someone whose principal aim is to justify the victory of one of the belligerents, and who, on the other hand, calls himself a pacifist, leave or defer these questions? How can he save them for other, constituted disciplines, that is, for institutions external to the one in which his own discourse is inscribed? Can one simply speak here of avoidance or denial? For this question is both posed and avoided by Cohen in a gesture that, while perhaps not rigorously Kantian, still maintains a Kantian style. Cohen says, in effect: I am renouncing here the philosophy of history, the theodicy of universal history as well as the regional sciences (economics, political science, etc.). But having thus fallen back on a neocritical gesture, I am still able to maintain a reflective and teleological attitude by asking myself: given that the event of the war *has occurred*, whatever its causes (for this see the historians, the economists, the political scientists) or final aims (for this see the philosophers of history or the theologians), "what may we learn from the fact of wars [*aus der Tatsache der Kriege*], and thus also from the fact of this war, regarding the *destiny of humankind* and, within that destiny, regarding the destiny of *Germanness* [*Bestimmung des* Deutschtums], in order to illuminate and fulfill the moral purpose of Germanness [*um den sittlichen Zweck des Deutschtums zu erhellen und zu erfüllen*]?" (§ 43).

Cohen calls this a "teleological" method (§ 43). It is only a method, for by renouncing the knowledge of ultimate ends, human or divine, one falls back on this question: What is the purpose of this war with regard to our national *Dasein* (*suchen wir den Zweck dieses Krieges für unser nationales Dasein zu erforschen*)? And the immediate reply is: from this war we expect a national rebirth (*nationale Wiedergeburt*) and *the social rejuvenation of our entire people* (die soziale Verjüngung unseres gesamten Volkes [Cohen's emphasis]). This is why, in the eyes of a German, a military victory is desirable.

2. But this German teleology is also a Jewish teleology. Because this war is taking place, the same question arises: Why should a Jew hope for the triumph of German arms? And what can this mean for the destiny of Judaism? In reply, this war is not far from being presented as a war of liberation. Such, at least, is the hope—or the trust (*DJ*, § 41). By the "heroes' victory of our fatherland," the "God of justice and love will put an end to the barbarous servitude" that the tsarist empire imposes on our brothers (ibid.). The political existence of these poor Russian Jews is a shameful defiance of human rights, dignity, and respect. But if he seems to place German Jews above the others, above the downtrodden Russian Jews, for example, Cohen hopes that the German victory will also advance the emancipation of the German Jews. He is well aware that there is room for progress on the German side as well, for example, concerning the recognition without reservation of the Jewish religion, for which mere legal equality is not enough. A German victory, Cohen thinks, should give even more life and truth to the Judeo-German psyche. We know why he was unable to submit his hypothesis to the test of experience.

3. Finally, how can this approval of a just war, this hope for a German—and one should say Judeo-German—victory, be reconciled with a funda-

mental pacifism, a pacifism associated with an originally Kantian cosmopolitanism? By means of this master idea, which at least resembles an Idea
in the Kantian sense: this war must be inscribed within the perspective
of a messianic idea and bring about an international agreement, peace
among nations. How should this peace be founded? Let us be attentive
here to the letter of these propositions. It gives to exemplarism—which
constitutes the very center of our reflection on nationality—one of its
most economic formulations. Our example (*unser Beispiel*), says Cohen (§
41), must serve as a model (*wird als Vorbild dienen dürfen.*). Our example
must serve as an example—in other words, as a model, an exemplary example, a paradigm, or an ideal: the *Beispiel,* as *Vorbild.* It must serve as an
example for the acknowledgement (*Anerkennung*) of German hegemony,
predominance, preponderance (*der deutschen* Vormacht [this last word is
emphasized by Cohen]) in all fundamentals or foundations of spiritual
and psychic life (*in allen Grundlagen des Geistes- und des Seelenlebens*). The
logic here is more extraordinary than ever: there will be no agreement and
no peace among nations unless our example is followed. But let us follow the progression, which is also a redundant tautology, between the a
priori synthesis and the analytic explanation: our example (*Beispiel*) must
be followed as an example (*Vorbild*) to recognize our *Vormacht,* German
hegemony or preeminence. The progression from *Beispiel* to *Vorbild* and
to *Vormacht* is tautologous, insofar as the example is not an indifferent
case in a series. It is exemplary, a pre-model, a pre-formative model. To
recognize it as such is to recognize German hegemony (*Vormacht*). Recognition cannot remain merely theoretical. It does not go without political
subjugation—in the spiritual and psychic order, of course, to which this
entire teleological discourse belongs, a discourse that proliferates purifying remarks regarding the foreign and foreigners, regarding "false literary
greats from foreign lands," and so on, that is to say, remarks that are rarely
pure of all xenophobia (see in particular *DJ,* § 45).

This spiritualist determination of national exemplarity does not belong
only to the German nation. What would one say to the statement that
this exemplarity does not belong to it except in an exemplary manner? In
Qu'est-ce qu'une nation? [*What Is a Nation?*], Renan also emphasizes this
spiritual characteristic. "Nothing material" is not enough to define the
nation. "A nation is a spiritual principle," and it is not its race, or even
its language, its interests, its religious affinity, its geography, its military

necessities that can exhaust its definition. Renan also calls this spiritual principle a "soul": "A nation is a soul, a spiritual principle."

For reasons that have to do not only with time and space I will point to two of the themes that lead me to quote Renan here. Both will lead us back to Cohen.

A. The first concerns memory and forgetting. For Cohen, to become conscious of a sort of spiritual Judeo-German nation is to give oneself over to an anamnesis of a rather peculiar kind. This anamnesis goes back to Plato, to Philo, to the Christian *logos*, to Maimonides, to Luther, to Kant and Fichte, and so on. Memory is possible. But it is also necessary and de rigueur, which means that it is not automatic: forgetting is therefore also constitutive of the history that will have formed a nation. Renan's thesis, both paradoxical and sensible, is that forgetting makes the unity of a nation, not memory. And, even more interesting, Renan analyzes this forgetting as a kind of repression: it is active, selective, meaningful, in a word, interpretive. Forgetting is not, in the case of a nation, a simple psychological erasure, a wearing out or a meaningless obstacle that makes access to the past more difficult, as if the archive had been destroyed by accident. No, if there is forgetting, it is because one cannot tolerate something that was at the origin of the nation, an act of violence, no doubt, a traumatic event, some sort of unavowable curse. In the midst of historical narratives that we should reread, whatever our nationality (I can count at least four here), Renan writes, for example:

> Forgetting, and I would say even historical error, are essential factors in the formation of a nation, and thus the progress of historical study is often a danger for nationality. Historical investigation, in fact, brings back to light the violent deeds that took place at the origin of all political formations, even those whose consequences have been beneficial. Unity is always achieved brutally; the unification of the north and south of France was the result of extermination and terror that went on for nearly a century. The King of France, who is, I dare say, the ideal type of crystallizer, the King of France who has achieved the most perfect national unity ever achieved, the King of France, seen from too close, loses his prestige; the nation he formed curses him, and today none but cultivated minds know what he was worth and what he did.

A series of examples (French, Slavic, Czech, and German) allows Renan to conclude:

Now, the essence of a nation is that all individuals should have many things in common and that all should have forgotten many things. No French citizen knows whether he is Burgunde, Alain, Taifale, Visigoth; every French citizen must have forgotten Saint Bartholomew, the thirteenth-century massacres in the South. There are not ten families in France that can furnish evidence of a Frankish origin, and any such evidence would still be totally defective, as a result of a thousand unknown interbreedings capable of undoing all our genealogical systems.

These truths, always worth repeating, remind us of at least two things. On the one hand, a nation does not exist until one is sure that all "have forgotten many things." As long as some remember originary deeds of violence, the nation remains unassured of its essence and existence. On the other hand, as long as some remember and can recall the purity of their ethnic origin (Burgunde, Alain, Visigoth, for example), the nation remains unassured of its essence and existence.

These truths, however, we should not forget. They did not prevent the French historian Renan from forgetting in turn (QED), and from being rather violent, when he dares to state the following blatant untruth: "An honorable fact for France is that it has never sought to obtain unity of language by coercive measures." We know that this is not at all true (QED). The objectivity of historical science, an interpretive discipline through and through, is here affected at a given moment in one of its representatives by his belonging to a national institution, the French language, to begin with. These are the limits of self-interpretation.

This discourse on forgetting is interesting not only for what it says about an originary violence, one that is constitutive and still silently active. One can also bring it to bear—even though Renan does not do this—on another comment located elsewhere in the same text. If a nation has a soul or a spiritual principle, this is not only, says Renan, because it is not founded upon anything that is called race, language, religion, place, army, interest, and so on. It is because a nation is both memory (and forgetting belongs to the very deployment of this memory) and, in the present, promise, project, a "desire to live together." Is this promise not in itself, structurally, a relation to the future that involves a forgetting—indeed, a kind of essential indifference to the past, to what in the present is only present—but also a gathering, that is, also a memory of the future? "A remembered future," one might say, twisting perhaps the title of a book you are very familiar with.[16] This is not Renan's language. I propose it nevertheless as a way of interpreting some of his statements:

> A nation is a soul, a spiritual principle. Two things that are in fact one constitute this soul, this spiritual principle. [Thus we have the spirit and the psyche, the latter being divided in two and reflected in time, as we will see: the past and the future turn around a present pivot.] One is in the past, the other in the present. One is the possession in common of a rich legacy of memories; the other is the actual consent, the desire to live together, the will to continue to exploit the heritage one has received undivided. Man, gentlemen, is not improvised.

"Actual consent," the "desire to live together" are performative engagements, promises that must be renewed daily, inscribing the necessity of forgetting in memory itself, one within the other, inseparably. Further in the text, Renan writes: "The existence of a nation is (forgive me this metaphor) a daily plebiscite, just as the existence of the individual is a perpetual affirmation of life. Yes, I know, this is less metaphysical than divine right, less brutal than a supposedly historical right." Is this so certain? I leave this question suspended here.

B. Another theme recalls Cohen's discourse: that of the European confederation. Following the war of 1870, and referring to it (something it has in common with Cohen's later discourse, with which it is contemporaneous from this perspective), Renan's text takes stock, in 1882, of what he calls the secession, the breaking up of nations:

> We have driven the metaphysical and theological abstractions out of politics. What remains after that? Man remains, his desires, his needs. Secession, you say, and in the long run, the breaking up of nations, are the consequence of a system that puts these old organisms at the mercy of wills that are often unenlightened. . . . Nations are not something eternal. They had a beginning and they will have an end. The European confederation will probably replace them. But such is not the law of the century in which we live. At the present time, the existence of nations is good, even necessary. Their existence guarantees freedom, which would be lost were the world to have but one master.

This leads us back to our third question: How can Cohen reconcile his hope for a Judeo-German victory with his cosmopolitan pacifism, inspired by Kant? How can the German spirit become the center of a federation that would guarantee world peace? How can one legitimize a war by claiming that it is just (*gerecht*) because it is also the preparation (*Vorbereitung*) for perpetual peace?

If the spirit of universal humanity is, *exemplarily*, the origin of *our* Judeo-German ethic, the German spirit is surely, from a moral viewpoint, the spirit of cosmopolitanism as it was formed in the eighteenth century. If a national development serves universal justice, the use of force is legitimate if it in turn serves this national development in its exemplary singularity. In this war, says Cohen, every German is conscious of both national right and of universal justice. From this consciousness he draws a "sublime energy" (*mit erhabener Energie* [*DJ*, § 46]), and in this too his letter to the American Jews definitely resembles a treatise on the sublime. (Let it be said in passing that this description of the soldier's "conscience" is undoubtedly correct enough to have been also the one into which the French soldier were inculcated at the same moment—like every non-mercenary soldier in every war in the world.) In this conscience, force is not opposed to right. Here there is an analogy between the individual and the state. "What the organism is for the spirit of the individual, is the same as the meaning of power for the state of the peoples" (*DJ*, § 46). Just as the individual must not thwart humanity, so the individual power of each state must not thwart the universal state, that is, the confederation of states that should be the ideal of every state. According to natural right or according to positive and historical right, the concept of state requires confederation. This requirement is inscribed in it and must lead to its maturity. The project of an international socialism must not remain a utopia. Thus war is what makes it finally emerge out of utopia! The power of the state is necessary to make socialism effective, to make it into something other than a "blunt weapon" and "half-truth" (*DJ*, § 47). One sees this same logic at work, a logic that is less and less Kantian, Hegelian rather, or quasi-Hegelian: the logic of effectivity or of actualization of the state, the very logic with which Rosenzweig broke. The force of the state should render effective a socialist and internationalist ideal that would otherwise remain abstract in a state of pure subjective representation.

Although he had bracketed the philosophy of history, Cohen now says just the opposite: the concept of "federation" or of "the achievement of the ideal of the state" must be erected into the "principle of *the philosophy of history*" (*DJ*, § 47). Let us temporarily conclude our discussion on this point. Like all the others, the problem of confederation is a current one everywhere.

Why does Cohen cease to take his cues from Kant when he broaches the problem of confederation and perpetual peace? Because he believes, unlike Kant, in the necessity of permanent armies. Kant, for his part, established as a principle that the constitution of permanent armies (*miles perpetuus*) must "gradually be abolished altogether": "No peace treaty shall be considered valid as such if it was made with a secret reservation of the material for a future war." Condemning any *reservatio mentalis* in peace treaties, he speaks of a sparrow, and this surely addresses itself to hawks and doves of all nations: "For a permanent universal peace by means of a so-called *European balance of power* is a pure illusion, like Swift's story of the house that the builder had constructed in such perfect harmony with all the laws of equilibrium that it collapsed as soon as a sparrow alighted on it."[17]

Cohen thinks, unlike Kant, that the existence of permanent armies is not in itself the cause of wars. He incriminates militarism instead and condemns those who see militarism wherever there is anything military. Militarism is a degradation of the military. It arises when people exalt an army that no longer serves a state worthy of the name, but only economic powers and the interests of capitalist expansionism. An antinomy may exist between the state and the military when the army puts itself in the service of private economic forces or a fraction of civilian society. But once it has become effective, the ideal state—that is, one that is ethical and federative in its orientation, thus German in its spirit—has no reason to give up its permanent army. Cohen opposes "our conception of military service" to that of the English enemy, whose social policy served as impetus to the war. It is true that in passing—and this will prevent us once more from simplifying the reading of this text—he brings a Kantian proposition into play in connection with right, if not morality: the exercise of right implies the ability to constrain.

> The individual state may thus—not only for its protection, but also for the protection of the idea of the confederation of states—not renounce its army, just as the confederation, like any constitution founded on right, also presupposes the power to protect itself. For this reason the individual state with and thanks to its army remains, for the correct causal as much as for the teleological consideration of the history of peoples, the *originary force* [ursprüngliche Kraft] from which the solution of the ethical task of humanity must *set out* and commence. But the *goal* of the task of the state is so certainly the confed-

eration of states that the idea of the state as such is only completed in itself through the confederation. (*DJ*, § 48)

Earlier (*DJ*, § 46), the state had been described as the summit (*Gipfel*), the summit of the nation as well as the summit of humanity. "The ideal of the state culminates in the confederation of states."

—*Translated by Moshe Ron and Dana Hollander*

Notes

1. Letter to a Japanese Friend

1. The following entry on "deconstruction" in the *Dictionnaire Bescherelle*, 15th ed. (Paris: Garnier, 1873) is also not without interest here:

DECONSTRUCTION.
Action of deconstructing, of disassembling the parts of a whole. The deconstruction of an edifice. The deconstruction of a machine.

Grammar: the displacement to which the words that make up a written sentence are subjected in a foreign language, by violating, it is true, the syntax of that language, but in order to bring it closer to the syntax of the mother tongue and thus better to grasp the meaning of the words in the sentence. The term refers precisely to what most grammarians improperly call "construction"; for in the work of any author, all sentences are *constructed* according to the particular genius of his or her national tongue; what is it that the foreigner does when he tries to understand, to translate this author? He deconstructs the sentences, he disassembles the words of these sentences, according to the genius of the foreign tongue; or, if one wishes to avoid confusing the terms here, there is *deconstruction* in relation to the language of the translated author and *construction* in relation to the language of the translator.

2. See "How to Avoid Speaking: Denials," Chapter 9 in this volume.

2. Geschlecht I

1. Martin Heidegger, *Sein und Zeit*, 12th ed. (Tübingen: Max Niemeyer, 1972); *Being and Time*, trans. John Macquarrie and Edward Robinson (New York: Harper & Row, 1962). Hereafter abbreviated *SZ* and followed by a page

number. When two page numbers are given, the first refers to the German text and the second to the English translation.—Tr.

2. Martin Heidegger, *Metaphysische Anfangsgründe der Logik im Ausgang von Leibniz*, in *Gesamtausgabe*, vol. 26 (Frankfurt a/M: Klostermann, 1978); *The Metaphysical Foundations of Logic*, trans. Michael Heim (Bloomington: Indiana University Press, 1984). Hereafter abbreviated *MA* and followed by a page number. When two page numbers are given, the first refers to the German text and the second to the English translation.—Tr.

3. Martin Heidegger, "Platons Lehre von der Wahrheit," in *Wegmarken*, *Gesamtausgabe*, vol. 9 (Frankfurt a/M: Klostermann, 1967), 236; "Plato's Doctrine of Truth," trans. Thomas Sheehan, in *Pathmarks*, ed. William McNeill (Cambridge: Cambridge University Press, 1998), 182.—Tr.

4. Martin Heidegger, "Vom Wesen des Grundes," in *Wegmarken*, 54; "On the Essence of Ground," trans. William McNeill, in *Pathmarks*, 122.—Tr.

5. For more on this point, see *Sein und Zeit*, 166; 209.

6. See Chapter 3 in this volume, "Heidegger's Hand (*Geschlecht* II)," and Jacques Derrida, *Of Spirit: Heidegger and the Question*, trans. Geoffrey Bennington and Rachel Bowlby (Chicago: University of Chicago Press, 1989), 107ff.

3. Heidegger's Hand (Geschlecht II)

1. Johann Gottlieb Fichte, *Reden an die Deutsche Nation* (Leipzig: Reclam, n.d.), 121; *Addresses to the German Nation*, ed. George Armstrong Kelly (New York: Harper & Row, 1968), 108. Hereafter abbreviated as *RN*, followed by a page number. When two page numbers are given, the first refers to the German text and the second to the English translation.—Tr.

2. Martin Heidegger, "Erläuterungen und Grundsätzliches," in *Gesamtausgabe*, vol. 16 (Frankfurt a/M: Klostermann, 2000), 414.—Tr.

3. Martin Heidegger, *Was heisst Denken?* 3d ed. (Tübingen: Niemeyer, 1971), 52; *What Is Called Thinking?* trans. Fred D. Wieck and J. Glenn Gray (New York: Harper & Row, 1968), 15. Hereafter abbreviated *WD* and followed by a page number. When two page numbers are given, the first refers to the German text and the second to the English translation.—Tr.

4. Martin Heidegger, *Qu'appelle-t-on penser?* trans. Aloys Becker and Gérard Granel (Paris: Presses universitaires de France, 1959), 92.—Tr.

5. Martin Heidegger, *Unterwegs zur Sprache* (Pfullingen: Neske, 1959), 252; *On the Way to Language*, trans. Peter D. Hertz (New York: Harper & Row, 1971), 122. Hereafter abbreviated *US* and followed by a page number. When two page numbers are given the first refers to the German text and the second to the English translation.—Tr.

6. Elsewhere I will study, as closely as possible, the developments Heidegger

devoted to animality in *Die Grundbegriffe der Metaphysik* (1929–30), in *Gesamtausgabe*, vols. 29–30 (Frankfurt a/M: Klostermann, 1983), pt. 2, ch. 4. Without any essential discontinuity, these developments seem to me to constitute the basis of those I am interrogating here, whether it be a question of (1) the classic gesture that consists in seeing zoology as a regional science that has to presuppose the essence of animality in general—which Heidegger then proposes to describe without the aid of this scientific knowledge (see § 45); (2) the thesis according to which "das Tier ist weltarm," a middle thesis between the two others ("der Stein ist weltlos" and "der Mensch ist weltbildend")—a very confused analysis in the course of which Heidegger has much trouble, it seems to me, both determining poverty, being poor (*Armsein*), and lack (*Entbehren*) as essential traits foreign to the empirical determination of differences of degrees (287), and explaining the original mode of this having-without-having of the animal that has and does not have the world ("das Haben und Nichthaben von Welt" [§ 50]); (3) the phenomeno-ontological modality of the *als*, the animal not having access to Being *as* (als) Being (290ff.). This last distinction would lead one to specify that the difference between man and animal corresponds less to the opposition between being-able-to-give and being-able-to-take than to the opposition between *two ways* of taking or giving: the one, that of man, is one of giving and taking *as such*, of Being or the present *as such;* the other, that of the animal, would be neither giving nor taking *as such.*

7. Émile Benveniste, "Gift and Exchange in the Indo-European Vocabulary," in *Problems in General Linguistics,* trans. Mary Elizabeth Meek (Coral Gables, Fla.: University of Miami Press, 1971), repr. in *The Logic of the Gift: Toward an Ethic of Generosity,* ed. by A. D. Schrift (New York: Routledge, 1997).—Eds.

8. Martin Heidegger, *Sein und Zeit*, 12th ed. (Tübingen: Max Niemeyer, 1972), 69; trans. John Macquarrie and Edward Robinson, *Being and Time* (New York: Harper & Row, 1962), 99. Hereafter abbreviated *SZ* and followed by a page number. When two page numbers are given, the first refers to the German text and the second to the English translation.—Tr.

9. Martin Heidegger, *Parmenides*, in *Gesamtausgabe*, vol. 54 (Frankfurt a/M: Klostermann, 1982), 118; *Parmenides*, trans. André Schuwer and Richard Rojcewicz (Bloomington: Indiana University Press, 1992), 80. Hereafter abbreviated *P* and followed by a page number. When two page numbers are given, the first refers to the German text and the second to the English translation.—Tr.

10. Martin Heidegger, *Holzwege* (Frankfurt a/M: Klostermann, 1950), 337; *Early Greek Thinking*, trans. David Farrell Krell and Frank A. Capuzzi (New York: Harper & Row, 1975), 51. Hereafter abbreviated *H* followed by a page number.—Tr.

11. Jacques Derrida, *The Truth in Painting*, trans. Geoffrey Bennington and Ian McLeod (Chicago: University of Chicago Press, 1987), 257ff.

12. If thinking and even the question (this "piety of thought") are a work of *the* hand, if hands joined together in prayer or in oath still gather together the hand in itself, in its essence with thinking, conversely, Heidegger denounces "clutch[ing] with both hands": haste, the eagerness of utilitarian violence, the acceleration of technology that disperses the hand into number and cuts it off from the thinking that questions. As if the taking with two hands lost or violated a thinking question that only *a* hand—*the* hand alone—could open or keep: (now) maintaining open. This is the end of *The Introduction to Metaphysics*: "To know how to question means to know how to wait, even a whole lifetime. But an age [*Zeitalter*] that regards as real [*wirklich*] only what goes fast and can be clutched with both hands [*sich mit beiden Händen greifen lässt*] looks on questioning as 'remote from reality [*wirklichkeitsfremd*]' and as something that does not pay [*was nicht bezahlt macht*], whose benefits cannot be numbered. But the essential is not number [*Zahl*]; the essential is the right time [*die rechte Zeit*]." Martin Heidegger, *Einführung in die Metaphysik* (Tübingen: Max Niemeyer, 1953), 157; *An Introduction to Metaphysics*, trans. Ralph Manheim (New Haven: Yale University Press, 1959), 206. I thank Werner Hamacher for having reminded me of this passage.

On the other "turn [*tournant*]" that I have tried to describe or situate around the question, and the question of the question, see *Of Spirit: Heidegger and the Question*, trans. Geoffrey Bennington and Rachel Bowlby (Chicago: University of Chicago Press, 1989), 129-36n5.

13. Perhaps you will be surprised to see me quoting a French translation of Heidegger in a lecture given in English. I am doing so for two reasons. On the one hand, in order not to erase the constraints or the chances of the idiom in which I myself work teach, read, or write. What you are hearing right at this moment is the translation of a text I first wrote in French. On the other hand, I thought that Heidegger's text might be still more accessible, might gain some supplementary readability, by reaching us thus through a third ear. The explication [*Auseinandersetzung*] with one more language may refine our translation [*Übersetzung*] of what is called the "original" text. I just spoke of the ear of the other as a third ear. That was not only to multiply to excess the examples of pairs (feet, hands, ears, eyes, breasts, etc.) and all the problems they should pose to Heidegger. It is also to underscore that one can write on the typewriter, as I have done, with three hands between three tongues. I knew I would have to speak in English the text I was writing in French on another I was reading in German. [*Nouvelle Revue Française* 6, no. 61 (1958); Martin Heidegger, *Acheminement vers la parole* [*Unterwegs zur Sprache*], trans. Jean Beaufret, Wolfgang Brokmeier, and François Fédier (Paris: Gallimard, 1976). Hereafter abbreviated *AP* and followed by a page number.—Tr.]

14. See "The *Retrait* of Metaphor," Chapter 2 in *Psyche: Inventions of the*

Other, vol. 1, ed. Peggy Kamuf and Elizabeth Rottenberg (Stanford: Stanford University Press, 2007).

15. David Farrell Krell, *Intimations of Mortality: Time, Truth, and Finitude in Heidegger's Thinking of Being* (University Park: Pennsylvania State University Press, 1986), 165.

16. See *Of Spirit*, trans. Bennington and Bowlby.

4. The Laws of Reflection: Nelson Mandela, in Admiration

1. Nelson Mandela, *The Struggle Is My Life* (New York: Pathfinder Press, 1986), 176. Unless otherwise noted, page numbers following quotations refer to this work. All emphases have been added by me.

2. Nelson Mandela and Breyten Breytenbach, *L'Apartheid* (Paris: Minuit, 1988), 19.

3. Ibid., 19–20.

5. No (Point of) Madness—Maintaining Architecture

1. Bernard Tschumi, *The Manhattan Transcripts* (London: Academy Editions; New York: St. Martin's Press, 1981). Published in connection with the exhibition of Bernard Tschumi's *Manhattan Transcripts Part 4* at the Max Protetch Gallery in New York, December 3, 1981–January 2, 1982.

2. Bernard Tschumi, "Madness and the Combinative," *Précis V*, 1984.

3. In *Margins of Philosophy*, trans. Alan Bass (Chicago: University of Chicago Press, 1984); see in particular the section titled "Paraphrase: Point, Line, Surface."

6. Why Peter Eisenman Writes Such Good Books

1. Peter Eisenman, *Moving Arrows, Eros and Other Errors: An Architecture of Absence* (London: Architectural Association, 1986).

2. Plato, *Timaeus*, trans. Peter Kalkavage (Newburyport, Ma: Focus 2001), 85; translation modified.

3. The drawings and models for this project were then published as "Œuvre chorale," in *Parc-Ville Villette: Architectures*, ed. Isabelle Auricoste and Hubert Tonka, *Vaisseau de pierres* 2 (Seyssel: Champ-Vallon, 1987).

4. "The pink edition, extra sporting, of the *Telegraph*, tell a graphic lie, lay, as luck would have it, beside his elbow. . . . " James Joyce, *Ulysses*, quoted in Jacques Derrida, *Ulysse gramophone: Deux mots pour Joyce* (Paris: Galilée, 1986), 67.

5. Jacques Derrida, "L'aphorisme à contretemps," in *Roméo et Juliette: Le Livre* (Paris: Papiers, 1986). See "Aphorism Countertime," Chapter 8 in this volume.

6. "So an endless play of readings: 'find out house,' 'fine doubt house,' 'find either or,' 'end of where,' 'end of covering' [In the wealth of reading possibilities, two of an 'inside' nature that have recently arisen might be interesting to indicate. 'Fin d'Ou T' can also suggest the French *fin d'août*, the end of August, the period, in fact, when the work on the project was completed. In addition, an English reader affecting French might well mispronounce this same fragment as 'fondue,' a Swiss cooking technique (from the French *fondu* for melted, also a ballet term for bending at the knee) alluding to the presence of a Swiss-trained architect, Pieter Versteegh, as a principal design assistant!], etc., is provoked by regulated manipulations of the spaces—between letters, between languages, between image and writing—a manipulation that is in every way formal, in every way writing, yet blatantly independent of the manipulations that the foundations (of French or English) would permit." Jeffrey Kipnis, "Architecture Unbound, Consequences of the Recent Work of Peter Eisenman," in Peter Eisenman, *Fin d'Ou T Hou S* (London: Architectural Association, 1985), 19.

7. Or the book to a monument. Hugo, for example, in *Notre Dame de Paris*: "The book will kill the edifice," but also "The bible of stone and the bible of paper," "the cathedral of Shakespeare," "the mosque of Byron."

8. Aphorism Countertime

1. In English as well as in French, "contretemps" signifies "an inopportune occurrence, an untoward accident; an unexpected mishap or hitch" (*Oxford English Dictionary*), but in French it also refers to being "out of time" or "off-beat" in the musical sense, to a sense of "bad or wrong time," "countertime."—Tr.

2. References to Shakespeare's *Romeo and Juliet* are to the Arden text, ed. Brian Gibbons (New York: Methuen, 1980)—Tr.

3. I have followed the text of Derrida's quotation here, thus preserving the colon at the end of the first line. The Arden version, already cited, gives a full stop. As Brian Gibbons points out (Arden, 129), there have been several variants and varying hypotheses regarding these lines of the play. Confusingly perhaps, Q2–4 and F in fact give: "ô be some other name / Belonging to a man."—Tr.

4. See G. W. F. Hegel, *Aesthetics: Lectures on Fine Art*, trans. T. M. Knox, vol. 1 (Oxford: Clarendon Press, 1975), 69.—Tr.

9. How to Avoid Speaking: Denials

1. Who has ever assumed the project of negative theology *as such*, reclaiming

it explicitly in the singular under this name, without subjugating and subor-
dinating it, without at least pluralizing it? On the subject of this title, negative theology [la *théologie négative*], can one do anything but *deny* it? Jean-Luc
Marion contests the legitimacy of this title, not only for the whole of Dionysius's
work—which goes without saying—but even for the places where it is a question of "negative theologies" in the plural (*tines ai kataphatikai theologiai, tines
ai apophatikai*) in chapter 3 of *The Mystical Theology*. Concerning "what is con-
ventionally called 'negative theology,'" Marion notes: "To my knowledge, Dionysius uses nothing that might be translated as 'negative theology.' If he speaks
of 'negative theologies,' in the plural, he does not separate them from the 'affirmative theologies' with which they maintain the relation described here." (Cf.
Pseudo-Dionysius Areopagite, *The Divine Names and Mystical Theology*, trans.
John D. Jones [Milwaukee: Marquette University Press, 1980], 1032c–1033d). See
Jean-Luc Marion, *L'Idole et la distance: Cinq études* (Paris: B. Grasset, 1977); *The
Idol and Distance: Five Studies*, trans. Thomas A. Carlson (New York: Fordham
University Press, 2001), 145n6.

2. This occurred in diverse passages and contexts. I will quote only one in
order to clarify a point and, perhaps, to respond to an objection that has the
merit of not being stereotypical. In "Différance" (first French publication in
1968 subsequently collected in *Margins of Philosophy*, trans. Alan Bass [Chicago:
University of Chicago Press, 1982]), I wrote: "So much so that the detours, lo-
cutions, and syntax in which I will often have to take recourse will resemble
those of negative theology, occasionally even to the point of being indistinguish-
able from negative theology. Already we have had to delineate *that* differance *is
not*, does not exist, is not a present-being (*on*) in any form; and we will be led
to delineate also everything *that* it *is not*, that is, *everything*; and consequently
that it has neither existence nor essence. It derives from no category of being,
whether present or absent. And yet those aspects of differance which are thereby
delineated are not theological, not even in the order of the most negative of
negative theologies, which as one knows are always concerned with disengaging
a superessentiality beyond the finite categories of essence and existence, that is,
of presence, and always hastening to recall that God is refused the predicate of
existence, only in order to acknowledge his superior, inconceivable, and ineffable
mode of being" (6). After having quoted this last sentence in *The Idol and Distance*, Jean-Luc Marion objects: "What is meant by 'one knows' here? We have
seen that, precisely, the so-called negative theology, *at bottom* [my italics—JD],
does not aim to reestablish a 'superessentiality,' since it aims neither at predication nor at Being; how, *a fortiori*, could it be a question of existence and essence
in Dionysius, when he still speaks a Greek original enough not to have either
the idea or the use of them?" (230n41). Here, too briefly, are some elements
of a response. 1. In speaking of presence or absence, of existence or essence, I

sought merely to specify, in a cursory manner, the different categories or modalities of presence in general, without precise historical reference to Dionysius. 2. Whatever may be the complex and quite enigmatic historicity of the distinction between essence and existence, I am not sure that it is simply ignored by Dionysius: how can one be certain of the *absence* of such a distinction at any stage of the Greek language? What does "a Greek original enough" mean? 3. What does "at bottom" mean here? What does it mean that "negative theology," at bottom, does not aim to reestablish a "superessentiality"? First of all, as Marion knows better than anyone else, it is difficult to consider accidental the reference to this superessentiality that plays a major, insistent, and *literal* role in so many texts by Dionysius and others, whom I will quote later. Next—beyond this obvious case, the only one to which I referred in a lecture that was not devoted to negative theology and did not even name Dionysius—it is necessary to elaborate an interpretive discourse as interesting and original as that of Marion, at the crossing, in the wake, sometimes beyond the thinking of Heidegger, Urs von Balthasar, Levinas, and a few others, to distinguish the "bottom" (the thinking of the gift, of paternity, of distance, of praise, etc.) from what in so-called "negative theology" still seems to be very concerned with superessentiality. Although I will not be able to develop this third point here, I will return to it below, at least in principle and in an oblique way.

3. Concerning a paradoxical writing of the word *sans*, notably in the work of Blanchot, I allow myself to refer to the essay "Pas" in *Gramma* (1976), nos. 3–4, reprinted in *Parages* (Paris: Galilée, 1986). *Dieu sans l'être* is the magnificent title of a book by Jean-Luc Marion (Paris: Fayard, 1982), to which I cannot do justice in the space of a note or the time of a lecture. This title remains difficult to translate. Its very suspension depends on the grammatical vacillation that only French syntax can tolerate—precisely in the structure of a title—that is, of a nominal or incomplete phrase. *L'* may be the definite article of the noun *être* (*God without Being*), but it can also be a personal pronoun—object of the verb to be—referring to God, from God to God himself who would not be what he is or who would be what he is *without being* (*it*) (*God without being God*, without being): God with and without being (*without, with and without*). On the subject of a title's syntax, Levinas preferred to say—also in a most singular syntax, no doubt in order to avoid this ultimate precedence of being or of the predicative sentence that would insinuate itself here—instead "being without being," "God with or beyond being," superessence or hyperessence: *otherwise than being*. Let us not forget what these two relatively recent titles are giving to be thought, Marion's *Dieu sans l'être* and Levinas's *Autrement qu'être ou au-delà de l'essence* (The Hague: Martinus Nijhoff, 1974–1978), which seek, in two very different ways, to avoid what Levinas calls the contamination by being, in order to "hear God not contaminated by being" for example. Grammar is not enough, but it

can never be reduced to an incidental instrumentality; by the word "grammar" one designates a discipline and its history, or more radically the modalities of writing: how one writes of God. The two cited titles lead the way to two major responses to the question I would like to raise: How to avoid speaking? How to avoid saying ? Otherwise, and implicitly: How to avoid speaking—of being? How to speak being otherwise? How to speak otherwise (than) being? And so on.

4. Meister Eckhart, *Meister Eckharts Predigten*, ed. Josef Quint, 3 vols. (Berlin: W. Kohlhammer, 1936), 1: 145–46; "Quasi stella matutina," trans. Frank Tobin in *Meister Eckhart, Teacher and Preacher*, ed. Bernard McGinn et al. (New York: Paulist Press, 1986), 256–57. "Quasi stella matutina" is hereafter abbreviated *Q.*—Tr.

5. Dionysius the Areopagite (Pseudo-Dionysius), *La Théologie mystique*, in *Œuvres complètes du Pseudo-Denys l'Aréopagite*, trans. Maurice de Gandillac (Paris: Aubier, 1990), 177. I have decided always to refer to this translation, which is easily accessible and was very valuable to me as a first reading of Dionysius. I shall sometimes quote several words from the original text for obvious reasons. [*Pseudo-Dionysius: The Complete Works*, trans. Colm Luinheid (New York: Paulist Press, 1987), 135, 998A. *The Mystic Theology* is hereafter abbreviated *MT*; *The Divine Names* is hereafter abbreviated *DN*. The English translations of works by Pseudo-Dionysius have frequently been modified to follow more closely Derrida's commentary—Tr.]

6. Meister Eckhart, *Meister Eckharts Predigten*, ed. Quint, 2: 305; "Adolescens, tibi dico: surge," trans. M. O'C. Walshe in *Meister Eckhart, Sermons and Treatises*, ed. M. O'C. Walshe, 2 vols. (London: Watkins, 1981), 2: 236.

7. Provenance of the call: Jerusalem. Sanford Budick had just called. He had to record a title, however provisional, on the program of the colloquium. I must associate the memory of this telephone call with that of a telegram. It also came from Jerusalem, it had already been signed by Sanford Budick, who was then preparing the volume, which has since appeared, *Midrash and Literature* (New Haven, Conn.: Yale University Press, 1986). Having learned that in Seattle, during a colloquium devoted to Paul Celan, I had given what he called in the telegram a "lecture on circumcision," he asked me: "could we have a portion of that lecture or some other piece you would be willing to give us however short stop midrash volume soon going to press?"

8. It is not possible here to get into this difficult problem of hierarchy directly, in particular concerning relations of translation or analogy—or rupture and heterogeneity between hierarchy *as such*, namely, the "sacred order," the principle or origin of sanctity, and, on the other hand, the sociopolitical order. One can follow Jean-Luc Marion very far when he dissociates the "*hierarchy*, understood starting from the theandric mystery for which the Church offers us the

sole place" and the "vulgar concept" or the "common concept" of hierarchy (*Idol and Distance*, 163–64). One might even agree with certain of his more provocative formulations ("The political model of hierarchy has nothing to do with the mystery of the hierarchy that opens to the communion of saints. Equivocation, deliberate or naïve, betrays the perversion of the gaze and does not even merit refutation. It is a question only of seeing, or of not seeing" [170]). No doubt, but it is also *necessary to see* the historical, essential, undeniable, and irreducible possibility of the so-called perversion that is perhaps the perversion of "the gaze" only because it was first observable, as one says, "in the facts." How was the "vulgar concept" constituted? This is also what it is necessary to see or not see. How can "distance"—in the sense that Marion gives this word and that also makes up the distance between the two hierarchies—have let itself be crossed or "traversed" and *given rise to the analogical translation of one hierarchy into the other?* Can one proscribe an "analogy" here that elsewhere seems to support this entire construction? And if the translation is bad, erroneous, "vulgar," what would be the good political translation of the hierarchy as a "sacred order"? This is only a question, but it is not impossible that its matrix holds others of the same type in reserve, on the subject of the trinitarian thearchy of which hierarchy would be "the icon, at once resembling and dissembling" (177; as well as the entire development on 163ff., beginning with the term "hierarchy," which Dionysius "mobilizes" and "our modernity forbids us straightaway from understanding correctly"); and thus on the subject of the trinitarian or patristic scheme underlying a thinking of the gift that does not necessarily require it or that perhaps finds in it a strange and abyssal *economy*, in other words, a fascinating limit. Here I must interrupt this lengthy note on the aneconomy or anarchy of the gift, which has occupied me elsewhere for a long time. In this regard, I feel that Marion's thinking is both very close and extremely distant; others might say opposed.

9. Dionysius the Areopagite (Pseudo-Dionysius), *The Ecclesiastical Hierarchy*, in *Pseudo-Dionysius: The Complete Works*, 255, 564a. *The Ecclesiastical Hierarchy* is hereafter abbreviated *EH*; *The Letters* is hereafter abbreviated *L*.—Tr.

10. "There are cinders there." On the recurrence of this phrase in his writings, see Jacques Derrida, *Feu la cendre* (Paris: Des femmes, 1987); translated by Ned Luckacher as *Cinders* (Lincoln: University of Nebraska Press, 1991).—Eds.

11. "The infinite differance is finite." See Jacques Derrida, *Speech and Phenomena and Other Essays*, trans. David Allison (Chicago: Northwestern University Press, 1973), 102.

12. The allusion is to a seminar on Jeremiah that had just taken place in Jerusalem (at the Institute for Advanced Studies), shortly before this colloquium, and to a large extent with the same participants. Concerning that which a question (be it the "piety of thought") must already contain in itself, and that no longer belongs to the questioning, see Jacques Derrida, *Of Spirit: Heidegger and the*

Question, trans. Geoffrey Bennington and Rachel Bowlby (Chicago: University of Chicago Press, 1989), 129-36n5.

13. Despite this silence, or in truth because of it, I may perhaps be permitted to reread this lecture as the most "autobiographical" discourse I have ever risked. One will attach to this word as many quotation marks as possible. It is necessary to surround with precautions the hypothesis of a self-presentation that passes by way of a lecture on the negative theology of others. But if one day I had to tell my story, nothing in this narrative would begin to speak of the thing itself if I did not come up against this fact: I have never yet been able—lacking the ability, the competence, or the self-authorization—to speak of what my birth, as one says, should have brought closest to me: the Jew, the Arab.

This small piece of autobiography confirms it obliquely. It is played out in all of my foreign languages: French, English, German, Greek, Latin, the philosophical, the meta-philosophical, the Christian, and so on.

In brief: how not to speak of oneself? But also: how to do it without letting oneself be invented by the other? Or without inventing the other?

14. A long introduction to this work in progress has appeared simultaneously under the title *Chora*, in a volume honoring Jean-Pierre Vernant. See also, more recently, Jacques Derrida, *Khôra* (Paris: Galilée, 1993), translated by Ian McLeod as "Khōra," in Derrida, *On the Name*, ed. Thomas Dutoit (Stanford: Stanford University Press, 1993).

15. See "The *Retrait* of Metaphor," Chapter 2 in *Psyche: Inventions of the Other*, vol. 1, ed. Peggy Kamuf and Elizabeth Rottenberg (Stanford: Stanford University Press, 2007).

16. Hans Urs von Balthasar quoted in Marion, *Idol and Distance*, trans. Carlson, 184n68. I refer the reader to this work, and in particular to the chapter "The Distance of the Requisite and the Discourse of Praise: Denys." I must admit that I had not read Marion's book at the time of writing this lecture, although it was published in 1977 and its author had been kind enough to send me a copy. Discouraged or irritated by a few signs of reductive misunderstanding or injustice that I immediately discerned regarding myself, I made the mistake of not continuing with my reading, thus allowing myself to be distracted by this very secondary aspect of a book (namely, its relation to my work) whose force and necessity I better perceive today, after rereading Dionysius and preparing the present lecture. Which does not mean, on my part, an agreement without reservation. Since the limits of this publication do not allow me to explain myself, I will defer the matter until later. Nonetheless, the few lines in which I distinguish between prayer and praise, like the references to *Dieu sans l'être*, were added later to the analysis devoted to prayer in the lecture read in Jerusalem. I did this in response and in homage to Jean-Luc Marion, who, it seems to me, gives the impression all too quickly that the passage to praise is the passage to prayer itself,

or that between these two the implication is immediate, necessary, and in some sense analytic. In particular, when he writes: "[Dionysius] tends to substitute for *to say* of predicative language another verb, [ὑμνεῖν], to praise. What does this substitution signify? It no doubt indicates the passage from discourse to prayer, for 'prayer is a λόγος, but neither true nor false' (Aristotle)" (184). What Aristotle in fact says in *Peri hermeneias* [On Interpretation] (17a), is that if every *logos* is meaningful (*semantikos*), only a *logos* in which one can distinguish the true and false is *apophantic*, and constitutes an affirmative proposition. And he adds: this does not obtain with all *logoi*: "thus prayer [*eukhē*] is, for instance, a sentence [*logos*], but neither has truth nor has falsity [*all' oute alethē oute pseudēs*]." But would Aristotle have said of praise (*hymnein*) that it was not apophantic? That it was neither true nor false? That it has no relationship to the distinction between true and false? That is doubtful. It is doubtful even in the case of Dionysius. For if praise or celebration of God does not in fact have the same rule of predication as every other proposition, even if the "truth" to which it lays claim is the supertruth of a superessentiality, it celebrates and names what "is" such as it "is": beyond being. Even if it is not a predicative affirmation of the usual sort, praise preserves the style and the structure of a predicative affirmation. It says something about someone. This is not the case of prayer that apostrophizes, addresses the other, and remains, in this pure movement, absolutely ante-predicative. It is not enough to stress here the performative nature of prayer and praise. The performative in itself does not always exclude predication. All the passages from *The Divine Names* or *The Mystical Theology*, to which Marion refers in a note (184n68) as "confirmation," involve praise or, as Maurice de Gandillac sometimes translates, a celebration that is not a prayer and that harbors a predicative aim, however foreign it may be to "normal" ontological predication. One may even risk the following paradox: sometimes the celebration can go further than the prayer, at least in supplementing it where it cannot accomplish itself, namely, as Dionysius says, in the "union" (*DN*, 2: 680b–d). Even if praise cannot merely bring to light (*ekphainein*) or say, it says and determines—as that which it is—the very thing that it cannot show and know, and to which it cannot unite itself even by prayer. If prayer, at least according to Dionysius, tends toward union with God, praise is not prayer; it is at most its supplement: what is added to it, when the union remains inaccessible or is lacking, in order to play the role of substitute but also to determine the referent itself, which is also the cause (the Requisite, Marion would say) of the prayer. It can incite to prayer, it can also follow it, but it is not identical with it. Among many other possible examples, I will recall only the one Marion in fact quotes, emphasizing a few words: "We must recall that this discourse does not aim to bring to light (ἐκφαίνειν) the superessential essence inasmuch as it is superessential (for it remains unspeakable, unknowable, and hence entirely impossible to bring to light, withdrawing from all union), but much rather to praise the procession that makes essences and that comes to all beings from the [trinitarian] Thearchy, the principle of essences" (*DN*, 5: 816b; cited by Marion, 184n68). This passage can be found on p. 128 of the (often different) translation of Maurice de Gandillac [*Œuvres Complètes du Pseudo-Denys l'Aréopagite* (Paris: Aubier-Montaigne, 1943)]. Not to bring to light, not to reveal (*ekphainein*), not to accede to it by a revelation that goes as far as "union" is not exactly not to speak, not to name, or even to abstain from attributing (be it beyond [*par-delà*] being). This is not to avoid speaking. It is even to begin speaking in order to determine the addressee of the prayer, an addressee who is also *aitia*, to be sure, and cause or requisite of the prayer, according to a trinitary beyond of being, a thearchy as principle of essence.

17. Repetition seems to be both forbidden and prescribed, impossible and necessary, as if it were necessary to avoid the unavoidable. To analyze the law of these paradoxes from the point of view of writing (especially in the usual sense of the word) or pedagogical initiation—and this is much more than a "point of view"—one would have to follow very closely the passage in *The Divine Names*, for example, that explains why it would be "mad" to "utter the same truth twice." For example, that of the *Theological Elements* of "our illustrious teacher Hierotheus." If Dionysius undertakes to write other treatises, and in particular "this present theology [*kai tēn parousian theologian*]," it is only to introduce *supplements* adapted to our powers (expositions, clarifications, distinctions), where Hierotheus had magisterially contented himself with an overall picture of the fundamental definitions. These supplements do not fill a lack, they repeat without repeating what was already said, virtually. They follow the order given and obey a given order. They transgress no law; on the contrary: "But, in fact, when he [Hierotheus] directed us and those with us who were teachers of the newly initiated, he urged us to judge by a discourse commensurate with our ability." But the order, the prayer, or the request also comes from the reader, from the immediate addressee, Timothy, *as if* he were reflecting Hierotheus's prescription ("he urged us to judge"): "Also, you have frequently urged us to do the same thing and have sent back his book to us as being too difficult for you." From the most difficult to the simplest, the *adjunction* of supplements only compensates for *our* weakness and not for a lack in what is to be read. Even before determining our relationship to the major text of Hierotheus, the first master, this supplementarity will have marked the relationship of Hierotheus's writing to God's writing, or rather, to God's "dictation." And thus the elite or the hierarchy—and analogy—are constituted: "For this reason, we judge that the instructions of his complete and presbyterial thoughts—which might be viewed as secondary writings [*Écriture nouvelle adjointe*] in conformity with the writings of those anointed of God—are for those beyond the many. Thus, we will transmit what is divine according to our logos to those who are our equals. . . . The eyewit-

ness vision of the intelligible writings and a comprehensive instruction in these require the power of a presbyter, but the knowledge and thorough learning of the reason which bear one to this are adapted to those dedicated and hallowed persons who are inferiors" (*DN*, 3: 681c). All of this is decided in view of greater blessedness, always, and thus of aging *well*, the consideration of age only taking on meaning from this analogy and this teleology.

18. *Meister Eckharts Predigten*, 3: 437; "Renovamini spiritu," in *Meister Eckhart: The Essential Sermons, Commentaries, Treatises, and Defense*, trans. Edmund Colledge and Bernard McGinn (New York: Paulist Press, 1981), 206; hereafter abbreviated *MEP*.

19. Martin Heidegger, "Was ist Metaphysik?" in *Wegmarken* (Frankfurt a/M: Klostermann, 1967), 1–19; "What Is Metaphysics?" in *Basic Writings*, trans. David Farrell Krell (New York: Harper & Row, 1977), 95–112.—Tr.

20. Martin Heidegger, *Einfuhrung in die Metaphysik* (Tübingen: Max Niemeyer, 1953), 50–51; *An Introduction to Metaphysics*, trans. Ralph Manheim (New Haven, Conn.: Yale University Press, 1959), 66.

21. Martin Heidegger, *Was heisst Denken* trans. Fred D. Wieck and J. Glenn Gray as *What Is Called Thinking?* (New York: Harper & Row, 1968), 227; translation modified.

22. Heidegger, *Einfuhrung in die Metaphysik*, trans. Manheim as *Introduction to Metaphysics*, 6; 7. Although this distinction is essential and stable, it does not always receive a terminological equivalent as clear as in *Hegel's Concept of Experience*; for example: "The science Aristotle has described—the science that observes beings as beings—he calls First Philosophy. But first philosophy does not only contemplate beings in their beingness [*Seiendheit*]; it also contemplates that being which corresponds to beingness in all purity: the supreme being. This being, (τὸ θεῖον, the Divine [*das Gottliche*], is also with a curious ambiguity called 'Being.' First philosophy, as ontology, is also the theology of what truly is. It should more accurately be called theology. The science of beings as such is in itself ontotheological." Martin Heidegger, *Hegels Begriff der Erfahrung*, in *Holzwege* (Frankfurt a/M: Klostermann, 1950), 179; *Hegel's Concept of Experience*, trans. Parvis Emad and Kenneth Maly (New York: Harper & Row, 1970), 135. See also Heidegger's 1936 course on *Schelling* (Tübingen: Max Niemeyer, 1971), 61–62. Insofar as it is distinct from the ontotheological theiology, theology was defined in *Sein und Zeit* a "more primordial interpretation" of man's Being in his relation to God, beginning with the "meaning of faith" (*SZ* 10; 30). See also Heidegger's *Nietzsche*, vol. 2 (Pfullingen: Neske, 1961), 58–59; *Nietzsche*, ed. David Farrell Krell, vol. 4. (San Francisco: HarperCollins, 1991), 26–27. In the preceding chapter, "Nihilismus, nihil und Nichts," Heidegger defines the essence of nihilism (from which Nietzsche supposedly did not escape): not taking the

question of the nothing seriously, "the essential nonthinking of the essence of the nothing [*das wesenhafte Nichtdenken an das Wesen des Nichts*]" (ibid., 53–54; 22).

23. See in particular the report of a meeting of the Evangelical Academy that took place in Hofgeismar in early December 1953, translated by Jean Greisch in *Heidegger et la question de Dieu* (Paris: Grasset 1980), 335.

24. "Es gibt die Zeit, es gibt das Sein," says "Zeit und Sein" in 1962. [Martin Heidegger, "Zeit und Sein," in *Zur Sache des Denkens* (Tübingen: Max Niemeyer, 1969), 1–25.—Tr.] There is no question of reversing a priority or logical order and saying that the gift precedes Being. But the thinking of the gift opens the space in which Being and time give themselves and give themselves to thought. I cannot enter into these questions here; I devoted a seminar to them at the École normale supérieure and at Yale University in the 1970s ("Donner le temps"); these questions have expressly oriented all the texts I have published since about 1972.

25. Heidegger sometimes quotes Meister Eckhart. And when he does it is often a matter of the thinking of the thing. "In what its language [i.e., that of things] does not say, there—says Eckhart, *old master of reading and life*—God is truly God" (my emphasis—JD). See Martin Heidegger, *Der Feldweg* (Frankfurt a/M: Klostermann, 1953), 4; "The Pathway," trans. Thomas F. O'Meara, O.P., and Thomas Sheehan, in *Heidegger, the Man and the Thinker*, ed. Thomas Sheehan (Chicago: Precedent Publishing, 1981), 70. It is always when he is on the subject of the thing that he associates the name of Dionysius (whom, to my knowledge, he cites nowhere else) with that of Eckhart: "Meister Eckhart uses the word *dinc* both for God as well as for the soul. . . . This *master of thinking* [my emphasis—JD] in no way means to say that God and the soul are something like a rock: a material object. *Dinc* is here the cautious and abstemious name for something that is at all. Thus Meister Eckhart says, adopting an expression of Dionysius the Areopagite: 'diu minne ist der natur, daz si den menschen wandelt in die dinc, di er minnet'—love is of such a nature that it changes man into the things he loves. . . . Kant talks about things in the same way as Meister Eckhart and means by this term something that is. But for Kant, that which is becomes the object of representation [*Gegenstand des Vorstellens*]" ("Das Ding," in *Vorträge und Aufsätze* [Pfullingen: Neske, 1954], 169; "The Thing," in *Poetry, Language, Thought*, trans. Albert Hofstadter [New York: Harper & Row, 1971], 176–77). I quote this sentence because it is not without relation, as we will see, to the reason for which Heidegger writes the word *Being* under erasure. As for the concept of *Gemüt* in Heidegger and a tradition that also leads back to Eckhart, among others, see my *Of Spirit*, trans. Bennington and Bowlby, 78ff.

26. By an analogous but no doubt radically different gesture, Jean-Luc Marion inscribes the name of God under a cross in *Dieu sans l'être* [God without

Being], "crossing God with the cross that reveals him only in the disappearance of his death and resurrection" (152–53; 105). This is another thinking of the gift and of the trace, a "theology" that wants to be "rigorously *Christian*" by opposing itself at times to the most kindred thinking, that of Heidegger in particular: "These interrogations could be gathered into a topical question, modest in appearance: does the name of the God, who is crossed because he is crucified, belong to the domain of Being? We are not at all speaking of 'God' in general, or thought on the basis of the divine, hence also of the Fourfold. We are speaking of the God who is crossed by a cross because he reveals himself by placement on a cross, the God revealed by, in, and as the Christ; in other words, the God of rigorously *Christian* theology" (107; 71–72). By placing a cross on "God" rather than on "Being," Marion proposes to remove the thinking of the gift, or rather of the *trace* of the gift—since it is also and still a matter of thinking of the *trace*—from the Heideggerian fourfold: "God *gives*. The giving [*donation*], in allowing to be divined how 'it gives,' a giving, offers the only accessible trace of He who gives. Being/being, like everything, can, if it is viewed as a giving, give therein the trace of another gift to be divined. All that matters here is the gift model that one accepts—appropriation or distance. In the first, naturally, the instance of God could not intervene, since the *giving* [donner] is included in the Fourfold. . . . It remains to be glimpsed, if not with Heidegger, at least in reading him, and, if really necessary, against him, that God does not depend on Being/being, and even that Being/being depends on distance" (153–54; 105–6). This thinking of the trace is thus also a thinking of a "distance" that would not be reducible to ontological difference.

27. Among many other places, see the first page of Heidegger's "Die Sprache im Gedicht: Eine Erörterung von Georg Trakls Gedicht," *Unterwegs zur Sprache*, 37; "Language in the Poem: A Discussion on Georg Trakl's Poetic Work," *On the Way to Language*, trans. Hertz, 159.

28. Martin Heidegger, "On the Question of Being," in *Pathmarks*, ed. and trans. William McNeill (Cambridge: Cambridge University Press, 1998), 210.—Tr.

29. "Metaphysics is ontotheology. Whoever has experienced theology in its own roots—both the theology of the Christian faith and that of philosophy—today prefers, in the realm of thinking, to *remain silent* [*schweigen*; my emphasis—JD] about God. For the ontotheological character of metaphysics has become questionable [*fragwürdig*] for thought, not on the basis of any atheism, but out of the experience of a thinking that has shown, in ontotheology, the as yet *unthought* unity of the essence of metaphysics." Martin Heidegger, *Identity and Difference*, trans. Joan Stambaugh (New York: Harper & Row, 1969), 121.

30. This seminar was translated and presented by F. Fédier and D. Saatdjian in the review *Poésie* 13 (1980), and the passage I quote was also translated in the

same year by Jean Greisch in *Heidegger et la question de Dieu,* 334. The German text of the privately circulated edition was quoted, for the passage that interests us, by Jean-Luc Marion, in *Dieu sans l'être,* 93n15; *God Without Being,* 211n16. [See Martin Heidegger, *Seminare,* in *Gesamtausgabe,* vol. 15 (Frankfurt a/M: Klostermann, 1986), 436–37.—Tr.]

31. *Heidegger et la question de Dieu,* 335.

10. Désistance

1. For example, in a passage that we will be quoting and reading again, Lacoue-Labarthe says: "For this reason, I have already proposed to speak of (de) constitution [in *The Subject of Philosophy*]. But this is makeshift. What should be noted here, with and against Lacan, and going back from Lacan to Reik, is that there is a constant though muffled breakdown of the imaginary, of the resources of the imaginary. The imaginary destroys at least as much as it helps to construct. This explains, perhaps, why the subject in the mirror is first of all a subject in 'désistance' (and why, for example, it will never recover from the mortal insufficiency to which, according to Lacan, its prematuration has condemned it). . . . The figure is never *one.* . . . [There is] no essence of the imaginary. What Reik invites us to think, in other words, is that the subject 'desists' because it must always confront *at least* two figures (or one figure that is at least double) . . . this destabilizing division of the figural (which muddles, certainly, the distinction between the imaginary and the symbolic, and broaches at the same time the negativity or absolute alterity of the 'real')" (Lacoue-Labarthe, "The Echo of the Subject," in *Typography,* 174–75; see also 141, and "Typography," in the same collection, e.g. 116). [Hereafter, all page numbers in parentheses in the text refer to this work. —Eds.]

2. "Heidegger's constant refusal . . . to take seriously the concept of mimesis. . . . It seems to me more and more difficult not to see a fundamental *mimetology* at work in Heidegger's thought" (297). "An unacknowledged mimetology seems to overdetermine the thought of Heidegger politically" (300).

3. "A thought can be less than infallible and remain, as we say, 'impossible to get around [*incontournable*]'" (269). In this essay, "Transcendence Ends in Politics," which can also be read as a very necessary meditation on *anankē* (*Notwendigkeit*) as it is interpreted in Heidegger's Rectoral Address, we can follow the thread of the ineluctable and the distribution of its terms: "avoided," "unavoidable," "not disavow," "incontestable" (268), "irreparable," "unpardonable," "inevitable," "unrenounceable," "impossible to circumvent," "difficult to avoid" (269), "not forbid," "not disavow," "inevitable" (271), "unyielding" (appearing in the Address and cited, 277), "undeniable," "unbreachable" ("cannot be broken

into"), "impossible to counter" (287), "inescapable" (in the passage quoted from the Address, 292).

4. The question of obsession, of the obsessive, of the obsessional returns quite regularly in all of these texts and at the heart of the problematic of mimesis, *typos*, and *Gestell*. It is even the question of the "style of questioning" (see, e.g., "The Echo of the Subject," 191). And it is the question of writing itself, beginning with the writing signed by Lacoue-Labarthe, who, in any case, never misses any of this. At the end of the essay "Obliteration," one reads: "One can always ascribe writing, especially when it is precautionary, to an exorcising mania or to the repetition compulsion. But perhaps it is strictly impossible to write anything but this: 'What forces me to write, I suppose, is the fear of going mad.'" It is a line from Bataille, and Lacoue-Labarthe adds that it applies as much to "Nietzsche" as to "Heidegger" (*The Subject of Philosophy*, trans. Thomas Trezise, Hugh J. Silverman, Gary M. Cole, Timothy D. Bent, Karen McPherson, and Claudette Sartiliot [Minneapolis: University of Minnesota Press, 1993], 98.) For example. Or: "[What vacillates is] the most basic narcissistic assurance (the obsessional 'I am not dead,' or 'I will survive')" (ibid., 195). Obsessionality, here, is no longer a clinical category.

5. One would have to know. What does it mean to know? And what does the supernegation of the ineluctable have to do with the knowledge of knowledge? Ten pages earlier, Lacoue-Labarthe was asking—already on the subject of Heidegger, and already in parentheses: "(does one ever know what he knows . . .)" (53). So we must also place quotation marks around this knowledge. "The Echo of the Subject": "But why does Reik, who 'knows,' want to know nothing about it?" (197).

6. "We have some reason to be suspicious of all the 'demagogic,' 'psychagogic' phraseology with which one claims today—without, it is true, too great a risk—to speak in the name of madness" (46).

7. At least since "L'Oblitération" (1973; subsequently included in Lacoue-Labarthe, *Subject of Philosophy*), which already ties the question of madness to that of the subject. The word *désistance* is not yet present there as such; rather, we find "(de)constitution of the subject" (73ff., 85). The word *déserter* [to desert] is perhaps the term that best announces the *désister* of which I will be speaking, for example, in this passage, which establishes in a remarkable fashion the axioms, so to speak, of this problematic: "As one might already have surmised, what interests us here is neither the subject nor the author [a question and a precaution taken up again in *Typography*, in the chapter "Diderot: Paradox and Mimesis," 257]. Nor is it the 'other'—whatever this may come to mean—of the subject or the author. Rather (and to limit ourselves for the time being to the question of the subject alone), what interests us is what is *also* at stake in the subject, while remaining absolutely irreducible to any subjectivity (that is, to any objectivity);

that which, in the subject, deserts (has always already deserted) the subject *itself* and which, prior to any 'self-possession' (and in a mode other than that of dispossession), is the dissolution, the defeat of the subject in the subject or *as* the subject: the (de)constitution of the subject, or the 'loss' of the subject—if indeed one can think the loss of what one has never had, a kind of 'originary' and 'constitutive' loss (of 'self')" (Lacoue-Labarthe, *Subject of Philosophy*, 81–82).

The placing in parentheses of the *de* in "(de)constitution" means that one must not hear it (any more than in the case of *désistance*) as a negativity affecting an originary and positive constitution. The italicizing of the *as* signifies that the "subject," as such, (de)constitutes itself in this movement of *désistance* and is *nothing other than* the formation of this movement. For this reason, the subject cannot simply be omitted or dissolved, or passed over in silence in the name of a deconstruction of subjectity—of the epoch of subjectity [*Subjectität*] in the sense defined by Heidegger. Hence, at this point already, the distance taken with respect to the latter; and this is what immediately follows after the passage that I have just cited. Lacoue-Labarthe calls into question, already, a certain Heideggerian "sublimation": "Now it is precisely this that Heidegger's text touches upon. But it does so only in order immediately (or even in advance) to take it back, to sublate it (meaning also to sublimate it) in and as thought. *This* is 'madness,' and 'madness' as it declares itself, or rather does not declare itself, in *Ecce Homo*" (*Subject of Philosophy*, 82).

8. Heidegger is almost never named by Foucault, who in any case never confronted him, so to speak, and never explained himself with regard to him. The same is true of Deleuze. This did not prevent Foucault from declaring in his very last interview: "My entire philosophical development [*devenir*] was determined by my reading of Heidegger." Nor did it prevent Deleuze, in the very last pages of his book on Foucault, from speaking of a "*necessary* confrontation between Foucault and Heidegger" (Gilles Deleuze, *Foucault*, trans. Seán Hand [Minneapolis: University of Minnesota Press, 1998], 108; my emphasis—JD). How, then, is one to interpret, retrospectively, this twenty-five-year silence? One must be brief: if, in listening to this silence, one thinks simultaneously of those who like Lacoue-Labarthe have constantly taken into account, in its most difficult, hazardous, indeed "necessary" dimensions, the said "confrontation" with Heidegger, one obtains a kind of film of the French philosophical scene in this quarter-century. To be deciphered: again the avoiding of the unavoidable. What does one avoid in this way? Heidegger? It is certainly not so simple.

9. See also the following: "From *Ge-stell*, among other things, not only *Gestalt* but *Darstellung* itself ([re]presentation, exposition, mise-en-scène, etc.) can be derived: Or, more precisely, *Gestalt* and *Darstellung* can both be derived from *Gestell*, among other things, even though Heidegger *never*, unless I am mistaken, *explicitly marks this relationship*, and to see it, we must link together and

at the same time make 'homogeneous' several relatively independent texts. Even though, in fact, everything happens here as if the commonality of origin, the homogeneity of *Gestalt* and *Darstellung*—symptomatically passed over in *silence*, I must insist, when it was a question of folding Jünger back upon Hegel—were, in one way or another, something very troublesome. Because, in effect, Mimesis is at play here" (62; emphases added—JD).

10. "One *inevitably* [my emphasis—JD] runs the risk of getting lost somewhere—or of losing all continuity of derivation. For example, *between* two or three texts, in the area of (the question of) *Darstellung*, or, to be more precise and to keep hold of the thread that we have already begun to follow, in the area where (the question of) *Darstellung* is, in effect, connected with Mimesis. In the beginning, however, everything goes rather well" (64–65). A long and careful analysis of numerous texts (I can only invite the reader to follow it) then demonstrates the process and the effects of this "loss of *Darstellung*," which "can scarcely be a simple matter" (72) and be limited to "the disappearance of a *word*" (73), even though there is the case of a text where Heidegger drops the word immediately after having cited it in the coupling *Her-* and *Darstellen* (73). That *Darstellung* should be "lost" does not mean that something has been lost—the term designates rather a certain inattention to the abyssal structure that can always divide it and fictionalize it. The question then becomes: "How, then, is *Darstellung* lost? And what is the consequence of this loss for the interpretation of mimesis?" (73). Cf. also "Typography," 79: "the loss of *Darstellung*."

11. One might reread the passage from *Was heisst Denken?* that Lacoue-Labarthe himself cites at the moment he comes to raise a second question of translation (60). The first concerned the untranslatable *Ge-stell*, where it is less a matter of knowing what it *means to say* [veut dire] than of knowing "how it functions" and "what purpose it serves." The other concerns the Heideggerian project of "translating" *Zarathustra* and submitting it to an "allegorical" treatment. This time, translation involves, beyond "expression" or "poetic ornament," an *unthought.* Heidegger: "To acknowledge and respect [the language of thinkers] consists in letting every thinker's thought come to us as something *in each case unique*, never to be repeated, inexhaustible—and being shaken to the depths by what is unthought in his thought. What is unthought in a thinker's thought is not a lack inherent in his thought. What is *un*-thought is such in each case only as the un-*thought*" (cited 60n22). (I have stressed "in each case unique," which is here the indispensable correlate of the very thinking of thought. Where unicity is lacking, thought itself, or even the un-*thought* of thought, will not come about. This is what Lacoue-Labarthe respects perhaps a bit more than I do: this unicity, and the affinity between this unicity and thought itself. On this point, my lack of respect, or what torments my respect, may signify two things: *either*

that I do not know (how to recognize) what thought is authentically and am not sufficiently concerned about it, *or else* that I do not exclude the possibility of some residue of *un*-thought [*quelque résidu* d'im*pensé*] in this Heideggerian determination of the un-*thought*, which still holds too much to the unique *site* of the gathering. What if one called thought (but perhaps another name is needed) the dislocation or even the *désistance*, of this unicity or this unity, of this *site* of gathering? For one might show that this question constantly returns to [*repasse par*] the topology of Being according to Heidegger and everything [it] gathers under the words *Ort* and *Erörterung*: precisely, the gathering.)

12. Lacoue-Labarthe will be more and more precise in subsequent texts about the paradoxical—hyperbological—constraints that "mimetological overdetermination" exerts on thought and discourse. He will even call the "thought of a *mimesis* without models or an 'originary mimesis'" the "'negative metaphysics' of the moderns." In this same text, he declares his reservations concerning a rehabilitation and a generalization of mimesis, be they modern or postmodern. See Philippe Lacoue-Labarthe, *L'Imitation des modernes* (Paris: Galilée, 1986), esp. 278, 281, 283.

13. See esp. Gilbert Kahn's translation of *Einführung in die Metaphysik* entitled *Introduction à la métaphysique* (Paris: Gallimard, 1958). Here is an excerpt from the index of German terms: "*Wesen*: essence, estance, lorsque ce sens est surtout verbal et, par là, exclut toute référence à la quiddité [when the meaning is especially verbal and hence excludes all reference to quiddity]. *Wesen*: ester, se réaliser historialement comme essence, sans donc que celle-ci soit donnée hors du temps comme modèle pour cette réalisation [to be fulfilled historially as essence, without the latter being given outside of time as model for this fulfillment]; *wesensmässig*: selon son [according to its] estance; . . . *anwesen*: adester; *An-wesen*: ad-estance; *Anwesenheit*: présence: *Ab-wesen*: ab-sence; *ab-wesend*: absent; *Unwesen*: inessentialité, désordre" (225).

14. Lacoue-Labarthe, *L'Imitation des modernes*, 271.

15. See "The Caesura of the Speculative," in *Typography*, 222. See also what immediately follows this passage on the subject of the double bind and Hölderlin's *withdrawal* or "madness."

16. Concerning the word "(de)construction," see below, n27.

17. These last three essays are collected in Lacoue-Labarthe, *L'Imitation des modernes.*—Tr.

18. A little further on, the inevitable is precisely *delay*. See on this point the entire paragraph that explains how "theorization, for the one who writes, is not only inevitable, but absolutely necessary," and why there is always a "mirror in a text," "the only conceivable means of overcoming the inevitable delay of the 'subject' in relation to 'itself' and of stemming at least to some extent that

inexorable lapse or failing in which something is stated, written, and so on"
(138). Once again, the "subject" thus written (in quotation marks) is not the
one Heidegger deconstructs. It is perhaps even the one against whose *désistance*
Heideggerian deconstruction protects itself (and seeks relief [*assistance*]). This
"subject" does not identify itself. Either with the other or with itself. Of course,
it seems to *do* nothing else, and in fact it does nothing other than identify itself. But this very fact, the *effect* of subjectivity, bears witness to the contrary.
It proves and undergoes [*fait la preuve et l'épreuve*] the contrary. If the subject
identifies itself, it is because it can never be identical, never identify itself—with
itself or with the other. The condition of possibility of identification is nothing
other than its impossibility, both of them ineluctable. Like mimesis. The subject,
which is thus desubjectivized, would not have to identify itself were it not for
the *désistance* that makes absolute identification absolutely inaccessible for it.

Delay and "prematuration," which go together—the belatedness with regard
to the subject's "own" birth—inscribe the subject in an experience of "abortion"
of which I will have to speak again.

19. I refer here to the entire passage surrounding this proposition: "the 'subject' *desists* in this, and doubly so when it is a question of man (of the male)"
(129).

20. At the heart of a thinking of rhythm, and as rhythm itself, the "One dif-
fering in itself" (*en diapheron eauto*): Lacoue-Labarthe often cites Heraclitus,
and Hölderlin quoting Heraclitus.

21. Jean-Luc Nancy and Philippe Lacoue-Labarthe, *Le Titre de la lettre (une
lecture de Lacan)* (Paris: Galilée, 1973); *The Title of the Letter: A Reading of Lacan,*
trans. François Raffoul and David Pettigrew (New York: State University of New
York Press, 1992).

22. Jacques Lacan, *Écrits* (Paris: Seuil, 1966); *Écrits,* trans. Bruce Fink (New
York: Norton, 2005).

23. I emphasize: "the book [Reik's *The Haunting Melody*] is a '*theoretical failure*'" (148). "It is as if Reik blurred all the divisions (often strict) to which Freud
submits, and got stuck in that sort of hole or gap between the 'symbolic,' if you
will, and the imaginary, which is not necessarily occupied by something like the
'real,' even if it be consigned to impossibility. This, of course, will not be without its consequences—even if the *theoretical failure* is certain" (153). We will see
that Reik the subject ends by *submitting* himself to that to which Freud himself
submits and to which Lacan himself *submits* (this is what "will not be without its
consequences")—an ineluctable chain of the same submission, the same failure.
A singular "rivalry" in mourning (157). "[Everything] that can and should hold
our attention in Reik, everything in his work that makes it more than a simple
repetition of Freud—that is to say, its '*theoretical failure.*' . . . Reik's *theoretical
failure,* or rather, working through him, the *general failure of the theoretical*"

(163). The latter consists in reflecting Freud in the repetition of the Goethean motif of "repeated reflection [*wiederholte Spiegelung*]," a specular reduction of the catacoustic. "He was seeking, in short, to define a kind of 'musical' essence of the subject. Nevertheless, he was not unaware of the fact that *to submit* to the theoretical was to lose all chance of reaching his goal. This is why the theoretical 'failure' is also a 'success' and the *inhibition* will never be truly lifted" (167). "The double *inhibition* at work here: both theoretical, by *submission*, and also literary, artistic" (173). "We must start again, here, from Reik's theoretical failure, or rather from his theoretical *quagmire* [enlisement] [Lacoue-Labarthe's emphasis], since 'inhibition' certainly has something to do with it. Why does he get bogged down? [*Pourquoi cet 'enlisement'?*]" (176). "This is not only why his theory of autobiography is *abortive*, but also why the autobiography itself cannot be written" (179). I have emphasized *abortive* because this word says something more with respect to the event of a singular failure: a birth, rather than an origin, takes place without taking place, a nameable subject will have been carried that is stillborn or "comes to itself only to lose itself." All of this is also carried in the "Maternal Closure" upon which the final pages open. But I also emphasized this word because it belongs to the title of a book announced by Lacoue-Labarthe (*L'Avortement de la littérature*). I would for the same reasons have emphasized the word *exemplarity*, another announced title, another major motif of this thinking. I extend my index (an introductory essay is a somewhat garrulous index, when it is not an irremediable betrayal): "We are on the verge of the *second theoretical floundering* [enlisement]. . . . The narrative recounting this second failure warrants our pausing for a moment" (180).

What the term *floundering* [enlisement] adds to the term *failure* [échec] and then to *abortion* [avortement] is perhaps the image of a slow sinking into a terrain whose limits are not distinct, whose sites cannot be set off against one another, whose ground is not solid. This has to do with the structure of a limit without opposition. And the slowness has to do with repetition, with the compulsion to repeat: one does not advance, one advances in place, one repeats the failure—the inhibition, rather than paralyzing one, obliges one to make the same gesture, and each movement causes one to sink further. Things do not happen just once, in running up against a limit, as the word "failure" alone might lead us to think. And above all, what produces and aggravates the floundering, namely, this situation in which the effort to get out by lifting oneself up only mires one further, is that the repetition grows heavier, takes on the autobiographic or autoanalytic *narrative*, as lucid as it is impotent, of the floundering itself. Reik is the first to recount, in repeating it, the "initial and repeated *mistake*": "'The failure of my attempt did not teach me a lesson in this direction'" (180). "'I must admit to myself that I have failed again because I have been too ambitious'" (189). Lacoue-Labarthe: "It is, in fact, to *submit* purely and simply to the Freudian programming. Nonetheless, it is not quite so simple either" (181). And here, formalized in the most economical fashion possible, is the scene of a *resistance to désistance, assistance*: "But it happens that in Reik's own text—on one occasion— these *three questions are assembled together* [how about that—there it is again]. Perhaps without his knowing it (although I am not so sure), and in any case without result. As though it were already *too late*, and as though the *theoretical submission to Freud* prevented Reik from *letting go* to the point of renouncing the renunciation—a renunciation which, despite everything, determines his fragile narcissistic *recovery* [(re)-saisie] in the demand for paternal *assistance* (whereby theory, here Oedipus, triumphs twice over)" (190). And the "too late" is still resonating.

24. The word "suspicion" itself, a "suspicion . . . hastily covered over," bears more strictly on the possibility of thinking rhythm *itself*, "before" music, almost without it. The word returns several times (203–4) in one of the striking passages on the shofar whose three groups of notes, as Reik specifies, "[are] distinguished only by a change of rhythm" (204). The shofar, Reik had remarked, is not a musical instrument. The sound it produces "'is more like the bellowing of a bull than music'" (204), and the Jewish tradition does not attribute the invention of music to a gift from God. But beyond the word, Reik suspects Freud—this time accusing rather than expressing an intimation—of having insisted "'one-sidedly [on] the determining role of the text'" (182) and of having in general "neglected" the "factor of the musical expression of a certain emotion in the tune" (186).

25. This would be the place for a patient analysis: too Greek or too "Platonic"? Can one connect what in a pre-"Platonic" or pre-"philosophical" Greece *would* not yet *be* ontotypological or mimetological with the Judaic vein toward which the experience of the shofar points? One would have to follow, in Lacoue-Labarthe's work, and more precisely in this context, at the very heart of psychoanalysis, the debate between the Greek, the German, and the Jew. It resonates everywhere. Can one say of the Jews or the Germans what is said of the Greeks in Lacoue-Labarthe's "Hölderlin and the Greeks": "*The proper feature of the Greeks is inimitable because it never took place*" (246)?

26. The resistance to *désistance* takes the form of inhibition—its general form, which no longer represents a clinical category or the definition of a "pathological" symptom. Inhibition is *unavoidable*. In general. No rhythm without it. One can say the same of the double bind. See on this point the pages already cited, in particular 167 and 173.

27. This *hyperbologic* is expressly defined in "Diderot: Paradox and Mimesis" (e.g., 260) and "The Caesura of the Speculative" (e.g., 233). It programs the inevitable effects of a "logic" of mimesis. In this precise context, where it is a matter of the actor, this hyperbologic regularly converts the gift of everything into the gift of nothing, and this latter into the gift of the thing itself. "The gift

of impropriety"—in other words, the "gift of mimesis"—is the "gift of general appropriation and of presentation" (260). But this is not, as we see, a "context" or an "example" among others. It is a matter of appropriation and (de-)propriation in general. The play of the *de-*, on which I have been working since the beginning of this preface, might well belong to this hyperbologic. Without being negative, or dialectizable, it both organizes and disorganizes what it appears to determine; it belongs to and yet escapes the order of its own series. What I said in the beginning about *désistance* would hold just as well for the hyperbologic of *disinstallation* (120, 133), (*de*) *constitution* ("L'Oblitération," "Typography," 259, 260; "The Echo of the Subject," 174), *disarticulation* ("The Caesura of the Speculative," 234; "Hölderlin and the Greeks," 245), *disappropriation* [(dé)propriation] ("Typography," 133, 135; "Diderot: Paradox and Mimesis," 265; "The Caesura of the Speculative," 231; "Hölderlin and the Greeks," 245), and *deconstruction* ("Typography," 65, 123; "The Echo of the Subject," 141; "The Caesura of the Speculative," 212, 234). Taking into account the supplementary ring [*anneau*] of which I have been speaking, the word "deconstruct"—a word that, as Lacoue-Labarthe says elsewhere, he does not consider "in the least 'worn out'" (*L'Imitation des modernes*, 282)—sometimes has the sense of a task, sometimes that of an event, of what occurs in any case in a "practical" situation, for example, in Hölderlin (cf. "The Caesura of the Speculative," 221). I have remarked that Lacoue-Labarthe sometimes writes (*de*)*construction* (123).

11. A Number of Yes

1. Michel de Certeau, *The Mystic Fable*, trans. Michael Smith (Chicago: University of Chicago Press, 1992), 1: 175. "That act does not postulate a reality or knowledge prior to its utterance. Also in that linguistic form, it is the accomplishment of a beginning. Among the performatives, it belongs more specifically to the order of the 'commissives.' The examples given by Austin (promise, am determined to, pledge myself, am dedicated to, declare my intention, etc.) are the same words that, in the mystic texts, mark the social manifestations of the initial *volo*" (ibid., 173). [References to this work hereafter included in the text in parentheses.—Tr.]

2. "The *Shekinah* implied a spiritual indwelling, a presence, a glory and, later, a femininity of God—themes that also played an important role in the Christian *mystics* of that era" (de Certeau, *Mystic Fable*, 303n3, 135). On this affinity between affirmation and femininity, I take the liberty of referring to *Éperons* (Paris: Flammarion, 1987), *Parages* (Paris: Galilée, 1986), and *Ulysse gramophone: Deux mots pour Joyce* (Paris: Galilée, 1986, 1987) and of quoting Blanchot: "Yet I have met people who have never said to life, 'Quiet!', who have never said to death,

'Go away!' Almost always women, beautiful creatures" (Blanchot, *Madness of the Day*, trans. Lydia Davis [New York: Station Hill Press, 1981], 7).

3. Franz Rosenzweig, *The Star of Redemption*, trans. W. W. Hallow (New York: Holt, Rinehart & Winston, 1971), 26–27.

4. *Unterwegs zur Sprache*, 175ff., 72ff. I touch on these questions of the *yes* in *Ulysse gramophone*, as to the Heideggerian movement to which I am alluding here, see my *Of Spirit: Heidegger and the Question*, trans. Geoffrey Bennington and Rachel Bowlby (Chicago: University of Chicago Press, 1989).

5. "When this situation manages to be said, it may still have as its language the ancient Christian prayer: 'May I not be separated from you.' Not without you. *Nicht ohne.*" At this point, Michel de Certeau adds in a note: "This Heideggerian category seems to me to permit a reinterpretation of Christianity." See Michel de Certeau, "La rupture instauratrice," *Esprit*, June 1971, 1177–1214.

6. See "Psyche: Invention of the Other" in *Psyche: Inventions of the Other*, vol. 1, ed. Peggy Kamuf and Elizabeth Rottenberg (Stanford: Stanford University Press, 2007).

7. Alliance and cut, Mount Carmel, whose name "means *science of circumcision.*" Here one would have to quote the pages devoted to the language of circumcision and the circumcision of language in mystical texts (see de Certeau, *Mystic Fable*, 133ff.). Concerning the "bloody signature of the body," which, according to Michel de Certeau, "marks access to the name of the father (to virility) by a submission to paternal power": "Just as Abraham raised his knife over his son Isaac to sacrifice him to Yahweh, that is, to produce meaning [*sacer facere*], so John of the Cross cuts into the quick of the flesh in order to describe the way of union. Cutting off is the procedure of the covenant when it is question of the absolute describing itself by what it takes away. A labor of sculpting, dear to John of the Cross. Negative theology: it *signifies* by what it *takes away*" (136–37).

12. Interpretations at War: Kant, the Jew, the German

1. The following summary was distributed, by prior arrangement, during the weeks preceding the conference:

Interpretations at War
Kant, the Jew, the German
or
The Judeo-German Psyche: The Examples of Hermann Cohen and Franz Rosenzweig

Insisting on the word *example*, I will introduce several questions:
(1.) What is exemplarity (rather than paradigm) in the history of national

self-affirmation? What happens when a "people" presents itself as "exemplary"? Or when a "nation" declares itself, by virtue of its very singularity, to be charged with an exemplary mission, testimony, responsibility, that is, with a universal message?

(2.) In what sense and how have the Jewish and German "peoples"—or those who refer to themselves in this way—been able to declare themselves exemplary of this very "exemplarity"? In what sense and how, since the Aufklärung (Mendelssohn, Kant, etc.) has a certain modern couple, both singular and impossible (that was judged "mythic" and "legendary" by Scholem), the Judeo-German couple, been doubly exemplary of this exemplarity? What happened, in this regard, in the politico-institutional context of the "emancipation," of the two world wars, of Zionism and of Nazism, and so on? What I am calling "psyche" is both the psychic space of a "fantasmatic impulse [*fantasmatique pulsionnelle*]" (love, hate, madness, projection, rejection, etc.), which has constituted the strange couple of these two "cultures," of these two "histories," of these two "peoples," *and* what is called in French *une psyché*, namely, a large pivoting mirror, a device of specular reflection.

(3.) In what way are these examples, and particularly the example of the corpus that we will be treating (a certain corpus signed Cohen and Rosenzweig), exemplary of the general questions that will be on the horizon of this presentation? What is a context? How does one determine its openness and its closedness? How does one delimit the institutionality of a context? What does it mean to take account of an institutional context in an interpretation, when a context always remains "open" and unsaturable? stabilizable, but only because it is essentially unstable and labile?

In the case of the texts we are going to analyze (Cohen's *Deutschtum und Judentum* [1915]; certain pages from Rosenzweig's *The Star of Redemption*), the contextual dimensions abyssally enveloped are at least the following:

(a) the "whole" of the two traditions (Jewish and German);

(b) the history of the "emancipation" of the German Jews;

(c) the history of Western philosophy (with Kant being privileged in an exemplary way by Cohen, Rosenzweig, and other German Jews [Benjamin and Adorno]; we will speak of "Kant, the Jew, the German");

(d) the respective situation of the two thinkers (in their relationship to each other, in their relationship to Judaism, to Zionism, to German culture, and—it should be emphasized—to the discourse or the tradition of the university, to academic philosophy in general);

(e) finally and above all the war of 1914–18: Cohen's nationalistic German (Judeo-German) text is in fact a very peculiar text, a powerful, violent, and troubling interpretation of the entire history of philosophy and of Western religions, and above all of the Judeo-German couple. This interpretation was addressed in the first place to American Jews to ask them to prevent the United States from entering the war against Germany. But what does "in the first place"—when it is a matter of destination—mean here for a text and a context? This text was said to be "cursed [*maudit*]." It is certainly not so simple. Is there an "actual" "context"—and which one—in which to reread it today? Instead of providing answers to these numerous and precipitous questions, I will instead multiply preliminary warnings as to the very positioning of these questions.

2. Franz Rosenzweig, "Ein Gedenkblatt" (1918), in *Der Mensch und sein Werk: Gesammelte Schriften*, vol. 3: *Zweistromland: Kleinere Schriften zu Glauben und Denken* (Dordrecht: Martinus Nijhoff, 1984), 239–40; "Un hommage," in *Les Cahiers de la nuit surveillée*, special issue "Franz Rosenzweig," 1982, 181. ["Lehranstalt" refers to the Lehranstalt für die Wissenschaft des Judentums (Institute for the Science of Judaism) in Berlin, where Cohen began teaching in 1912, having stepped down from his chair in philosophy at the University of Marburg. All English translations from the original German of Hermann Cohen and Franz Rosenzweig are by Dana Hollander, unless otherwise noted. The original German texts were always consulted, even where Derrida refers only to French translations.—Tr.]

3. Franz Rosenzweig, letter to Helene Sommer, January 16, 1918, in *Der Mensch und sein Werk. Gesammelte Schriften*, vol. I.1: *Briefe und Tagebücher, 1900-1918* (The Hague: Martinus Nijhoff, 1976), 508.—Tr.

4. French translation by Stéphane Mosès, in *Archives des sciences sociales et religieuses* 60/61 (1985); I will propose a reading of this letter elsewhere. ["Bekenntnis über unsere Sprache" ("A Confession on the Subject of Our Language"), Scholem's contribution to a portfolio of short handwritten texts and images presented to Rosenzweig on his birthday and published in a facsimile edition as *Franz Rosenzweig zum 26. Dezember 1926*, ed. Martin Goldner (New York: Leo Baeck Institute, 1987). English translations by Ora Wiskind in *History and Memory* 2, no. 2 (Winter 1990) and by Gil Anidjar in *Acts of Religion* (New York: Routledge, 2002), 226.—Tr.]

5. Hermann Cohen, *Deutschtum und Judentum: Mit grundlegenden Betrachtungen über Staat und Internationalismus*, 2nd ed. (Giessen: Töpelmann, 1916); "Germanité et judéité," trans. Marc B. de Launay, *Pardès* 5 (1987); hereafter cited in text as *DJ*, followed by section number. [The French translation by de Launay from which Derrida quotes seems to be based on the 1916 edition. The critical edition of this work, which reflects the variants between the 1915 and 1916 versions, is in Hermann Cohen, *Werke*, vol. 16: *Kleinere Schriften V: 1913–1915*, ed. Hartwig Wiedebach (Hildesheim: Olms, 1997), 465–560.—Tr.]

6. Theodor Adorno, "Auf die Frage: Was ist deutsch?" in *Stichworte: Kritische Modelle 2* (Frankfurt a/M: Suhrkamp, 1969), 103; "On the Question: 'What is

German?'" *Critical Models: Interventions and Catchwords*, trans. Henry W. Pickford (New York: Columbia University Press, 1998), 206.

7. The language between brackets is not found in the French text as printed in *Psyché*, vol. 2. We here follow the translation, which was based on an earlier version of Derrida's essay, because the passage makes more sense as rendered. —Eds.

8. See Jacques Derrida, *Of Spirit: Heidegger and the Question*, trans. Geoffrey Bennington and Rachel Bowlby (Chicago: University of Chicago Press, 1989).

9. Benedict de Spinoza, *Tractatus Theologico-politicus*, trans. R. H. M. Elwes as *A Theologico-Political Treatise and a Political Treatise* (New York: Dover, 1951), 121, translation modified.—Tr.

10. I refer the reader to long developments devoted to this scene in my *Glas*, trans. John P. Leavey Jr. and Richard Rand (Lincoln: University of Nebraska Press, 1986).

11. Franz Rosenzweig, "Die Bauleute: Über das Gesetz" in *Der Mensch und sein Werk. Gesammelte Schriften*, vol. 3: *Zweistromland*, 699–712; "The Builders: Concerning the Law," in *On Jewish Learning*, ed. and trans. Nahum Glatzer (New York: Schocken Books, 1965), 76–77.

12. At this point Derrida inserts the following comment: "[Having no access, at the moment, to the original, I am quoting a French translation which seems strange and may be inadequate.]"—Eds.

13. Johann Gottlieb Fichte, *Addresses to the German Nation*, ed. George Armstrong Kelly, trans. R. F. Jones and G. H. Turnbull (New York: Harper & Row, 1968), 40.

14. Franz Rosenzweig, *Der Stern der Erlösung*, 4th ed. (The Hague: Martinus Nijhoff, 1976), 23; *The Star of Redemption*, trans. William W. Hallow (South Bend, Ind.: University of Notre Dame Press, 1985), 20, translation modified. Also see *The Star of Redemption*, trans. Barbara E. Galli (Madison: University of Wisconsin Press, 2005), 27–28.

15. See Maurice Blanchot, "Les intellectuels en question," *Le Débat* 29 (March, 1984).

16. The allusion is to a book by Harold Fisch, a professor at Bar-Ilan University in Israel, who participated in the conference.

17. Immanuel Kant, "On the Common Saying: 'This May be True in Theory, but it does not Apply in Practice,'" in *Political Writings*, ed. Hans Reiss, trans. H. B. Nisbet (Cambridge: Cambridge University Press, 1991), 92.

Sources

Chapter 1, "Letter to a Japanese Friend," translated by David Wood and Andrew Benjamin, originally published in *Derrida and Différance*, edited by David Wood and Robert Bernasconi, Northwestern University Press, 1988. Copyright © 1988 by Northwestern University Press.

Chapter 2, "*Geschlecht* I: Sexual Difference, Ontological Difference," translated by Ruben Berezdivin, originally published as "*Geschlecht*: Sexual Difference, Ontological Difference," *Research in Phenomenology* 13 (1983): 65–83. Used by permission of Brill Academic Publishers.

Chapter 3, "Heidegger's Hand (*Geschlecht* II)," translated by John P. Leavey Jr., originally published in *Deconstruction and Philosophy*, edited by John Sallis, University of Chicago Press. Copyright © 1987 by The University of Chicago.

Chapter 4, "The Laws of Reflection: Nelson Mandela, in Admiration," translated by Mary Ann Caws and Isabelle Lorenz," originally published in *For Nelson Mandela*, edited by Jacques Derrida and Mustapha Tlili, Henry Holt, 1987 For permission to reprint, we thank Marguerite Derrida.

Chapter 5, "No (Point of) Madness—Maintaining Architecture," translated by Kate Linker, originally published as "Point de folie—maintenant l'architecture" in *AA Files* 12 (Summer 1986): 65–75. Used by permission of the publisher, AA Publications.

Chapter 6, "Why Peter Eisenman Writes Such Good Books," translated by Sarah Whiting, originally published in *Architecture and Urbanism* (1988): 112–24.

Chapter 7, "Fifty-Two Aphorisms for a Foreword," translated by Andrew Benjamin, originally published in *Deconstruction: An Omnibus Volume*, edited by A. Papadakis, C. Cooke, and A. Benjamin, Rizzoli, 1989. Reprinted by permission of the publisher.

Chapter 8, "Aphorism Countertime," translated by Nicholas Royle, originally published in *Acts of Literature*, edited by Derek Attridge, Routledge, 1992. Reproduced by permission of Routledge / Taylor & Francis Books, Inc.

Chapter 9, "How to Avoid Speaking: Denials," translated by Ken Frieden, originally published in *Languages of the Unsayable: The Play of Negativity in Literature and Literary Theory*, edited by Sanford Budick and Wolfgang Iser, Columbia University Press, 1989. For permission to reprint, we thank Marguerite Derrida.

Chapter 10, "Desistance," translated by Christopher Fynsk, in *Typography: Mimesis, Philosophy, Politics*, by Philippe Lacoue-Labarthe, edited by Christopher Fynsk, 1–42 (Cambridge, Mass: Harvard University Press, 1989). © 1989 by the President and Fellows of Harvard College.

Chapter 11, "A Number of Yes (*Nombre de oui*)," translated by Brian Holmes, originally published in *Qui Parle* 2, 2 (1988): 120–33. For permission to reprint, we thank the editors of *Qui Parle*.

Chapter 12, "Interpretations at War: Kant, the Jew, the German," translated by Moshe Ron, originally published in *New Literary History* 22, 1 (1991): 39–95. For permission to reprint, we thank Moshe Ron.

Index of Proper Names

MERIDIAN

Crossing Aesthetics